EVENINGS WITH
CARY GRANT

EVENINGS WITH
CARY GRANT

Recollections in His Own Words and by Those Who Knew Him Best

Nancy Nelson

CITADEL PRESS
Kensington Publishing Corp.
www.kensingtonbooks.com

CITADEL PRESS BOOKS are published by

Kensington Publishing Corp.
850 Third Avenue
New York, NY 10022

First published in 1991 by William Morrow and Company, Inc.

All Kensington titles, imprints, and distributed lines are available at special quantity discounts for bulk purchases for sales promotions, premiums, fund-raising, educational, or institutional use. Special book excerpts or customized printings can also be created to fit specific needs. For details, write or phone the office of the Kensington special sales manager: Kensington Publishing Corp., 850 Third Avenue, New York, NY 10022, attn: Special Sales Department, phone 1-800-221-2647.

CITADEL PRESS and the Citadel logo are Reg. U.S. Pat. & TM Off.

First Kensington printing: December 2002

10 9 8 7 6 5 4 3 2 1

Printed in the United States of America

Library of Congress Control Number: 2002110879

ISBN 0-8065-2412-X

To the Memory of Cary Grant

Knowing him, and then preparing this intimate portrait,
are cherished highlights in my life.
Inside these covers you will hear his friends say,
one way or another,
"I've never had so much fun."

Neither have I.

FOREWORD

We join with the many people who thought that this book captured the spirit of Cary best. He was remarkable: full of humor, warmth, love, intelligence, fun, and humility. He was generous, sensitive, and supportive in everything that he did. Rather than talk about his extraordinary career, Cary preferred to listen to others or talk about his own many and varied interests: He never wrote an autobiography. *Evenings with Cary Grant,* however, is written using his own recollections, those of his friends and loved ones, and with access to his personal papers. It gives a true understanding of this wonderful man.

We are delighted that Nancy Nelson has so accurately portrayed the husband and father that we love. We are thrilled that not only will you get to know Cary but that you will have the pleasure also of meeting his marvelous friends.

Barbara and Jennifer

ACKNOWLEDGMENTS

The nicest things happen because of Cary Grant.

This book would not have been possible without the support of Barbara Grant. I am enormously grateful to her for her confidence and trust, making this project a blissful experience. Never once did she look over my shoulder. I am elated that she and Jennifer are pleased with the finished work.

In an effort to avoid adding to the errors already recorded as part of the mythology of Cary Grant, I have relied wherever possible on primary sources—Cary Grant's papers and the people who knew him best. I was privileged to receive candid, loving, and amusing observations and contributions from the following people, many of whom I interviewed several times. My regret is that some did not live to see their contributions and that some interviews had to be cut or omitted for reasons of space or of repetition. My deepest gratitude to:

HSH Prince Albert of Monaco, Valerie Allen, Bobby Altman, Cleveland Amory, Richard Anderson, Johnny Andrews, Binnie Barnes, George Barrie, Ralph Bellamy, Milton Berle, Richard Bienen, Nicky Blair, Peter Bogdanovich, Mary Brian, Phyllis Brooks, Richard Brooks, George Burns, Sammy Cahn, Gemma Camins, Leslie Caron, Virginia Cherrill, Cy Coleman, Robert Cox, Judith Crist, Jean Dalrymple, Mary Lawrence Daves, Marvin Davis, Angie Dickinson, Stanley Donen, Betsy Drake, Irene Dunne, Clarice Earl, Marjorie Everett, Douglas Fairbanks, Jr., Irving Fein, Harry Fender, José Ferrer, Greer Garson Fogelson, Betty Ford, Charlotte Ford, John Forsythe, Stanley E. Fox, Betty Furness, Dr. Seymour J. Gray, Merv Griffin, Henry Gris, Florence Haley, Jack Haley, Jr., Monty Hall, Lesley Harris, Dr. Mortimer A. Hartman, Dr. Curtis Haug, William Randolph Hearst, Jr., Dr. Richard Henning, Audrey Hepburn, Katharine Hepburn, Robert Hutton, Rick Ingersoll, Quincy Jones, Frederique and Louis Jourdan, Garson and Marion (Seldes) Kanin, Sylvia Fine Kaye, George Kennedy, Kirk Kerkorian, Deborah Kerr, Stanley Kramer, Perry Lafferty, Dorothy Lamour, Hope Lange, Ralph Lauren, Steve Lawrence, Irving Lazar, Peggy Lee, Ernest Lehman, Mrs. Mervyn LeRoy, Jerry D. Lewis, Rich Little, Sophia Loren, Myrna Loy, David Mahoney, Roderick Mann, Johnny Maschio, Walter Matthau, Everett Mattlin, Audrey Meadows, Dan Melnick, Dina Merrill, Douglas Miller, Dick Moore, Gary Morton, Mrs. Ken (Bette Lou) Murray, Adolpho Navarro, Jamie Niven, Peter O'Malley, Thelma Orloff, Dr. Francis Page, William Paley, Vicky Palmer, Gregory Peck, Judy Quine, HSH Prince Rainier III of Monaco, Nancy Reagan, Burt Reynolds, Maurice Richlin, Hal Roach, Leighton Rosenthal, Steve Ross, Roy, of Siegfried and Roy, Jill St. John, Richard Schickel, Martha Scott, William Self, Irene Mayer Selznick, Walter Sharp, Bea Shaw, Sidney Sheldon, Siegfried, of Siegfried and Roy, Barbara and Frank Sinatra, Alexis Smith, Ray Stark, George Stevens, Jr., James Stewart, Peter Stone, Frank Tarloff, Elizabeth Taylor, David W. Tebet, Pat Ullman, Jack Valenti, Abigail Van Buren, Robert Wagner, Ray Walston, Billy Wilder, Robert Wise, Fay Wray, Sylvia Wu, Jane Wyatt, Michael York, Loretta Young, and Micky and Norman Zeiler.

In March 1989, working at the Margaret Herrick Library and Academy Film Archives in Los Angeles, the beneficiary of Cary Grant's papers, I was engulfed by boxes and boxes of material, much of which was still in the sorting process. An archivist offered her assistance. This book is imprinted with her skill and sensitivity. Dr. Joanne Yeck's Ph.D. in communications and her knowledge of early Hollywood proved invaluable. She helped me transform my material into a book. I bless the day we met.

Samuel S. Vaughan, as Nancy Sinatra's editor for her book

about her father, had occasion to speak to Cary Grant many times. Sam and I first met in 1984, when he, like all publishers, was trying to persuade Grant to write a book. After Grant's death, Sam encouraged me to make an outline and subsequently brought me to William Morrow. I will always be indebted to him for his unwavering interest in this project. At Morrow, he introduced me to Howard Kaminsky, the publisher, and Lisa Drew, vice-president and senior editor. Like Sam, they were devoted Cary Grant—and movie—fans. Not only had I found the right home, but also Sam became my editor. Enthusiastically, he improved the book, almost beyond recognition. Lisa good-humoredly and ingeniously made dozens and dozens of artistic and marketing decisions.

Pearl Hanig's painstaking and tasteful copyediting gave the book its final polish. Robert Shuman, Lisa Drew's chipper and cooperative assistant, walked me through each step of the publishing process, and Deborah Weiss Geline, chief copyeditor, went the last miles with me. The Morrow gang is fabulous.

Appreciative thanks to the helpful and spirited staff of the Margaret Herrick Library and Academy Film Archives—Linda Mehr, library director, Sam Gill, special collections archivist, Howard Prouty, acquisitions archivist, Robert Cushman, photograph curator, and Val Almenderez, processing archivist.

For patience, interest, and intelligence beyond anything I could have wished, I am indebted to Crystal Brian and Chris van Ness for transcribing hundreds of hours of taped interviews. When someone had difficulty remembering a date or name, they volunteered the information when they knew it and researched it when they didn't.

Special thanks to: Metta Hake, former historian at San Simeon; Cecil Saxby, Scotland Yard's former Detective Chief Superintendent; the *Ladies Home Journal;* the British Cabinet Office; and the British Foreign and Commonwealth Office.

The photograph captions by Ingrid Bergman, David Niven, and Rosalind Russell came from previously published material: *Ingrid Bergman: My Story* by Ingrid Bergman and Alan Burgess (Delacourt); *Bring on the Empty Horses* by David Niven (G. P. Putnam's Sons); and *Life Is a Banquet* by Rosalind Russell and Chris Chase (Random House).

Deborah Kerr graciously gave me permission to use her poem, written on the occasion of the Princess Grace Foundation

ACKNOWLEDGMENTS

Tribute to Cary Grant in 1988; and Joseph L. Mankiewicz and Ted Donaldson happily consented to the use of their letters. The children of Grant's friends were equally generous. Isabella Rossellini (Ingrid Bergman's daughter), Dr. Walter Odets (Clifford Odets's son), Jill Schary Robinson-Shaw (Dore Schary's daughter), and Lance Brisson (Rosalind Russell's son) were delighted to let me quote from letters found in Grant's papers.

Peter Bogdanovich voluntarily gave me his unpublished interviews with Howard Hawks and Alfred Hitchcock; George Stevens, Jr., willingly provided me with his notes from conversations with Grant about George Stevens, Sr; and Henry Gris and Jerry D. Lewis gave me carte blanche access to their numerous interviews with Grant.

Especially helpful were Katharine Hepburn, who introduced me to Betsy Drake (who had not talked previously about Grant), and Marje Everett, who paved the way for my conversations with Nancy Reagan, Elizabeth Taylor, and Walter Matthau.

My sincere thanks to Bea Shaw, one of Grant's most intimate friends, for many kindnesses, not the least of which was her patient reading of my first draft. Bea had never before talked about Cary Grant. Her almost total recall is exceptional. I treasure our mutual trust and friendship.

Heartfelt thanks to my special friends: Ray and Yvette Ellis for use of their Volvo and duplex apartment during the first leg of research in Los Angeles; Rita Battat-Silverman for her certainty; Dan Green for his wit and wisdom; Walter Bode for his steadfast reassurances; Judy Quine, with whom I shared many confidences; and Linda Civitello, a seasoned writer and techie, for encouragement, her introduction to Crystal and Chris, and for opening up another world for me with WordPerfect. And thank you, Phyllis Wright, for teaching me how to use it.

My mother, Ellen Hultgren, enjoyed her role of English teacher once again, correcting my spelling and grammar in the early draft. She also laughed in all the right places.

Finally, I most heartily thank Randy Lanchner, my confidant, agent, and savvy lawyer for his spirit, enthusiasm, and endurance. He survived the red-eye from Los Angeles to New York on weekends and selflessly stood by me during these years of my preoccupation with Cary Grant. Even though I called him Cary a few times, he's still my marvelous husband.

CONTENTS

CONTENTS

THE BACKGROUND OF THIS BOOK

June 1981. Ginger Rogers had agreed to make lecture appearances under the aegis of the New York lecture bureau where I was senior vice-president, and during one of our talks we discussed a publicity brochure for the announcement of her appearances. She wanted to avoid the obvious, a photo with Fred Astaire, and provided instead a still of her with Cary Grant. It was a great idea. Now all we needed was his approval.

I wrote to him and asked if we could use the picture.

Within days the office receptionist buzzed me. "There's a woman on line three who says she has a call for you from Cary Grant. . . . Ha-ha-ha-ha."

Of course, I knew it was Cary Grant. I had just written to him, and I knew he didn't hesitate to pick up the telephone to conduct business, often startling the person at the other end of the line.

Still . . . I pressed the button on my phone. A female voice said, "One moment, please, for Mr. Grant." The news of the call had spread through the office instantly, and I was surrounded by five women eager to overhear.

The famous staccato voice came through loud and clear. "Hello, this is Cary Grant. I have your letter about Ginger. How is Ginger? I haven't talked to her in such a long time. Tell me, do you have a number where I might reach her?"

We went back and forth about Ginger, and I almost forgot to ask him about the photograph. "Go right ahead," he said.

He was inquisitive. Where did the lectures take place? What were the audiences like? How often would Ginger give one?

I found him very easy to talk to and quickly took the opportunity to tell him how exciting it would be for me to have *him* as a client. His response was an equally quick but gracious no. "You're very kind, but I'm retired. And besides, I don't like to give speeches. No one is going to sit still for anything I have to say anyway."

I protested that *everyone* would be interested in what Cary Grant had to say. But he didn't want to listen. I persisted and explained that he didn't have to make a speech. He could simply take questions from the audience. "Yes, I know," he replied, "but I don't want to."

Hanging up the phone, I felt more inspired than defeated. I dashed off a lengthy letter describing lecture audiences. I guaranteed Grant kid-glove treatment, some fun, and the flexibility of doing as many or as few "lectures" as he liked.

Grant called back as soon as he received my letter. He thanked me for all the things I had to say. However, he thought I was making a terrible mistake by spending so much time on him because he wasn't interested. I said, honestly, "If you'll just try one evening, I know you'll be hooked."

For almost a year and a half this was my relationship with Cary Grant. I wrote. He called. Gradually I could tell he was becoming intrigued.

He became more open as time passed. He told me his wife Barbara was British and hadn't seen a great deal of the United States. Maybe an occasional lecture could double as a sight-seeing trip for Barbara.

I also learned he was extremely nervous about the idea of public speaking. Charm and humor masked his shyness. "Who would come to see an old geezer like me?" He argued, "I can't commit to anything because I don't know when I'll be available. I don't have the vaguest idea of where I want to be next week." Once he said he didn't need an agent. "Why, if I wanted to go to some colleges, I would just go."

Finally, in May 1982, he conceded, "I might be willing to break in my act if you get a cancellation. Or if you come up with something last minute near Los Angeles. In that case, by all means call me. But I'm not promising anything."

He explained that board meetings took him away from California. There were occasional trips to Washington, D.C., for the Kennedy Center. Once a year he went to Denver for a diabetes fund raiser. New York was always on his itinerary because of his affiliation with Fabergé. I was starting to get a still-better sense of him. If I could get a convenient date, one he would consider "on the way to" somewhere he was going, Grant might be ready to say yes.

Dick Henning's forum at Foothill College, which used the twenty-six-hundred-seat Flint Center for the Performing Arts in Cupertino (an hour south of San Francisco), was perfect for Grant's maiden lecture. Henning was well known for his red-carpet treatment. Notables from Henry Kissinger to Walter Cronkite to former U.S. Presidents had graced his stage. However, Henning booked a year in advance, and he seldom had a cancellation.

I decided to call anyway. "Would you be willing to try a booking without much lead time and simply advertise a mystery guest?" I asked. Henning said he had too many seats to take that risk. When I told him the guest would be Cary Grant, he promised to call the instant he had an opening.

Just two months later Henning had his first cancellation in seven years. Steve Allen was bowing out of an October 23, 1982, date to appear in his own Off Broadway revue. "It's just two months away!" Henning whooped into the telephone.

Perfect. I knew that Barbara Grant had not been to San Francisco. Henning listened patiently while I explained how nervous Grant would be. If I could get Grant to commit, there might be some unusual conditions. He wouldn't want any advance publicity, and he didn't like to be fussed over by the press. Henning was emphatic. No matter what it took, he wanted Cary Grant.

I laid everything out for Grant over the telephone. The theater was already sold out, so he didn't have to worry about filling twenty-six hundred seats. Henning assured me he would not use Grant's name in any advertising but would simply mail an announcement to ticket holders. There would be no press releases or invitations. All precautions would be taken to ensure that no tape recorders found their way into the theater. And Grant's contract would prevent Henning from taping the evening's proceedings. "I don't want a copy of the evening ending up in Taiwan," Grant said.

As part of the package, the Grants would have three days at his favorite Nob Hill hotel and a limousine for sight-seeing. When I finished the details, Grant responded, "Now that's what I call a discreet proposal."

He didn't seem the least bit hesitant. He was eager to go. However, October 23 fell on a Saturday, and he wouldn't work on a weekend. I felt sure Henning could change the date. "All right," Grant replied, "but I don't want that man to go to a lot of trouble. Hold on while I find out if Barbara wants to go to San Francisco." He came back with a "go ahead," provided we changed the date. A quick call to Henning, and the date was changed to Thursday, October 21.

When I got back to Grant, he presented a problem I hadn't anticipated. He was having second thoughts about the fee. "It's too much to charge that poor man," Grant demurred. "I'm not Pavarotti, with a big production. I'm just a guy who's going to sit on a stool and answer some questions. You give me that man's telephone number, and I'll tell him I'll come for a lower fee." I sidestepped and told Grant I would send him a letter with all the details. I understood how he felt. He didn't want to charge much for his first engagement. He'd never specified an amount, and I had negotiated the standard in the industry, not what I knew Cary Grant was worth.

My letter was unyielding. I told him he was welcome to call Henning and tell him how he appreciated this opportunity to "break in his act" so close to home. But if he intended to tell Henning he was getting too much money, I wanted to drop the whole thing. "The amount of money might be too much for you, Mr. Grant, but, in my opinion, it is not enough. That's my side of it, and I have tried to understand yours. However, it is done. If you were to change it, you will make me look foolish." The letter went by overnight mail.

The following day Grant was on the telephone. "I have your letter. I don't know quite what to say. I don't think I have ever received a letter quite like this one. I thank you for your clarity . . .

your honesty . . . and for putting me in my place."

God, he was wonderful.

The concept and format of *A Conversation with Cary Grant* (*Conversations*) was entirely his. He'd had some experience with a question and answer format. In the 1950s he promoted *To Catch a Thief* by appearing onstage at movie theaters. Grant explained, "I know people have a lot of questions. When you make a speech, you may bore the whole crowd, but if you answer a question, then you know at least one person is interested."

He wanted to set the tone for the evening with an eight-minute film clip. The Academy of Motion Picture Arts and Sciences had assembled a composite of Grant's films in 1970, when he was awarded an honorary Oscar. He chuckled. "I'll show some film clips in which I look moderately young and then come out on stage looking incredibly aged."

He didn't want anyone onstage with him. No moderator. No interviewer.

Keeping someone of Grant's phenomenal popularity a secret was like sneaking an elephant into a telephone booth. He was furious when he found out that the press was reporting he was coming to Cupertino. When Glenn Lovell, the entertainment writer for the San Jose *Mercury News,* called him, Grant was testy. "Look," Grant said, "I had an arrangement with the people there—absolutely no advance publicity. I'm distressed the word got out. When it comes down to it, the public doesn't really give a good hoot what I do. . . . It's the press. Why don't they just let me get on with it?"

On October 21 Grant walked onstage to tumultuous applause and a standing ovation. People yelled. They screamed. They laughed. And they cried. The questions flowed out. They unabashedly told Grant how much they loved him.

I wondered whether Grant had ever admitted to himself the kind of effect he had on people. He had spent much of his life avoiding public contact, yet there he was, bantering with twenty-six hundred strangers. He sat on a stool for two and one-half hours. And for what must have been the rare awkward moment in his public life, he couldn't figure out how to get off the stage. He hadn't prepared an exit.

When he was asked why he was onstage, he replied, "To regain my self-confidence."

He seemed genuinely surprised by the reaction of the adoring crowd. He appeared to be even more impressed with his favorable "notices." But when I asked him when he would be ready to do another, he laughed. "Now, don't get carried away."

Could I see him in New York the following month? He said, "You'll be wasting your time, Nancy. I really can't say I'll ever do another one of these things."

It was cat and mouse all over again.

November 1982. It took a few more telephone calls and some prodding, but Grant had a change of heart. We agreed to meet for breakfast in his suite at the Pierre Hotel.

Flustered, I left my apartment early that morning without applying lipstick. It upset me that I didn't look pulled together. Grant would think I had just fallen out of bed.

When I rang the bell to his suite, he opened the door himself. I tried not to look nervous. He was dressed simply and impeccably in dark gray trousers and a long-sleeved white shirt. There wasn't one gray hair out of place. And he was so lively. In California it was only six in the morning. I was to learn he never suffered from time changes or jet lag. He complimented me on my knitted sweater-jacket. I told him I had become a compulsive knitter when I gave up smoking. He said his wife also liked to knit and sew. Little did I know these details of our first meeting—my lack of makeup, my fondness for knitting, and especially the fact that I had given up smoking—all were in my favor.

He poured my coffee. At seventy-eight he was handsomer than ever. And he had more sex appeal than men half his age.

He smiled and laughed. His eyes, yes, twinkled. I felt at home. It was easy to talk with him. He was very intelligent, sincere, and interested, asking question after question.

At one point in the conversation his wife Barbara came into the room. She was young and very beautiful. Her natural brown hair was pulled back in a classic chignon. She wore not a hint of makeup but looked as though she had stepped from the pages of an ad for Ralph Lauren. She was stunning in that year's "riding suit"—a navy blue jacket fitted at the waist, a long navy blue skirt, and navy boots. A Chanel bag rested on a chair.

Mrs. Grant greeted me warmly. A gracious and proper Englishwoman, I thought, as she moved about the room. It was quickly apparent that she was organized and competent. Clearly she made things run. She had letters to mail, a car to order for the trip to the airport and their flight to Washington, where they would attend a dinner that evening in the White House, and someone to meet in the public rooms of the hotel. They seemed a devoted couple, constantly looking at each other adoringly.

Every twenty minutes or so I tried to excuse myself. I didn't want to overstay my welcome. Each time I did, Grant had more questions. I was flattered by the attention.

He admitted that his experience at Cupertino had been relaxing and enjoyable. In fact, it was an unexpectedly stimulating experience. He couldn't commit to any future dates, but he did say he was interested in showing his wife the United States—New Orleans, New England, Santa Fe, Florida. He might even go back to San Francisco . . . . "My daughter, Jennifer, is at Stanford, you know."

I left him walking on air. I was completely bedazzled. I didn't know where it would all lead.

Late May 1983. Tenacity pays. The company with which I was associated moved to Connecticut. Grant called me in June and encouraged me to start my own agency. "Do that, Nancy, and you can have me as a client. I won't be the biggest one you'll ever have. After all, I'm not going to do very much. But it'll be good for you to have me" were his exact words. *I wasn't dreaming.*

From late 1982 until his death on November 29, 1986, Grant made thirty-six public appearances. One thousand, two thousand, sometimes three thousand people rocked with laughter and poured out their love.

Accompanying Grant and his wife, I was struck by the richness, the warmth, and the intimacy of these evenings. Soon word of Grant's extraordinary agility as a storyteller, both off and on-stage, spread to performing arts presenters the world over. My office was deluged with requests for him—in person and on tape. However, Grant himself determined where he would go. And when. Usually with only a month's notice. No tapes were made.

From the beginning I felt compelled to make extensive and

detailed notes about those evenings and my travels with the Grants. Because I knew he would never write a full autobiography (he was adamant about that), my plan was someday to convince him to produce a memoir. I would prepare it with him—a "from the back seat with" kind of book. I casually mentioned the idea in Oklahoma City in March 1984.

"Only if we're all standing in a breadline, Nancy," was his response.

I was not disheartened. I had heard this before. I just kept making notes.

November 1986. The news from Davenport, Iowa, where he was preparing for his program, was sudden and sad. Cary Grant was dead at eighty-two. It wasn't possible.

My plans to help with his memoir were abandoned. Since Grant had refused all publishing offers for his life's story, the three-article series he had done for the *Ladies' Home Journal* in 1963 and these *Conversations* would be the closest his admirers would ever get to an autobiography.

May 1987. Even though Grant was gone, I continued to get calls and letters asking for transcripts from his evenings. This unfailing interest in him encouraged me. I envisioned a modest memoir based solely on the *Conversations*, but after a lunch in New York in the fall of 1988 with Jill St. John and Robert Wagner, I had a new idea. Their stories about Grant stirred up gales of laughter—and a few tears. I had found a new dimension for the project.

March 1989. Barbara Grant made it possible for me to interview many of Grant's friends. In New York I spoke with Katharine Hepburn, Burt Reynolds, Douglas Fairbanks, Jr., and Audrey Hepburn. By April I was in Beverly Hills, talking to Jimmy Stewart, Irene Dunne, George Burns, Gregory Peck, Elizabeth Taylor, Betsy Drake, Quincy Jones, Nancy Reagan, Loretta Young, Walter Matthau, Louis Jourdan, Abigail Van Buren, John Forsythe, and Dorothy Lamour.

Barbara Grant also made available Grant's important letters, family papers, early contracts, scripts, jokes, speeches, notebooks, and photographs. The book grew and grew.

My notes from Grant's *Conversations* have been enhanced by selections from his articles and from Grant's personal papers. The one hundred fifty interviews proved to be invaluable.

October 1991. As it now stands, this book is a sort of memoir with various voices, some famous, some not. The cast of characters at the back of the book offers a minibiography for each of the speakers. But one voice predominates.

Evenings with Cary Grant is not a biography. It is a celebration, a tribute. As an author I have shunned most vest-pocket psychoanalysis, conjecture, rumor, secondary sources, and supposition and have done my best to step aside, giving center stage to those to whom it belongs—to Cary Grant and his friends.

CG: I think that being relaxed at all times, and I mean re-laxed, not collapsed, can add to the happiness and duration of one's life and looks. And relaxed people are fun to be around.

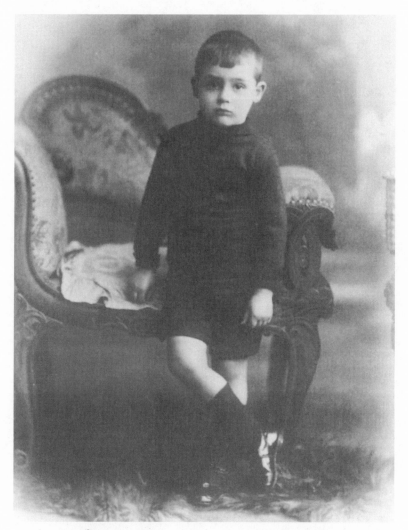

Grant selected and signed this picture of himself at age five for the front cover of his New York Friars Club tribute program on May 16, 1982. He also sent the picture in sterling silver Cartier frames as gifts to special friends.

CHAPTER ONE

ARCHIE LEACH

CG: I first saw the light of day—or rather the dark of night—around 1:00 A.M. on a cold January morning, in a suburban stone house which, lacking modern heating conveniences, kept only one step ahead of freezing by means of small coal fires in small bedroom fireplaces; and ever since, I've persistently arranged to spend every possible moment where the sun shines warmest.

Elsie Maria Kingdon, twenty-one, and Elias James Leach, twenty-five, were married on May 30, 1898, by Vicar Charles E. Perkins at the parish Church of St. Matthias-on-the-Weir in the seaport town of Bristol in the southwestern part of England.

A son was born on January 18, 1904. His parents named him Archibald Alexander. Vicar E. W. Oakden baptized the child in the Episcopal faith on February 8, 1904, in the Horfield parish church. His baptismal certificate states his middle name as Alec. His birth certificate (which Grant said was lost in a Bristol fire during World War I) identified it as Alexander. Nonetheless, it was a child called Archie Leach who would become a man known as Cary Grant and achieve international fame.

Possibly because Grant himself had a lasting affection for his original appellation (he even named one of his dogs, a Sealyham terrier, Archie Leach), the public has long been aware that Cary Grant started out life as Archie. When he ad-libbed lines in *His Girl Friday* and *Gunga Din* referring to Archie Leach, they were

27

inside jokes the audience understood. And when John Cleese played "Archie Leach" in *A Fish Called Wanda*, it was an homage to a beloved thespian.

According to DAVID W. TEBET, Grant never lost his fondness for his birth name: "When the New York Friars Club paid tribute to Cary in 1982, I asked him what he'd like on the front cover of the program. He gave me a picture of himself at age five with a facsimile of his boyhood signature, Archie Leach."

Many people have claimed to be related to Cary Grant. Some were named Leach. Some were named Grant. Whatever their motivation and whatever their name, the desire to be connected to the rich legacy that was the exquisite blend of Archie Leach and Cary Grant was universal. Millions of moviegoers felt it.

Elias and Elsie Leach reared a proper son. They taught him to be polite to strangers and to observe the law and manners of the time. He learned to speak only when spoken to and that money did not grow on trees. They were churchgoing people. JEAN DALRYMPLE remembers that one of Grant's earliest acting efforts was in a Bible class play. "In Bristol Archie played Joseph with his coat of many colors. I always thought he was quite religious. He often told me he relied on and believed in God."

PEGGY LEE found Grant to be "religious but never pious." RICHARD BROOKS tells of their never-ending theological debate: "Faith, religion, and God were important to Cary. Our usual discussion was the difference between reality and faith. If you have faith, you don't question God or his actions. Cary couldn't see why it should be left to faith. . . . Our discussion went on for years. To this day I don't know what his faith was. I never had the temerity to ask."

Archie grew up in a working-class family. They lived in a gaslit stone row house. Small fireplaces kept them warm during the cold, damp English winters. On his marriage license Elias Leach stated his occupation as "tractor's presser." He pressed men's suits for a living. Grant's paternal grandfather, John Leach, was a potter; his maternal grandfather, William Kingdon, a ship's carpenter.

In time Grant's friends observed an interesting correlation between the actor's personality and his origins. MAURICE RICHLIN "knew three people who became giant stars: Charlie Chaplin,

Maurice Chevalier, and Cary Grant. All three started out poor."
JOHN FORSYTHE sees parallels particularly with Charlie Chaplin's
childhood: "Chaplin came from a broken home, slept in hallways,
and very often had to rummage in garbage pails for things to
eat. . . . I don't know if Cary came from such an impoverished
background, but he was a poor kid. He did scrape his way to the
top. That meticulous quality he had—knowing how to best use
himself—was one of the key things to his nature."

BETSY DRAKE notes that "in Cary's day you got nowhere—
*no*where—with a lower-class accent. The fact that he survived all
that speaks very well for him."

QUINCY JONES believes that when Grant was growing up, "the
upper-class English viewed the lower classes like black people.
Cary and I both had an identification with the underdog. My perception is that we could be really open with each other because
there was a serious parallel in our experience."

Elsie and Elias Leach were an attractive couple. One of
Grant's earliest and best memories of his mother and father was
of waking up one night in a thunderstorm and seeing his parents
standing together at the window with their arms around each
other's waists. Yet the adult Cary Grant could see their underly-
ing unsuitability reflected in photographs.

> CG [describing a photograph of his parents]: My father
> was a handsome, tallish man with a fancy moustache,
> but the photograph does not show that he possessed an
> outwardly cheerful sense of humor and, to balance it, an
> inwardly sad acceptance of the dull life he had chosen.
> My mother was a delicate black-haired beauty, with
> olive skin, frail and feminine to look upon. What isn't
> apparent in the photograph is the extent of her strength
> and her will to control—a deep need to receive unre-
> servedly the very affection she sought to control.

In 1912 Grant's father was offered a better-paying job in
Southampton, about eighty miles from Bristol. There he worked
for a firm that made khaki uniforms for the expanding British
army.

> CG: Odd, but I don't remember my father's departure
> from Bristol. Perhaps I felt guilty at being secretly

Elias Leach, CG's father. CG: *"He possessed an outwardly cheerful sense of humor and, to balance it, an inwardly sad acceptance of the dull life he had chosen."*

pleased. Or was I pleased? Now I had my mother to
myself . . . but I missed him very much.

Grant and his mother moved to a larger house in Bristol. They
shared the house and expenses with two young female cousins.
Grant's mother arranged for piano lessons. He played at school as-
semblies and throughout adulthood maintained his love of the piano. THELMA ORLOFF says, "He played a real beer hall piano, a real
jazzy piano. He never had any music in front of him. He would doo-
dle on the keyboard and play and sing and carry on like crazy." And
BEA SHAW remembers that when Grant was in vaudeville, the performers played the piano for one another at rehearsals. "The danc-
ers and singers liked him to play because he could keep the beat.
Also, he didn't just play by ear. He could read music."

> CG: My piano teacher, an unhandsome irascible woman,
> came to the house specifically, I think, to rap the knuck-
> les of my left hand with a ruler. Curiously, although I
> was left-handed, my interpretation of the bass notes was
> decidedly weak. If my bass hand were as strong as I
> suspect my base nature to be, I'd be a virtuoso.

Grant was grateful he had not been forced into right-handed-
ness. One of his favorite books, *A Social History of Left-Handers,*
was written by a technician with the BBC.

> CG: This technician was editing the recorded speeches
> of King George VI, erasing the King's stammer. He
> knew that many people stammer because they're frus-
> trated, but wondered what could possibly frustrate a
> king. He did some research and found out. It seems
> George had been naturally left-handed but was forced
> as a child to use his right hand. I realized when I read
> the book how very lucky I was that my teachers in Bris-
> tol didn't have the same intolerance. If I'd grown up
> with a stammer, it might have proved something of a
> hindrance to my film career.

Elias Leach's new job in Southampton lasted only a few
months. Despite the increased salary, he was not able to support
two households. He returned to Bristol and his old job. The family, including his cousins, moved to a smaller house. Grant told

Elsie Leach, CG's mother, in Bristol, England. CG: *"What isn't apparent . . . is the extent of her strength . . . a deep need to receive unreservedly the very affection she sought to control."*

JEAN DALRYMPLE that "his parents didn't pay much attention to him. Cary said they used to go to the pub and 'drink it up,' but he never said mean things about them."

Young Archie was filled with wanderlust and decided to investigate the larger world.

> CG: I was about eight years old when another little chap and I built a trolley (just a wooden plank on wheels). We set off adventuring with no money and no food. We got as far as Bath [about twelve miles] on the thing before we decided to turn back. When we reached home, it was about three o'clock in the morning. My father was waiting up for me and the police were conducting a search.

In 1913 Grant's mother disappeared. One day she was there squabbling as usual with Elias. The next day she was gone. When she didn't return, he naturally asked why. He was told his mother had gone for a rest at a nearby resort. Grant thought this unusual but accepted it. As the weeks went by, however, he realized that she was not coming back at all. There was no further discussion of her absence. HENRY GRIS describes Grant's bewilderment: "Cary told me it wasn't until many years later that he realized the depth of his guilt complex about his mother's disappearance. He believed *he* was the subject of his parents' many bitter quarrels."

By the time he learned his mother had been committed to a sanitorium for the mentally ill, following a nervous breakdown, Grant was an adult.

> CG: I was not to see my mother again for more than twenty years, by which time my name was changed and I was a full-grown man living in America, thousands of miles away in California. I was known to most people of the world by sight and by name, yet not to my mother.

He speculated that the tragedy of her first son, John William Elias Leach, born on February 9, 1899, was the basis of her illness.

> CG: He was in my mother's arms when a door slammed on his thumbnail. It was torn off, and he developed gan-

grene. My mother stayed up night after night to be with him, suffering severe exhaustion. When she finally took her first sleep, the child died of convulsions.

Grant believed she never forgave herself for that small, exhausted nap.

School portrait, Class I, Bishop Road Boys' School, Bristol, England. Archie is standing in the back row, the sixth child from the left.

When he was four and a half, Grant started school. He didn't like school, and he dreaded homework. Nevertheless, his 1913 report card from the Bishop Road Boys' School shows Grant was an excellent student. He was never late and never absent; indeed, he was credited 117 times for being early. He earned

excellent grades in reading, writing, arithmetic, dictation, drawing, and conduct. His class mistress, R. E. Pinkard, praised his
performance in the all-male class of forty-one students.

Not long after his mother's sudden, long-unexplained absence, Grant's world was disrupted a second time by Britain's
entry into the Great War. Food was rationed, and Grant learned
to take his tea without sugar. Often alone, Grant joined the first
Bristol YMCA Boy Scout Troop and was assigned air-raid duty.
His job was to climb up the gaslit streetlamps and extinguish
them as quickly as possible. He applied for war work wherever
his services as a Scout could be used. Eager to escape Bristol, he
welcomed any assignment promising travel. He was given work
as a messenger and guide on the Southampton docks, where no
one was permitted unless he was wearing a uniform or carrying
a special pass.

> CG: I saw thousands of young men sail away into the
> night toward France, packed into transport ships that
> were, prayerfully, fast enough to outdistance the enemy
> submarines that waited for them in the English Chan-
> nel; and if I was on gangplank duty I sadly noted the
> quick moment of apprehension cross each face, the first
> premonition of danger, as I issued every soldier a life
> belt and accompanied it with a few cheerful notes of in-
> struction to hide my feelings. Hundreds of those men
> drowned only a few miles from their homeland before
> even reaching the battlefront.
>
> Although it was not part of our duties, the scouts
> often delivered messages and mailed letters for the sol-
> diers waiting in the dock sheds on their last day in En-
> gland. It was a point of honor among us not to take
> money for our small services. So, as we had no other
> way of escaping their touching gratitude, we accepted
> mementos instead—a military button or regimental
> badge—and displayed them with the pride of collectors,
> attached to our belts, which were heavy with tokens.
>
> All military movement into and out of the docks was
> made throughout the night. Soldiers poured through
> Southampton and the rows of sheds were filled and re-
> filled. There were no seats and the men sat or lay

around the floor among their kits. Some of them had already been out to the front once and lost an arm or leg, yet were returning to fight again. One officer, a Guardsman, had been to the front twice before and had lost an arm, and a leg at the knee, but was still going back again to rejoin his regiment in the trenches.

In 1915, when Grant was eleven, he and his father moved to the house of his father's mother on Campbell Street in Bristol.

CG: We lived in the lower floor front and upstairs back bedrooms and my grandmother lived in the lower back part and upstairs front bedrooms. However, I didn't see a great deal of her and took care of my own needs as best I could, sharing Saturday and Sunday breakfast and midday dinner [with his grandmother and father], and scrounging around in the kitchen, or stone larder, for other meals on my own.

That same year he won a scholarship to the local Fairfield Secondary School. The Liberal government offered tuition to a limited number of children whose parents could not afford to pay. Grant thought it would lead to one of England's great universities, an aspiration that faded when he realized such costs were beyond his father's means.

Although he never finished his secondary education, Grant remembered Fairfield and in 1953 donated money to the Old Fairfieldians' Society.

His lack of formal education was one of Grant's lifelong regrets. JEAN DALRYMPLE says, "One time, Cary and I were having lunch at Romanoff's in Los Angeles. He commented what a great pity it was that he had not been properly educated. Then he spoke in French. I said, 'But you've learned French.' 'Oh, I've picked it up,' he said. And I said, 'Well, you've done a wonderful job of educating yourself, haven't you?'"

Despite his acceptance to Fairfield, Grant continued to dislike school, especially Latin and mathematics. He preferred geography, history, art, and chemistry. But his real love was the cinema. On Saturday afternoons Grant queued up on Castle Street to see Charlie Chaplin, Ford Sterling (who headed the famous Keystone Kops), Fatty Arbuckle, Mack Swain, John Bunny with Flora Finch, and his idol, Bronco Billy Anderson, the cow-boy star.

On rainy days when he couldn't play fives (English handball), Grant sometimes loitered in the school's chemistry lab. In that room the science professor's part-time assistant, an electrician, helped the young Archie Leach take a first step toward becoming Cary Grant.

> CG: He was a jovial, friendly man with children of his own, and one day, in kindly response to my eagerness to learn about anything electrical, he invited me to visit the newly-built Bristol Hippodrome, in which he'd installed the switchboard and lighting system. The Saturday matinee was in full swing when I arrived backstage; and there I suddenly found my inarticulate self in a dazzling land of smiling, jostling people wearing and not wearing all sorts of costumes and doing all sorts of clever things. And that's when I *knew*! What other life could there *be* but that of an actor? They happily traveled and toured. They were classless, cheerful and carefree. They gaily laughed, lived, and loved.

His friend introduced him to the manager of another Bristol theater, the Empire, where he was invited to assist the men who worked the arc lamps, the limelights. While working there, Grant conceived a new theatrical lighting effect that so interested the manager of the Empire that he was allowed to install and operate it. He was only thirteen years old.

At the Empire he saw star attractions, including the famed magician the Great David Devant, originator of many spectacular illusions. Young Leach's fascination with things magical never waned. Years later in Los Angeles he joined the board of the Magic Castle (a private magicians' dinner club) and its Academy of Magical Arts. Lines such as "Come up and saw me sometime" livened up the occasional speech he made at award dinners. Grant took an interest in and aided talented young magicians. Illusionist SIEGFRIED, of Siegfried and Roy, holds him in high esteem: "Cary was our inspiration. He is the only person to whom we showed illusions before we finished them."

Always full of shenanigans, Grant liked to surprise others with the wonders of magic. LESLEY HARRIS found Grant mischievous when they went to the Magic Castle together. She says: "Cary had me sit on a barstool. He stood there laughing as it went down into the floor and disappeared with me on it." And Grant taught LORETTA YOUNG an impressive trick on the set of *The Bishop's Wife:* "Cary said he could take off [director] Henry Koster's shirt without removing his coat. I said it was impossible. To prove it to me, Cary had Henry sit on a chair, take his tie off, and unbutton his cuffs. Then Cary grabbed the back of Henry's shirt and pulled it right up. His coat was still on and his shirt was off!

"So Cary said, 'I'll teach you the trick, and the next time we go to a party, we'll be all set.' Well, the next party was at my house, for about forty people. After dinner I asked a couple of my guests if I could take their shirts off. Each one said, 'No. You'll ruin my shirt.' Finally Cary said, 'Well, Loretta's been so wonderful to us tonight, I'll let her take off my shirt.' We took bets from the guests on whether I could do it. I don't remember how much money we won, but we turned it all over to charity."

Grant himself, however, was not an accomplished magician. "I'm interested in magic," he said, "but I can't do a blessed thing."

While the young man's smile became known to millions of people, one fact went practically unnoticed. At thirteen he fell face forward on an icy playground, changing his grin forever.

CG: My tooth snapped in half. Straight across. I didn't want my father to know, so I had the remaining piece pulled out at a dental school, where extractions were either free or reasonable enough for me to pay out of my weekly pocket money. I was left with a gap right in the middle of my upper front teeth, but by keeping my mouth shut (quite an unusual accomplishment) at home that weekend, I kept father from noticing the gap, and by the next weekend it had already begun to close up.

The only person who ever remarked upon that tooth's absence, including even dentists, was Mack Sennett, the great comedy-picture producer, who came backstage to visit me in New York years later, and surprised me by saying that his camera-trained eye had noticed it from the audience.

During 1918, at the early age of fourteen, Grant recorded his activities. His Boy Scout's Notebook and Diary, a handbook that includes instructions on all sorts of things, from sending smoke signals to developing individuality, also contains a journal bearing his adolescent scribbling.

The four-by-three-inch leather-bound volume shows he was no longer the diligent scholar. He was spending a great deal of time out of school and at the Empire Theater. Entries from January reveal the pattern of his days. And nights.

14 Monday. After school I went and bought a new belt. And a new tie. Empire in evening. Daro-Lyric Kingston's Rosebuds.

17 Thursday. Stayed home from school all day. Went to Empire in evening. Snowing.

18 Friday. My birthday. Stayed home from school. In afternoon went in town. In evening, Empire. Second house . . . out to King's Hall. Snowing. Letter from Mary M.

19 Saturday. Had a new suit. A new pair of shoes. And a new cap. Seen show. In evening went to Empire. Great fuss in review. Two people did not turn up.

20 Sunday, second after Epiphany. Wore new suit. Went out to tea.

21 Monday. School. Wrote letter to Mary M. Empire in evening. Not a bad show. Captain De Villier's wireless airship at the top of bill. Bale [not legible] flies around hall twenty feet long. Alec Fountain and Delia at bottom of bill. Mr. Macane gave me pass for two in stalls [for] Thursday, second house.

22 Tuesday. School all day. In evening, Empire. All went well, first house. But second house, wireless balloon got out of control and went on people in circle. Good comedy cyclist called Lotto.

23 Wednesday. School. In afternoon came to school, got my mark, and went to matinee. Miss [name not legible] didn't notice it. Stayed at hall for tea, and went over Olympia till they finished matinee. Then worked first and second house.

24 Thursday. School again. Only a month to claim

five-pound note. Went to Empire in evening. All right
first house. Second house was a row between Saunders
and Billiers.

25 Friday. Conversion of St. Paul. Late for school
in morning. In evening, Empire as usual.

26 Saturday. Strolled about. Empire evening. Did
well in tips [presumably from escorting people to their
seats].

So, at fourteen, Grant was evaluating shows and forming
likes and dislikes of music hall performers. As the year pro-
gressed, he skipped school more frequently, attending matinees
as well as pantomimes in the evenings. In March he records that
he had a whiskey.

"Exams febanams (worse luck)" is written in the front of the
book. In the back are a cash account and a list of his friends' addresses, many of them "on tour." His letter register reveals the
start of a habit he maintained the rest of his life. On December 16,
1917, he notes that he received a letter from Marion Siehohar,
54 Ackland Road, Kensington, London. With a pen he wrote across
the entry that he had answered it. He remained meticulous about
recording his response to a letter or document, noting whether he
wrote or telephoned, although he almost always omitted the substance of the response.

During these years he was unaware his father was corresponding with his mother. Elias Leach wrote to her on May 5,
1918, from 12 Campbell Street, St. Paul's, Bristol:

MY DEAR WIFE,
I am very sorry that I have not written to you before. . . . I am very pleased to say that Archie is going along
alright and also that he is in the very best of health and that
he is enjoying himself alright. I am very glad to know that
you are going along alright and that you are getting better
which I hope will continue for you. I am also pleased to say
that I am enjoying the best of health at present, which I also
hope will maintain with me. Archie is going up to see Joe
and Emmie this afternoon for he goes up now very often to
see them. They are always asking after you and your health
and hope that you will soon be with us once again.

I remain your loving husband ELIAS.
With kind love and kisses from Archie xxxxxxxxxx

Sometime in 1918 Grant learned about Bob Pender's troupe of knockabout comedians. Too young to be released from school, he wrote a letter about himself to Pender, enclosed a snapshot, and signed Elias Leach's name. He neglected to tell Pender he was only fourteen.

Grant diligently watched for letters addressed to his father, and soon back came an answer from Bob Pender. He suggested that Elias Leach's son, Archibald, meet the troupe in Norwich. Pender even enclosed the railway fare. Grant quietly left in the middle of the night bound for Norwich. Since he and his father were accustomed to leaving the house at different hours without seeing each other, he knew it would be some time before he was missed.

CG: [Pender] was a stocky, strongly built, likable man of about forty-two who had been renowned as the great Drury Lane clown. I suspected that he suspected that Archie and Elias James Leach were the same correspondent, but he introduced me to his kind wife, Margaret, a well-known dancer whom he'd met when she was ballet mistress at the Folies-Bergère in Paris.

Pender agreed to take him on. Grant lived with Mr. and Mrs. Pender and two or three of the youngest members of the company and began instruction in ground tumbling and acrobatic dances. He practiced makeup and thickly covered his face with greasepaint. (Later in his career he wore no makeup at all.)

Within ten days of Archie's joining Pender's troupe, Elias Leach caught up with them in Ipswich and reclaimed his son. But Leach and Pender sat down and discussed the boy's future. Both men were Masons, were of like mind, and agreed that Archie should finish his education.

Leach and his son returned to Bristol and Fairfield, where Grant did everything he could to be expelled. Determined to rejoin Pender, he cut class after class.

CG: One afternoon another boy of equal curiosity and I decided to sneak over the girls' side of school to investigate the inside of the girls' lavatories. . . . No one was around. I kept watch at the end of the corridor while he went in to see what it looked like. And then, just as it came my turn to explore the inner sanctum, I was suddenly, out of nowhere, shrilly nabbed by a powerful female who must have been the hockey teacher at least.

The following morning when the school filed in for morning prayer in the assembly hall my name was called and I was marched up the steps onto the dais and taken to stand next to [Augustus] Gussie Smith [the headmaster], where, with a quivering lip that I did my best to control, I hazily heard such words as "inattentive . . . irresponsible and incorrigible . . . discredit to the school." . . . I was being publicly expelled in front of the assembled school.

Young Archie Leach had achieved his goal. Three days later he was back with the Pender troupe, this time with Elias Leach's permission. The father realized it was futile to try to keep the boy in school against his wishes.

The contract between Pender and Leach, now yellow with age, is written in longhand:

MEMORANDUM OF AGREEMENT

Made this day 9th of Aug. 1918 between Robert Pender of 247 Brixton Road, London, on the one part, *Elias Leach* of 12 Campbell Street, Bristol, on the other part.

The said Robert Pender agrees to employ the *son* of the said *Elias Leach* Archie Leach in his troupe at a weekly salary of 10/- [approximately $2.38 in U.S. currency] a week with *board* and *lodgings* and everything found for the stage, and *when not* working full board and lodgings.

This salary to be increased as the said *Archie* Leach *improves* in his *profession* and he agrees to *remain* in the employment of *Robert Pender* till he is 18 years of age or a six months notice on either sides.

Robert Pender undertaking to teach him dancing & other accomplishments needful for his work.

Archie Leach agrees to work to the best of his abilities.

Signed, BOB PENDER

CG: Over the years I've signed many lengthy, involved typed contracts calling for me to earn great sums of money, but no employment contract since has ever matched the thrill of that one sheet of ordinary notepaper stating that I was to have the opportunity of learn-

The Bob Pender Troupe, with whom Archie, fifteen (in front, extreme right), *toured the English provinces. When CG turned eighty, he wanted to go home again and tour with his evening* Conversations. *However, the impresario chosen as the most "reliable" wanted to use a dubious contract. "I've never ducked income tax in my life," Grant said, "and I'm certainly not going to do that now. We won't deal with that man. . . ."*

ing a profession that appealed to me more than any other in the world.

Three months after joining Pender, he was back in Bristol, this time onstage at the Empire Theater.

CG: Touring the English provinces with the troupe, I grew to appreciate the fine art of pantomime. No dialogue was used in our act and each day, on a bare stage, we learned not only dancing, tumbling and stilt-walking under the expert tuition of Bob Pender, but also how to convey a mood or meaning without words. How to establish communication silently with an audience, using the minimum of movement and expression; how best immediately and precisely to effect an emotional response—a laugh or, sometimes, a tear. The greatest pantomimists of our day have been able to induce both at once. Charles Chaplin, Cantinflas, Marcel Marceau, Jacques Tati, Fernandel, and England's Richard Herne. And in bygone years Grock, the Lupino family, Bobby Clark, and the unforgettable tramp cyclist Joe Jackson; and currently Danny Kaye, Red Skelton, Sid Caesar, and even Jack Benny with his slow, calculated reactions. Surprisingly, Hitchcock is one of the most subtle pantomimists of them all.

While playing the great Gulliver circuit of vaudeville theaters in London, Grant and most of the other boys lived with the Penders in their home in Brixton, sleeping dormitory-style.

When World War I ended, Pender expanded to two complete troupes, including former members of the company who had returned from the front. With this expansion Grant finally graduated from minor performer to stilt walker and pantomimist.

In 1920 Grant's excitement at touring the English cities and countryside was eclipsed by a totally new adventure. Bob Pender booked an engagement with a Charles Dillingham production at the Globe Theater in New York City. Eight boys were chosen to go.

In July Archie Leach, sixteen, carrying British passport 5016, sailed to America aboard the SS *Olympic*.

CHAPTER TWO

A SPRINKLING OF STARDUST

CG: New York City. There it was; but was I *there*? Was I actually there at the ship's rail, neatly scrubbed and polished, standing with a small, solitary band of Pender-troupe boys—none of whom had slept all night for fear of missing the first glimpse of America?

The troupe crossed the Atlantic in the SS *Olympic*'s affordable second class. In first class the most celebrated newlyweds in the world, Douglas Fairbanks and Mary Pickford, were returning from their European honeymoon.

Grant's glimpses of Fairbanks provided him with the perfect example of elegance and style. Tanned and fit, the star epitomized the gentleman. Grant found his dress tasteful and timeless. He never forgot Fairbanks's style, and dozens of years later he described it down to the last detail to RALPH LAUREN, who says, "Cary tried to convince me to make a double-breasted tuxedo like the one worn by Fairbanks, same lapel and all."

On board Grant was photographed with Fairbanks during a game of shuffleboard. Some years later, when Grant played vaudeville in Los Angeles, Fairbanks invited him to the set of *The Thief of Baghdad*. When Grant achieved his own stardom in Hollywood, he became friendly with DOUGLAS FAIRBANKS, JR.: "Cary's relationship with my father was en passant. My father and I were always very cozy, but we didn't see much of one another. My crowd and his didn't mix."

The Pender troupe was met by a Dillingham representative, who took them directly to the Globe Theater. A change of programs put the act into another Dillingham production at the world's largest theater, the Hippodrome. It stood on Sixth Avenue, between Forty-third and Forty-fourth streets. There they were to play matinees and evenings every day, except Sundays, to ten thousand people a week.

> CG: The most renowned and spectacular acts of the day appeared: "Poodles" Hanneford and The Riding Hanneford Family; Marceline the clown; The Long Tack Sam Company of Illusionists; Joe Jackson the tramp cyclist; and Powers Elephants, an amazing water spectacle in which expert girl swimmers and high divers appeared and reappeared in an under-stage tank containing 960,000 gallons of water.

Though not a star, Grant was part of the magic for one young member of the audience, STANLEY E. FOX: "I was at the Hippodrome in the early 1920s, when I was fourteen or fifteen years old. There was a huge stage. In one show there were fifteen or twenty Hippodrome diving girls, swimmers who dove into a great big pool and vanished. As it turns out, Cary was the person who tended the trapdoor through which they disappeared."

Still a minor, Grant lived with the Penders and the other boys in an apartment near Eighth Avenue.

> CG: We had rotating duties. I learned to keep accounts for, cater for, and market for, to wash dishes for, to make the beds for, and to cook for every other occupant of that apartment. . . . Thanks to my Boy Scout training, I knew how to cook a stew.

From the Bronx Zoo to the Battery, Grant traveled around New York City. He spent hours on Fifth Avenue's open-air buses. Gladys Kincaid, a ballet dancer and a Hippodrome girl, had caught his fancy, but their shyness thwarted a romance.

After the show closed in 1921, the troupe departed for Philadelphia to begin a tour of the B. F. Keith vaudeville circuit. They played theaters throughout the East, including Cleveland, Boston, Chicago, as well as the Palace, in New York City.

Back in England, Elias Leach was living in Bristol with

Mabel Alice Johnson. Their son, Eric Leslie Leach, was born on September 5, 1921. Grant barely knew his half brother but one day was to support him and set him up in business.

By 1922 Grant's travels enabled him to step into the world of celebrities. He met Jack Dempsey, the heavyweight champion of the world, and, earlier, toward the end of his presidency, Woodrow Wilson (when, in his wheelchair, Wilson attended a performance at the Keith Theater in Washington, D.C.). Among the would-be celebrities Grant knew was GEORGE BURNS, who says: "Before I met Gracie, she was doing an act with Larry Reilly, and he introduced us to Archie.

"We met sometime in the 1920s. He was the best-looking guy I'd ever seen. . . . We used to have dinner together once in a while. At the Automat everything was cheap. The most expensive thing they had was beef stew for fifteen cents. I didn't have any money then, but I never paid for the beef stew. I had seven sisters and used to take one of their hairpins with me to the Automat. Somebody would put in three nickels, and the little window would open. They'd take out the beef stew, and before the little window closed, I'd put in the hairpin. So I got beef stew for nothing. In fact, I got so much beef stew, I was selling it for ten cents.

"Cary didn't have any money either. He said, 'Well, why didn't you tell me about that? I'm poor, but I can buy a hairpin.'"

CG: I knew George when he was called Nat Burns and was courting his beloved Gracie. He and Jack Benny were the very closest of friends. . . . When I was a teenager and in an acrobatic troupe, I worked on the bill with Jack when he did his first single. He was second on the bill and never played the violin. He probably held it for the same reason that George holds his cigar—for timing.

Jack did topical jokes. I can't imitate Jack, but one of his first jokes was "How do you like the suit? It came with ten pairs of pants. Y'see, I walked up ten flights of stairs." That was when a clothier advertised that if you walked up two flights of stairs to his establishment, you would get two pairs of pants. The laugh that greeted that particular joke may have been the original of Jack's self-proclaimed stinginess, which anyone close to him knows is the opposite of his true character.

A member of the troupe taught Grant to box. He learned the stances, enjoyed the physical workout, and got some extra money from his bets. He retained an interest in boxing but grew increasingly disturbed in his later years by the injuries fighters suffered in the ring.

Grant's romance with baseball also started in the early 1920s, when he played in his first game. In 1984 he fondly recalled his experience for his friend Jerry D. Lewis:

> CG: It happened in New Orleans. I was still rather young for some of the city's other pleasures. Our vaudeville troupe was playing the Del Mar circuit, and on one warm spring day we actors got up a baseball team and challenged the stagehands. I hadn't even seen a baseball game . . . and there I was playing in one. I wasn't afraid to try, though, because I'd played cricket back home in England and I knew how to handle a bat—left-handed. I led off the first inning, and I hit the first ball pitched to me. It looped over the shortstop's head and landed in left field. I stood at home plate waiting for the next pitch while my teammates were yelling, "Run, run." I turned and calmly guaranteed them I could hit a ball further than that. I couldn't get them to understand that I wanted to wait and pick another pitch. A batsman in cricket is allowed to do that. That's my first baseball memory.

Grant continued to play on tour, and when he was in New York, he sat in the sun behind third base at games at the Polo Grounds. JERRY D. LEWIS recalls, "In the 1980s, remembering his first exposure to American baseball, he told me, 'I still spoke English English, and I knew that to get jobs here, I'd have to learn American English. In those days, of course, movies were silent, so I couldn't learn from them. I've always had a pretty good ear, and soon I was yelling at the umpire like a native. I was also daydreaming about playing for the team.'"

He followed baseball for the rest of his life, first as a New York Giant fan and then as a Dodger fan, when the Brooklyn team moved to Los Angeles. According to Dodger owner PETER O'MALLEY, "Cary loved the game. He understood it. He appreciated all sports, but baseball might have been his favorite. He said, 'Once you've seen a movie, that's it. The script doesn't change. But in baseball every night it's a different story.' He appreciated the performance of the players who played well. He realized how difficult it was to hit a moving baseball with a round bat. He knew the umpires, the sportswriters, and the players. He would follow changes in our team. If we had a young player coming up, he would know about him before the player was on the field."

When the Pender tour ended, Grant and Bob Pender's younger brother decided to remain in the United States. They were determined to find work on their own. Grant's independent spirit was more than just a youthful whim. It was an expression of his emerging strength of personality. JACK HALEY, JR., puts it succinctly: "He was constantly a maverick, rebelling against what everybody expected him to do. He had the confidence to say good-bye to Pender and look for work in the theater. Later he'd walk out on the Shuberts. Then he walked out on Paramount, which offered him a great deal of money to stay. And that was right toward the end of the Depression. It took *cojones* to do that."

The boys, however, were not entirely honest in their split from Pender. They had led him to believe they would be returning home to England. Bob Pender wrote to Elias Leach:

244 West Thayer Street
Philadelphia, PA
May 21, 1922

DEAR MR. LEACH:

I am writing this to inform you that Archie is coming home. He leaves New York by the Cunard Liner Berengaria on May 29th and should arrive Southampton June 2 or 3. He has made up his mind to come home. I offered him 35 dollars a week which is about G8 [eight guineas] in English money, and he will not accept it, as he says he cannot do on it so I offered him £3/10 a week clear and all his expenses paid but he says he wishes to come home. The wage I have offered him is the same as my daughter and also another of my boys have been getting so I know he could do very nicely on it but I must tell you he is most extravagant and wants to stay at the best hotels and live altogether beyond his means.

I promised him if he improved in his work and was worth it, I will give him more money, but he is like all young people of his age. He thinks he only has to ask and have. I must tell you he has very big ideas for a boy of his age, and he seems to have made up his mind to come home.

He has been a good boy since he has been with me and I think he is throwing away a good chance but *he* does not think so. Mrs. Pender has talked to him but it is no use. He will not listen. So I should like to hear if he arrives home safely. . . . I shall be glad to do anything for him when I return to England.

I remain,

Yours truly, BOB PENDER

Jobs in vaudeville were scarce that summer and Grant spent his days close by the National Vaudeville Artists Club on West For-ty-sixth Street, hoping for word of a job. While he waited, he survived by becoming the forerunner of today's sidewalk salesman. He amused LESLIE CARON with his tales of his early entrepreneurism. She recalls: "Cary would tell stories about himself—how he used to sell ties out of a suitcase on Broadway with one eye watching for the police. If he saw a cop, he would close the suitcase and run." GEORGE BURNS remembers Grant's exploits firsthand: "Orry-Kelly (who later became the head costume designer for Warner Brothers) would buy a dozen ties for a dollar apiece and paint them. Then Archie sold the ties for three dollars apiece. They made twenty-four dollars' profit on twelve dollars!"

Just when his money was running out, Grant was invited to a dinner party and was asked to escort Lucrezia Bori, a lyric so-prano for the Metropolitan Opera. BEA SHAW recalls, "He said Lucrezia Bori kindly suggested they walk to the party and then back to her apartment afterward because 'it was such a beautiful evening.' Actually they both knew he couldn't afford the cab fare. Throughout his life Cary made a point of helping struggling actors because he remembered how people such as Lucrezia Bori had helped him when he was struggling."

At that dinner he met George Tilyou, who owned Steeple-chase Park at Coney Island. The meeting resulted in a job. Tilyou hired Grant to walk around Coney Island on stilts while wearing a "sandwich board" that advertised the racetrack. He was paid forty dollars a week, providing him with some steady cash while he looked for vaudeville bookings.

When BURT REYNOLDS admired Grant's athletic ability, Grant attributed his agility to those days spent stilt walking. "We used to talk about his films a great deal," Reynolds says, "and I asked him how he learned to fall. He told me he had a job carrying a placard while walking on stilts. Kids used to run between the stilts and push him. Sometimes he'd fall. He told me he had to learn to tuck and roll when he'd hit the ground because it was a long way down. . . . Cary didn't have a gymnast's body. He had the body of a swimmer—long and muscular but not tight in any way. But he had a gymnast's attitude."

Grant carried this attitude with him throughout his career. KATHARINE HEPBURN witnessed Grant's gymnastic confidence while they were making the movie *Holiday:* "Cary was physically very competent—a good stunt man and gymnast. He had to pick me up, and then I had to somersault off his shoulders."

DR. FRANCIS PAGE observes that Grant never lost his agility: "At a party one night in Bristol Cary knelt on his toes and knees, keeping his body upright. With one sudden spring he was back on his feet, knees fully bent. This trick would have been difficult for anyone to perform, but Cary was a man in his sixties! We were astonished. His body was still fit. He moved as quickly as he had when he was a boy."

The stilt-walking career didn't last long, and Grant was soon back at the Hippodrome in a show called *Better Times*. When it closed, he and other ex-members of the Pender troupe prepared a new vaudeville act. He eventually toured the Pantages circuit of theaters, which took him on weekly tours through Canada to the West Coast and back across the United States.

Grant loved to reminisce about those days of vaudeville. He said he had been influenced by many performers, particularly GEORGE BURNS, who says: "Cary even got up at a dinner in my honor and said he stole my delivery. He said he took my style. Well, he stole my delivery, but he never touched my cigars."

> CG: I watched him and Gracie every night I could when they were at the Palace. For their opening night five of us got together and chipped in five dollars apiece and bought them twenty-five dollars' worth of flowers, a

princely sum in those days. I asked George when we should have the usher bring up the flowers, and he said, "After the *third* encore!" Now, that's confidence! . . . George is an absolute genius . . . timing his laughs with that cigar. He's brilliant.

GEORGE BURNS: "What is timing? Timing is this. You're working with somebody. When the people laugh, I smoke. When they stop laughing, I stop smoking and I ask the questions. I talk. So what's so great about timing? If I talk while the people are laughing, they'd have to put me away. So I use the cigar. It works for me."

CG: George was a straight man, the one who would make the act work. The straight man says the plant line, such as "Who was that man I saw you with?" and the comic answers it: "Oh, that was not a man, that was my uncle." He doesn't move while that line is said. That's the comedy line. The laugh goes up and up in volume and cascades down. As soon as it's getting a little quiet, the straight man talks into it, and the comic answers it. And up goes the laugh again.

GEORGE BURNS: "Now, that's one way of being a straight man. Another way is to do nothing. Gracie and I worked together for forty years. I said to Gracie, 'How is your brother?' And Gracie talked for forty years."

CG: George is still quick with a quip as anyone around. Recently [1984] we were invited to a dinner. I asked him if we should go. After the absolutely perfect pause, he replied, "Only if it's downhill."

While Grant was on tour, a letter from his father reflected Pender's anger about Grant's deceptive departure from the troupe. What the letter lacked in punctuation and grammar, it made up for in affection. Elias Leach openly expressed his love and concern for his son, even surrounding his signature with little crosses and kisses.

April 17, 1923
70 Kingston Road
Bristol

MY DEAR SON:

Once again I have the greatest pleasure of answering your most and ever welcome loving letter dated April 2, received April 16 containing another ten shillings note which I thank you very much for it only shows me how much you must think of us at home in sending us the money. I hope my boy that you will never be in want for your generosity towards us.

Well Archie I was rather surprised to get the news about the rumor of Mr. B. Pender action towards you that is if there is anything in it. Well if he does try and get you out of your engagements while you are over there it only shows how jealous he must be of your success and being on your own bat. Now Archie directly you get information about what he intends to do to you try and get in touch with the national vaudeville artists institute and ask them if they take up such cases as yours for these kinds of artists clubs generally employ a lawyer if needed to fight a case for a member without the member paying him as they have what is known as a sinking fund for these things and are only too willing to do their best for their member's welfare. So Archie this is all I can advise you to do if he tries his game on. Of course you would have to explain the true facts of your case and how you left him so don't be afraid to tell the truth for it will mean everything in your favour and will only show up Mr. B. Pender meanness because you did not come home when he paid your passage home. It only shows to one how plucky you are to have done what you did and how you have got on. Now Archie I only hope that T. Pender will stick by you if his brother does what you have hinted to me about for myself he ought to stand by you as you have been working with him and getting along together. Now if I get any letters from B. Pender or anybody else from New York I will do as you have asked me to do, not take any notice of them. So don't worry about me doing any wrong for you. Now I think I have told you all I can about how to act.

The weather over here is still very cold and inclined to be stormy. I am more than glad to tell I am quite well and hardy and getting on famous in health. Mabel [with whom Elias was living] I am glad is still enjoying good health. She sends her best love to you and the very best of good luck. If there is anything we can do for you and if it lays in our power we shall be only too willing to help you.

So take heart and be joyful and take Beecham's as they say. Get me. Ha. Bury all your troubles for the while. Goodnight God bless you, my boy Now I must close with our best wishes and greatest love to you.

From your ever loving DAD

The vaudeville group returned to New York and disbanded in 1924. Grant lived at the National Vaudeville Artists Club, where he met all types of performers and often teamed with young comedians to obtain a day's work here and there.

CG: Doing stand-up comedy is extremely difficult. Your timing has to change from show to show and from town to town. You're always adjusting to the size of the audience and the size of the theater. We used to do matinees, supper shows, and late shows. . . . The response would change from night to night and from town to town. The people in Wilkes-Barre and the folks in Wilmington don't necessarily laugh at the same things.

Grant played a series of small towns across America. He was twenty-one years old. Still, there were signs of progress and fateful meetings, including one with MILTON BERLE, who says: "I met Cary as Archie Leach in 1925. He was with a group that opened the show in vaudeville. He was the stilt walker, and I was doing a single act at Proctor's in Newark, New Jersey. We played the stage show and a second show up on the roof garden. I remember they had a lot of trouble getting the stilts upstairs! I didn't see him again until the early 1930s, when he had changed his name. I walked up to him, and said, 'Weren't you in vaudeville?' And Cary said, 'Yes, I was.' He was flabbergasted that anyone remembered him."

Grant's first paid speaking role was in *The Woman Pays,* a vaudeville sketch that ran for about a year, playing during "family time" on the vaudeville circuit, mostly at junior Orpheum, Keith, and Proctor houses. Written in 1926 by JEAN DALRYMPLE, "it was about a girl who was engaged to a dull but awfully nice fellow.

Then she meets another man. He is the most charismatic, good-looking guy she's ever seen. The casting people kept sending me Rudolph Valentino types, and I kept saying, 'No. I want a nice American boy who's very good-looking and full of charm. Not a Spanish-looking type.' So then they sent me a lot of very dull-looking farm boys. And I said, 'No. I've got to have somebody I could fall for, someone women in the audience would be crazy about.'

"In came Archibald Leach. He was absolute perfection. He was a little shy, had a peculiar walk and a strange accent, but he was ideal.

"I could feel he was a little in awe of me. Especially, as he told me afterward, because I was so young myself. I was his age, but I looked younger.

"Well, the men thought he was terrible. Don [her partner, Don Jarrett] was particularly indignant. He didn't look neat. He looked haphazard. They agreed he was good-looking, but thought he couldn't act. And that voice! That accent! Well, I was ready to make the character an Englishman, if necessary. Archie had never played a speaking part but had always wanted to act. He'd used his acrobatic talent to get his foot in the door of show business. Oh, he enchanted me! He was the man I wanted. We cast him opposite Thelma Parker."

In the end DALRYMPLE's selection was vindicated: "Archie surpassed everyone's expectations. He couldn't have been better."

During these years Grant was sometimes mistaken for an Australian, and various people have perpetuated the tale that Grant and his vaudeville troupe toured Australia. Yet when Grant applied for U.S. citizenship on June 26, 1942, he presented a meticulously detailed list of all his trips to and from the United States to immigration authorities, and Australia was not mentioned. While Grant's accent was decidedly not Australian, it was highly distinctive. During his early years with the Pender troupe, Grant had picked up a tinge of cockney. This, blended with his efforts at an American accent, resulted in his now-famous staccato enunciation. In the years to come, it was a pleasure for Grant's fans, in every walk of life, just to hear him talk.

CG: The phone would ring, and it would be Bobby Kennedy on the line calling from the White House. We'd talk, and then he'd put his brother on. Inevitably their call would come right in the middle of my lunch. But I didn't mind. They had such enthusiasm for life. It was a real joy for me to have their friendship.

The regard was mutual. JERRY D. LEWIS relates, "A Hollywood producer once told President Kennedy he intended to film his life after his stay in the White House and asked who should be cast in the role. 'Cary Grant,' the President replied."

In the autumn of 1927 Grant worked in his first Broadway show. Through his friendship with the musical comedy player Max Hoffman, Jr., he had met Reginald Hammerstein, a stage director and the younger brother of Oscar Hammerstein II.

CG: Reggie Hammerstein cheerfully took me to the offices of his uncle, Arthur Hammerstein, who was soon to begin rehearsals of his expensive, well-produced but ill-destined operetta *Golden Dawn*, which opened the newly built Hammerstein Theater at Broadway and 54th Street in 1927. I played a small part and understudied the leading man, Paul Gregory.

Grant was living uptown in the Yorkville section of New York, at 325 East Eightieth Street, when he agreed to give his exclusive services to Arthur Hammerstein. The January 12, 1928, contract called for seventy-five dollars per week (eight performances) for the balance of the 1927–28 season. Hammerstein had options to renew yearly through 1933. Grant's salary was to increase to two hundred dollars during 1928–29 and top at eight hundred for 1932–33.

Golden Dawn closed after 184 performances, but his personal success won Grant a lead in *Polly*, the musical version of the comedy *Polly with a Past*. Nonetheless, his lack of musical comedy experience "did not go unnoticed." Hammerstein took him out of the show before it opened on Broadway.

However, Grant was around the *Polly* cast long enough to make a hit with FLORENCE HALEY, who says: "Fred Allen was breaking in *Polly* in Philadelphia, and Cary was in the show. My husband, Jack, was working, but I accompanied Fred's wife, Portland Hoffa, to the opening. All the girls had a crush on Cary. Besides being good-looking, he was a gentleman. Cary had a lot of class. Everybody in the cast liked him, and he had great audience appeal."

Despite his popularity with fellow thespians, Grant thought it wise to reserve his charms for the audiences.

> CG: So many girls who played in a musical comedy with me claimed we had a relationship. Stories would come back to me about how I had lived with someone in Cincinnati or some place. The one thing you learn is to never have an affair with a girl in a show because that can get you in a lot of trouble.

This was a rule Grant broke a few times, and he cautioned his friend Peter Bogdanovich against making the same "mistake." BOGDANOVICH recalls: "When Cybill Shepherd and I were going through a rough time with the press, Cary said to me, 'It's not a good idea to get romantically involved with somebody you're involved with professionally.'" Then, recalling his affair with Sophia Loren, Grant added, "We tore up a few bullrings in Spain on that one, I'll tell you."

Grant was out of *Polly*, but he wasn't out of work—or admirers—for long. Marilyn Miller, the popular musical comedy star, chose him to replace her leading man in *Rosalie*.

> CG: The male star of the show, of course, was the great comedian Jack Donahue, whom I knew and greatly admired. But Mr. Hammerstein and Mr. Ziegfeld, who produced Miss Miller's show, were hardly on friendly terms and, over my complaining voice, my contract was taken over by the Messrs. J. J. and Lee Shubert, managers and owners of a vast theater chain and countless original plays, musical comedies, and other theatrical properties.

Grant's first production with the Shuberts opened in New York at the Casino Theater in January 1929. Spotted by a Fox Film Corporation talent scout, he was asked to take a screen test.

> CG: I was in a show called *Boom Boom* with Jeannette MacDonald, Frank McIntyre, and Stanley Ridges. J. J. Shubert named it that in rivalry or retaliation to Florenz Ziegfeld's successful *Whoopee*. It was soon after the be-

ginning of talkies, when they were after anyone who could talk. We all were tested.

But Grant flunked the test. Fox's talent scout reported he was "bowlegged and his neck is too thick." His collar size was seventeen and a half inches.

One of his most embarrassing moments happened during a performance of *Boom Boom*. The show had just opened, and so, in a sense, had he.

CG: Opening night in Philadelphia, I was dancing on stage when the drummer told me my fly was open. Naturally I thought he was joking, and I just kept on dancing. Then an actress told me the same thing. I tried to make my way to the side of the stage to fix the problem but was pushed back onstage by a chorus of dancing girls. Lee Shubert, one of the owners of the Shubert chain of theaters, a very prim and proper kind of man, was in the audience. He came backstage red-faced, and I thought I was going to be fired. It was just the opposite! He liked it so much that he asked me to keep it in the show.

(More than forty years after, in February 1973, Grant contributed his silver-topped walking stick from *Boom Boom*, initialed A.A.L., to a charity auction.)

The male lead in an adaptation of *Die Fledermaus* called *A Wonderful Night* was Grant's next Broadway role. The play opened at the Majestic in October 1929, just days after the Wall Street crash and closed in February. Fortunately for Grant, the Shuberts cast him in the touring company, providing him with a job that lasted into the summer months.

In May 1930 Grant purchased a 1927 Packard sport phaeton. He lived at the Hotel Belvedere, at 319 West Forty-eighth Street, New York City. Proud of his beautiful automobile, he drove down to spend summer weekends with friends in Deal, New Jersey. Fifty-six years later, after a technical rehearsal for an evening *Conversation* in Red Bank, New Jersey, Grant drove to Deal, retracing his route in the Packard. He eagerly showed his wife Barbara the lovely old houses with his favorite, long, wraparound porches.

His next show, *The Street Singer,* opened in the fall of 1930, but the Shuberts were in serious financial trouble. While the show was playing at the Royal Alexandria in Toronto, the producers asked Grant to take a reduction in salary from $400 to $275 a week, then thanked him for his "splendid cooperation . . . and the assistance given us during these trying times."

In 1931 the Shuberts sent Grant to work the summer season of operettas at the open-air St. Louis Municipal Opera in Forest Park. He played in several shows, including *Music in May* and *Nina Rosa,* and that summer began a love affair with the city that was to last until the end of his life. He returned often over the years. The operettas provided another opportunity for growth in his career.

> CG: I realized that to get anywhere in my work, I had to go onto the legitimate stage. I began to do musical comedies—for less money than I had been earning. I was taking a chance because I had never done any serious singing. I sang only English music hall ballads, and those were mainly for my own amusement.

While he never grew confident of his singing voice, its unique qualities were ultimately appreciated by professionals like STEVE LAWRENCE: "It was a style. The tones he reproduced were not far removed from his speaking voice, which was very distinct. It was not crooning. His attitude toward the song was not unlike Rex Harrison's in *My Fair Lady,* except I think Cary's was better because Rex's style was more talk-sing. Cary had more musicality. He was more sing-talk."

He enjoyed singing for his own pleasure and sometimes entertained costars, including LESLIE CARON, who recalls: "He kept the ball up in the air on the set of *Father Goose.* In between scenes he sang music hall songs—with a cockney accent. He was so funny. We could see the comic talent he had when he was a boy. He sounded like Stanley Holloway, an old music hall entertainer. He wasn't a crooner. It wasn't the singing that mattered. It was the words and the humor and the way of phrasing. It kept his mind light, and it kept us bubbling. He was very keen on making everybody laugh."

PEGGY LEE knew him as a more reticent vocalist: "Cary was shy about singing. His singing voice was very much like his

CG, twenty-seven, in Nina Rosa, *a musical play by Otto Harbach, produced under the personal direction of J. J. Shubert and presented by The Municipal Theater Association, St. Louis, Missouri, June 22 to 28, 1931.*

speaking voice. It quavered a little, I think because of nerves. I was surprised he sang as well as he did." But the secret of Grant's singing success was clear to composer CY COLEMAN: "When Lucille Ball sang, people liked it because it was Lucille Ball singing. Everybody loved Louis Armstrong's voice because it was Louis Armstrong. It was the same with Cary Grant. Cary's was not a trained voice, but he had something essential. You wouldn't want him to sound like an opera singer. He talked some, and then he sang some. Singing is really another form of acting. The rest is technique. Some people add great vibrato or great sustained tones, but if you're musical at all and you can stay on the melody, the rest is an acting job. Cary had that. He could make people believe what he was singing."

A big moment came on May 8, 1931, when Grant was engaged for six days by the Paramount Publix Corporation to appear in a motion-picture short entitled *Singapore Sue*. He was paid $150. In the 1930s short subjects not only served to fill out an exhibitor's bill but also enabled studios to test new talent. Grant's first film work, *Singapore Sue*, might have been Archie Leach's ticket to Hollywood. Nothing came of it.

In 1970, when a composite of Grant's films preceded Grant's acceptance of an honorary Oscar, the assemblage included a clip from *Singapore Sue*. JACK HALEY, JR., who produced the awards show, remembers that Grant wasn't overjoyed when he saw those early efforts at screen acting: "A great Sturm und Drang began with Cary saying he didn't want clips from *Singapore Sue* or *She Done Him Wrong*. . . . As far as I know, he's the only person who's ever been privy to the film clips for an Academy show. I didn't do it for Laurence Olivier or anybody. But that was part of Cary's deal in accepting the Oscar. So I told him I'd make them as brief as I could."

GREGORY PECK, who as president of the academy was sympathetic to Grant's point of view, says, "In that early short Cary hadn't acquired the poise and confidence, the kind of looseness before the camera that he later had. He still looked like English music hall. I know how I would feel if someone showed a lot of footage of me before I had smoothed out my craft. It was his night. I wanted him to be happy with every inch of film and be sure he was represented at his best. And why not? We arrived at something I thought was right. When Cary saw it, he liked it.

The first thing he said was, 'I'm glad you didn't use any more of that early footage.'"

Grant was so pleased with the finished product that a decade later he carried the composite of films with him for his *Conversations*. He showed the footage twenty-three times before he edited it. He finally got his way. On November 19, 1985, at Trinity University in San Antonio, Texas, he asked Pat Ullman, Trinity's audiovisual production manager, to cut out *Singapore Sue*. Ullman followed his instructions. Grant said he couldn't bear to see himself with all that makeup, looking green and inexperienced.

In August 1931 Grant asked to be released from his Shubert theater contracts. The Shuberts obliged. At the end of that month Grant was engaged to play a character named Cary Lockwood opposite Fay Wray in her husband John Monk Saunders's play *Nikki*. It opened on September 29, 1931, at the Longacre Theatre. Grant was paid $375 for each of the first three weeks and was raised to $500 a week for the rest of the run. The show closed after only thirty-nine performances, but Archie Leach had taken another step toward stardom on the stage. FAY WRAY remembers his professionalism and grace: "When we had scenes together, he would move downstage and turn toward me as if he wanted me to have all the focus of the audience. He was extremely generous.

"He always called me Nikki. And I always called him Cary, even though his name was Archie when we met. He was absolutely magical. His eyes would flash as he looked at me. They said, 'I love what you have to say. I like you.' But I was married. The timing was not right for romance.

"About three years after *Nikki*, Randolph Scott told me, 'Cary is in love with you.' Many years later, in 1945, after I had married Bob Riskin, I overheard Cary at a party say to Bob, 'Be good to her. I was so in *love* with her! But I wouldn't have been a good husband. I pay too much attention to the position of a sofa!'"

In November 1931, shortly after *Nikki* had closed in New York, Grant went to California. He drove across country, full of ambition and excitement about the prospects of a movie career.

Grant shared his aspirations with his early supporter JEAN DALRYMPLE, who says: "I had lunch with him at the Algonquin just before he went to California. He was so excited. He felt it was his great opportunity. I remember telling him not to get

LONGACRE THEATRE

L. LAWRENCE WEBER, PROPRIETOR AND MANAGER
FRAND THEATRE CO., INC., LESSEES

PROGRAM · PUBLISHED · BY · THE · NEW · YORK · THEATRE · PROGRAM · CORPORATION

FIRE NOTICE: Look around now and choose the nearest exit to your seat. In case of fire, walk (not run) to that exit. Do not try to beat your neighbor to the street.
JOHN J. DORMAN, Fire Commissioner.

<table>
<tr><td>BEGINNING
TUESDAY EVENING,
SEPTEMBER 29, 1931</td><td></td><td>MATINEES
WEDNESDAY AND
SATURDAY</td></tr>
</table>

HARRISON HALL

PRESENTS

"NIKKI"

BY JOHN MONK SAUNDERS

WITH

FAY WRAY

MUSIC BY PHILIP CHARIG
LYRICS BY JAMES DYRENFORTH
DANCES AND ENSEMBLES BY PALMERE BRANDEAUX
ORCHESTRATIONS BY LOUIS KATZMAN
SETTINGS BY P. DODD ACKERMAN AND KARLE O. AMEND
ORCHESTRA CONDUCTED BY JULES LENZBERG
STAGED BY WILLIAM B. FRIEDLANDER

CAST

(In the order in which they speak)

SHEPARD (SHEP) LAMBERT.........*Played by*	DOUGLASS MONTGOMERY
NIKKI .... " "	FAY WRAY
FRANCIS (THE WASHOUT) .... " "	JOHN BROOKE
WILLIAM (BILL) TALBOT ....*Played by*	NATHANIEL WAGNER
CARY LOCKWOOD .... " "	ARCHIE LEACH
WILLARD (WIFFIE) CROUCH .... " "	LOUIS JEAN HEYDT
KISS-ME-QUICK .... " "	BOBBIE TREMAINE
BENJ .... " "	RUDOLFO BADALONI

ACT I.
PARIS, FRANCE

Scene 1—Claridge's Bar

Scene 2—A Sidewalk Cafe
Setting designed by James Morcom, executed by Karle O. Amend.

stuck in California but to come back to the theater from time to time.

"I didn't know he was going to be a sensational hit. He didn't always have that marvelous, debonair personality. He was often very quiet and reserved. But when he got in front of a camera, his eyes sparkled and he was full of life. The camera loved him.

"He was born a star. Some people just are. His image evolved from the parts he played and the direction he took. The audience loved him, and he glowed."

He also confided in IRENE MAYER SELZNICK, who remembered: "I had a long talk with Cary before he went to California. We sat next to one another at a party at the Waldorf after *Nikki* had closed. He had only two things on his mind that night: whether he should go to Hollywood and Fay Wray. He was very stuck on her.

"We didn't meet again until 1943 and *None but the Lonely Heart*, when I visited the set with Clifford Odets. I think perhaps Cary was the best present Clifford gave me."

Grant had his first glimpse of Southern California with its vineyards and orange groves from a train window during his vaudeville days in the 1920s. He had seen palm trees for the first time. He was impressed by Hollywood's wide boulevards and their extraordinary cleanliness. He was strongly attracted to its beauty and climate and knew, even then, that someday he would go back.

FAY WRAY wished her dear friend the best of luck, recalling, "He called to tell me that he and Phil Charig, the man who wrote the music for *Nikki*, would be driving to California.

"Cary had a sense of joy—about the world, about himself. He could inspire the moment with great pleasure and fun and appreciation of life. He gave you the feeling that life was delicious. Hoagy Carmichael's 'Stardust' seemed a natural piece of music to relate to Cary. He wrote it just about the time of *Nikki*, and I immediately thought of Cary. Even today when I hear it, I think of him."

CHAPTER THREE

A STREETCAR NAMED HOLLYWOOD

CG: Becoming a movie star is something like getting on a streetcar. Actors and actresses are packed in like sardines. When I arrived in Hollywood, Carole Lombard, Gary Cooper, Marlene Dietrich, Warner Baxter, Greta Garbo, Fred Astaire, and others were crammed onto the car. A few stood, holding tightly to leather straps to avoid being pushed aside. Others were firmly seated in the center of the car. They were the big stars. At the front, new actors and actresses pushed and shoved to get aboard. Some made it and slowly moved toward the center.

When a new "star" came aboard, an old one had to be edged out the rear exit. The crowd was so big you were pushed right off. There was room for only so many and no more.

One well-known star, Adolphe Menjou, was constantly being pushed off the rear. He would pick himself up, brush himself off, and run to the front to fight his way aboard again. In a short time he was back in the center only to be pushed off once more. This went on for years. He never did get to sit down.

It took me quite a while to reach the center. When I did make it, I remained standing. I held on to that leather strap for dear life. Then Warner Baxter fell out the back, and I got to sit down.

When Gregory Peck got on, it was Ronald Colman who fell off. The only man who refused to budge was Cooper. Gary was firmly seated in the center of the car.

He just leaned back, stuck those long legs of his out in the aisle, and tripped everyone who came along.

When Joan Fontaine got on, she stood right in front of me and held on to one of those leather straps. I naturally got to my feet, giving her my seat. Joan sat down and got an Academy Award!

Cary Grant loved this allegory and told it often over a period of more than forty years, first to friends and later during his *Conversations*:

> CG: George Stevens and I made up the story one day when we were waiting around on the set of *Talk of the Town*. We were talking about great jokes. One of them was a scene from a Chaplin picture in which Charlie takes his girl home and then tries to get on the last tram. We took the scene, added the actors, and said, "My God, that's the story of Hollywood!"

Soon after Grant's arrival in Los Angeles an introduction to director Marion Gering led to a dinner with B. P. Schulberg, head of production at Paramount. A screen test and the offer of a long-term contract were the result. FAY WRAY recalls: "After he signed with Paramount, he called to tell me he was using my old dressing room. I liked that he wanted to do that."

As with many young contract players, the studio doubted the marquee value of his name. So, with the signing of his first motion-picture contract, "Cary Grant" was born.

> CG: I changed my name at the behest of the studio. They said Archie Leach had to go. John Monk Saunders, a friend and the author of *Nikki*, a play I'd done in New York, suggested I take the name of the character I played in the show: Cary Lockwood. Well, Cary was all right, but Lockwood wasn't; there was already an actor named Harold Lockwood under contract to the studio. What went with "Cary"? It was an age of short names—Gable, Brent, Cooper. . . . A secretary came

KATHARINE HEPBURN: *"I liked the way he looked when he had that chunky, slightly pudgy face."*

with a list and put it in front of me. "Grant" jumped out at me, and that was that.

There were immediate advantages to the new name, which he later related to RODERICK MANN: "Cary told me he used to telephone Clark Gable each Christmas and say, 'Did you get any monogrammed stuff you don't want? If he said yes, I'd hurry 'round and we'd exchange initialed presents.'"

During Grant's first few weeks at the studio he found a friend in Jack Haley. "When Cary was first at Paramount, he made a beeline for my father, who had already done six or seven pictures there," says JACK HALEY, JR. "Cary wanted to know what making movies was all about. My father told him, 'The first thing you learn is not to use your stage makeup. So find a good makeup person. And don't talk to the leading actress. She'll steer you wrong. She's your competition. Talk to the character people. They'll teach you the ins and outs.'

"Cary loved Charlie Ruggles, Arthur Treacher, and all those character people who came from Broadway or vaudeville. He felt secure with them. Years later Cary told me, 'Your father was the only one who gave me advice for my first picture.'"

CG: To play yourself—your true self—is the hardest thing in the world. Watch people at a party. They're playing themselves . . . but nine out of ten times the image they adopt for themselves is the wrong one.

In my earlier career I patterned myself on a combination of Englishmen—A. E. Matthews, Noel Coward, and Jack Buchanan, who impressed me as a character actor. He always looked so natural. I tried to copy men I thought were sophisticated and well dressed like Douglas Fairbanks or Cole Porter. And Freddie Lonsdale, the British playwright, always had an engaging answer for everything.

I cultivated raising one eyebrow and tried to imitate those who put their hands in their pockets with a certain amount of ease and nonchalance. But at times, when I put my hand in my trouser pocket with what I imagined was great elegance, I couldn't get the blinking thing out again because it dripped from nervous perspiration! I guess to a certain extent I did eventually become the characters I was playing. I played at being someone I wanted to be until I became that person. Or he became me.

Ultimately Grant and his image became a model for others, including writers like SIDNEY SHELDON, who recalls: "In writing *Bloodline*, I used Cary as the prototype for Rhys Williams, an uneducated man from the coal mines of Wales. He has no background and no manners. In London he goes to restaurants and watches people eat and observes how they dress. He needs an image for himself and creates Rhys Williams, a sophisticated, urbane man. I told Cary about it, and I think he was rather pleased."

Grant's first feature film was *This Is the Night*, and before the end of 1932 his name had appeared in the credits of six more films with some of the biggest stars and finest actors on the trolley: Carole Lombard, Fredric March, Tallulah Bankhead, Gary Cooper, Charles Laughton, and Sylvia Sidney.

Perhaps Grant's most interesting film that first year was *Blonde Venus*, which reteamed the talents of director Josef von Sternberg and the captivating Marlene Dietrich. Von Sternberg's unique vision turned a conventional romantic triangle into an opulent, steamy melodrama—and made a small but significant change in Grant's appearance.

CG: The first morning of shooting he [Von Sternberg] suddenly stopped everything, grabbed a comb, and parted my hair on the "wrong" side, where it's been ever since.

Still new to motion pictures, Grant wisely demurred to the dictates of Von Sternberg, says PETER BOGDANOVICH. "Von Sternberg writes in his autobiography that Cary didn't try to argue with him. Dietrich and Von Sternberg were very close. He said [Bogdanovich imitating CG], 'I knew what was going on, and I just did what I was told,' which perhaps means Dietrich was vamping him a bit. Cary didn't want to get involved because Von Sternberg was the director and also Dietrich's lover."

Grant was making $450 a week, an enormous salary by Depression standards, and in May 1932 he invested in a smart men's apparel shop called Neale, at 3161 Wilshire Boulevard, just west of downtown Los Angeles, near the new Bullock's Wilshire and I. Magnin department stores. Grant's personal records dated

BEA SHAW: *"He didn't just play by ear. He could read music."*

May 1 through July 16, 1932, show payments due to Lester W. Neale totaling $579.25 and to various employees, including the bookkeeper ($15) and the stenographer ($22.50).

In early August Grant received a distressing report from his lawyer, Charles E. Millikan. No bank account existed for the business, and all deposits had been made to Neale's personal account. Not all the cash received at the store had been deposited. Sales slips were missing, and invoices could not be found.

When Neale wrote Grant for additional money to pay creditors, Grant refused until an audit was completed. In November the Citizen's National Bank informed Grant that a $750 ninety-day loan was overdue, and eventually Grant was personally responsible for a $5,700 debt. The business was liquidated. According to STANLEY FOX, this was a valuable business lesson that Grant never forgot. "Cary never had any debts. He paid all his bills." BEA SHAW saw Grant's business acumen reflected in his personal bookkeeping: "He kept meticulous records of how much he owed as well as how much was owed him. He never wanted to be in debt."

The assignments Grant got during 1933 did not improve much over the previous year. The majority of his roles simply capitalized on his good looks, dressing him in evening clothes at every opportunity. Despite the glamorous treatment the studio was giving Grant's "look," the more substantial side of his career was floundering. His thankless roles were castoffs from Paramount's more established stars. In retrospect, JACK HALEY, JR., diagnosed the shallowness of Grant's apparent success: "It must have been miserable for Cary. As a foreigner he didn't know many people here. And he was at the bottom of the barrel in terms of parts. The first choice went to Gary Cooper. The second went to George Raft. Even Fred MacMurray was getting better parts than Cary."

But Peter Bogdanovich points out two important exceptions in 1934, *She Done Him Wrong* and *I'm No Angel*. Both films starred Mae West. According to BOGDANOVICH, "*She Done Him Wrong* featured the most misquoted line of Mae West's career, spoken to Cary Grant: 'Why don't you come up sometime and see me? I'm home every evening.'"

The white-blond buxom actress liked to claim she discovered Cary Grant, overlooking the fact that *She Done Him Wrong* was his eighth picture for Paramount. He always denied her claim. MAURICE RICHLIN found Grant firm on the subject: "Cary hated that story about Mae West having made his career—when she reportedly said, 'If that man can talk, I want him for my costar.'"

If she didn't discover Grant, Mae West's films certainly helped make him a star, though Grant barely acknowledged it. As a rule Grant subscribed to the axiom "If you don't have anything nice to say, don't say anything at all." Mae West was the exception.

> CG: She always got a great deal of publicity for herself. She was intent upon what she wanted to do and did it. Everyone else suffered the consequences. . . . I could never understand the woman. I thought she was brilliant with that one character she portrayed, but she was an absolute fake as a person. You would shudder from it. I never knew anyone like her. She wore so much makeup and all that figure and those tall high heels. You couldn't find Mae West in there. I'm not attracted to artificiality. I'm not attracted to makeup. And certainly Mae wore more of it than anyone I've ever seen in my life.

Despite his personal reaction, Grant respected her unique persona and her extraordinary appeal. In the 1950s he encouraged friends to see her nightclub act at Ciro's. Grant even went to the show, taking along RICHARD ANDERSON, who recalls: "Cary felt everybody should see her. She was one of a kind."

His feelings for the actress did not escape the wit of his close friend Noel Coward. Grant's copy of the music to *Bitter Sweet* bears Coward's wry inscription: "For Cary, In memory of Mae West."

In May 1933 Grant bought another Packard, a 1932 Coupe 8 roadster. He was living near Griffith Park at 2285 West Live Oak Drive in a house he leased with his friend Randolph Scott, also an up-and-coming Paramount contract player. Amiable, handsome, and successful, Grant and Scott presented a perfect portrait of glamorous Hollywood bachelors.

When Grant met Virginia Cherrill, his bachelor days were numbered. Cherrill, a stunning blonde, had become an overnight success in 1931, when she was featured with Charlie Chaplin as

First wife, Virginia Cherrill (pictured here at San Simeon in 1933), made CG's hypothetical list of twelve ideal female dinner companions twenty-one years after their divorce.

the poor but beautiful blind girl the Little Tramp befriends in *City Lights*. Then twenty-five, the twice-married Cherrill met Grant at the palatial Santa Monica beach house William Randolph Hearst had bought for his mistress, the actress Marion Davies.

On November 17, 1933, Grant and Cherrill sailed for England aboard the SS *Paris*. It was Grant's first trip to England since his move to America in 1920. According to his records, the couple was married in London's Caxton Hall registry office on February 9, 1934. He was thirty years old.

Their marriage was not to last. His personal papers show that their divorce was final on April 25, 1936. Cherrill claimed Grant was too possessive.

Born on April 12, 1908, Cherrill had five husbands: Irving Adler, a wealthy Chicago attorney; William Rhinelander Stewart; Grant; George Villiers, the ninth earl of Jersey; and Florin Martini, a Sicilian whose name she uses today. Now in her early eighties, Cherrill lives quietly in California. Misquoted in the past, VIRGINIA CHERRILL no longer wishes to talk about her marriage to Cary Grant: "I read a few pages in a recent [1989] book about Cary and knew right away it was a complete fabrication. . . . I don't know why people have to destroy someone's name after he's dead."

Other stars share Cherrill's antipathy toward and dislike for posthumous books of misunderstanding and misinformation. "I don't like the idea of dying at all," says DOUGLAS FAIRBANKS, JR., "but one of the worst things about dying is wondering what they are going to say about you after you're dead. They say all the things they don't dare say when you're alive."

To BURT REYNOLDS it is clear that one emotion often creates detractors. He says: "Cary had everything. He was handsome, talented, funny, intelligent, wealthy, and had all kinds of beautiful women. So the envy barrier around him just got higher and higher."

In the spring of 1935 Grant was separated from Virginia Cherrill and dated another beautiful blue-eyed blonde, an eighteen-year-old named BETTY FURNESS, who remembers: "One day Cary said to me, 'I'm going to New York tomorrow.' As it happened, so was I. He was flying, and when I told him I was taking the train, he said, 'Why don't you fly with me?'

"My mother gave me her permission, and we took off in a little ten-seater plane. I think TWA was the only carrier flying coast to coast. This was long before cabins were pressurized. . . . The airports didn't have terminals, just hangars and an occasional shack which sold hot dogs. The plane had eleven scheduled landings between Los Angeles and Newark. I threw up at every one of them. You must admit, this was a marvelous way to get acquainted with someone.

"Before we got to Newark, Cary asked if I was busy that night. I was flying to New York to spend two weeks with my father, whom I hadn't seen in a year, but I chanced my father's understanding and said I had no plans. My father was indeed understanding, and Cary took me to the theater.

"I ended up spending only four nights in New York because MGM called me back to start a film. Three of those evenings I spent with Cary, and only one was with my father. When Cary returned, we dated for the next few months."

They were also seeing each other in the neighborhood. Grant lived next door to Furness in an apartment at the Colonial House. She and her mother were at La Ronda, at 1424 North Havenhurst. They were living in the heart of Hollywood, around the corner from the celebrity apartment-hotel the Garden of Allah, and a block away from the famous Schwab's drugstore on Sunset Boulevard. For two years they had been members of the Santa Monica Swimming Club, where they spent time on their days off.

FURNESS remembers those days with great fondness: "He was beyond any question the most attractive, charming, funny, sweet, marvelous man I've ever known. It's been awhile since 1935, and I haven't met his rival yet. He was absolutely extraordinary. We laughed and laughed and laughed. One thing has rankled me. Writers, Brendan Gill included, have said we were set up by the studios. I would simply like to state that my relationship with Cary was a romance on both parts. It was not set up by anyone."

Professionally the years 1934 and 1935, despite Mae West, did not significantly improve for Cary Grant. His films continued to be ordinary, his parts uninspired, although the high caliber of his leading ladies may have been a consolation. Sylvia Sidney, Elissa Landi, and Myrna Loy shared his plight. LORETTA YOUNG also suffered from haphazard casting: "My part in Born to Be Bad was written for Jean Harlow, who died before production began.

CG, thirty-one, and Betty Furness at a movie premiere, 1935. FURNESS: "He was beyond any question the most attractive, charming, funny, sweet, marvelous man I've ever known. . . . I haven't found his rival yet."

I was under contract to Darryl Zanuck. When he gave me the script to read, I burst out laughing. It was so obviously written for Jean Harlow. I looked like a fourteen-year-old dressed up in my mother's clothes. I was so uncertain. I was acting my head off and not getting any place. I thought it was perfectly terrible. Cary was not pleased with his part either. We didn't communicate much on the set except to play the scenes. We each had our own problems. When the picture was previewed, one critic said, 'We saw a picture last night called *Born to Be Bad*. It is.'"

BEA SHAW recalls Grant's sense of humor about these films: "Some of Cary's early movies were pretty awful. I caught *Enter Madame* one night on the late show, and when I told Cary I had seen it, he said, 'That wasn't me! That was some other fellow.'"

There were, in fact, four films Grant wished had been made by another fellow. Over the years he kept a typewritten list of his feature films. Before 1937 he noted merely the film's title and production studio. After that he included the picture's starting date—the day he reported for work. By anyone's count, Grant made seventy-two feature-length films. That is, by anyone's count but his own. When journalists reported "seventy-two," Grant scratched out the number and wrote in "sixty-eight." His personal record omits: *The Devil and the Deep* (1932), *Born to Be Bad* (1934), *When You're in Love* (1937), and *People Will Talk* (1951).

During the mid-1930s this series of uninteresting assignments was broken by a new excursion. On May 5, 1935, Grant starred in the first of a series of radio shows called the *Lux Radio Theater*, sponsored by Lever Brothers. The shows were scripted with material adapted from current movies. On *The International Silver Hour* he played in *Wings in the Dark*, with PHYLLIS BROOKS who says: "I played Myrna Loy's part. Radio was eager for drama in those days, and it was not uncommon to play one another's roles."

In 1939 Grant appeared on a talk show called *Circle Broadcasts*, which aired on NBC and was sponsored by Kellogg's cornflakes. He later appeared over CBS on *The Hollywood Guild*, sponsored by Gulf Oil, and did so through 1953.

Over the years Grant worked on radio with some of the best talent in town. His costars included Constance Cummings, Grace Moore, Irene Dunne, Jean Arthur, Thomas Mitchell, Rita Hayworth, Claudette Colbert, Robert Young, Jeanette MacDonald,

Robert Taylor, Ronald Colman, Chico Marx, Lawrence Tibbett, Groucho Marx, Carole Lombard, and Betsy Drake.

Even an undistinguished career in Hollywood was not as easygoing as it appeared. Grant worked hard cranking out one picture after another. Long hours and workweeks made up a contract player's schedule. "In the early days Cary worked on more than one picture at a time," recounts STANLEY E. FOX. "He went from one studio to another. Later, when pictures were made more and more on location, it was impossible to do more than one at a time."

While Grant was shooting a film, any offscreen glamour was relegated to Saturday nights. As for most people, it was the only night for loosening up and real enjoyment. The consolation was that his Saturday nights were spent at Ciro's or the Trocadero or the Cocoanut Grove.

In the mid-1930s JAMES STEWART's opportunities for socializing were similar. He recalls: "I got to Hollywood in 1935 . . . [and] did twenty-five pictures between 1935 and 1941. We worked six-day weeks and had Sundays off. On Saturday nights we went to the Trocadero, which is where I think I met Cary."

DOUGLAS FAIRBANKS, JR., remembers that even these star-filled evenings ended early: "Los Angeles was a blue town. Everything closed at midnight on Saturday. You weren't allowed to have drinks on Sunday."

BETTY FURNESS recalls, "Cary and I went to the Trocadero and to parties. We drove around a lot with the top down. We did silly things. Cary was a very sophisticated-looking man, but a part of him wasn't that way at all."

Not everyone had Grant's interest in or energy for touring the nightclub circuit. LORETTA YOUNG explains, "You didn't have a chance to do anything except work and sleep. At least the women didn't. I don't know how the men managed." And KATHARINE HEPBURN rarely went to nightclubs, recalling: "I preferred instead to have dinner parties in my home and to go to friends' homes."

Grant and his friends—and often his dates—spent Friday nights at the American Legion Stadium in Hollywood. His interest in boxing also resulted in what was to be a fifty-year friendship with Charles Rich, who later owned the Dunes Hotel in Las Vegas. (In the 1970s Grant had a calling card that read: "The

Dunes Hotel and Country Club, Cary Grant, Talent Scout, Telephone 702-734-4110, Las Vegas, Nevada." It typified his and Rich's mutual sense of humor.)

BEA SHAW remarks on Grant's affection for Rich: "Cary adored Charlie Rich. He was a small, very quiet, impeccably dressed man. He was a very close friend. Cary was devastated when Charlie died."

At Rich's memorial service in Las Vegas on April 18, 1986, Grant spoke of their first meeting.

CG: A *Look* photographer requested that I sit on the aisle for a photo session. Charlie sat next to me. The photographer explained that during each fight the people around us were standing up excitedly whereas Charlie and I sat quietly watching the strategy of the fighters. So the photographer asked *us* to jump up and down. I declined since we never jumped up and down, and to my mind, our sitting still and expressionless made the photographs more interesting.

I asked Charlie if he wanted to jump up, and he said, "Why? Is there a fire?"

"Well, will you yell?"

And he said, "Only if I have to bet on the short end."

Sundays were the star's only day off, and Grant knew how to enjoy them. In late summer 1935 he and Randolph Scott rented the Santa Monica beach house producer Joseph Schenck had built for his wife, the silent-screen great Norma Talmadge. Over the next few years 1018 Ocean Front hosted many star-studded Sunday parties. HAL ROACH says, "When Cary and Randy moved next door to Townsend Netcher's place, we became very friendly. Netcher's family owned the Boston Store in Chicago. Cary and Randy were just starting in the picture business. They didn't even have a maid in the beginning. Girls came in to cook dinner." WILLIAM RANDOLPH HEARST, JR., recalls the beach house as a bachelor's paradise—and not just for guest cooks: "There were girls running in and out of there like a subway station."

Grant's dissatisfaction deepened with his situation at Paramount. The studio, either at a loss for how best to utilize his talents or lacking suitable parts, began to "lend" Grant to other

CG and Mary Brian, 1936. BRIAN: *". . . the most romantic man I've ever known."*

studios. Two of these loan-outs had an impact on his future, the first on his personal life and the second on the development of his screen personality.

On November 7, 1935, Grant made another trip to England, sailing on the SS *Aquitania* to make the film version of E. Phillips Oppenheim's novel *The Amazing Quest of Ernest Bliss*. It had been two years since his last visit, and he was eager to go home again.

Released by Grand National in the United States as *Romance and Riches*, the film also starred the young, petite, very pretty brunette MARY BRIAN, who had won fame in 1924, when she appeared as Wendy in the screen version of *Peter Pan*. During production Grant's and her professional acquaintance soon ripened into friendship. She comments: "Naturally I was bowled over. Not only was Cary good-looking, but he had a great knack for making you feel as if you'd known him forever. He was so fun-loving and enjoyed renewing his English ties. Soon we started seeing one another for dinner. He was the most fun and the most romantic man I've ever known.

"When we had a day off, we went prowling around London, using buses for transportation. One very rainy day [agent-producer] Freddy Brisson, Cary, and I took off for Brighton Beach, stopping at pubs all along the way—not to drink but just because they were such fun. They were almost like character studies. Also, Cary and I saw every show in London, including the spectaculars in the music halls—choruses, acrobats, and pantomime, in which men played women. When there were no seats available for Noel Coward's *Tonight at 8:30,* Noel invited us to stand in the wings. It was so exciting. After Noel's show he joined us, and we went to parties together.

"We danced at the Dorchester and went to private parties. We were invited everywhere. At a very formal party at the Savoy I told Cary about a crazy game played with tissue paper. You put it against your nostrils and then hold your breath to keep it there. Your partner has to get into a strange position and take it off your nose. Cary thought it was uproarious. He started it at our table, and soon the whole ballroom was doing it."

When Grant had first arrived, before shooting started, he made a trip to Bristol to visit his father. The brief reunion was their last. On December 2, 1935, Elias Leach died at the age of sixty-three.

Although Grant lost his father while he was making *Romance and Riches,* he did not share his grief with MARY BRIAN, who recalls: "We stopped production, and he went to Bristol. I don't think it was as traumatic as it might have been because he hadn't seen that much of his father for quite a number of years. I don't mean he wasn't fond of him, but it wasn't as if he'd been with him day after day. He never discussed his mother or his father with me. And it wasn't that he was drawing back. He just wasn't ready. If he learned his mother was alive at this time, he never spoke to me about it."

CG: [The cause of my father's death] was recorded as extreme toxicity, but what was more probably the inevitable result of a slow-breaking heart, brought about by an inability to alter the circumstances of his life.

Afterward Grant went through his father's belongings and lovingly took possession of his pocket watch. It remained a keepsake dear to him for the rest of his life.

After finishing the picture, MARY BRIAN stayed in London to work on another film while "Cary returned to California. When I was on my way home, Cary called the ship, and asked, 'When are you getting here?' I had to stop off in New York for about four or five days. And he kept saying, 'Don't stay any longer than that.'

"The train from New York to Los Angeles took three or four days. The dining room was set with beautiful silver, linen, and crystal, and they stopped for fresh trout along the way. Year after year the waiters were the same. They knew the people who traveled back and forth. It wasn't as elegant as the *Orient Express*, but it wasn't Amtrak.

"When I returned, Cary and I saw one another steadily. I started a picture with Henry Fonda called *Spendthrift*. Cary started, I think, *The Last Outpost*.

"On Sundays he drove over the mountains to pick me up and bring me to his beach house. Townsend Netcher always had a lot of friends from the East and Chicago. Members of the beach club would come by and play handball and swim. Douglas Fairbanks, Jr., and David Niven would pop in and out. Also Reggie Gardiner. . . . Often during the week Cary drove over and brought me back for dinner. By then Randy Scott had married Marion du Pont, the Virginia heiress.

"We had fallen in love and talked about marriage and children. Cary talked about going to Las Vegas to get married, but he was torn between devoting all his time to his career and committing to marriage. I thought he should make up his mind. I felt the time was not right for him to marry. So I went to New York, where I did a couple of Shubert shows and stayed eight or nine months. We had been seeing one another for about a year and a half, and I wanted a full commitment. When I came home, he was going with Phyllis Brooks."

On the set of Sylvia Scarlet, *1935.* KATHARINE HEPBURN: *"We had wonderful cooks who prepared lunch at home for about twenty people every day and then brought it out. We took turns and paid for it ourselves. Cary, George [Cukor], and I liked good food."*

In 1935 the second of Grant's loan-outs from Paramount proved to be the most important development in Grant's screen persona since his arrival in Hollywood. *Sylvia Scarlett*, made at RKO and directed by George Cukor, was the first of four films to team Grant with a formidable talent, KATHARINE HEPBURN, who remembers: "That was really the beginning for Cary. George Cukor had seen him and thought he was wonderful. George told me, 'We're going to have this unknown fella, but he's absolutely great.' Cary was grateful to George for that."

CG: *Sylvia Scarlett* was my breakthrough. It permitted me to play a character I knew. Thanks to George Cukor. He let me play it the way I thought it should be played because he didn't know who the character was.

KATHARINE HEPBURN thought that Grant gave an excellent performance: "He was the only reason to see *Sylvia Scarlett*. It was a terrible picture, but he was wonderful in it. He was very secure in his work. And God, he was fun. He had a tremendous vitality. He was heavier and huskier then. I liked the way he looked when he had that chunky, slightly pudgy face."

George Cukor once told PETER BOGDANOVICH, "*Sylvia Scarlett* was the first time Cary felt the ground under his feet as an actor. He suddenly seemed liberated. It was very exhilarating to see."

In 1936, after making two pictures with Joan Bennett (*Big Brown Eyes* and *Wedding Present*) at Paramount and *Suzy* with Jean Harlow at MGM, Grant ended his five-year contract with Paramount and became one of the first stars to free-lance successfully at a time when most actors' careers were controlled by exclusive contracts. The agent Frank Vincent represented Grant, along with Rita Hayworth, Mary Martin, Rosalind Russell, Claire Trevor, Louis Jourdan, Nigel Bruce, Joel McCrea, and Edward G. Robinson. Grant stayed with him until Vincent's death in 1946.

When Grant announced that he would not re-sign with Paramount, Adolf Zukor, who didn't want to lose his rising star, offered Grant thirty-five hundred dollars a week to stay (jumping his next salary raise, which was scheduled to be three thousand dollars). Grant, however, was convinced his future lay in independence and the freedom to pick and choose not only his roles but his co-workers.

CG: If I had stayed at Paramount, I would have continued to take pictures that Gary Cooper, William Powell, or Clive Brook turned down. Refusing a renewal of my contract wasn't the first time I took what seemed like a step backward. When I came to America, I was fairly successful as a pantomimist but began to do musical comedies.

In those days each studio had its roster of players. You always worked with the same people. Joan Crawford and Clark Gable. William Powell and Myrna Loy. I figured I'd change the equation. Harry Cohn gave me a three-year contract with Columbia that allowed me to make pictures for other studios. As it turned out, other studios wanted me. That was nice.

PETER BOGDANOVICH explains how Grant took artistic control of his career: "He became responsible for his material and formed the arc of his career, shaping his own movie persona, in a way that Cagney or Bogart or Cooper or Tracy was not as free to do."

JACK HALEY, JR., admires Grant's keen business sense as well: "He maneuvered an unheard-of deal. He did one picture for Columbia, one for RKO, and then he had a freebie. He could go anywhere. Then he had to go back to Columbia. At the time it was unbelievable freedom. Today everybody's independent. Or they have a deal with one studio. But they're not under contract with two separate studios, getting a weekly check and then going off and doing one on their own. How did he have the guts to do that? I've never ever heard of a career like Cary's."

At one point during these months Cary Grant learned that his mother was alive.

The earliest letter from her among his papers is dated September 30, 1937, when Mrs. Leach was sixty years old. It comes from Grantchester, Westbury-on-Trym, Bristol:

> MY DEAR SON,
>
> Just a line enclosing a few snaps taken with my own camera. Do you think they are anything like me Archie? I am still a young old mother. My dear son, I have not fixed up home waiting to see you. No man shall take the place of your father. You quite understand. I am desperately longing waiting anxiously every day to hear from you. Do try and come over soon. . . .
>
> Fondest love, your affectionate MOTHER

PHYLLIS BROOKS recalls that "as soon as Cary finished making *Gunga Din*, he went to see her." He sailed to England via Italy on October 22, 1938, aboard the *Conte de Savoie*.

Once Grant discovered his mother was alive, he supported her for the rest of her life. Through the London solicitors Davies, Kirby & Karuth, he arranged for an allowance and moved her to a house at 93 Whiteladies Road, Clifton.

Remembering Grant's affection for his mother, BROOKS said, "Cary called his mother a dear little woman. But he didn't talk much about her. I didn't probe. It was such a traumatic thing to have happen to anybody."

Elsie Leach at sixty. LEACH: *". . . a few snaps taken with my own camera. Do you think they are anything like me, Archie?"*

Over the years Grant saved hundreds of postcards, cables, and letters from his mother. The earliest cables from Elsie Leach to Grant were imprinted with beautiful color photographs: holiday scenes with Christmas trees; people walking in the snow; or a family at a sumptuous-looking dinner with geese and hams on the table. Her letters were chatty and detailed her daily routine. She always asked about his next trip to England. She addressed him as "Archie" or "My Darling Son" and closed with "Kisses," "Fondest Love," and "Your Affectionate Mother." One time she addressed an envelope to "Mr. A. A. Leach, Cary Grant, Actor, Paramount Studios, Hollywood, California, America."

In Grant's cables and letters, he addressed her as "Darling" and signed "All my love," "Love Always," and "God Bless." He insisted that his cables be delivered and not telephoned.

Presents flowed back and forth. Mrs. Leach sent Grant a cigarette lighter for his birthday in 1939. Pudding, mince pies, and shortbread were forwarded at Christmas that year. "It is all made with good stuff. I have not made any since six years so I hope you will like it," she wrote. Another time she sent Easter eggs containing "a sweet miniature clock."

After the war Sundays were reserved for telephone calls. If Grant couldn't phone, he cabled and explained why. BEA SHAW was particularly sensitive to the difficulties in the unusual late-blooming mother-son relationship: "Cary was devoted to his mother, but she made him nervous. He said, 'When I go to see her, the minute I get to Bristol, I start clearing my throat.' He used to call her every Sunday before noon California time. During the 1960s and early 1970s she was in a nursing home, and the switchboard closed at eight o'clock. I talked to him one Sunday, and he said, 'Something is wrong with my throat.' I said, 'It's Sunday. You just talked to your mother.'"

Despite the fact that Grant was never fully comfortable with his mother, he was happy his financial security guaranteed proper care for her.

The winter of 1936–37 marked the beginning of Grant's independence with a film for Columbia, *When You're in Love*. This was followed in the spring by *Topper*, a charming comedy produced by Hal Roach, in which he and Constance Bennett play ghosts who torment Cosmo Topper (Roland Young).

CG: I enjoyed making *Topper*. I liked the people I was working with, but I wasn't very good. I didn't enjoy myself in it at all.

If these months were filled with the satisfaction of a new freedom, they were also brightened by a romance with Fred Astaire's costar in a series of hit musical comedies. HAL ROACH remembers that during the making of *Topper* "Cary was head over heels in love." Grant told BEA SHAW, "I was crazy about Ginger Rogers. She was a beautiful girl. Howard Hughes and I were both crazy about her. Howard bought RKO just because of Ginger, to impress her. She was working there, and he was her boss. And then she dumped both of us for an Indian guy. After that any time Howard and I were dating the same girl, we'd say, 'Look out for the Indian!'"

While still dating Ginger Rogers, Grant met the equally engaging PHYLLIS BROOKS, who recalls: "The first time I saw Cary was at Marion Davies's beach house. He was there with Ginger Rogers. He was so tanned he was almost black. Ginger was lobster red. It was funny.

"My best friend was the debutante singer Eleanor French. One night we went to a nightclub called Mocambo. Cary was there, and Eleanor was quite taken with him. So I arranged for a good friend to take us to one of Cary and Randy's Sunday brunch-buffets at the beach. After a few Sundays Cary asked me out instead of Eleanor.

"When Cary came into my life, I changed my mind about Tyrone Power. Ty was going with Sonja Henie. We wanted to be together, but he was afraid of her. She was older and very sophisticated, and he didn't want to confront her. She was going to Europe, and we were biding our time.

"So it was Cary who became the love of my life."

For the next two and a half years PHYLLIS BROOKS joined the beach parties, traveled with Grant to Europe, spent weekends with him at San Simeon, and nearly married him. "David Niven and Errol Flynn shared a house called Cirrhosis-by-the-Sea," says BROOKS. "The houses were very close together. Cary's was not huge, but it had two bedrooms, a large living room with a wonderful sea view, a small dining room, and a kitchen. In the back, facing the roadway, there was a room with a grand piano and a built-in bar and tables for backgammon. Cary and I played

Phyllis Brooks with CG in Santa Monica, 1938. BROOKS: *"We were so much in love. This picture says it all."*

all the time. There was a Ping-Pong table next to a large pool in front of the house. And Cary's darling little Sealyham terrier, Archie Leach, was always around.

"Cary loved to bang away at the piano. He was invariably trying to get through *Rhapsody in Blue*. As far as I know, he never made it.

"At the house you'd find Cesar Romero, Reggie Gardiner, and Gloria Vanderbilt's first husband, an agent named Pat de Cicco—a very amusing fellow. And Cubby [Albert R.] Broccoli, De Cicco's little cousin. Cubby, of course, went on to make all those Bond films. Cary, David Niven, and Bob Coote were marvelous storytellers. And Bobbie Mullineaux, a darling girl, would often be there. . . . God, we had fun.

"Other girls and boys would come and go. Randy was seeing Dorothy Lamour. Then he met Pat, who became his second wife. This pretty much made up the nucleus."

To be sure, DOROTHY LAMOUR spent many memorable days at the beach ho ʌe. She recalls: "Randy and I were both working at Paramount. It was 1936, and I was in the middle of *High Wide and Handsome*.

"One Sunday, after the others had left for the day, their cook prepared dinner for just the four of us—Randy, Cary, Phyllis, and me. We had a beautiful dinner of fried chicken, which I love. I was devouring it. . . . I looked up at Cary and said, 'I'm from New Orleans, so I should know good fried chicken. This is the best I've ever had.' He looked at me with a twinkle in his eye. 'Dorothy, he said, 'it's not fried chicken. It's fried rabbit.'"

Noel Coward was one of the many famous visitors to the beach house.

CG: I was on the set one day when Noel Coward, who was staying at my house, called and asked me to come home right away. He said that Garbo was there having tea. She had a film she wanted to discuss making with me. I was very nervous about meeting her.

PHYLLIS BROOKS: "He was out of his mind! He called me and tried to get me to leave work to accompany him to meet Greta Garbo."

CG: I had idolized her for years. I got off at five and arrived just as she was leaving. In my nervousness, I thrust out my hand and heard myself saying, "Oh, I'm so happy you met me."

DOUGLAS FAIRBANKS, JR., and Robert Benchley were renting a house farther down the beach. FAIRBANKS remembers: "Gertrude Lawrence was a lady friend of mine, and I wanted to give a party for her. Cary and Randy said they wanted to help and would split the costs. They had a bigger house than we did. Ours was just a little cottage. Mitchell Foster, a nice, fine-looking fella, one of what we used to call FFVs [First Families of Virginia], was helping Randy out. He presented me with my share of the bill for the party, which came to X dollars and thirty-five and a half cents. I asked Mitch, 'How do you write out a check for half a cent? Can't you make it one cent? Or two cents?' Those guys were *keen* students of the dollar. And I say that affectionately."

PHYLLIS BROOKS remembers that "Randy was very smart with money. He said, 'You know, Cary, you and Brooksie should invest in uranium. It's going to be the thing.' I didn't. But Randy had a lot of uranium stock early on."

According to DOUGLAS FAIRBANKS, JR., Grant was equally skillful: "Cary used to do a lot of arbitrage. He would buy Japanese yen and sell English pounds and buy Italian lire or German marks. He did that every morning before work on *Gunga Din*. He'd look over the paper and buy and sell things and send messages to buy so many pounds and then sell so many yen, and so forth. I was fascinated. But I didn't have the patience to go into it."

During these years Grant and Phyllis Brooks were frequent visitors at another, somewhat larger house where the parties were given on a slightly grander scale. To be entertained at William Randolph Hearst's home in San Simeon (a hundred-room Mediterranean revival-style estate Hearst affectionately referred to as the Ranch) was tantamount to being feted by royalty.

"We went there many, many times," says PHYLLIS BROOKS. "We had so much fun. Mr. Hearst felt paternal toward me because my cousin Charles Carstairs collected art for him." BEA SHAW knew Grant and Hearst to be special friends: "Cary was also friends with Mrs. Hearst. He said to his knowledge, he was the only person welcome at both San Simeon and Mrs. Hearst's Sands Point house in New York."

On the weekends at San Simeon WILLIAM RANDOLPH HEARST, JR., unwound with Grant: "Cary was a good, steady tennis player. None of us were professionals, although Pop had a couple of pros up as guests to help with *his* game. We also rode horses. And watched movies at night."

More than fifty years later Grant proudly showed San Simeon to his wife Barbara. He remembered the 103-foot-long Neptune's Pool—before the addition of columns and cypress trees. He took great delight in showing her Azalea Walk, which couldn't be seen from the main house. As lover's lane it had served as a rendezvous spot for the amorous guests. He also recalled the Richelieu bed under which David Niven hid his liquor bottle—and the Hearst semidry ordinance.

> CG: David would eat mints as he walked across the main terrace in case he ran into Mr. Hearst. I would sometimes bring a bottle or two in my suitcase and unpack quickly. You couldn't let the servants find any extra liquor.

During the golden days of San Simeon guests met before dinner in the Assembly Room, the largest of fourteen sitting rooms, where they were surrounded by objects of art dating back to the fifteenth century and where Hearst prepared *very* weak daiquiris for his guests. "Mr. Hearst was a teetotaler," says PHYLLIS BROOKS. "When he'd come down to join his guests, Marion Davies would quickly put her drink in my hand, and I'd look for the nearest potted palm."

> CG: I would drink mine fast, and then serve myself another one. It was difficult to get too much liquor. Mr. Hearst would measure it with a jigger into the big wine cooler, which was filled with punch.

Over the years Grant slept in almost every bedroom on the estate. He asked Colonel Joe Willicombe, the majordomo who sent the invitations, to assign him a different room each time he visited. Like Grant, Jean Harlow also requested different room assignments.

> CG: At dinner in the Refectory, the estate's only dining room, your place card was moved further and further

down the table away from Mr. Hearst (who sat in the center) as your stay became longer. The table was always full.

Once Grant joined Hearst for a trip to Europe. Hearst picked up the tab and gave his guests a packet of currency for the country of entry. Grant was irritated by people who accepted Mr. Hearst's hospitality and then talked behind his back about his parsimony. They ignored his generosity and commented on the fact that he turned out the lights as he left a room.

Grant once played "bombardier" in a biplane flown by the younger Bill Hearst.

CG: Bill purloined and piloted [San Francisco banker] Herb Fleishhacker's airplane at San Simeon one morning and induced naive me to come along. . . .

WILLIAM RANDOLPH HEARST, JR., had just gotten a private pilot's license. "Cary was foolish enough to come with me," he recalls. "We got the kind of paper bags one found at the corner candy store and filled them with flour. We buzzed around and threw the bags on the hangar's asphalt roof. It was great fun because you could see where they hit . . . see the splash when the bag broke. We made a few more passes, throwing out more bags."

BEA SHAW adds, "Cary said that what they didn't realize was that sacks of flour dropped from that height could do tremendous damage. They damaged the roof, made a terrible noise, and frightened all the guests.

"When they got back to the house, Cary's bags were packed and on the front porch, which was the way Mr. Hearst let a guest know he was no longer welcome. Someone interceded, however, and Cary was allowed to stay."

WILLIAM RANDOLPH HEARST, JR., recalls that "after the airplane escapade, George 'Rosie' Rosenberg, who was a very close friend of mine, dubbed Cary Ace. The name stuck with him in our bunch. I liked Cary very much. He was a very clean-cut, decent person."

Grant never lost his great capacity for fun. BURT REYNOLDS claims that "the two best audiences I ever had for telling a story were Cary Grant and Jack Benny. Comedians are usually an impossible audience. They don't laugh. They don't even smile. But Cary and Jack were the best at what they did, so they didn't have any insecurity about listening. Cary was a fabulous listener. He didn't interrupt. When some people listen, they look bored. Cary looked like someone who was loving it. And he was a giggler."

JEAN DALRYMPLE knows that Grant had always been a giggler. "When he first did *The Woman Pays*, he would say a funny line and giggle."

According to RICH LITTLE, Grant would "hear jokes, tell jokes, laugh, giggle. When you think of him as the suave, sophisticated man that he was on the screen, it took you aback, in real life, when he laughed himself into hysterics."

"He'd laugh so hard, he'd get tears in his eyes," says PETER BOGDANOVICH. "I never saw him giggle or laugh in a movie the way he did in life. It was something really open and giving. The most memorable thing about Cary for me was his sense of joy."

CHAPTER FOUR

JUDY ... JUDY ... JUDY

CG: Comedy holds the greatest risk for an actor, and laughter is the reward. You must be laughed at. You know right away that you're a flop if no one laughs. An actor in a drama doesn't get that kind of immediate feedback. Unless it's a great tearjerker, you can't tell how you're doing. People think it's easy to get a laugh. It's not. There's a story about a dying actor who was asked how it felt to die, and he said, "Dying's easy; comedy's hard."

I liked making comedy films even though there was little flexibility. Your timing had to be modified for the screen. Since a laugh rolling up the aisles of a big-city movie theater took longer than one bouncing off the walls of a tiny rural vaudeville house, you had to time what you thought would please all audiences. And you had to think about theater audiences because the film crews don't laugh. They are too busy doing their own jobs.

GARSON KANIN agrees: "Comedy is very serious. It's difficult. In the theater you get laughs. In the movie business you don't get any laughs. You're guessing. You're hoping. You're thinking, 'This'll be funny, or this line will get a laugh, this reaction will get a laugh, this scene will get a laugh.' But you don't *know*. That's what makes acting comedy in films infinitely more difficult than on the stage."

The vehicle that made the most visible advance in Cary Grant's career was *The Awful Truth*. When it was released in the fall of 1937, reviewers praised the film as "the season's funniest and smartest drawing-room comedy." Costarring with Irene Dunne and Ralph Bellamy under Leo McCarey's eccentric but brilliant direction, Cary Grant was at last the elegant, graceful, yet pratfalling comic screen personality that brought him international fame.

PHYLLIS BROOKS recalls the film's impact: "*The Awful Truth* came out, and Cary suddenly became very important. He was so happy. Everybody who knew him was thrilled."

With hindsight, given the film's inception and McCarey's sometimes unintelligible directorial demands, no one would have guessed this film would catapult Grant into stardom.

RALPH BELLAMY witnessed the film's haphazard genesis: "Leo McCarey was a charming, wonderful, great little guy with dancing eyes. He looked as if he were about to bust out laughing. After we shook hands, I said, 'I don't know what I'm doing. I don't even know what clothes I'm going to wear.' McCarey said, 'The jacket and trousers you have on are just what I want! Can you sing?' I said, 'I can't get from one note to another.' 'Oh,' he said, 'wonderful! Come with me.'

"We went over to a grand piano where Irene Dunne was looking at the sheet music for 'Home on the Range.' She said, 'I don't read music, Leo. This is unfair of you to ask me to do this.' The camera was set up across the piano, shooting at Irene. McCarey said, 'Just play it the best way you can, and Ralph, you blast it out with your Oklahoma accent.' Well, she played, and I sang. We finished what we knew of 'Home on the Range,' and nobody said 'cut.' I looked up, and Leo McCarey literally was on his hands and knees, laughing under the camera. He said, 'Cut. Print it.'"

HAL ROACH describes Leo McCarey as an "odd" kind of director: "He kept improving on things. He'd give Cary something in the morning and then tell him, 'I'm not going to do that.' Cary decided that Leo didn't know what the hell he was doing and tried to get out of the picture." RALPH BELLAMY recalls, "We were all as mad as could be. Irene was in tears. And Cary offered to do another picture for nothing, if Cohn would let him out of it. I couldn't do anything. I was under contract." And IRENE DUNNE admitted that "Cary had some trouble getting used to Leo McCarey. I told him that if he would just stay with it, he would give a wonderful performance, which he did. It upset him that McCarey didn't have a script. I was able to calm him down."

RALPH BELLAMY details the chaos of shooting a scene: "McCarey came in every morning with a small piece of brown wrapping paper on which he'd written his ideas. He'd say, 'Cary, you come in that door on the right, and Ralph, you come in over there on the left. I'll run the dog through, and Irene, you come through. . . .' But after four or five days we realized he was a comedy genius."

The blending of McCarey's gifts and Grant's blossoming comedic talent influenced a whole genre of films, as PETER BOGDANOVICH describes it: "In the films of the 1930s it was very unusual for a romantic lead to do what was considered comedy relief—especially physical comedy. It was very successful in *The Awful Truth*. McCarey gave Cary direction, which Cary used from then on. But that's what an actor does. If you get something from a director and it works, you use it again. And he did. Why not?"

GARSON KANIN thinks Grant found his screen personality in *The Awful Truth*. He says: "How much of that personality was directed into him by Leo McCarey, I'm not prepared to say. I didn't know him well then. He polished that personality, and he played it over and over and over again—each time more skillfully and more successfully." HAL ROACH sums it up: "*The Awful Truth* turned out to be one of the best pictures Cary ever made, and Leo got an Academy Award for best director."

According to Ralph Bellamy, Grant was not out just for himself—or for McCarey. "I am a profound admirer of Cary's," says BELLAMY. "He was eager for everyone to have what was coming to him. There was no upstaging. Quite the opposite. He would give you your moment. He was always laughing and great to work with—friendly and receptive. But after a while you realized he was a little . . . shy isn't the right word . . . reticent. Cary had a polite sort of reticence."

In February 1938 *Bringing Up Baby* was released. The first of four films Grant made with director Howard Hawks, it has become one of the classics of screwball comedy. His costar for the

On the set of The Awful Truth, *1937.* ROBERT WAGNER: *"Cary had a great sense of nonsense and playfulness. There was a circus going on in his head all the time."*

second time was Hepburn, and the two now were working as a well-practiced team.

Both Grant and KATHARINE HEPBURN were meticulous about details. She recalls: "We wanted it to be as good as it could possibly be. Nothing was ever too much trouble. And we were both very early on the set. Howard Hawks was always late, so Cary and I worked out an awful lot of stuff together. We'd make up things to do on the screen—how to work out those laughs in *Bringing Up Baby*. That was all Cary and me."

> CG: Kate's a joy. At the end of *Bringing Up Baby* she climbs up high on a ladder next to the brontosaurus, to apologize for what has happened. The ladder falls, and she climbs to the back of the brontosaurus, where I'm standing on a platform. She had to get over the brontosaurus. As she moves, the brontosaurus starts to collapse. I told her when and how to let go. I told her to aim for my wrists, an old circus trick. You can't let go of that kind of grip, whereas if you go for the hands, you'll slip. She went right for my wrists, and I pulled her up. Kate was marvelously trusting if she thought you knew what you were doing.

Brontosaurs were one thing, but HEPBURN knows that Grant never warmed up to the leopard in *Bringing Up Baby:* "He didn't like cats, so he would have none of it. I was the only one who would work with the leopard because Cary was so scared of it. I was too dumb to be afraid. They blocked the scene and caged in the leopard. Olga Celeste, the trainer, was hidden off camera—with a whip. I had three scenes to do with the leopard. The first was a walk-through. In the second I'm in a negligee with the leopard trailing after me. And in the third I'm in a short dress with weights on the bottom, so when I turned, the skirt flicked. And by jiminy, when I turned—and I was much too sure of myself—that skirt *flicked*. The leopard sprang at my back. I didn't see it. That was the end of shooting the leopard with an actor.

"During the filming we dropped a fake leopard through the top of Cary's dressing room. He was furious at us—but amiable, of course."

(Decades later Grant had noticeably overcome his fear of cats. ROY, of Siegfried and Roy, relates that "Cary and Barbara came to our home in Las Vegas, where we have about twenty animals—leopards, tigers, great Danes—living freely. Cary would sit with us in the garden room, with a tiger sitting at his feet and watch the others swimming in the pool. He was fascinated with our commitment to preserving the white tiger, which is almost extinct.")

KATHARINE HEPBURN appreciated Grant's humor offscreen as well as on: "Cary was a lovely, very generous actor. A good comedian. And so *funny*. He had a wonderful laugh. When you looked at that face of his, it was full of a wonderful kind of laughter in the back of the eyes. Of course, he was also very serious." Howard Hawks was fully aware of Grant's wider range, as he told PETER BOGDANOVICH, "Cary is a great comedian and a great dramatic actor. He can do anything."

When LOUIS JOURDAN first saw Cary Grant on the screen in *Bringing Up Baby*, he found him irresistible: "I discovered this extraordinary presence. I was in awe of this persona on the screen—the look, the walk. But mainly it was his extraordinary, innate sense of the absurd. He was a master of the absurd, a pioneer before the theater of the absurd arrived. The Cary Grant I fell in love with on the screen hadn't yet discovered he was Cary Grant. He was absolutely in the raw. All those mannerisms—everything that has been imitated for forty years—he didn't know yet.

"Pauline Kael, the critic, made me see what makes Cary unique. At the same second that he is delightful and charming and irresistible, there is also the threat he could have a black side. He is constantly in conflict. Behind the construction of his character is his working-class background. That's what makes him interesting. That's what makes him liked by the public. He's close to them. He's not an aristocrat. He's not a bourgeois. He's a man of his people. He is a man of the street pretending to be Cary Grant!"

Grant confided to JACK HALEY, JR., the origins of one of *Bringing Up Baby*'s funniest sequences: "It was the scene in which Cary steps on the tail of Katharine Hepburn's dress and tears out the rear panel. He based it on a real-life happening. He went to the Roxy Theater in New York. Sitting next to him were the head of the Metropolitan Museum and his wife. At some point he gets up to go to the men's room and returns. A little while later the woman gets up and crosses in front of him. They're right at the edge of the balcony, he starts to stand, and he sees that his fly is open. So he zips his fly shut and catches her frock in it. They had to lock step to the manager's office to get pliers to unzip his fly from the dress. He told Howard Hawks the story, and Hawks used it. He couldn't use the fly joke, but he used the lockstep."

Hawks liked to tell another story. "It may be apocryphal," explains PETER BOGDANOVICH, "but Cary never refuted it. There's a scene where Cary's supposed to get angry, and Howard said, 'That's pretty dull. You get angry like Joe Doakes down the block. I know a guy, when he gets angry, he kind of whinnies like a horse. Why don't you do that?' So Cary went like this . . . [makes whinnying sound]. And then *that* became a part of his persona. Now, you could say that Hawks could have given that direction to anybody. But it wouldn't necessarily have worked. It wouldn't have worked with Bogart or Cooper or Gable. It worked with Cary Grant. Perhaps Hawks was inspired by the qualities Cary brought to the scene and knew Cary could make it work."

Grant not only enjoyed a happy working relationship with KATHARINE HEPBURN but also counted her among his friends. She recalls: "Cary was linked with many women in those days. He knew all the girls and introduced many of them to Howard Hughes, whom I met through Cary. But during the making of *Bringing Up Baby,* Phyllis Brooks was the woman in Cary's life. She was quite fascinating."

PHYLLIS BROOKS was equally intrigued with Miss Hepburn: "I thought Kate and Howard Hughes were a wonderful couple and would end up together. They were very much in love. Howard was very serious about Kate, and she returned that affection. The four of us, Cary and I and Howard and Kate, would go out together. It was always a triumph to get Kate to go someplace like the Cock and Bull [a Los Angeles restaurant]. She was a highly intelligent woman. She enjoyed small gatherings with good conversation and didn't care to be looked at."

Grant had met Howard Hughes in 1932, when they were introduced by Randolph Scott. It was a lifelong friendship.

CG: Howard was the most restful man I've ever been with. Sometimes we'd sit for two hours and never say a word. He owned only two suits. He never owned a tuxedo. If he needed one, he'd borrow one of mine. I'd show up at the airport with matching luggage. Howard would drive up in an old car and a brown paper bag with a change of underwear. He was a little deaf, but for some reason he could hear better in an airplane. I would forget and yell so he could hear me, and he'd say, "Why are you shouting?" He was a brilliant man. Way ahead of his time. I would listen to him for hours, not always understanding at the time exactly what he meant. But as time went by, his thoughts would be proven correct.

Grant once said to BEA SHAW, "I think Howard Hughes and I were friends because he didn't want anything from me and I didn't want anything from him."

On January 24, 1938, Grant reported to the set of *Holiday*, again to work with Katharine Hepburn and director George Cukor. Her pleasure in the combination was directly transmitted to audiences. HEPBURN remembers: "We got on well, Cary and I. It was fun to play with him, and I think he had a good time, too. People liked us together, so we enjoyed it." PETER STONE observes that Grant was a bit more ambivalent about one aspect: "Cary liked working with Cukor, but he always figured Cukor was filming the lady and not him. Well, he was."

This talky comedy about New York society was followed by Grant's first adventure picture, *Gunga Din*. Finally Cary Grant was out of the drawing room and into an Errol Flynn–style rollicking story. Loosely based on the poem by Rudyard Kipling, it costarred Douglas Fairbanks, Jr., Victor McLaglen, and an up-and-coming ingenue named Joan Fontaine.

DOUGLAS FAIRBANKS, JR., has Grant to thank for one of the best-remembered roles of his career: "It was Cary's idea for me to be in the picture. He wanted to make it a three-star vehicle. He didn't even have a script at the time—only a draft of the synopsis. He told me he'd play whichever part I didn't want. Cary chose the material first and then worried about the part. That was the secret of his success. Ultimately we tossed a coin."

Howard Hawks was intended to direct *Gunga Din* but was replaced by George Stevens, who ended up making the most expensive film RKO had ever released. Shooting began in June

1938 in Lone Pine, California, at the largest location camp in motion picture history. At the base of Mount Whitney, in the High Sierras, were fifteen hundred actors, featured players, and extras. The production department shipped twenty six thousand gallons of crude oil to the location and dyed the soil black to replicate the sands of India.

Whether Grant played the role of Sergeant Archibald Cutter by luck or by choice, it gave him a wonderful opportunity to sink his teeth into a slightly eccentric, cockney role—and to go on developing. According to DOUGLAS FAIRBANKS, JR., Grant was always giving other people ideas and trying to be helpful: "He was wonderful, and the most generous player I've ever worked with. He wasn't just taking his salary. He was concerned that the picture be a good picture. He thought that what was good for the picture was good for him, and he was right. He was very shrewd that way. He was a master technician, which many people don't realize, meticulous and conscious of every move. It might have looked impetuous or impulsive, but it wasn't. It was all carefully planned. Cary was a very sharp and intelligent actor who worked out everything ahead. I called him Sarge or Sergeant Cutter, and he called me Ballantine right to the end of his life."

The film wasn't without mishap.

CG: The fight was choreographed. Victor McLaglen hit me so hard in a scene we were shooting for *Gunga Din* that he knocked me out cold. I meant to miss his fist, but my timing was off; instead of moving back, I went right into it. He carried me off the set over his shoulder, not even knowing that he had knocked me out. He could have killed me. When I came to, I chased after him with a bottle. It was lucky I didn't catch him.

Lucky for McLaglen or Grant? "McLaglen was a big man," explains DOUGLAS FAIRBANKS, JR. "He had been the heavyweight champion of the British army in the First War. He could have taken both of us with one hand. He was very physical. Very strong."

While shooting at Lone Pine, Grant and McLaglen played a joke on Fairbanks. It wasn't until late 1985 that Grant told the story to his public. It was as bawdy as he would ever be in front of an audience.

CG: We were dressed in heavy boots and uniforms, and waiting around the set dressed this way could get tedious. We'd amuse ourselves by taking a handful of gravel and letting the pebbles slowly fall onto one another's boots. When the pebbles made contact with the boots, it sounded like someone relieving himself. One day we were up shooting on a cliff. It was about a hundred and ten degrees. We drank a great deal of water on those kinds of days. And I had to go to the loo. Vic said, "Well, why don't you just pee on Fairbanks's boots?" I said, "I can't do that." And McLaglen said, "Why don't we both do it?" [Fairbanks was meanwhile distracted, looking down, taking directions from George Stevens, says his son.] Doug, thinking he heard pebbles again, said, "Oh, come on fellows. Cut it out."

Years later *Gunga Din* was colorized by computer. It was the beginning of the film colorization controversy, and Grant had a definite opinion. He was not a purist.

CG: They are coloring films that were classics in their time. I thought *Topper* turned out very well, true to the way I remembered the sets and costumes. And I've seen a reel of *Gunga Din* in color. It's absolutely marvelous. The uniforms are exactly what they should be. It's rather an expensive process. And some films should be left untouched.

PHYLLIS BROOKS visited Grant on the *Gunga Din* location, and they continued to see each other through the fall of 1938. Their relationship appeared to be heading toward marriage. "We were in New York in late 1938. I had gone there to meet Cary, who was coming from Europe after seeing his mother. We were staying with Olive and Bert Taylor, Dorothy di Frasso's brother. (Bert was treasurer of the New York Stock Exchange. Dorothy had married Count Carlo di Frasso, a Roman nobleman, in the 1920s.)

"Olive arranged for a furrier to come to the apartment, and Cary chose a mink coat for me.

"We came home from *Hellzapoppin'*, and I had a temperature of a hundred and five. I was in bed with my hair in twenty-five pigtails. Cary said, 'Brooksie, I have the treat of the world for you,' when Noel Coward walked in. Noel was darling. He did cheer me up.

"Cary had to go back to the Coast to start *Only Angels Have Wings*, and I insisted on returning home. I went on a stretcher by ambulance to the train. The nurse accompanied me to Pennsylvania Station [on the west side], and we couldn't find the train. Cary was at Grand Central [on the east side], ready to board the *Twentieth Century*. Cary got them to hold the train. Oh, was he wild. You can imagine the embarrassment. The train was being held for half an hour, and he's standing there waiting for the stretcher to arrive. I had double lobar pneumonia, which was something in those days. They didn't have penicillin. I was the second person ever to get sulfa. That's how new that was. It's a strange illness. You don't know you're sick. I was in bed at home with a nurse for a long time. It was a close one. Cary thought I was dying. He was cheerful in my presence, but I knew he was desperately worried because our friend Bob Coote said he cried like a baby."

In 1939 the studio system was at its peak. Actors and actresses at every studio had been groomed throughout the decade. Bette Davis, James Cagney, James Stewart, Ginger Rogers, Henry Fonda, Claudette Colbert, Gary Cooper, Clark Gable, Edward G. Robinson, Fred MacMurray, Carole Lombard, and Rosalind Russell had worked their way up from character actors, ingenues, comedians, and juveniles to some of the biggest stars in the world. Archie Leach had taken a similar path.

The Depression was lessening. Admission to neighborhood theaters cost twenty-five cents. More people had a quarter to spend, and they got more for their quarter than ever before or ever again. Not only did a moviegoer get an A picture (a big-budget film with big stars), a B budget film (which had a shorter running time and less production value), a newsreel, a comedy short, and a cartoon, but they also saw many of the finest films Hollywood would ever make.

No one could have anticipated that 1939 would be the culmination of the best aspects of the studio system. It was the peak year in American motion-picture history. *Gone With the Wind*, *The Wizard of Oz*, *Stagecoach*, *Wuthering Heights*, *The Women*, *The Story of Alexander Graham Bell*, *Goodbye Mr. Chips*,

Mr. Smith Goes to Washington, and *The Hunchback of Notre Dame* were among the most popular pictures ever made. *Gunga Din* was no less outstanding. The movies had come of age. And so had Cary Grant.

Grant had significantly expanded his capacity as a performer with *Gunga Din,* and this was immediately followed by the more serious adventure film *Only Angels Have Wings.* This time he combined his abilities as romantic lead with a strong masculine story so typical of the film's director, Howard Hawks. Grant co-starred with the acerbic Jean Arthur and a relative newcomer to A pictures, Rita Hayworth. The movie, which began shooting on December 20, 1938, was Grant's thirty-third film in seven years.

More than a decade later impersonators were imitating Grant by saying "Judy, Judy, Judy." PETER BOGDANOVICH believes that the genesis of the imitation came from Grant's delivery of several lines in *Only Angels Have Wings.* "In the film his former girl friend is called Judith or Judy (played by Rita Hayworth). Cary has lines like 'Hello, Judy. Come on, Judy. Now, Judy.' But he never said 'Judy, Judy, Judy.'"

JUDY QUINE has an another explanation: "Cary told me back in 1955 that when he did the *Lux Radio Theater,* they used his voice introduction for Judy Garland, who was a guest for the following week. He recalled some banter where he could have said 'Judy, Judy, Judy,' but he wasn't sure."

Although Grant must have tired of being constantly asked to say the line, he always obliged when women named Judy asked him to say "Juday, Juday, Juday." And RICH LITTLE admires Grant's sense of humor about it: "Cary said [Little imitating CG], 'Where is this "Juday, Juday, Juday" coming from? I don't know anybody named Juday-Juday-Juday. The only Judy I knew was Judy Garland. And when I saw her, there weren't three of 'em!'"

During the making of *Charade* PETER STONE used to joke with Grant about "Judy, Judy, Judy." He recalls: "While we were shooting the taxi scene—right near the end of the picture where Audrey's feet are up in his lap and he's massaging them—Cary looked at the camera and said [Stone imitating CG], 'Juday, Juday, Juday. There. Now you've got it on film!'"

As late as the 1980s Grant was still answering questions about the phrase, and during one of his *Conversations* he offered still another speculation on how it came about.

CG: We looked up track after track and outtake after out-take. As far as we can tell, I never said it. We think it started with a celebrity impersonator by the name of Larry Storch. He apparently was appearing in a night-club and doing me when Judy Garland walked in. And that's how he greeted her.

In the end, no matter which story comes closest to the truth, "Judy, Judy, Judy," like "Play it again, Sam," has become one of those famous lines we fondly remember but never really heard.

Grant applied for American citizenship while he was doing *Only Angels Have Wings*. But when Great Britain declared war against Germany, he didn't think it right to forswear allegiance to his native country at a time when it was in trouble. So, although he still wanted to become an American, he held off.

A letter from his mother shows she was pleased:

December 12, 1938

MY DARLING SON,

I was delighted to receive your cablegram this morning very early I read in newspaper suggestion you thinking of changing your nationality. I hope and trust you will do what's right in the sight of God. I have always trusted in him. My darling I am sending you this Christmas parcel hoping you will be pleased to find it useful. It is very fashionable colours I like. I do my darling so wish you were nearer. I could see you more often and do for you. I felt ever so confused after so many years you have grown such a man. I am more than delighted you have done so well. I trust in God you will keep well and strong. . . . I remain your affectionate mother fondest love wishing you all the best.

On April 11, 1939, Grant and Carole Lombard reported to the set of *In Name Only*. The plot involved a rather routine trian-gle in which Grant's love for Lombard is thwarted by his marriage to Kay Francis. The movie was more reminiscent of his earlier vehicles for Paramount than it was in keeping with his new, more spirited roles.

Meanwhile, PHYLLIS BROOKS accepted an assignment to make two pictures in England. She recalls: "At the last minute he tried very hard to make me change my mind. Freddy Brisson was my agent for foreign films, and he said, 'You can't back out now. It's all set.' So, Freddy and I sailed off on the *Queen Mary*. Cary sailed later [June 14, 1939] on the *Normandie*."

Grant's mother's letters repeatedly referred to his visit to Bristol, his last before the war. It was seven years before he again saw her.

Noel Coward entertained PHYLLIS BROOKS in London. She recalls: "Cary set it up. Noel was the most adorable man. He and Gertie Lawrence gave a performance of *Tonight at 8:30*, his series of one-act plays, on a Sunday night just for actors. It was the most exciting evening I will ever remember in the theater. The electricity was enormous.

"When Cary arrived, we went to Paris, where we visited my cousin Betty Carstairs, who had a beautiful home on the Left Bank. We motored down to the south of France and into Italy, where we went to Venice and ended up with Dorothy di Frasso at her villa in Rome. She was a fascinating woman. There was nobody she hadn't met. An amazing raconteur, she talked all evening. Cary and I listened and laughed."

> CG: Dorothy's escapades were the gossip's delight, and her palatial Villa Madama in Rome was the scene of indescribably lavish parties. The Villa Madama, the classic site of so many Hubert Robert paintings, was taken over by Mussolini's Fascist government for Hitler's use during the war. In light of events to come, it was Dorothy's haunting grief that she didn't arrange to leave a time bomb in the place before departing to live in America. She died in her sleep in 1954—on a train returning to Los Angeles from Las Vegas, where she had visited Marlene Dietrich. It was my unhappy mission to accompany her body to New York for the funeral and a gathering of those who, like myself, would miss her amusing presence and the loyalty of her friendship.

Grant was scheduled to start filming *His Girl Friday*. He and Brooks sailed back on the *Île de France*. It was the second to the last ship before the war started. Brooks's agent for American films, JOHNNY MASCHIO, explains that her family condemned the couple's open relationship: "They raised hell, complaining their friends were saying, 'What's Cary Grant doing running around with your daughter in Europe?' Today nobody would mention it. If her family had not interfered, they would have married."

PHYLLIS BROOKS confirms her parents' frame of mind: "My mother was a tight-thinking person, a strict Victorian. She felt she *had* to be with me, even when I was over twenty-one. Things were a lot different in those days. There were moral clauses in your contract. Nobody dared live together. Good Lord, no. It would have been utterly scandalous. I lived with my mother and my brother."

From the outside the couple's life was as glittering as any in Hollywood. She remembers the good times and the difficult ones: "We loved to dance. Always to a live band. And always black tie. It was a much more formal society than we know today. Boxing matches were on Friday nights. Cary enjoyed them a lot. I didn't. But I'd go anyplace he wanted to go. I just wanted to be with him. Once we had a misunderstanding about meeting each other for a date. I thought Cary had stood me up. The following day I was playing and listening to music in a record store in Westwood, and Cary found me. He was wearing a porkpie hat. He gave me a ruby and diamond cigarette case and asked my forgiveness."

Their relationship did have an on again, off again quality. Their engagement was announced more than once, but when Grant was asked by the press whether he would marry again, he said only, "I hope so."

When they finally decided to marry, Grant presented PHYLLIS BROOKS with a prenuptial agreement. She says: "In it Cary made sure my mother could never come to our house. I didn't blame him. She was so hostile to Cary that he didn't come into the house. When I saw his car pull up, I'd go out. I was twenty-four, and my mother was in my house dictating to me. Cary wanted to get married and have a family. We both wanted children. He wanted me to give up my career. I really didn't care if I worked or not. I was very much in love with Cary. However, my income was important because my father, who was an industrial engineer, was just beginning to reestablish himself in his profession after the Depression. And my mother's inheritance had been lost in the crash. The thought that I would quit work and marry Cary made my mother blow her stack. It became an impossible situation for me. We were enormously happy together. It was a joyous time . . . and it disintegrated into something awful."

By 1940 they were seeing each other only occasionally. "It wasn't that we didn't love each other," BROOKS admits. "It was just the ghastly situation. Then Cary was to make *The Howards of Virginia,* and he decided to take a tramp steamer through the Panama Canal and up the East Coast. A few good friends came to his house the night before he left—Bob Coote, Reggie Gardiner, a few others, and me. Cary said, 'Oh, I'm going to bring Brooksie back topazes from Mexico and things from all the ports I visit.'"

Grant sailed to Panama from Los Angeles on March 15, 1940, aboard the *Europa,* a Danish liner, and BROOKS went to see him off. She recalls: "I went home, looked at my mother, and saw the whole situation was still there. It disturbed me so much, I didn't go with him. It was too painful to stay in California. So I went to New York for a year, where I did *Panama Hattie.* I saw Cary shortly after I got back at a benefit at the Hollywood Bowl. Cary was on the program. I was so nervous just breathing the same air. Louis Schurr, my agent, and I were sitting down front. Cary was just across the aisle. When he made his way from the stage, he saw me. And Louis, who surmised how we must be feeling, said, 'Why don't you meet us at Mike Romanoff's after the show?' Cary said, 'Why, I'd love to.' Louis and I were sitting at the back of Romanoff's. Cary drove me home, and we talked. It was very sad. It's painful even today. But I could not live and be hostile to my mother. She thought she was doing the right thing.

"In the early years of my [subsequent] marriage to Torbert Macdonald [John F. Kennedy's Harvard roommate and Massachusetts congressman], I kept all the letters and my photos from Cary at my parents' house in Syracuse. I didn't want Cary's letters in the house with my husband. I was afraid he might run into them. But I certainly didn't want to lose them. Some years later I went up to the attic and opened the trunk, and they were gone. I came downstairs, and I said, 'Mother!' She told me she had burned them.

"My mother never liked anybody I went out with, but Cary presented the biggest threat. In her mind she had saved my life. She died believing that."

CHAPTER FIVE

WORKING WITH THE BEST

CG: I think most of us become actors because we want affection, love, and applause.

On September 2, 1939, the day after Germany invaded Poland, a cable to Grant read: "DARLING TELEPHONE DELAY TO LONDON HOPE YOU SAFE DON'T WORRY ABOUT MOTHER PULLED THROUGH LAST WAR GOD WATCH OVER YOU LOVE ALWAYS LEACH."

For millions it was the beginning of World War II; for Grant, it was the first day on the set of *His Girl Friday*. More in the style of *Bringing Up Baby* than of *Only Angels Have Wings*, this clever remake of *The Front Page* was Grant's third picture with director Howard Hawks. Grant was cast as the newspaper editor and, with a clever role reversal on the original, Rosalind Russell played Grant's ace reporter (and former wife). Ralph Bellamy costarred as Russell's long-suffering fiancé.

BELLAMY recounts his first viewing of one of Grant's famous ad libs: "On my day off I went to see the rushes from the previous day. What I saw was a complete surprise. Cary was asked to describe my character and says, 'He looks like, er, that fellow in the movies . . . you know, Ralph Bellamy.' Well, that was Cary's contribution. It was one of the biggest laughs in the picture."

CG: When I first started in pictures, an actor didn't have the freedom to interrupt the dialogue. But in *His Girl Friday*, Rosalind Russell and I were constantly interrupting each other. The sound men would say, "We can't hear you." And we'd say, "Well, you're not supposed to hear us. People do interrupt each other, you know."

Filming *His Girl Friday* marked the beginning of another lifelong friendship. Rosalind Russell not only enriched Grant's life but made a profound difference in the future of his friend Frederick Brisson. Grant introduced the couple, and in October 1941, during the filming of *Arsenic and Old Lace*, Brisson and Russell were married in Solvang, a Danish community in the Santa Ynez Mountains, north of Santa Barbara. Grant, accompanied by Barbara Hutton, was the best man. Russell thanked Grant for his contribution to her life.

DEAREST CARY,

Now look what you've done! You black-eyed cupid! For the remainder of my life, I'll hold *you* responsible and when I go to Reno (and I shall if I can't get the great Dane's haircut properly), I'll scream at the judge: "Grant did this to me."

But, seriously, Cary, you will never know the great joy you have helped bring us both and how much we shall always love you for it. You must know, too, that the wedding would not be complete without you. You who brought us together.

All love to you, Cary, darling.

Devotedly, ROSALIND

At Russell's funeral on November 28, 1976, Grant gave a eulogy for his cherished friend:

CG: Roz always held her head high. Who had a better right than she? She seemed to be aiming at a place I couldn't get to. At the rosary service preceding her funeral, when the priest suggested she was on her way to paradise, I realized: that's where she had been aiming. . . .

I know of no one better qualified to enter paradise, and I can imagine her in a glorious place telling everyone where to be and what to do, properly, yet with kindness, because Roz never missed a trick. . . .

On December 7, 1939, Grant started work on *My Favorite Wife*. Columbia didn't waste any time cashing in on the box-office

With Rosalind Russell and director Howard Hawks making His Girl
Friday, *1939.* RUSSELL: *"Hawks was a terrific director; he encouraged us
and let us go. Once he told Cary, 'Next time give her a bigger shove onto
the couch,' and Cary said, 'Well, I don't want to kill the woman,' and
Hawks . . . said, 'Try killin' 'er.'"*

response to *The Awful Truth* and cast him again with Irene Dunne in the new comedy. Chosen to direct was GARSON KANIN, who says: "*The Awful Truth* was enormously successful, and the studio was eager to come up with a second picture for Cary and Irene. Leo McCarey had a contract with the studio but, for complicated business reasons, did not want to direct. He asked me if I would like to do it. And of course, I was delighted. They were both big stars, very able, and full of personality. They had developed instinctively a fascinating team rapport—something that cannot be directed, written, or inspired."

IRENE DUNNE recalled, "I loved working with Cary—every minute of it. Between takes he was so amusing with his cockney stories. I was his best audience. I laughed and laughed and laughed. The more I laughed, the more he went on."

KANIN continues, "When Cary read the script for *My Favorite Wife*, he asked, 'Who is going to play the other part? I think Randy could do it.' I didn't know Randolph Scott, so I sent for him. He was certainly a very attractive fellow and very personable indeed. It was, by far, a secondary part, but when he said that he would like to do it, we engaged him at once.

"Cary was not one of those movie stars who gets out there just because he's handsome and has a flair for playing one key or another. He worked very hard. I remember that indelibly. Almost more than any other quality was his seriousness about his work. He was always prepared; he always knew his part, his lines, and the scene. And he related very well to the other players. He took not only his own part seriously; he took the whole picture seriously. He'd come and look at the rushes every evening. No matter how carefree and easygoing he seemed in the performance, in reality he was a serious man, an exceptionally concentrated man. And extremely intelligent, too. Still, he played far more on instinct than he did on intellect. I don't recall him ever intellectually discussing a role or a scene or a picture or a part. He trusted his own instincts, which had worked for him so well. He just polished that up and used it."

ROBERT WISE, who edited the film and found the cast and crew exceptional, recalls: "Garson liked to have his film editor on the set with him when he was shooting to be sure he got plenty of coverage. Cary was always up. And very generous with the crew. At the end of the filming he gave everybody gifts. I got a nice set of gold cuff links. I hadn't been in the business too long, and it was quite a thrill to get that from him. I still have them."

On the set THELMA ORLOFF observed Grant's professionalism: "He knew the lighting well, and he knew his best side [for the camera]. He understood exactly how to maneuver. He had grasped every aspect of the business. I never saw him stutter. He never did anything that wasn't right on the button.

"I first got to know Cary when Gar Kanin gave me the job as his secretary. Cary asked me, 'Do you play backgammon?' And I said, 'What's that?' And he said, 'I'll teach you.' He bought a backgammon set and gave it to me when the picture was finished. He was an excellent teacher. He knew the game well. Cary was such a perfectionist that he wouldn't have played if he couldn't play well. We used to play a lot of backgammon at the beach."

Years later Grant was still playing backgammon, often with GEORGE BARRIE, who remembers: "He was a good but extremely conservative player. He made sure everything was covered. He wouldn't leave anything open. He didn't play cards or backgammon for money. The highest stake was ten cents a point."

Still a bachelor and still interested in marriage, Grant was reintroduced to Barbara Hutton by his friend Countess Dorothy di Frasso. He had first met the Woolworth heiress sailing to England from New York on the *Normandie* in mid-June 1939. They had dined together on board ship; but at the time Grant was seeing Phyllis Brooks, and Hutton was still married to her second husband, Count Court Haugwitz-Hardenberg-Reventlow. Hutton was now returning from a visit to Honolulu and had decided to stay in Los Angeles. She moved into a house at 1044 North Hartford Way in Beverly Hills.

THELMA ORLOFF was first aware that Grant was interested in Hutton when she saw her picture sitting out at the beach house. She recollects, "She looked very elegant in the photo, and Cary said, 'That's Barbara Hutton.' And I said, 'So I see.' And he said, 'What a lady.' He loved the way she dressed. He loved the way she got herself together."

The interest was mutual, and Hutton and Grant saw each other regularly even though she was not yet divorced.

The next month Grant went to work on *The Howards of Virginia*, costarring with MARTHA SCOTT, who remembers: "When I was asked whether I was interested in doing the picture with

With Martha Scott in The Howards of Virginia, *1939.* SCOTT: *"During a shot, if somebody mumbled, he'd mumble too, forcing another take."*

Cary, I said, 'I'd give anything to work with him. No matter what size part.' And my agent said, 'It isn't that simple. Mr. Grant has full approval of the cast, will look at some film, and then make up his mind.' I later learned Cary chose me because he thought I looked like Barbara Hutton.

"It was my second film, and I think Cary knew, having seen *Our Town*, what a switch it was for me to go from a little New England girl to a very elegant British woman. But he never made me feel he knew I was nervous. Once in a while, in a close shot over his shoulder, in a full-head close-up of me, he would put his foot next to mine so I wouldn't move my body out of the frame. Sometimes he'd reach over and touch my elbow—to remind me not to move out of the light. I was so used to the theater that I was apt to do my scenes and not care about anything. But Cary wanted it to be right for me. He was conscious of body movement, like a dancer. It was wonderful to watch. Working with him was such a loving and happy experience. The most outstanding thing was his commitment to perfectionism, his help in surreptitious ways. During a shot, if somebody mumbled, he'd mumble, too, forcing another take.

"In 1981 I sat next to Cary at the luncheon which proceeded the Kennedy Center Gala. He was receiving the award that night. He leaned over and whispered, 'Will you ever forgive me? I was so bad in *The Howards of Virginia*. I don't belong in costumes.' I said, 'Cary, you astound me. You were marvelous. You were so much that man, and it's so unlike all the things you've done since.' It's only because he felt uncomfortable. He thought he was terrible, but he wasn't."

On July 8, 1940, Grant reported to the set of *The Philadelphia Story*, which reunited him for the last time with George Cukor and Katharine Hepburn. It was the only time he worked with James Stewart. Cukor's direction resulted in a wonderful blend of comedy and romance. The film's success reestablished Hepburn as a viable marquee name (she had been pronounced "box-office poison" and had left Hollywood after *Holiday*), and Stewart won an Academy Award.

JAMES STEWART remembers filming one scene in particular: "I play a writer who falls in love with Katharine Hepburn. The night before her wedding I have a little too much to drink. This gives me the courage to go and talk to Cary, who's playing her ex-husband. So I go to Cary's house and knock on the door. It's obvious I've had too much to drink, but he lets me in.

"It was time to do the scene, and Cary said, 'George, why don't we just go ahead? If you don't like it, we'll do it again.' So, without a rehearsal or anything, we started the scene. As I was talking, it hit me that I'd had *too* much to drink. So, as I explained things to Cary, I hiccuped. In answer to the hiccup, Cary said—out of the clear blue sky—'Excuse me.' Well, I sort of said, 'Umm?' It was very difficult for me to keep a straight face, be-

CG and Katharine Hepburn in The Philadelphia Story, *1940.* HEPBURN:
"We got on well, Cary and I."

cause his ad-libbed response had been so beautifully done. . . . Cary had an almost perfect humor."

Grant held Stewart in equally high esteem.

CG: Jimmy simply mesmerized me on the screen. When I watched him act, I felt like a triangle player in the orchestra who keeps watching the conductor and then, when he finally gets the baton signal, he misses his triangle.

Grant donated his entire salary for *The Philadelphia Story*, $125,000, to the British war effort. When the picture was released, Joseph L. Mankiewicz (the producer) sent Grant a letter:

> This is essentially a happy birthday note and many more happy ones by the way, but more than that, I want to add to my previous expressions of gratitude to you for your work in *The Philadelphia Story*.
>
> Whatever success the picture is having, and it is a simply enormous smash, is due, in my opinion, to you in far greater proportions than anyone has seen fit to shout about. As what is laughingly called "the producer" of the film, but still, perhaps, closer to it than anyone—believe me, your presence as Dexter, and particularly your sensitive and brilliant playing of the role, contribute what I consider the backbone and basis of practically every emotional value in the piece. I can think of no one who could have done as well or given as much.
>
> I don't know what moved me to this outburst except that your birthday seemed as good a time as any for me to air my private feeling that you have been unjustly slighted in the general hysteria at Kate's comeback—and a desire to express once again my thanks and to remind us both of the great pleasure it was to work with you—I hope we can again soon.
>
> This probably makes suckers out of all the men who have bitten dogs—but producer thanks actor, and, brother, that's news!
>
> Happy Birthday, Cary.
>
> Sincerely, JOE

STANLEY DONEN, who later directed Grant, agrees with Mankiewicz: "Two of the greatest performances ever given by an actor were Cary's in *His Girl Friday* and *The Philadelphia Story*.

Cary is not really appreciated for the remarkable actor that he was. He's thought of as a man who achieved a certain elegance and savoir faire. But in truth he was a fantastic actor. It's not just the persona which he had developed over the years; it was his ability to act. He was absolutely the best in the world at his job.

"Cary was unique. You see it and feel it in the reactions and the characterization. There's not a false moment. And it seems like it's just happening, that he's experiencing it at that moment. He projected ease and comfort, and he was always concentrated. You never saw any fear in him when he was acting. His scripts were full of little notes to himself. The minute detail of it all: That's really what all art is about. The tiniest details: That's what he was great at. He always seemed real. It wasn't a gift from God. It was the magic that came from enormous amounts of work."

And he continued to work. Grant's next picture was *Penny Serenade*, a sentimental story of a marriage about to break apart. On October 15, 1940, he reported to work with his friend Irene Dunne for director George Stevens. The picture was released in April 1941, and this time it was Grant who was nominated for an Academy Award.

IRENE DUNNE said Grant's mind was on domestic issues, on screen and off: "During the filming—it was before he married Barbara Hutton—Cary said, 'I know what my children are going to look like. They're going to be blond with brown eyes.'"

GEORGE STEVENS, JR., who met Grant for the first time on the set of *Penny Serenade*, remembers: "I was eight years old. He made three pictures with Dad, who was very important to his life. In June 1981, when I was making the film about my father, *A Filmmaker's Journey*, I went to Cary's house to interview him. He talked about my father for two hours. He told stories, laughed, and wept. He was brilliant. And then I said, 'Well, Cary, I'd like to come back and film a little—to illustrate. . . .' 'Oh, George,' he said [Stevens imitating CG], 'I couldn't do that. I loved George, but if I do it for George, I'd have to do it for Hitch and for Hawks. I'd have to do it for everybody.' I was really shocked because his feeling had been so fully demonstrated, but I also knew how stubborn he could be. . . . After several telephone calls he said, 'George, I'll do a little bit of narration for you, but I won't be photographed.'

"Well, Cary was in Washington for the Princess Grace Foun-

CG, thirty-six, with Irene Dunne, working on Penny Serenade, *1940.*
DUNNE: *"Cary told me I was the sweetest-smelling actress he had ever played with."*

dation, and I asked him if he would do the narration while he was in town.

"Now parenthetically, I had promised my son Michael (who was in high school) that he could have a car if he earned a B average. Well, he did, and I gave him my Volvo station wagon, and I'd been driving an old wreck that belonged to my wife Liz's mother.

"So the next day I got in this old minicar wreck and drove down to the L'Enfant Plaza. I told the guy in front I was just going upstairs to pick up Cary Grant. He was suspicious, but he gave me ten minutes. So I squeezed in between the Mercedes limousines and went upstairs. Cary opened the door. 'Come on in,' he said. 'Barbara's here, won't you have some coffee?' Well, we had an enchanting conversation, but I did not participate vigorously because all I could think about was the son of a bitch downstairs who told me I only had ten minutes. Finally, Cary said, 'Okay, let's go.'

"I decided not to apologize for my car. Cary climbed in, closed the door, and the handle fell off. We drove away in silence. After what seemed like ten minutes Cary turned to me and said, 'George, the only other man I know who drove a car like this was Howard Hughes.'

"In 1984 my film was released theatrically. In Los Angeles it was shown at the Motion Picture Academy theater. Cary agreed to host the evening along with Fred Astaire, John Huston, Frank Capra, and Warren Beatty. Army Archerd wrote [for *Variety*] that it was the longest standing ovation he could remember for a film in all his years in Hollywood. There was an enormous outpouring of emotion at the end. And as we walked up the aisle, Cary said, 'Oh, George, I should have done that interview.'"

Grant's next picture began his classic association with Alfred Hitchcock. The first of four films they made together, *Suspicion* was the least successful and least satisfying. Grant did not feel the rapport with his costar, Joan Fontaine, that he had with Rosalind Russell or Irene Dunne, and adding to the tension on the set, the script was not finished when they started production on February 11, 1941.

Suspicion's script continually underwent changes during filming—right down to the film's final scenes. In the original ending Grant gives his wife (Fontaine) a glass of poisoned milk. Just before she drinks it, she hands him a sealed envelope to mail. The letter names him as her killer. Then, still in love with her murderer, she drinks the poison.

> CG: I thought the original was marvelous. It was a perfect Hitchcock ending. But the studio insisted that they didn't want to have Cary Grant play a murderer.

Hitchcock was inarticulate with his actors and his cinematographers. He had a reputation for not giving direction. "One doesn't direct Cary Grant," he once told PETER BOGDANOVICH; "one simply puts him in front of a camera. He enables the audience to identify with the main character. He represents a man we know. He's not a stranger. He is like our brother."

JAMES STEWART says, "There was no discussing a scene with Hitchcock. That wasn't the way he worked. In my day you just didn't talk about the acting profession very much. I've had people ask, 'Well, how did you approach this part in this picture?' I really didn't know what the hell they were talking about. To my generation acting was a business. I have a feeling Cary felt that way, too."

He did. Nevertheless, Grant occasionally had ideas about his character development.

> CG: Hitch and I sat down one day and worked out a certain character which became the basis of all the comedies I played in after that. In the films I made with Hitchcock, the humor relieved the suspense. People laugh in the theater because what's on the screen is not happening to them. I played my role as though it wasn't happening to me. And I think that's how I got the audience on my side.

"I never saw Hitchcock look through a camera," JAMES STEWART remembers Grant saying. Stewart's own experience paralleled Grant's: "When I worked with Hitch and we finished blocking a scene, he would say, 'All right, that's fine.' And his cameraman, Bob Burks, knew exactly what to do. Hitch would go and sit down in his chair. Burks would light the scene, come over to him, and say, 'It's lit.' And Hitch would say, 'All right, everybody, let's go over this scene. Move around and see if you can keep from running into each other.' And that was about the size of Hitchcock's direction."

Grant told JOHN FORSYTHE many stories about Hitchcock, "and I had one he hadn't heard. . . . Hitchcock was making *Lifeboat*. A ship had sunk, and a handful of people—including Tallulah Bankhead, Hume Cronyn, and John Hodiak—are stranded in the small boat. Now Hitch never went to the dailies. He said, 'I know what I have. It's not like going to the Beverly Hills camera shop and picking up your snapshots from yesterday.' So, after about five or six days of shooting, Hitch still hadn't seen any dailies. The director of photography, Glen MacWilliams, came to him and said, 'Hitch, I'm very upset.' And Hitch said, 'Easy, now. Why?' And he said, 'Because of the confines of the lifeboat, I have to have my camera down low and we're shooting up a lot. Well, er, Miss Bankhead doesn't wear any panties. She has nothing on underneath. What am I going to do? I can see everything, and it's there on the film.' Hitchcock paused for a moment and said, 'Well . . . I don't know whether this is a problem for wardrobe, makeup, or hairdressing.' Cary almost fell out of the car."

Grant made a trip to Mexico on August 13, 1941, to join Barbara Hutton, whose divorce from Count Reventlow had become final. This was his first trip to Mexico and his last outside the United States until the war was over. During the monthlong visit he met the artist and muralist Diego Rivera and later acquired Rivera's "Girl with Lilies," an oil painted in 1941.

When BURT REYNOLDS was invited to Grant's house, he was struck by the Rivera painting on the living-room wall. "I'd never seen a painting like it. Cary told me it was a picture of a painting. He said, 'I had the painting, then I sold it, and Barbara [Harris] had a photograph taken of it. Now I have the money and the picture.' He was playing up to the fact that he had a tight rein on his money. I thought it was a put-on—like Jack Benny."

It was. Grant had donated the painting, along with two oils by Eugène Boudin plus sixteen French riding prints, on July 7, 1978, to the Norton Simon Museum in Pasadena, California.

On October 18, 1941, Grant began *Arsenic and Old Lace* with Josephine Hull, Jean Adair, Raymond Massey, Peter Lorre, and Priscilla Lane. Its release was held until September 1944, when the highly successful Broadway run was over. While the Frank Capra-directed comedy is still popular today, it never was with Grant.

CG: I did not enjoy the role. It's my least favorite film. It wasn't my kind of comedy. Frank Capra, who was a great director, thought I could do it. I tried to explain to him that I couldn't do that kind of comedy—all those double takes. I'd have been better as one of the old aunts!

GREGORY PECK felt Capra pushed the limits of Grant's comic style: "Capra was a very strong, determined, hands-on director, and he had Cary doing a lot of squirrely things. When a director imposes on an actor or persuades or cajoles the actor to do something that doesn't feel right, that's not good direction. It's all right to ask an actor to stretch to his limits but not to go off into an area where he does not feel comfortable doing it. It becomes fake. I would never say that Cary was faking in that picture, but I understand why he was not comfortable. I think Capra pushed him too far in the direction of old farce—the kind of farcical playing that was a bit strained."

ROBERT WAGNER, on the other hand, admires Grant's broader moments: "Cary was the best ham in the world. He had a wonderful sense of the joy of the moment. Cary took risks. Look at the things he did in *Arsenic and Old Lace*."

But Grant himself was uncomfortable in the role.

CG: I was embarrassed doing it. I overplayed the character. It was a dreadful job for me, and yet the film was a very big success and a big money-maker, perhaps because of the reputation it had as a play. The fellow who played the role onstage in New York, Allyn Joslyn, was much better than I was. Jimmy Stewart would have been much better in the film. One of the reasons I did it was because they could get me in and out in three weeks, and I wanted to give my salary to various charities, including the British War Relief.

As large as this gesture seems, it is small compared with the way he lived his life. HSH PRINCE ALBERT OF MONACO observes: "Cary was a subtle blend of elegance, sensitivity, poise, and charm, wrapped around a soul filled with wit, generosity, and concern for others. It is not surprising for me to find the word 'care' in his name."

Chapter Six

THE WAR YEARS IN HOLLYWOOD

cg: There is nothing I wouldn't do for this country, which, because of its type of government and the opportunity it affords each and every individual, has allowed me to gain whatever measure of success I've achieved.

Grant had not worked for almost a year when the camera rolled for *The Talk of the Town* on January 28, 1942. It was the last picture he made with George Stevens, and its story was the antithesis of the romantic *Penny Serenade*. In it Grant plays Leopold Dilg, a freethinking radical, involved in an unusual triangle of ideas with Jean Arthur and Ronald Colman. It was a timely discussion of the applications of justice and the sometimes conflicting letter of the law. Under Stevens's direction, it blended wonderfully comic moments with serious philosophical and political questions. In 1981, as George Stevens, Jr., was preparing the film about his father, Grant fondly recalled the director's sensibility.

cg: Your father had a very serious exterior, but deep down he possessed a great deal of humor. I see the same qualities in Burt Reynolds and James Garner. And perhaps even in myself at one time. . . .

Your father struck me as a one-purpose man. Nothing and no one stopped him from accomplishing his purpose. Not other producers, not studio heads. He did it his way. Now, he might permit you to believe that you did it your way. But he was in control, and we all knew that. He was always dedicated to his purpose. If we got off the subject, he got right back on it.

When George Stevens, Jr., showed him a photograph of his father, Grant said:

CG: I find this very touching. I think we all loved each other in a manner we possibly couldn't express to each other. You shouldn't have sentiment on a set. You don't have time for it. But then you don't know how much you loved a person until he's not there.

Both *Penny Serenade* and *The Talk of the Town* were done at Columbia Pictures under the hard, watchful eye of studio head Harry Cohn. Cohn was notorious for his ruthlessness and vulgarity, but despite his crudeness, he had an innate sense of picture making.

CG: Poor Harry. He was always in a dither about something. He had a bad temper and blew off steam. He was not George's kind of man. . . . George had imagination. The others dealt with numbers. All that mattered was the numbers.

STANLEY E. FOX remembers Grant's attitude about producers: "Cary said, 'They don't understand actors. If they gave us a bigger dressing room, we'd take less money. All we want is comfort.'" Grant also amused FOX when he told him he "once appeared in a theater in New York that had been beautifully designed and built. But somehow they managed to forget to put in dressing rooms. The actors had to go down an alley to another theater."

On April 25, 1942, Grant started work on *Once Upon a Honeymoon*. Leo McCarey directed Grant and Ginger Rogers in this topical film set in war-torn Europe. Openly propagandistic, the picture dealt with the Nazis and the growing threat of the fifth column.

Grant earned $6,250 a week plus 2 percent of the gross receipts for the film. His success as a free-lance actor was secure, but the government was taking the vast majority of his wages. By 1943 his income had reached $327,166.66. He was now in the 93 percent income tax bracket. Only charitable donations could drop him to the 88 percent bracket. Grant once said that out of every $100,000 he earned, he took home exactly $12,000.

During the spring of 1942 RKO filed for an occupational deferment for Grant so he could finish *Once Upon a Honeymoon,* at which time he planned to enlist in the Army Air Corps. But he was thirty-eight years old. To increase his chances of acceptance, he asked Lieutenant Colonel Jack Warner (production chief of Warner Bros.) to contact the Army on his behalf. On June 24, 1942, the Army wrote to Warner:

> At the present time it is practically impossible to obtain a commission in the Army Air Forces due to the temporary "freezing" order on any new appointments. However, it is felt that Mr. Leach's case is an exceptional one and his services to the Army Air Forces will be of inestimable value. Consequently, there should be no great obstacle to overcome in having his papers processed within a comparatively short time.

On June 26, 1942, Grant became an American citizen, under naturalization certificate 5502057 and legally changed his name to Cary Grant.

"He was very proud that he had become an American," says JERRY D. LEWIS. "He was very patriotic, yet he remained very pro-British."

Grant maintained close ties with his British friends, such as BINNIE BARNES, who says: "Cary would get with his British pals and talk about London and the early days. Even though he was very pro-America, he was terribly British-minded. If it had anything to do with the queen or royalty, he was very upright about it."

The day after Grant received his citizenship documents, he signed enlistment papers, hoping to report to the Army's officer candidate school, in Miami Beach, Florida. He was given a physical and was classified 2-A.

He measured six feet one and a half inches and weighed 180 pounds. He *still* wore a size seventeen and a half collar. He reported his childhood diseases as measles and mumps. The famous mole on his left cheek was listed as his most prominent characteristic.

On August 4, 1942, the War Department notified Grant that "We have today forwarded your file to the Adjutant General's Office for consideration of your commission as a 1st Lieutenant in the Army Air Forces." On August 19, 1942, the War Department wrote him again:

> Please be informed that this directorate has requested that authority be secured from the Adjutant General's Office permitting you to enlist in the armed forces on September 15, 1942, at the recruiting office, Washington Building, Los Angeles, California, and that upon such enlistment you be ordered to report for duty to the commanding office, Officer Candidate School, Miami Beach, Florida. Upon receipt of such authority, you will be advised accordingly.

The enlistment never took place. By December 11, 1942, Grant's classification had been changed to 1-H, and an RKO Radio Pictures memorandum in Grant's files describes his final status:

> Washington suggests that they would like to have Cary Grant's name on their list of people who from time to time might do some temporary service. In each instance, if he is called upon, he will have an opportunity to say "yes" or "no" to whatever job is proposed and it is not at all certain that they will call upon him in any case. We understand that the type of work that he might be called upon to do would not be the sort that would require him to drop out of whatever other activities he may be engaged in and the fact that he was doing the work would be publicized.

Washington had made its decision. Whatever Grant's personal feelings about the conclusion of his enlistment, he enthusiastically supported the war effort.

Grant also released a statement explaining his position:

World War II, U.S. Army Signal Corps, Camp Polk, Louisiana. JACK
HALEY, JR.: *"He went on the victory caravans too, but he preferred a low-
profile, unpublicized one-on-one. . . ."*

The business of and the livelihood afforded by the motion picture industry is dependent upon the publicity given it. The business of working for one's country should be done without such fanfare, and with the dignity it so rightly deserves. I therefore have no intention of mixing the two. . . .

It follows, then, that a man gratefully should do everything toward helping this war effort in order to protect those very standards which allowed him the privilege of living under this form of government.

Wherever Uncle Sam orders my utilization to the best purposes, there I will willingly go, as should every other man. I feel that Uncle Sam knows best.

During the war years Grant was on the board of the Hollywood Victory Committee (clearinghouse for all picture talent for servicemen shows), United Nations War Relief, and Jesterate of Masquers (a theatrical group that did war work). He went to committee meetings several nights a week and appeared in shows at nearby Army camps. With Myrna Loy, Rosalind Russell, and Charles Boyer he sold peanuts at a Buy-a-Bomber Benefit.

While Grant sought a commission, he continued to pursue Barbara Hutton. Her divorce final, she and Grant were married on July 8, 1942. The ceremony was performed at the Lake Arrowhead home of his agent and best man, Frank Vincent. The witnesses were Madeleine Hazeltine, the wife of sculptor Herbert Hazeltine; Termaine Tocquet, Hutton's former governess and companion; Frank Horn, who had been in the cast of *Nina Rosa* with Grant in 1931 and later became Grant's secretary; William Robertson, a mutual friend of Grant's and Hutton's; and Perry Lieber, RKO's publicity chief.

The Reverend H. Paul Romeis, of the Lutheran Church of San Bernardino, performed the ceremony. When Grant told him he didn't know the customary fee, the minister said the church needed an organ. Its cost was eighteen hundred dollars, but the church had raised only twelve hundred. Grant wrote out a check for six hundred dollars.

Born on November 14, 1912, in New York City, Barbara Hutton was eight years Grant's junior. She was the granddaughter of F. W. Woolworth (founder of the five-and-ten-cent store chain) and the daughter of Edna Woolworth and stockbroker Franklyn Laws Hutton. When she was five, Barbara's mother died, and the child inherited approximately forty million dollars. She had been married twice before, first to Georgian Prince Alexis Mdivani (1933–35) and then to Count Reventlow (1935–41). She and Reventlow had a son. "Lance was born in London on February 24, 1936," says JILL ST. JOHN. "He grew to be six foot one and had ash blond hair and black eyes."

DINA MERRILL's father (E. F. Hutton) and Barbara Hutton's father were brothers. Dina recalls: "Cary and Barbara Hutton came to visit us in Washington right after they married. My mother [Marjorie Merriweather Post] loved Barbara, and since Barbara's mother was dead, I think she tried to take her place. Mother and I thought Cary was absolutely divine. I was thrilled my cousin had married this eminent movie star."

HAL ROACH remembers that "the house Cary had with Barbara Hutton [1038 Ocean Front] was only about four doors from where he lived originally."

Hutton's decorating was innovative. In the dining room, instead of one big table, she had six tables, each of which seated four. "She had the walls mirrored with glass and gold," THELMA ORLOFF says, describing the design. "There were little oval tables all around and lots of red velvet. It looked like a nightclub. Cary was amazed. He kept saying, 'Look at this.'"

Soon the couple moved into DOUGLAS FAIRBANKS, JR.'s, house in Pacific Palisades. He says: "When I went off to the war, I rented my house to Cary and Barbara Hutton for something like five hundred dollars a month. I'd gotten it from a bankrupt estate which let everything go for what was owed in taxes. I picked up the house and twelve acres for peanuts."

As the war worsened in Europe, Grant and his mother stayed in touch by cable and letter. In her notes she wondered when they would meet again and prayed, "God keep us safe from enemies."

Grant wired his solicitor, asking him to communicate the following to his mother: "IS MONEY OR ANYTHING NEEDED FOR YOUR WELFARE OR FOR ANY RELATIVES OR FRIENDS AS WITH ONLY NEWSPAPER ACCOUNTS OF BRISTOL TO GO BY AM GREATLY CONCERNED."

The solicitor paid all of Mrs. Leach's bills. Grant also wanted her to have extra spending money so she could shop for special occasions. When the solicitor learned she was putting this money in the bank to save for a trip to America, he took it upon himself to choose and send her various presents.

On November 21, 1942, Mrs. Leach wrote to her son:

> I hope you are not experiencing the blitz like here. We have not had an alert for a couple of weeks. I expect Mr. Davis will tell you I am a fire-watcher. I wish I could do more. My age against me. It is a lingering war. I shall be glad when it is over. . . . Darling, if you don't come over as soon as the war ends, I shall come over to you. I am pleased you are married and you have a nice wife and someone to love. I have no one. Only my little dog. I think of you always, darling. We are so many thousands of miles from each other.

Throughout the war Grant made applications for a passport and requested permission to go abroad for an entertainment tour—a tour he hoped could include a visit to his mother.

On February 10, 1943, he wrote the passport office in San Francisco and again requested a passport. His records do not show one was ever issued. On October 14, 1943, Grant cabled his mother of his uncertainty about obtaining permission for an entertainment tour. And again, on December 28 he cabled: "STILL NO LUCK GETTING PERMISSION FOR TRIP."

Unable to go abroad, he toured camps in the United States. In March 1943 he visited Camp Crowder in Missouri, Camp Robinson in Arkansas, and Camp Claiborne in Louisiana, where he had "real discussions" with the soldiers.

CG: These kids are interested in everything. After I left, they sent me letters telling me that they're still thinking about what we discussed.

JACK HALEY, JR., found Grant's war effort admirable. He says: "Cary would go to places you never heard of where there'd be forty GIs. He would sit and talk with them by their beds. He went on the victory caravans too, but he preferred a low-profile, unpublicized one-on-one with the guys."

On June 23, 1943, Grant reported to the set of *Destination Tokyo*. It was his first and only bona fide war film, a prime example of Hollywood propaganda. Grant played the commander of a submarine and headed an ensemble cast, which included John Garfield and newcomers John Forsythe and Robert Hutton. The film was written and directed by Delmer Daves.

"Delmer was a successful writer and longed to direct," explains his wife, MARY LAWRENCE DAVES. "He had done some acting and directing as a student at Stanford. Well, Warner Brothers *begged* him to direct *Destination Tokyo* because he [and Albert Maltz] had turned in a very technical script, approved by Washington and the FBI. But would the star agree? Cary did immediately." From that day on they were fast friends.

Destination Tokyo was ROBERT HUTTON's film debut. He recalls: "There were no women on the set. Boredom set in, and people started coming in late. So Johnny Garfield said, 'Let's paddle them for every minute they're late.'

"The prop department made a great big heavy wooden paddle, which we all signed, including Cary and Delmer Daves. The first one late was Cary. He was driving a little Austin to conserve on gasoline. He looked bigger than the automobile. He came tearing down the main street at Warner Brothers to the stage where we were working. And we thought, '*Oh, my God! We can't paddle* him!'

"Cary went through this whole rigmarole. 'Look, guys, I live down in Pacific Palisades. It's a hell of a long drive, and I'm just three minutes late,' et cetera. Delmer Daves came out, took the paddle, and said, 'Cary, bend over.' And we belted the daylights out of him. From then on he was one of the guys.

"The studio wouldn't let newcomers see the daily rushes. They felt you wouldn't like what you saw and you'd become inhibited. One day Delmer Daves invited me to the rushes of a scene I'd done with Cary. It was the biggest scene in the movie, the one where I remove a bomb and become the hero.

"I was so excited and walked over to the projection room. I was all alone, so I went to the first row and waited. Finally Cary came in with Delmer Daves, Jerry Wald (the producer), and a whole bunch of guys. I slid down in the seat, to make myself as little as possible. The lights went down, and the movie came on.

"There were various cuts—close-ups and long shots. Then

DAVID NIVEN: *"Cary's enthusiasm made him search for perfection in all things, particularly in the three that meant most to him: filmmaking, physical fitness, and women."*

came a long shot of me crawling through the submarine to the bomb. I was way up in the foreground. And way off in the background was a little tiny head of Cary Grant. And I thought, 'Look at that. I got the close-up, and there's Cary way in the back.'

"Then they showed a choker of me and cut to another little tiny shot of Cary Grant. He looked about an inch tall. That was it. One after another—all close-ups of Bob Hutton and tiny shots of Cary Grant. I was so embarrassed I slid way down in the seat. The lights came up, and there was deathly silence.

"I heard Cary clear his throat. The first thing he said was, 'Why does that son of a bitch get all the close-ups and I get nothing?' That's when I died. I wanted to go home to Kingston [New York] and forget the whole thing.

"In the back Daves and Wald argued with Cary. Cary insisted, 'I'm the star. Why does that kid get all the close-ups?' Jerry Wald said, 'But the scene belongs to Bob Hutton.' And Cary said, 'Then I quit. I'm walking off the movie.'

"I heard the door slam, then hushed tones between Jerry Wald and Delmer Daves. Then they left. I thought, *This is ridiculous. Because of* me, *Cary Grant has walked off the movie? What's Jack Warner going to say? What is Louella Parsons going to print in her column?*

"I finally walked out. Delmer Daves, Jerry Wald, and Cary were waiting outside—dying laughing. Cary had put them up to it. Delmer Daves said, 'Look, Cary wanted me to shoot the scene that way from the very beginning. It's your scene.'"

The young actor was distantly related to Barbara Hutton, as ROBERT HUTTON explains: "We'd been working together for three or four weeks when I told Cary we were cousins."

When Grant told his wife that Robert Hutton was working with him on *Destination Tokyo*, she was delighted and invited him and his fiancée, Natalie Thompson, to dinner. HUTTON recalls: "From then on we dined with them twice a week. I wore a business suit on Wednesdays and black tie on Saturday. Among the regulars at these dinners were Freddy Brisson and Rosalind Russell; Gene Tierney and Oleg Cassini; Louis Jourdan and his beautiful wife; Alexander Korda and Merle Oberon; June Duprez and the Baron Guy de Rothschild.

"I always sat on Barbara's left; the guest of honor, on her right. One Saturday night, and for no apparent reason, Cary, who had been sitting at the other end of the table, got up and walked over to Barbara. While she was talking to her guest of honor, he leaned over and kissed her. He said, 'I love you so much.' Then they looked at each other, and he walked back to his seat. I thought, That's great. What a nice gesture."

In the summer of 1943, during the filming of *Destination Tokyo*, Grant and Barbara Hutton appeared to be very much in love. In the months to come, however, their differences gradually cracked the happy surface of their marriage.

"Cary was most attentive," JOHN FORSYTHE recalls, "and he introduced her to everybody. But she was a rather remote woman, certainly not the kind you would expect an actor to marry."

JOHNNY MASCHIO saw one of the couple's problems: "I think they were very much in love. But every single night she had a dinner party. She had nothing else to do. She played tennis in the daytime and had dinners at night.

"Cary would come in, beat, and say, 'Darling, send me up a bowl of soup. I've got a five o'clock call in the morning.' "And Barbara would say, 'God, Cary, give it up. It's getting to be the season for the south of France—or skiing in Switzerland.'

"If he had not been working so much, I think they would have stayed together . . . and God knows she was a beautiful girl."

CHAPTER SEVEN

ARCHIE LEACH IMITATING CARY GRANT

CG: You don't lose your identity up on the screen. It's always you. . . .

Since his break with Paramount in 1936 the image of Cary Grant had been steadily (and very successfully) honed. Independent of a long-term contract, he was able to select precisely the roles he wanted and build a unique screen persona: witty, urbane, thoughtful, shrewd, confident—and always attractive to the opposite sex. The result was a complex, multifaceted personality that he carried with him from film to film, gracefully—and made part of his life.

JOHN FORSYTHE comments on the difficulty of making acting look simple and natural: "The hardest thing to do is to be yourself. Someone asked Spencer Tracy, 'Why are you always yourself, Mr. Tracy?' His response was 'Who do you want me to be, Humphrey Bogart?'"

CG: It's difficult to be yourself within the confines of the plot when you're going to be blown up on a theater screen and hear your voice amplified.

You don't lose your identity up on the screen. It's always you, no matter how you behave. How can you lose your own identity, because you're there, in the flesh, photographed and blown up?

It's rather stupid for critics to knock Gary Cooper or Duke Wayne for playing themselves because they were both number one in the business for many years. It's much more difficult than anyone could possibly imagine. None of this comes naturally. It comes from experience. It takes practice. Just as a writer says he improves from year to year—and looks back upon his old stuff and says, "My God!" well, so does an actor.

Destination Tokyo was followed by *Once Upon a Time*, a comedy for Columbia. Grant went to work on September 11, 1943, this time with Janet Blair and a child actor named Ted Donaldson. While the film did not prove to be one of Grant's most memorable, Donaldson was greatly affected by Grant's friendship. Decades later, in 1979, he wrote to Grant revealing his feelings:

> In two or three days it will be thirty years since you and Betsy Drake [who married Grant in 1949] came to the Beverly Hills Hotel to attend my high school graduation. You sat on the aisle and turned as we walked very slowly to the strains of "Pomp and Circumstance." One girl nearly crushed her corsage when she saw you, and I was so pleased and proud that the few people I wanted most to be there were all there: my parents, my agent, Lew Deuser, my teacher, Lillian Barkley, and you.
>
> From the first day on the set of *Once Upon a Time* you made everything easy for me. You didn't wait for me to be brought to you by my agent, or a studio representative. You came over to me and my father and introduced yourself. You supervised a fitting at Macintosh's. You insisted that a Kavanaugh hat be made for me. (I must have been the only ten year old in the world wearing a Kavanaugh.) I suppose I thought it was all being done just for me, while you probably wanted everything just right. Whatever; it was a givingness that went beyond the personal and yet had enormous personal affect. For one of the last scenes [cinematographer] Franz Planer had taken his usual two hours to light a two-shot of us. We were ready to roll, when you waved your hand and told [director] Alexander Hall that the set-up was all wrong, that it just wouldn't do: "It should be a close-up of the kid" with just your shoulder to establish the scene.

You would not be persuaded otherwise, so Mr. Planer had another happy two hours, and I a story I would tell a hundred times.

. . . it seemed past time to put down some memories, to say that once upon a time I received the gift of working with you, and that all I have written here is but a hint of the respect and love I have felt for you these past thirty-six years.

In March 1944 Grant picked a role that contrasted strongly with the type he had been playing. Ernie Mott in *None but the Lonely Heart* was a dark, cynical character who came from London's lower classes. ROBERT HUTTON remembers his first impressions of the film: "Barbara Hutton called and asked us to have dinner with her and Cary at Romanoff's. She said, 'I've got a surprise for you.'

"After dinner we drove down to the RKO studios and went into a cramped projection room. Cary and Barbara sat about two rows in front of us. And on came *None but the Lonely Heart*.

"We expected to see Cary Grant with dapper clothes and smart dialogue and were disappointed. When the lights came on and Cary turned around and looked at me, the only thing I could say was 'Boy, what a movie!' Cary loved the picture. He thought it was wonderful."

According to HAL ROACH, Grant, like many actors, was not always the best judge of his work: "Every time Cary thought he was making a great picture, it was not so good, and when he tried to get out of making a picture because it was so bad, they were the best ones he made."

"I don't think *None but the Lonely Heart* and *Father Goose* were Cary's milieu," says JOHN FORSYTHE. "When you're a leading man with the kind of stamp he had, it's hard to hide it with beards and funny caps and cockney accents. It doesn't work."

His peers in the Motion Picture Academy did not agree with his friends; he received his second Oscar nomination for the performance. Grant costarred in the film with Ethel Barrymore, Jane Wyatt, and June Duprez. The script was based on a novel by Richard Llewellyn and was adapted for the screen by playwright Clifford Odets. At Grant's suggestion, Odets was hired by RKO as the film's director.

CG, thirty-nine, Barbara Hutton, Robert Hutton, and Natalie Thompson, 1943. HUTTON: *"Cary was an usher. Natalie's family owned the house originally built by William Powell for Jean Harlow. During the reception Barbara took Natalie's mother aside, brought out her checkbook, and said, 'I'll give you a blank check for the house right here and now.'"*

JACK HALEY, JR., sees the film as a major collaboration between Odets and Grant: "Cary sat for hours with Odets and talked about Bristol. He had a wonderful love of writers. That's why he helped several of them become directors. It was extraordinary the way he put his career on the line to give all those guys their first shot."

Clifford Odets was equally proud of Grant's performance. On June 28, 1944, Odets wrote to Grant:

> Just this hour I received your gift of the script so beautifully bound, so pictured, so inscribed; and it has put me in a soup of an emotion. Anyway, putting it simply, thank you! And that is to say
>
> Thank you for the very beginning of the film. For the intuition which made you feel the novel as a picture, and for what seemed to me the surprising fact that you thought I could direct it as well as write it.
>
> Well, Cary, the film is almost cut, ready for sound and music. It is predictions which are odious, not comparisons, but I will make a prediction concerning your reactions to the film when you see it: you will be proud of your performance. I know that I am! Such reality, constantly moving and warm, I have seldom seen in any film of any nation. It is simply something new in films, that's all.
>
> And, in closing, one other thing struck me as I watched the picture: you yourself are a hero out of a Joseph Conrad novel. Have you ever read "Lord Jim" or "Victory" or "The Rescue"? You share with the heroes of those novels a strange quality of decency, which is not a poor word when used this way. It is a quality of goodness that comes from the heart, whether one wills it or not; and it is everywhere evident in the film. . . .

Despite the darkness of Grant's role, life on the set was brighter. As JANE WYATT recalls it, "Cary was an absolute delight to work with. Witty and wonderful, he entertained us by walking on his hands! But he was serious about his work. He was always prepared. He was just so good. He should have gotten an Academy Award."

A quarter of a century later, when Grant was awarded his

honorary Oscar, he requested that a clip from *None but the Lonely Heart* be included in his film composite. GREGORY PECK, who was going to leave the scene out of the assemblage, says: "It was a little scene with Ethel Barrymore. Cary cried on the screen, and he wanted that in. I didn't think it was one of his greatest moments. But he insisted. He said, 'Well, I didn't do much of that kind of emotion, but I think that was rather good.'"

Grant's comments on it reveal a view of, or knowledge of, himself that few shared:

> CG: I thought the picture showed a successful bit of acting. I was usually cast as a well-dressed, sophisticated chap. This time I was an embittered cockney. In many ways the part seemed to fit my nature better than the lighthearted fellows I was used to playing.

None but the Lonely Heart marked the beginning of a long friendship between Odets and Grant, observes PETER BOGDANO-VICH: "They stayed in steady touch throughout the years. Odets always spoke very fondly of Cary. He told me his ideal casting for the damned and doomed film star lead in *The Big Knife* was not John Garfield, who had played it in the original Broadway production, but Cary Grant."

Their correspondence reflects a respect for the other's talents. In 1957, when Grant and his third wife, Betsy Drake, were in Europe, Odets lived in the house they had bought in Palm Springs as well as the one on Beverly Grove.

Throughout the 1950s Odets hoped Grant would present one or another of his projects to a studio. He wrote to Grant, "Such advance notice on your part could possibly lift me out of [a] profound hole."

Out of true friendship and concern for Odets's economic difficulties, Grant lent Odets thousands of dollars. Grant's files contain several letters from Odets, either asking for money or thanking him for a check.

During the shooting of *None but the Lonely Heart*, Grant learned the advantages of keeping the writer handy.

> CG: In one scene, I asked a girl in a restaurant, "Would you like to have a cup of tea?" I wasn't clear about my motive. So I asked Clifford, "Why am I saying this? I

don't understand. What's the point of asking her to have a cup of tea?" Odets smiled. "Don't you know why I wrote that? You're saying, 'Would you like a cup of tea?' but you're actually thinking 'How can I get her into bed?'"

From then on I saw the value of having the screenwriter on the set!

JANE WYATT remembers Grant's kindness after the film was completed: "When we had finished making the film, my husband and I gave a party. Barbara Hutton called to say she was terribly sorry but she and Cary wouldn't be able to come. Then Cary called and said, 'Barbara won't be able to be there, but I would love to come.' I'll never forget he did that. It was darling of him."

During the next few years Grant's involvement with the film resulted in some surprising, even ludicrous consequences. On May 11, 1944, long before Senator Joe McCarthy's public witch-hunt, the Los Angeles office of the FBI issued a memorandum entitled "Communist Infiltration of the Motion Picture Industry." It listed the personnel of *Citizen Tom Paine*, *The Master Race*, and *None but the Lonely Heart*.

The FBI also claimed that the following people, among others, had "Communist connections": Lucille Ball, Ira Gershwin, John Garfield, Walter Huston, and Cary Grant. A list of films produced or released in Hollywood between January 1 and November 20, 1944, said to be "loaded" with Communists, included three starring Cary Grant. They were *Mr. Lucky, None but the Lonely Heart,* and *Destination Tokyo*.

In 1947 Lela Rogers (Ginger Rogers's mother) testified before the House Un-American Activities Committee in Washington, D.C., that the story of *None but the Lonely Heart* was Communist propaganda. Mrs. Rogers was working for RKO as an "expert" on Communist infiltration in the industry. She claimed the film was "filled with despair and hopelessness." In it Ernie Mott says to his mother (who runs a secondhand store), "You are not going to get me to work here and squeeze pennies out of little people poorer than I am." Lela Rogers claimed this was a blatant anticapitalist sentiment.

Cary Grant was not a Communist, of course. However, his name was indexed in the investigations of other individuals or subject matters. For example, in the files on Barbara Hutton, the FBI's primary interest was in Barbara Hutton's relationship with Baron Gottfried von Cramm, the well-known German Davis Cup tennis player, and in her fifth marriage to Dominican playboy-diplomat Porfirio Rubirosa, but Grant is occasionally mentioned.

Despite Grant's involvement with films that had "questionable" content, today the federal agency says that "Grant has not been the subject of an investigation conducted by the FBI" and "the central files of the FBI contain no additional pertinent information" about Grant.

During the summer of 1944 Grant's relationship with Barbara Hutton became increasingly difficult. In addition to marital problems, Hutton was in the middle of a custody fight over her son, Lance, whose father had taken him across the border into Canada, claiming he was not getting proper care.

Shortly afterward Grant and Barbara Hutton separated, reconciled, and moved to 10615 Bellagio. During 1944 and early 1945 they went through a series of separations and reconciliations. His second marriage was falling apart, and it was draining his energy to perform.

When Grant started *Night and Day* on May 12, 1945, he had not worked for more than a year. Now he was faced with portraying Cole Porter, a role he felt ill prepared to play.

> CG: Cole Porter [was] probably the world's best-known living composer of contemporary music . . . [whose life] I so ineptly portrayed, with little understanding of such extraordinary talent or the graciousness of its possessor. Although Cole must have sensed my lack of insight, he appeared genuinely pleased about the picture, and frequently invited me to his home and many entertaining parties there.

To add to Grant's difficulties, the script was undergoing constant revision. Costar ALEXIS SMITH remembers the endless changes: "The shooting script for *Night and Day* was a rainbow of color because the changes were coming down constantly. When you start a film, you're given a white script. Changes are added first on blue paper and then maybe on yellow, and so on. There had been so many writers on the project that Mike Curtiz, the director, had a big cardboard box in his dressing room filled with unorganized pages from various drafts."

It was Grant's habit to make meticulous notes on his scripts during the shooting of a picture. But most of the scripts he saved are final shooting copies—what's actually in the movie—and are practically clean. His working copy was of no permanent value—to him.

ALEXIS SMITH had played leading ladies for several years, but she was overwhelmed by the prospect of working with Grant: "In our first scene together, Cary kissed me. We are being introduced and, unbeknownst to me, are standing under mistletoe. The line following the kiss was mine. Well, when we came out of the kiss and I looked at him, I couldn't remember my name, much less my line. There was a big pause, and finally the director said, 'Cut. Alexis, what's the matter?'

"I was in a state of shock. It hadn't been very long since I'd been a schoolgirl, sitting in the balcony at Saturday matinees on Hollywood Boulevard, swooning over Cary Grant.

"There was such an intense quality and focus about his work. It was all encapsulated in that moment. He was mesmerizing and very exciting. It was so strong that I—and I'm sure anyone who ever worked with him—felt you were his whole universe."

During the shooting Grant's domestic problems weighed heavily on his mind, and ALEXIS SMITH has never forgotten Grant's advice on marriage: "Craig Stevens and I had married just before *Night and Day*. Cary told us, 'Never get divorced. You may as well stick with this one because you just keep marrying the same person over and over.'"

In July 1945, one month before the end of the war, Barbara Hutton filed for divorce. She claimed that she and Grant didn't share the same friends. "On more than one occasion, when I gave dinner parties," Hutton said, "Cary would not come downstairs. When he did come down, he was not amused."

Stanley E. Fox handled Grant's side of the case. Grant had first consulted Fox about a real estate problem. His firm, Fox, Goldman & Cagen, was located on the second floor of the building now occupied by the restaurant Le Bistro, in Los Angeles. Grant's agent, Frank Vincent, was in the same building on the third floor.

The divorce did not include any financial settlement, says

STANLEY E. FOX. "Cary never got a dime from Barbara Hutton."

"He didn't need to," GEORGE BURNS confirms. "But when your wife's that rich, maybe the only way she knows you love her is if you take money from her. Cary didn't depend on her, so she left him."

> CG: Well, I did take money from her—when we played gin rummy and I took a dime here, a quarter there. It mounted up.

Grant's divorce from Hutton did not, however, sever their ties. ROBERT HUTTON was well aware of this: "In 1948 I passed Cary coming out of Barbara Hutton's suite at the Ritz Hotel in Paris as I was going in." BEA SHAW remembers Grant's devotion: "Sometime in the late 1960s Cary was staying in my guesthouse when Barbara Hutton had cataract surgery and couldn't read. At that time of her life all she did was stay home and read. So she would talk to him on the telephone for hours. She'd say to him, 'You're falling asleep.' And he'd say, 'No, I'm not, I'm listening.' He felt sorry for her because while she had a radio and television to listen to, she had no one to listen to her."

Indeed, until her death on May 11, 1979, at the age of sixty-six, Grant maintained a relationship with Hutton (who had married seven times). He also remained close to Lance, whom he loved as a son. JILL ST. JOHN says, "Cary referred to Lance as 'my son.'"

Lance called Grant General and wrote to him often. His letters were witty, literate, and beautifully constructed. Obviously intelligent, he seemed older than his middle teens. Grant sent him films regularly, convinced him to stop smoking, and talked to him frequently by telephone. In the early 1950s, when Lance was attending the Southern Arizona School for Boys, he often made vacation visits to Grant and Betsy Drake in their Beverly Grove home.

Lance and his first wife, Jill St. John, were married in San Francisco on March 24, 1960. After their divorce Lance married the tall, pretty blond actress and former Walt Disney Mouseketeer Cheryl Holdridge.

Lance died on July 24, 1972, at the age of thirty-six, in a plane crash outside Aspen, Colorado. THELMA ORLOFF attests to Grant's devotion to his stepson: "Cary worried and cared so much about Lance. He was devastated when he died." Grant invited JILL ST. JOHN to fly with him in the Fabergé jet to the memorial service. She recalls: "At six o'clock in the morning we climbed into his old Rolls-Royce for the trip to the airport. On the way he handed me a big manila envelope. He said, 'Here, darling, look at this while we're driving.' He had saved everything Lance ever sent him—cards, letters from camp, letters from school, postcards, gift enclosures, Christmas cards, Easter cards—from about the age of six years to maybe twelve.

"On the plane we discussed the fact that Cary was there and Barbara Hutton wasn't. And he said, 'You know, part of the problem when you're that wealthy is that everybody treats you differently. They accept eccentricities that would not be accepted in the rest of us.' It didn't excuse her, but it did help to explain her aberrant behavior.

"There was lunch at a friend's house, an all-Mozart concert in the music tent, and a wake. Cary didn't act as host, but he definitely was the éminence grise."

On October 22, 1945, Grant reported to the set of *Notorious*, in which he was to play a federal agent who gets involved in a romantic triangle and espionage. This sophisticated, suspenseful melodrama, Grant's second film with director Alfred Hitchcock, was his first with Ingrid Bergman.

CG: I was very fond of Ingrid. She was an amazing woman. She was one of the world's most talented women, completely secure and happy. She didn't care a thing about clothes. She used no makeup, not even lip rouge. Why don't more actresses imitate her instead of going the other way?

She took acting so seriously. She was a splendid, splendid performer, but she wasn't very relaxed in front of the camera. Ingrid spoke English beautifully, of course, but she would occasionally have problems with some of its nuances.

One morning, when we were working on *Notorious*, she had difficulty with a line. She had to say her lines a certain way so I could imitate her readings. We worked on the scene for a couple of hours. Hitch never said anything. He just sat next to the camera, puffing on

CG and Ingrid Bergman in Notorious, *1945.* BERGMAN: *"A [approved] kiss could last three seconds. We just kissed each other and talked, leaned away and kissed each other again. . . . But the censors couldn't and didn't cut the scene because we never at any one point kissed for more than three seconds. We did other things: We nibbled on each other's ears, and kissed a cheek, so that it looked endless, and became sensational."*

his cigar. I took a break, and later, when I was making my way back to the set, I heard her say her lines perfectly. At which point Hitch said, "Cut!" Followed by "Good morning, Ingrid."

When STANLEY DONEN directed Grant and Bergman in *Indiscreet*, he found their tempos were different: "He was always quick off the trigger. Bang. It was there. That was delightful. Ingrid just had a slower tempo. But it wasn't a problem. They were magic together."

Years later Grant insisted on taking a young director to Hitchcock for advice. "I was having a technical problem lining up a shot in the midst of shooting *Elmer Gantry*," RICHARD BROOKS recalls. "Cary drove me to Hitchcock's house on the golf course at Riviera, near the beach. Hitchcock was a genius with a camera. He listened while I explained that I wanted to make a shot with the same kind of sharpness that he had achieved in *Notorious*. (Ingrid Bergman is in bed. And in comes a cup of poisoned coffee. The cup of coffee is sharp, and so is she.) Hitchcock says, 'Well, dear boy, that cup of coffee was three feet high. I moved the camera back twenty feet, making both Ingrid and the cup sharp.'

"'A three-foot-high cup of coffee? I saw it being carried in.'

"'But you didn't see a hand carry it in.'

"'I saw part of a hand, around the cup.'

"'But that was a piece of statuary.'

"I had learned from the *master*, through Cary."

On March 24, 1946, a Western Union telegram, imprinted with "For Victory, Buy War Bonds Today," went to Hollywood's most important and glamorous people:* "WE FIGURE IT'S ABOUT

---

*Invitations had gone to: the Fred Astaires, the Vincent Astors, Lew Ayres, the Richard Barthelmesses, Constance Bennett, the Jack Bennys, the Edgar Bergens, the Richard Berlins, the Frederick Brissons (Rosalind Russell), the Humphrey Bogarts, the Frank Capras, Lady Adele Cavendish, the Charles Chaplins, the Gary Coopers, Joan Crawford, the Bing Crosbys, George Cukor, Olivia De Havilland, the Douglas Fairbanks, Jrs., Geraldine Fitzgerald, the Henry Fondas, Joan Fontaine, Kay Francis, Lady Thelma Furness, Clark Gable, Lillian Gish, the William Goetzes, the Samuel Goldwyns, the Averell Harrimans, the Rex Harrisons, the Howard Hawkses, the Leland Haywards, Rita Hayworth, William Randolph Hearst, Mark Hellinger, Sonja Henie, Betty Hensel (Cary Grant's date), the Alfred Hitchcocks, the Lou Holtzes, the Bob Hopes, Hedda Hopper, John Houseman, Howard Hughes, John Huston, Barbara Hutton, Van Johnson, John Kaufman, the Danny Kayes, Sir Alexander Korda, Jack and Charlie Krindler, the Mervin LeRoys, Anita Loos, Ida Lupino, the Fred MacMurrays, the Herman Mankiewiczes, the Joseph Mankiewiczes, the Harpo Marxes, the Zeppo Marxes, Elsa Maxwell, L. B. Mayer, the Ray Millands, the

TIME WE THREW A PARTY, SO WILL YOU COME TO THE OLD CLOVER CLUB, 8477 SUNSET BOULEVARD, 8 PM, NEXT SATURDAY, MARCH 30TH. SORRY ABOUT THE SHORT NOTICE BUT WE'VE ONLY JUST BEEN ABLE TO HIRE THE JOINT. PLEASE ANSWER EARLY. WE ARE NERVOUS. BLACK TIE, LOW CUT DRESSES. ARDMORE 8-6056. EDDIE DUCHIN, CARY GRANT, JOHN MC CLAIN, AND JIMMY STEWART."

JAMES STEWART had come back from the war in November 1945. He recalls: "I'd been away for four years, and we were at Mike Romanoff's restaurant when Cary came up with the idea. Cary said, 'All these people have been giving parties and inviting us. I think we ought to return the favor. The four of us—[pianist] Eddie Duchin, [screenwriter] John McClain, Cary, and I—met at Cary's house. Mike Romanoff, who catered the food, also came over.

"The Clover Club had been closed during the war, and McClain got them to open it up for us. It had been kept in very good shape. We didn't have to do anything.

Elsa Maxwell sent this response: "ACCEPT WONDERFUL INVITATION FOR TONIGHT MY BLACK TIE IS LOW, MY DRESS IS HIGH BUT SO ARE MY SPIRITS DARLINGS AND YOU CAN JUST DANCE WITH MY LITTLE GHOST THROUGHOUT THE NIGHT. . . ."

"We made a big show out of it and decided the four of us should be in tails," STEWART recounts. "We hired guards. And I remember Cary saying, 'Let's have a receiving line.' So we stayed at the front door and received everybody. It was a hell of a job. Mike was at his best as far as the food was concerned. Everybody mentioned it. And the orchestra was amazing."

They feasted on green turtle soup and vichyssoise; oysters, shrimp, cracked crab, and trout in jelly on carved ice; baby chicken, roast stuffed turkey, roast ribs of beef, and baked sugar-cured ham; green goddess salad and potato and egg salad; shrimp newburg, coq au vin, and boned squab à la Jacques; gnocchi, romaine, French peas paysanne, and wild rice. For dessert they

Robert Montgomerys, the George Murphys, David Niven, the Gregory Pecks, Cole Porter, the Tyrone Powerses, Otto Preminger, the Basil Rathbones, the Hal Roaches, the Edward G. Robinsons, Cesar Romero, the Randolph Scotts, David O. Selznick, Irene Mayer Selznick, Ann Sheridan, Toots Shor, the Frank Sinatras, Sam Spiegel, the Spencer Tracys, Lana Turner, the Walter Wangers, the Jack Warners, the Lew Wassermans, Clifton Webb, the Lowell Weickers, the John Hay Whitneys, the Keenan Wynns, and the Darryl Zanucks.

were served fresh pears Lucien, petits fours, small French pastries, fancy cakes, and coffee.

They danced to a hand-picked group of radio musicians led by Hal Reese. And Edith Gwynn wrote in the *Hollywood Reporter* that the "standouts in the low cut dress division were Pat Scott [Mrs. Randolph Scott], Connie Moore, Frances Fonda [Mrs. Henry Fonda], Paulette Goddard, Joan Crawford, and Rita Hayworth." She continued, "Cary Grant and Betty Hensel were closer than half past six by half past two in the A.M. And Ida Lupino and Bing Crosby did a marathon rhumba."

JAMES STEWART's date was Rita Hayworth. He says: "Around two o'clock or so, Rita said, 'We've been working all week, and I'm tired.' So I took her home—and came back alone.

"As I came in, everything seemed to be quiet, except for some music. There, *sitting* on the dance floor, were about two hundred and fifty people. Up on the orchestra platform, Hoagy Carmichael was playing the piano and Bing Crosby was singing. This went on until five o'clock in the morning . . . with Bing and three or four others singing and Hoagy playing. No microphone. Everybody sitting on the floor, after all the hoopla of the party.

"I'll never forget it."

CHAPTER EIGHT

ALWAYS WITH A LIGHT TOUCH

CG: If you want to be an actor, my advice is to learn your lines and don't bump into the other actors. Just get out there and act. You have to have the courage to make mistakes. It takes courage to be bad. You can only be good with experience. If you are really interested in a film career, you should get all the training and experience you can. You won't be wasting your time. Practically all films have someone young and someone old in them. You can work until you're one hundred years old.

The war was over, and Grant made his first trip to a liberated Paris, arriving on April 21, 1946. He also visited his mother in Bristol.

On June 13, 1946, he was on the set of *The Bachelor and the Bobby-Soxer*, a picture that costars Myrna Loy, Shirley Temple, and Rudy Vallee. In it Grant played the object of Shirley Temple's adolescent romantic fantasy. The script called for him to act like a teenager in order to discourage her. Some scenes were undignified but very funny.

At the time of the film's release Grant's friend producer Alfred Zeisler wrote to him, praising his performance.

I am so enthusiastic about your delightful performance in *The Bachelor and the Bobby-Soxer* that I have to follow my impulse to write you a letter of sincerest admiration.

The Bachelor and the Bobby-Soxer, 1946. JOHNNY MASCHIO: *"Cary didn't like the script at first. He said, 'Look what they've given me to do next.' Dore Schary, a good friend of Cary's, was running the studio and begged him to do it. It was one of the best pictures Cary ever made."*

You played your part to such perfection and with such an abundance of *human* humor that I went to see the picture for a second time. And this time I found myself analyzing and dissecting your performance with much the same enjoyment which I felt when—as a little boy—I took a huge grandfather's clock in my parents' home apart.

I have always realized that for an actor "underplaying" and yet keeping all the color, all the subtle scales of emotion, all the twinkling, all the modulations of true-to-life reactions and all the relaxed charm means the paragon of his achievement. I honestly feel that you gave an unrivaled perfection of comedy-playing such as I don't remember ever having seen before, either in Europe or in this country, and I have seen quite a lot.

May I add that I was not influenced by my personal friendship and admiration for you. Just to the contrary: Next to myself, I am more critical about my friends than about strangers.

Frank Vincent, Grant's agent, also represented a smoothly handsome young French actor, Louis Jourdan. In 1946 a gin rummy game with Vincent brought Grant and Jourdan together for the first time. "Subsequently I was interviewed by Louella Parsons on her radio show," says JOURDAN. "She asked me who was my favorite actor. . . . Two days later I received a case of champagne with a note: 'Thank you for the tribute. Cary Grant.' For forty years, until his death, the originality of my relationship with Cary Grant was that there was no relationship! I assume he felt as I would in a similar situation. If someone had said I was their favorite actor, I would have been extremely embarrassed to meet him, not to disappoint him. Cary was a very shy man. So was I. He didn't make any effort at most parties. He let people come to him. I'm the same way. He was always charming toward me, but we exchanged fifteen words, or twenty-five, and whoop—we never [claps hands] got into contact. But he did have a marvelous relationship with my wife."

FREDERIQUE "QUIQUE" JOURDAN counts Grant as one of her first friends in Hollywood. She recalls: "I came with a lovely wardrobe from Paris and went with Louis for my first black-tie dinner. I got as far as the middle of the living room, and when I turned, Louis had disappeared. All alone, I looked around and saw Cary. His was the nicest face I saw. I went to him and said, 'I'm Quique Jourdan. I don't know anybody. Can I sit with you?' And he said, 'Please do.' From that moment on, each time I saw him at a party, he would ask if I was all right. He danced with me and talked to me. He always took care of me because he was touched that he was the first man I went to when I first arrived."

"She loved him, and he loved her," admits LOUIS JOURDAN. "In between his marriages he would go out with her. They would go to dinner, to the races, or she'd spend a day with him on the set."

Grant escorted FREDERIQUE JOURDAN to parties as well. She remembers: "One party stands out. . . . Deborah Kerr had a little crush on Cary, and Doris Vidor, Charles Vidor's wife, organized a party. Cary was alone, and she thought he could take Deborah Kerr home. Louis was working in Europe, so I went with the Billy Wilders. At one point I was talking to Cary and Audrey Wilder came to me and said they had to leave because Billy was shooting in the morning. Cary offered to take me home.

"When I went to the ladies' room, Doris told everyone she couldn't wait for the end of the evening to see Cary take Deborah home. I was totally speechless and didn't say anything. When Cary and I got up to go, everybody was watching. I had spoiled Doris's plans."

When Frank Vincent died in 1946, Lew Wasserman (then at MCA) became Grant's agent, but Grant did not sign with the agency. He became MCA's only nonexclusive client. Both Wasserman and Stanley Fox represented him on each negotiation and split the customary 10 percent agency commission.

CG: Closest to me of all [is] my lawyer-manager, Stanley Fox, without whose friendship and counsel I'd be adrift.

THELMA ORLOFF says, "I don't think Cary made a move without him. And I think Stanley was even more conservative than Cary. He made no mistakes, believe me. When they were young, they looked alike. Stanley was gorgeous. When they walked together, it was hard to tell the actor from the lawyer. Stanley watched everything for Cary. He was impeccably honest."

"Cary was my best friend," says STANLEY E. FOX, "right from the start. We grew up in the same era. We knew the same old jokes and liked the same kinds of music. We would laugh about how the mosquitoes would absolutely eat you alive on a summer's night at the Muny Theater in St. Louis."

Grant eventually persuaded Fox to give up private practice and represent him exclusively. Together they formed a series of companies with which Grant produced several of his pictures. FOX describes their formation: "Ninety percent of Cary's income was being taxed, but we never took advantage of any dodges. We thought the dangers involved in those deals could, in the end, cost more money than the high taxes. So we formed different corporations for different situations. When Cary did a film, he was employed by the company for a salary that was less than he could get if he were working for a studio. But we owned the picture. The company would get seventy-five percent of the profits, and the studios would get the other twenty-five percent for putting up all the money and giving us whatever backing we needed. We got offices and an expense account."

In 1946 Grant bought Frank Vincent's house on Beverly Grove Drive from his estate. Modeled after an old French farmhouse, it sits high in the hills overlooking Beverly Hills, just below the houses of Charles Boyer and Miriam Hopkins. Over the years the house had been home to more than one celebrity. Katharine Hepburn rented it from Vincent, and when Grant was in Europe, he lent it to Howard Hughes. Grant lived in the house when he was a bachelor and from time to time while married to Betsy Drake. In the early 1970s he started renovating it for his daughter, Jennifer, and completed it when he married his fifth wife, Barbara Harris.

As Cary Grant developed his suave, confident persona during the 1940s, there were residues of Archie Leach he still fought to eliminate. As a child Grant had two phobias: a fear of knives and a fear of heights. The first resulted from an incident when his father was shaving. Elias Leach gestured toward the young Archie with a straight-edged razor. The boy was terrified and never forgot it.

The root of Grant's fear of heights also resulted from an experience with his father.

CG: In one section [of a long garden] there was a large patch of grass surrounding a fine old apple tree near which my father lovingly sank strong, high, wooden supports for a swing. I took pride in the fact of that swing, the possession of it, but lacked the daring and abandon of a free swinger; and my father's rhythmic shoves, although gentle, seemed much too perilous. Either I have always lacked bravery or, as I prefer to regard it, never been foolhardy.

Since then I have attempted gradually to overcome my fear of heights—even by learning, years later, to walk on stilts in a theatrical troupe specializing in pantomime and acrobatics.

Grant started to address his acrophobia by the time he was sixteen. Little by little he succeeded in overcoming his fear, especially his fear of flying. Eventually he grew to love air travel and flew in all sorts of weather and in all sorts of planes, including open cockpits, transcontinental Ford trimotors, and unscheduled small airmail planes through snowstorms over the Alleghenies. He frequently flew with Howard Hughes in a converted bomber, sometimes landing in abandoned fields in Mexico.

In January 1947 Hughes and Grant went on a trip to Mexico City via Guadalajara, where they were forced to turn back because of darkness. Ten days later they made a second attempt. On the first leg they were reported missing along with Hughes's mechanic, Earl Martin.

CG: We read in the local newspaper that we were dead. It's quite a blow to read about your own death. But after you get over the initial shock, it makes a great story.

He often flew with Sir Alexander Korda, the imaginative power behind London Films. Most actors bored Korda, but Grant was a major exception and a good friend.

CG: A man of old-world charm and an amused regard of life. . . . During the early years of transoceanic flying, Alex and I crossed the Atlantic many times and, accustomed to the unreliability of planes' heating systems in those days, we learned to bring along heavy sweaters.

On one trip, in 1946, after comfortably settling ourselves, we both began fumbling around in our airplane bags beneath the seats, and simultaneously came up, grinningly pleased with ourselves, holding two identical pairs of brown fleece-lined zipper-fronted slipper boots we'd bought at Abercrombie & Fitch as a surprise for each other. We had four pairs between us.

And SYLVIA WU found Grant fearless. She recalls: "In 1985 Cary, Barbara, Jennifer, and I were on a cruise around the Hawaiian Islands. Cary organized a little plane to fly over the Kilauea volcano, which was erupting, and I thought he was crazy. I was too terrified to go with him."

Grant made trips to New York and Europe with Kirk Kerkorian on his private plane. BOBBY ALTMAN describes it as the "finest, most handsomely equipped private plane in the air." Grant was introduced to Kerkorian during the early 1960s in Las Vegas by Charles Rich, and their relationship resembled his long-standing friendship with Howard Hughes. In fact, Grant served on the board of directors for both men, first in the 1940s, for Howard Hughes's Southwest Airlines and later for Kerkorian's Western Airlines.

"I could see why Cary and Kirk Kerkorian were good friends," says BEA SHAW. "Cary admired Kirk for his honesty and thoughtfulness. They were both intensely loyal, self-made men with a great zest for living. Both came from poor backgrounds, with little formal education, and they both anonymously helped people in distress and gave large sums of money to charity without seeking publicity."

Grant loved to sleep on planes, recalls PETER STONE. "It was the most restful thing he did. He always got off refreshed." DAN MELNICK found Grant's ability to relax on planes remarkable: "When we were marketing *That's Entertainment, Part II,* we were invited to open the Cannes Film Festival. Quite an entourage got off the plane in Nice—Cary, Gene Kelly, Fred Astaire, Donald O'Connor, Leslie Caron, Johnny Weissmuller, Kathryn Grayson, and Howard Keel. After a long overnight flight everyone was rumpled, wrinkled, and looked bedraggled. Cary and Fred got off as if they just stepped out of a shower into freshly laundered clothes. Those two just couldn't wrinkle."

On February 1, 1947, Grant began *The Bishop's Wife,* directed by Henry Koster and produced by Samuel Goldwyn. His costars were Loretta Young and David Niven. In this charming fantasy Grant plays an angel named Dudley, whose mission it is to restore hope and faith in the lives of an Episcopalian bishop and his wife.

LORETTA YOUNG sees aspects in Grant's personality that suited him for the role: "He was extraordinarily sensitive. He watched out for himself but never to the point where he stepped on anyone else. That's unusual. I've been lucky to work with seven or eight really top actors, and it's a pleasure when you get one like Cary. He was so professional he seemed to have three or four heads working at the same time.

"I remember one scene where we were going through a door. Just before the director yelled, 'Camera,' Cary said to me, 'It's supposed to be cold outside. Why isn't there frost on those windows?' Well, when the camera rolled, I walked in the room, and blew my dialogue, saying, 'What did you say about the frost on the windows?' Henry Koster, the director, said, 'Oh, for heaven's sakes, Cary.' But he told the prop people to put frost on the windows. I said, 'Cary, please don't do that to me. Do all the talking you want before we start a scene but not just as we're doing one. You may have a ten-track mind, but mine's only one-track.' He was very apologetic, saying, 'Oh, Loretta, I'm so sorry.' From then on he never did that again."

Years later STANLEY E. FOX found that Grant's attention to detail paid off: "Sometimes he was so meticulous that people he worked with would often become exasperated, but in the end he was always right. For example, when Cary was in *Walk, Don't Run*, he came back from Tokyo on a Saturday, called me, and said, 'Let's go to the studio tomorrow and check out the set.' This was not an uncommon thing for him to do. Well, when we got there, he was appalled. He said, 'I can walk through this door standing up. When I'm in the scenes we shot in Tokyo, I have to stoop everywhere. Everyone will laugh us right out of the picture when they see this.' The set designers were not at all happy. They had to work the whole night through to change all the doors on the set.

"And when Cary was making *An Affair to Remember*, he was critical of a costuming detail. In the dance sequence on board the *Queen Mary*, Cary took one look at the steward's jacket and said, 'Wait a minute. The stewards on the *Queen Mary* don't have buttons that look like that.' Everybody tried to appease him by saying nobody would know the difference. But Cary said, 'Yes, but I'll know it.' So of course, they replaced the buttons."

SIDNEY SHELDON remembers incidents during the filming of *Dream Wife:* "When Cary walked on the set, he said, 'That's *not* the way it looks in the Middle East.' He got into everything—the architecture, the costumes. And in spite of it all, he was a joy to work with."

But when it came to rehearsals, Grant's desire for freshness in a scene, like his fondness for the ad lib, overrode his perfectionism. JAMES STEWART recalls, "He just came in and said, 'Here I am. I know the lines. Let's go.' He came to work fully prepared. He didn't like rehearsals, and neither did I. Some people need them and feel they're important. Cary and I went along with that, and it turned out that most of the time I would learn something which added to my understanding of the scene. This was true of Cary, too."

For all his involvement in the details of production, Grant had no ambition as a director:

> CG: I liked being where I was in front of the camera, especially when there was a man I respected on the other side. Directing is a long, long haul. You start with the script and have to be able to work with everyone connected with the film—actors, the scenic designer, the cameraman. . . . And when the picture's finished, you still have to edit it. That step can take months and months. As a director you have to spend a great deal of time on one film. An actor, on the other hand, is in and out. A director gives a great deal of his life to his craft. I was never attracted to that aspect of filmmaking. I was much more interested in the economics of the business.

The role of the producer did appeal to Grant not only because owning the picture meant the possibility of higher profits but also because he wanted more control of the final product:

> CG: I did like to butt in and put in my two cents' worth.

According to Stanley Donen, Grant brought in considerably more than two cents. "And why not?" asks DONEN. "Let's tell it like it is. If you were trying to make a movie and needed twenty million, you'd have a hell of a time getting it. But if you could say, 'I've got Cary Grant,' there was no more money trouble. Cary was entitled to have an opinion. He was more than the star. He was the reason the picture got made!"

STANLEY E. FOX adds, "In Cary's contracts, the studios had the final cut of a film. However, we had a handshake deal so that Cary got the final cut. He would sit day after day with the film editor. He wanted a film to move and did not want it to run more than a hundred and twenty minutes. His sense of good timing extended to the pace of the film itself."

While working on *The Bishop's Wife*, Grant renewed his old friendship with Niven.

CG: David was a great friend and a very dear man. He was never without humor, even when he faced death. I deeply miss him.

RODERICK MANN, a friend of both men, says: "My friendships with them overlapped. They had been chums for a long, long time. There was a tiny bit of jealousy between them. It was not voiced, but it was obvious. Niven was closer to my age. Cary was more the older brother. David was the sophisticated man everybody thought Cary was, and I think David was a little jealous of Cary's star stature.

"I worked with David a bit on his book *The Moon's a Balloon*, and when it was published, I think Cary was a bit teed off. He felt David had stolen from his stories. He said, 'That happened to me, not him.' But everybody knew David took stories that happened to other people and melded them as though they had happened to him."

JACK HALEY, JR., remembers Niven's memorial service: "Cary and I were ushers. There were about sixty people there. Cary kept asking, 'What do we do?' I said, 'Just stand here and watch what I do. Just funnel them down front.' He looked at me. '*Funnel them down front?*' He'd get nervous about the simplest things. He wanted to know exactly what was expected of him. Here's a man who took pratfalls and fell out windows, but in real life he wanted to be proper.

"After the service we went up to Irving Lazar's for lunch. Cary and Barbara and the Pecks were there. Cary told wonderful stories and had us all in stitches. Then [Peter] Ustinov got going,

163

and it was very funny. It was exactly the way David would have wanted it. It was like an old Irish wake."

During the Academy Awards ceremony on April 9, 1984, Grant paid tribute to his old friend:

> CG: David was a gentle man, a gentleman of wit, and he'll be missed by all of us who value style, and taste, in the lives of those we love. . . . A dear, unforgettable man. We were all lucky to know him.

"It could have been Cary's own epitaph," says JACK HALEY, JR. "He was all those elements that he loved in David."

JAMIE NIVEN remembers, "Cary read it majestically, and then he turned to the audience and said, 'And David Niven was never more at his finest than when he was streaked [a naked man ran across the stage] up here as master of ceremonies.' Then they rolled the footage of Daddy being streaked in 1976, and Cary walked off the stage.

"My father told me that many of the movies he made were because Cary didn't want to do them or was busy doing something else. He said, 'I was always lucky that Cary Grant was such a success. I got some very good roles.'"

Niven wasn't the only one to benefit. LOUIS JOURDAN says, "Starting with *The Awful Truth*, and for the rest of his career, there wasn't one part around that was not offered first to Cary Grant. There are actors in this town who made important careers for a long, long period just by taking the parts Cary Grant turned down."

When Grant finished *The Bishop's Wife* in August 1947, he sailed for England. On the trip over he met ELIZABETH TAYLOR, who was fifteen. She recalls: "My mother and I were traveling on the *Queen Elizabeth* from New York, and we met Cary in the Veranda Grille. Cross-eyed with awe, I couldn't stop looking at him. I was just a kid, but he took notice of me. He was so sweet to me, giving me all his attention and making me feel special."

At the end of the month Grant headed back to New York with playwright Frederick Lonsdale, author of *The Last of Mrs. Cheyney* and other Broadway hits. This time it was Grant who was eager to meet another passenger. He had just seen Betsy

CG, forty-three, autographing for Elizabeth Taylor, fifteen, aboard the Queen Elizabeth, 1947. TAYLOR: *"He made me feel as though I were the most interesting and witty person. He had that unique ability to make you feel as though you were the only person in the room."*

Drake onstage in London in *Deep Are the Roots* and admired her performance.

CG: Merle Oberon, who, propelled by my cowardly insistence and her own irresistible sense of the romantic, approached Betsy Drake on the deck of the *Queen Mary* and introduced herself; then, while I hid in the nearest companionway, she invited Betsy on my behalf to join us at lunch . . . [Freddy], like me, was deeply attracted to

Betsy . . . In fact, had Freddy been 20 years younger, I would certainly have lost her to him.

It was a pleasant surprise for Grant to find that Drake was not only an attractive young woman but also very intelligent with a broad spectrum of interests.

She was born in Paris on September 11, 1923. Her parents were Americans. Her father, Carlos Drake, whose family had founded the Drake and Blackstone hotels in Chicago, was a writer. When she was six, her family moved to the United States, where the precocious child spoke English with a French accent.

They moved frequently, and at the age of seventeen Drake quit high school and looked for work in the theater. Instead, she found work as a Conover fashion model and began supporting herself. She didn't particularly like the work. The incessant fashion chatter bored her.

Betsy Drake got her first opportunity on Broadway as an understudy and assistant stage manager for *Only the Heart*. After appearing in *The Moon and the Yellow River* for an experimental theater in Holyoke, Massachusetts, she understudied in *Therese*, a Broadway production with Eva Le Gallienne, Victor Jory, and Dame May Whitty.

In 1946 she signed with film producer Hal Wallis, who brought her to Los Angeles for a screen test, but a film contract was not forthcoming. In New York she auditioned for the English production of *Deep Are the Roots*. Following a successful run with the London company, she was returning to New York. Drake was twenty-three years old.

Grant returned to Los Angeles and his house on Bellagio Road. He was enraptured by Drake but ready to go to work on October 1, 1947, on his next picture, *Mr. Blandings Builds His Dream House*. His costars in this bright comedy were Melvyn Douglas and Myrna Loy. At the film's conclusion, the producer, Dore Schary, wrote to his star:

I had been getting a series of memos to which I paid little attention but I read one concerning you and for the record, I just want to tell you that you are the most cooperative and nicest, the fairest and the best actor in the entire United States of America.

In case of emergency, just call.
Your devoted admirer—

Grant moved from Bellagio Road to his house on Beverly Grove when Betsy Drake came to live with him following their initial courtship. Convinced of her talent and her potential on-screen, he encouraged her and introduced her to RAY STARK, who recalls: "Charlie Feldman and I had tried to get Cary as a client. I never did, but he got me Betsy Drake, a lovely lady for whom I worked out a deal with David Selznick."

On May 24, 1948, Betsy Drake arrived on the set of her first film, *Every Girl Should Be Married*. She was cast in the central role of an overly romantic department store clerk who sets her cap for an attractive pediatrician. Grant played the doctor. Franchot Tone played Drake's wealthy boss.

As IRENE MAYER SELZNICK observed, comedy was not Drake's forte: "Betsy Drake was an intelligent, studious, wellborn woman of talent and dignity. She was a lady. But she had no comedic talent. She was a dramatic actress. My impression is she really wanted to be in the theater and only went to Hollywood because of Cary."

Grant's next picture, *I Was a Male War Bride*, took Howard Hawks's company to England and Europe. Betsy Drake joined Grant on location in September 1948. He and his costar, Ann Sheridan, both became seriously ill during the picture. Drake nursed Grant through his illness.

In 1948 Grant was clearly at the top of his career. He made *Fame Magazine*'s list of the top ten actors and was in excellent company, sharing the honor with Bing Crosby, Betty Grable, Abbott and Costello, Gary Cooper, Bob Hope, Humphrey Bogart, Clark Gable, Spencer Tracy, and Ingrid Bergman. He made handsome salaries, plus 10 percent of the gross on these pictures: *The Bishop's Wife* ($150,0000+), *The Bachelor and the Bobby-Soxer* ($50,000+), *Mr. Blandings Builds His Dream House* ($50,000+), *Every Girl Should Be Married* ($50,000+), and *I Was a Male War Bride* ($100,000+).

GEORGE BURNS admired Grant's business sense: "He'd agree to make a picture and in the negotiation ask for the rights at the end of seven years. The studios gave it to him. The companies thought he was jerky. Who the hell was going to look at a film seven years later?" Indeed, when television started buying "old movies," those starring Cary Grant were worth a fortune.

During 1949 Grant returned to radio. Drake costarred with him in a series based on *Mr. Blandings Builds His Dream House*, and she wrote some of the episodes.

On December 25, 1949, Grant and Betsy Drake were married at the ranch of Mr. and Mrs. Sterling Hebbard. Howard Hughes flew them to Phoenix and stood up for Grant as his best man. The witnesses were the Hebbards (Sterling Hebbard was a prominent Phoenix real estate man), Will Hinckle (a Phoenix attorney), Colonel C. A. Shoop (the chief test pilot for Hughes), and Richard Mason (also a Phoenix attorney). Grant was forty-five and Betsy Drake twenty-six.

Clifford Odets sent his best wishes from New York.

> Your wire today about your marriage to Betsy Drake, it came this morning and took away the bitterness of a wet wily New York afternoon.
> Let me use one of your favorite phrases & say, "Bless you, bless you, bless you!!!"
> How much happiness and human love I wish you both.
>   As ever—

Katharine Hepburn wrote: "I don't know why the hell I should be so thrilled at the idea of you two being married, but I am pleased as can be for the look of you together seemed a very good sight. . . ."

Grant and his new bride gave up their honeymoon because on January 1, 1950, Grant had to be on the set of *Crisis*. The film marked an important turning point in the career of RICHARD BROOKS, who recalls: "After World War Two I wrote three or four movies: *Brute Force* and *Swell Guy* and—my only collaboration, with John Huston—*Key Largo*. I asked him, 'What will I do if I haven't got John Huston to make movies out of my screenplays?' Huston said, 'Well, kid, I guess you'll have to direct 'em yourself.'

"Sometime in 1949, when I had about seventy pages of still another script, I went to the track on a Saturday and was introduced to Cary Grant. He had just read my unfinished script and said he liked it. I told him I wanted to direct but no one would let me. He asked how I got along with people. I told him, 'Okay.'

He said, 'Well, if the rest of it turns out like this, I'll do it.' That day I became a director."

IRVING LAZAR made the deal for Brooks to direct and then met Grant for the first time. He recollects: "Cary was correct about Brooks, who subsequently directed many good and successful pictures. He became an important director under the auspices of Cary's approval."

During the casting of *Crisis*, Grant met Nancy Davis, who later became the wife of an actor and a President. NANCY REAGAN remembers, "There was a huge bunch of stars at Metro, and we were awed by them. Sometimes they tested someone with a stand-in. But not Cary. He tested with me for the role I desperately wanted. He was so sweet and nice and helpful. Of course, I was crushed when I didn't get the part.

"He took me to lunch, and as we walked toward the commissary, I told him how terrified I was to go there alone. He told me, 'You shouldn't feel that way about yourself. You should feel good about yourself.' He gave me a real pep talk. And he consoled me about the part. He said, 'I know you are disappointed. But let me tell you something I notice about you. You have the ability to listen when someone is talking. Not many actors have that.' I treasure that he said that to me. That was my Oscar."

While shooting *Crisis*, RICHARD BROOKS found Grant a loyal friend. He recalls: "We were using a crane that must have weighed tons. The crane's trucklike tires ran on two-by-twelve wooden tracks. As we were dollying in to Grant and José Ferrer, I [walking alongside the camera] stopped walking. The camera kept going. It ran over my foot. I didn't say anything because I didn't want to spoil the scene. When the shot was over, I asked, 'Okay for camera?' The operator said, 'Not for me. There was some kind of a bump.' Cary was already running toward the camera. He saw what had happened. Cary said, 'Get him to the hospital.'

"I said everything was fine. He said, 'You're not fine; there's blood all over your foot.' I took him aside and said, 'If I go to the hospital, there'll be another director here in fifteen minutes. I'll be out.' Cary said, 'If they get a new director, they're going to have to get a new actor. Now, go to the hospital!'"

During the filming Grant and Betsy Drake became mentors for a twenty-three-year-old actor named RICHARD ANDERSON, who

169

recalls: "I was on an NBC talent show called *Lights, Camera, Action* in the fall of 1949.

"One day, after my appearance, the telephone rang. The voice said, 'Hello, this is Cary Grant. My wife and I saw you on television. We think you're pretty good, particularly in comedy. Why don't you come to the studio for lunch?' I met him on the set of *Crisis*. I'll never forget it. He said, 'I'd like to help you. You're a very good actor.'

"Metro-Goldwyn-Mayer tested me with Sally Forrest in a scene from *The Cowboy and the Lady*, an old Gary Cooper movie. Two weeks went by, and because I hadn't heard anything, Cary called the front office and learned I had been accepted. The head of the studio later told me he was stunned that a leading man would recommend another leading man. He told me it was unheard of in this business."

RICHARD BROOKS also saw Grant's generosity during the casting of *Crisis:* "For three Spanish-speaking roles, Cary wanted us to hire actors who had been stars in silent pictures. 'They speak Spanish. They'd be glad to get the work.' One of them was Ramon Navarro, the man who played the original Ben Hur. Others were Gilbert Roland and Antonio Moreno. Cary saw to it they were hired.

"One afternoon Cary came to see me in my little forty-dollar-a-month one-room walk-up apartment in Laurel Canyon. . . . He looked around. 'Where can we sit?' I didn't have any furniture. I pulled up a couple of boxes. Two days later he arrived with a truckful of furniture. I still have the couch he gave me.

"There were two brain surgeons in America who were specialists, the kind we were simulating in *Crisis*. One of them was Nancy Davis [Reagan]'s stepfather, and the other was a doctor from Chicago, who was in Los Angeles to perform surgery. I asked him whether Cary and I could watch. . . . At first, Cary and I were seated in a small balcony, with a number of students. Then the doctor invited us to come closer, giving us surgical masks, et cetera. The doctor's own nurse ended up in the movie because Cary wanted to avoid mistakes. He knew she would handle the instruments properly and could also act as a technical adviser. That's how Cary approached the role."

Many of Grant's friends learned to seek his advice. DAN MELNICK says, "I think Cary enjoyed mentoring. It made him feel

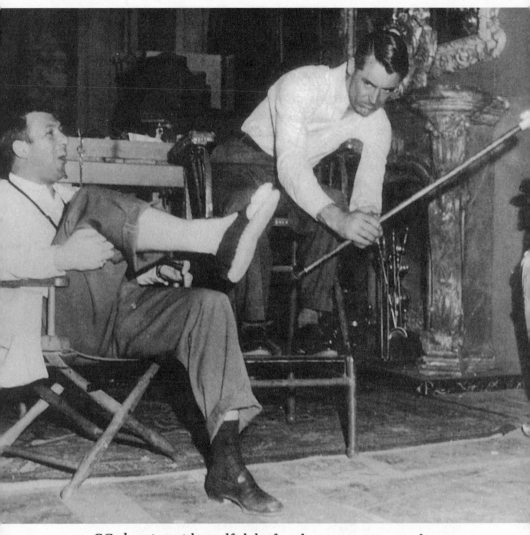

CG clowning with a golf club after the camera ran over director Richard Brooks's foot on the set of Crisis, *1950.*

good to pass on his insights, the kind that can only come with a lot of mileage and time." RICHARD BROOKS found Grant especially knowledgeable about scripts: "Cary was very good at story structure, and over the years I'd call him to talk about a tough story point. We were free enough to discuss a problem and not let vanity interfere with getting at the truth." And Cleveland Amory benefited from Grant's long experience working within the studio system. "When I went out to Metro in 1956 to work on *High*

Society," says AMORY, "Cary gave me a couple of tips. He said, 'Watch the wastebaskets. Metro has a new efficiency expert. He checks the writers' wastebaskets at the end of the day. Be sure your wastebasket has a lot of half-written papers in it. Even if you're not doing anything all day, which you're probably not, just scribble a lot of stuff and crumple up the paper and put it in the basket.' I did it every day."

When Richard Anderson first started at MGM, Grant told him, "Play all the parts. Play doctors, lawyers, sailors, or soldiers." ANDERSON, who took his advice, says, "I ended up doing thirty pictures in six years. When he went to see *Just This Once,* a picture I did with Janet Leigh, he liked it. He said, 'From now on, be careful of the parts you play because if they like you in a part, that's the part you'll play forever. You should concentrate now on the roles you want to play.' Cary's really a sponsor. To this day I feel grateful to him."

Grant also gave John Forsythe some good advice about leading ladies. "Always allow the woman to come to you in a love scene," Grant said. "Don't make the move to her. It puts you in a very commanding position."

"He was absolutely right," FORSYTHE says. "If you watch the love scenes Cary played with Grace Kelly, you'll see she made the first move. Her image was a schoolmarm or high society lady, but when you peeled off a couple of layers, she was quite a different lady—sensuous and fascinatingly hungry. He did that as often as he could. He couldn't do that with somebody like Rosalind Russell or Irene Dunne; they were too wise. But with the young ones, like Eva Marie Saint, he could."

STANLEY DONEN, who recalls that young actors frequently asked Grant for help with their lines, says, "They'd tell me it was the most wonderful experience, just being able to sit and talk to Cary about a part. They ate it up and remembered everything he said. Unlike a lot of big stars, he wasn't afraid of other people being good. He wanted everybody to be sensational and tried to help them. Many actors do the opposite. You hear stories of one actor changing the tempo of a reading in order to throw the other actor off—but not Cary. He wasn't afraid he was going to be overshadowed."

"I think he understood me better than I did myself," says AUDREY HEPBURN. "He was observant and had a penetrating

Friend of forty-one years, artist-writer FLEUR COWLES MEYER (right):
"*My husband and I were in Spain when Cary was filming* The Pride and
the Passion. *Our picnic on a hill overlooking Toledo—interrupted when
it began to rain—was brought back to the hotel at Cary's insistence.
Betsy [Drake, left] and I kept our hats on. The waiter thought we were
mad!*"

knowledge of people. He would talk often about relaxing and getting rid of one's fears, which I think he found a way to do. But he never preached. If he helped me, he did it without my knowing, and with a gentleness which made me lose my sense of being intimidated. I had this great affection for him because I knew he understood me. It was an unspoken friendship, which was wonderful. He would open up his arms wide when he saw you, and hug you, and smile, and let you know how he felt about you. We lived at other ends of the world, but it was always the same."

RICHARD ANDERSON concludes, "He was a concerned and caring man and very generous with his time. If you asked advice, most of the time he'd say, 'I don't have a crystal ball.' It was always with a light touch. He was always the cockney. . . . Up, up, up!"

Settled into marriage, Betsy Drake greeted Grant each morning with a poem. Lovingly placed on his breakfast tray were such selections as "Silence" by Marianne Moore, "The Character of Happy Life" by Sir Henry Wotton, "Salutation" by Ezra Pound, and "Remember" by Christina Georgina Rossetti. When she chose "Good and Bad Children" by Robert Lewis Stevenson, she attached this greeting. "DEAREST CARY, Good Morning and a very happy day to you! Enclosed is your first morning poem, which you must feel free not to read and at liberty to tear up. My love to you—BETSY."

In December 1950 Grant started *Monkey Business*, working again with Howard Hawks and Ginger Rogers. Grant is a chemist who has developed a formula for rejuvenation much to the delight of his boss, played by the veteran comedian Charles Coburn. Grant held Coburn in high esteem and years later fondly saluted him:

> CG: I learned how to steal a scene from Charles with no other prop except a cigar. He has screwed up more scenes for more leading men than I would care to name. Charles discovered that a good puff of cigar can settle around and obliterate any fellow player; he becomes no more distinguishable than Los Angeles City Hall from two blocks away on any moderately smoggy day. If the wind is not in the other actor's favor, then a slight extra

puff from those powerful and expert lungs of Mr. Coburn's can easily place it exactly on target. His accuracy with a triple puff is astounding.

On only one occasion have I known Charles to exhibit nervousness during a scene. When we were filming *Monkey Business*, he had to chase and squirt Marilyn Monroe with a siphon of soda, a moment he approached with glee. Any seeming reluctance, he later explained, was only his indecision about *where* on Marilyn's . . . um . . . *ample* proportions to *squirt* the soda. Miss Monroe seemed to present so many inviting parts. Everyone on the set awaited the moment with goggling eyes. You could have heard a pin drop. Eventually Charles gave it a healthy squirt, and missing Miss Monroe, he hit me full in the puss, thereby completely obliterating me from a scene again.

Even early in her career Grant could see a suggestion of Monroe's psychological and emotional difficulties:

CG: I had no idea she would become a big star. If she had something different from any other actress, it wasn't apparent at the time. She seemed very shy and quiet. There was something sad about her. She came to the set early, went into her room, and read. She would stay there until we called her. When the studio workers whistled at her and made remarks that I certainly did not want to hear, it would embarrass her a lot. People don't realize how distressing that sort of thing is. I'm sure they don't or they wouldn't do it. She was a victim of the Hollywood system. It's difficult for a girl to get used to being chased around all the time by the press. They never really leave you alone.

Since the war Grant had dramatically decreased the number of films he was making. Now that he was married again, he started to withdraw even further from his career as an actor. Between mid-1950 and the fall of 1952 Grant worked on only three films: *People Will Talk, Room for One More* (his second film with Betsy Drake), and *Dream Wife*.

With *Dream Wife*, Grant helped another screenwriter,

SIDNEY SHELDON, establish himself as a director. He recalls: "During the shooting of one scene he was waggling his eyebrows like Groucho Marx, and I told him to play the scene straight. It was a love scene with Deborah Kerr, but he kept very subtly doing the eyebrow thing. I was behind the camera and had to put my fingers in my mouth and bite them to keep from laughing. Cary's back was to me. He couldn't hear me and couldn't see me, but in the middle of the scene he stopped, turned around, looked at me, and said, 'If you're going to laugh, I can't do the scene.' Cary knew exactly what was going on—even behind his back!"

Unfortunately the audiences weren't laughing. Beginning with *People Will Talk,* his films did not command big box-office receipts. For the first time since Grant had left Paramount in 1936, he was failing with the public.

Grant's was not the only career to take a downward turn in the early 1950s. The industry as a whole was adjusting to the changing tastes of the postwar audience, and many of the great stars of the 1930s and 1940s were having to adjust as well. Major studios were not renewing the expensive long-term contracts of actors like Clark Gable and Errol Flynn, believing their popularity had run its course. There were new stars rising on the horizon, among them William Holden, Marlon Brando, Kirk Douglas, and Burt Lancaster. Not only were these men younger than Grant, Gable, and Flynn, but they also represented a new style, the antihero who suited the gritty, realistic dramas that were gaining popularity over the light, romantic comedies that had made Cary Grant a star.

Some of the actors of Grant's generation, Humphrey Bogart and Spencer Tracy, for example, were able to adapt to the tough-guy hero. Grant's image, however, was inextricably tied to a romanticized world of tuxedoes and champagne.

When *Dream Wife* was concluded, Grant decided to retire. He was forty-eight years old and had been working since he was fourteen. Now, he thought, it was time to put his marriage first and his career behind him.

Chapter Nine

"DON'T COUNT ON IT, HITCH"

CG: If I can understand how I became who I am, I can use that to shape my life in the future. I want to live in reality. Dreams aren't for me.

In 1952 Cary Grant retired from motion pictures. Encouraged by Betsy Drake's intellectual curiosity, Grant embarked on a new path—one of erudition and introspection. Through extensive reading and study, he strove to shed some light on the complexities of his life.

In December the Grants booked passage on a freighter headed for the Orient. Perhaps in part to separate themselves from what Grant called the "hypocrisies of Hollywood" and in part to satisfy their wanderlust, the couple decided to pursue a different kind of life. They crammed their bags with books, leaving the illusions of moviemaking to explore the realities of the Far East. They would also visit wounded soldiers in Army hospitals in the Pacific's Southwestern Command.

RICHARD ANDERSON, who saw them off, says, "They left from the San Pedro pier and went to the Orient. Cary figured his career was over. He was wrong, but he thought audiences didn't like his stuff any more, that the whole business had changed and the style of Marlon Brando and the others had taken over."

Indeed, Grant's desire for knowledge had been propelled by the fact that he felt to some degree he had failed in his profession. He was more than simply modest about his importance as a "movie star." He belittled his position as an actor. In the weeks he traveled and studied with his wife, Grant attempted to resolve his relationship with the imposing figure "Cary Grant" had become.

PETER BOGDANOVICH speculates on the pressures of stardom: "People don't know what it does to a person's private life and private thoughts to be blown up so many times your actual size—on screens all over the world. It must be mind-boggling. Sometimes Cary would put it down. He'd say to me, 'Oh, it's just a movie. Who cares about movies? Why don't people read books?'

"I don't think he ever really came to peace with it all. There was something so huge about being a star of that magnitude. He became mythical. What did it feel like to incarnate a myth? It had never happened before in the history of the world, except perhaps in some kind of pagan religions, and even then one was the elected representative of a deity, not the deity incarnate.

"Cary had to be aware he wasn't the person he was playing on the screen. He couldn't be all those different people. The person he played for Hawks was different from the person he played for Hitchcock. It was Cary, of course, but it was Cary seen from each director's point of view—especially with those major directors.

"When Cary was in charge of his pictures, he could decide what he wanted to do with himself. He played a wide range of characters, some quite different from others. It's hard to know which one was the most like Cary. He must have asked himself many times, 'Which of those Cary Grants am I?'"

Grant and Betsy Drake visited the Tokyo Army Hospital on January 5, 1953. He carefully saved the name of each man he visited, along with a picture of himself with a patient named Lawrence DeBenedictis. Letters from the hospital staff thanking him said the patients often remarked about how "down-to-earth" Grant was. By January 31 Grant had visited hospitals in Kyoto, Osaka, Fukuoka, Itazuke, and Nagoya. On February 14 he was in Kowloon at the Thirty-third General Hospital, and later, in Hong Kong, at the Royal Naval Hospital.

Grant's bookshelves contained an incredibly eclectic range of titles, including Dr. Ernest Jones's three-volume *The Life and Work of Sigmund Freud*. In their Palm Springs home the Grants assembled an impressive library. Clifford Odets, who frequently used the house when they were away, wrote to them after enjoying the variety: "I've gone thru all the old *Verve* magazines and, reading about Edgar Cayce, the clairvoyant medical man, last night I took a hot epsom salts bath and continued reading in the bath. This morning I was with Lord Byron after a few murmurs with Wordsworth."

As a guest, KATHARINE HEPBURN also read in the bath. She wrote, "I would lie in Betsy's bathtub and read Sophocles . . . and then open the shutters, clear the daddylong legs out of the tub, and sit for hours reading Greek plays."

Grant had begun dabbling in philosophy some years earlier. In 1949 Spencer Tracy introduced Grant to Dr. Seymour J. Gray, a professor of medicine at the Harvard Medical School and the head of the gastrointestinal department at the Peter Bent Brigham Hospital in Boston.

Grant and the doctor struck up an immediate friendship. Their mutual interest in philosophy became the essence of many conversations, in person and by telephone. At Gray's suggestion, Grant read Albert Schweitzer's autobiography. The French humanitarian's principal concept, "reverence for life," fascinated Grant. Grant was equally interested in Plato's Dialogues, another of the doctor's recommended readings.

> CG: I was a self-centered bore until the age of forty. I didn't have time for reading. Now I'm reading, absorbing, listening, and learning about the world and myself. Understanding is as important to growth as patience is necessary to understanding. One must have perspective.

"He was a thinking person," DR. GRAY says. "He talked a great deal about the values of life, the acceptance of life. We talked about success and immortality, as it were, in respect to one's work. Cary wondered about the meaning of life and asked, 'What is success? When you think about money, it really doesn't mean much. You need it to survive, but it doesn't buy happiness. If you already have all the money you need, what's the point in continuing?'

"I had the feeling Cary wasn't primarily interested in money. His main concern was doing a good job. He was proud of his work. He always pointed out to me in these discussions his humble beginnings. He wanted to impress his mother, I think, to be loved by her. I'm not sure she recognized how much he had accomplished."

Over the years Grant occasionally revealed the inner man. When BURT REYNOLDS met Grant, Reynolds was number one at the box office. He recalls: "Cary told me, 'Enjoy the moment, but understand this is not the summit. You haven't gotten where you're going.' I thought he was talking about my career, but he was talking about my life—children and happiness. I wish I could tell him now that he was absolutely right."

Grant also saw Dr. Gray and his wife, Ruth, socially. The Grants, the Grays, and Spencer Tracy and Katharine Hepburn enjoyed each other's company. HEPBURN says, "I got to really know Cary when he started to see Betsy Drake. Betsy and I really hit it off. We still see each other." And DR. GRAY fondly remembers evenings spent with his friends: "Katharine Hepburn invited us to dinner at the old Charles Boyer house, above Cary's. Howard Hughes had taken it over from Boyer and let Kate use it. Spencer Tracy, Jimmy Cagney, and Cary were there. Kate pressed a button, and the roof opened up over the dining-room table. We had our dinner under the stars, with a view of the whole city."

Grant's leap into the world of ideas never included politics, although RICHARD ANDERSON recollects that Grant's sense of justice was taxed by the witch-hunts of the McCarthy era: "When Charlie Chaplin was ostracized in this country, Cary was one of the first to come to his defense." Grant told a reporter at the time that he did not believe Chaplin was a Communist and that Chaplin's value as a great entertainer was more important than his politics. In general, if Grant had political beliefs, he kept quiet about them. In 1950 he made the rare public political statement that he "would like to see a woman as President," but that was about as far as he would go on the subject.

CG: I'm opposed to actors taking sides in public and spouting spontaneously about love, religion, or politics. We aren't experts on those subjects. Personally I'm a mass of inconsistencies when it comes to politics. My opinions are constantly changing. That's why I don't ever take a public stand on issues.

"He kept his politics to himself," says DAN MELNICK. "I can't remember Cary's ever discussing a specific politician running for a specific office. I felt he was a traditional conservative, one who believed in the Bill of Rights and took it seriously. The thing that did characterize Cary in any discussion about politics was his humanism and compassion. When we discussed the McCarthy era, he talked about the horror of people not being able to work and of the hysteria of the industry's reaction."

Gregory Peck and Grant stayed off the subject. PECK says: "Cary knew that my views are quite liberal, so we avoided the topic. I didn't try to convert him, or try to win a point with him, and I don't think he would have enjoyed a political argument or confrontation." Grant told BEA SHAW, "Nobody really knows I'm a Republican. I don't make an issue of it because I have friends who are Democrats and Republicans."

During these months away from the work schedules the Grants lunched frequently with friends but rarely entertained in their home. When they did have a dinner party, their guests were likely to be comfortable, easy friends like Richard Brooks, Jean Simmons, Janet Gaynor, and Richard Anderson.

In 1953 Drake read *Hypnotism Today* by Jean Bordeaux and Leslie M. Le Cron. She was fascinated by the power of hypnosis to change human behavior. Grant wanted to stop smoking, so she hypnotized him and cured him of the habit. Like many converts to a smoke-free life, Grant became a staunch antismoker and advocated hypnosis as a simple way to end the addiction.

In a letter Grant confidently promises a friend a better life, with his smoking days behind him:

> You are a dear kind man, admired and loved by those who know you, particularly now that you have given up smoking. As well as being harmful—as you know—it is a disgusting, dirty habit, which leaves a foul smell on your breath, your fingers, in your hair, and on your clothes. It offends many people near and dear to you—and that has always troubled you. We all like to please, especially those we love.
>
> So, now that you are beginning to like yourself, to take care of yourself, you will find that you will enjoy everything and everyone around you. Each day becomes better and happier.

Your life will improve in every way as you continue to stop poisoning yourself. You are now breathing clean, fresh air and are able, at last, to relax and appreciate the peace and beauty of life. To *enjoy yourself*—which means to *enjoy being you*.

IRVING LAZAR comments that Grant didn't tolerate smokers: "Once he offered to give me a dinner and told me to invite anybody I wanted for the following Sunday. Then he called me on Friday or Saturday and asked who I had invited. They were all people I knew Cary liked. His response was, 'They're all smokers. I can't have dinner with them. I'll pay for it, but you have the dinner.'"

"He lectured me all the time," recalls GEORGE BARRIE. "He really overdid it and was sometimes obnoxious. I said, 'Cary, when I decide to quit smoking, I'll quit.'"

Soon the Grants were using hypnosis to relieve tensions and induce sleep. Eventually, when Grant returned to acting, he used self-hypnosis to learn his lines in his sleep.

Almost two years after Grant's departure from filmmaking, Alfred Hitchcock tried to convince him to come out of retirement to star in one movie. "Don't count on it, Hitch," Grant said at first. Hitchcock finally enticed him with a good script, a location in the south of France, and a costar who was zooming to the height of her meteoric career, the twenty-six-year-old Grace Kelly.

To Catch a Thief brought Cary Grant out of retirement. He boarded the train to New York "with too much baggage" and headed for the Riviera. Still reluctant, he recorded en route his thoughts on the backs of pages from his script. Badly typed, the end of each line disappearing from the page, he wrote out ruminations about the perplexities of modern life.

At last a leisurely moment. It's amusing to recollect the last-minute detail—contracts, tax forms, powers-of-attorney, insurance data, the "whereases" and "notwithstandings" that harass and bedevil a poor human who makes the mistake of informing his lawyer that he is leaving to make a picture in Europe. The endless social notes, the "so sorry, cannot attend," and "thank you so much for your kind thoughts, etc." The hypocrisy of it all; the fear of us all. Why are we so browbeaten into believing that attention to such so-called politeness is important? Important to whom? You? The person who receives the note?

Grant clearly saw the many false fronts that went with life in Hollywood, and his goal in the coming years was to rid himself of the casual hypocrisies he had internalized. He had read Freud and was familiar with the language of psychoanalysis, but there is no evidence that he ever underwent psychotherapy. Instead, he chose self-analysis through introspection, reading, and, in the late 1950s, medically supervised experimentation with LSD. Aside from that Grant learned what he knew from books and from discussions with friends. As in almost every aspect of his life, he was self-taught.

DAN MELNICK sees what might be unexpected depths in Grant's character: "He was as introspective and troubled as any sensitive person growing up in our society. He knew I had been through classic analysis at an early age, so we shared a psychoanalytical frame of reference. He gave me advice. in metaphorical or allegorical terms but was more specific when we had analytical discussions."

PEGGY LEE had many serious talks with Grant, about which she says, "We had a mutual respect for one another and shared some of the same philosophies. I got the impression that Cary had a great deal of love and reverence for life. I believe he and Betsy Drake counseled with Ernest Holmes, the founder of the Church of Religious Science."

By November 18, 1954, Grant was in Monaco and on the set. He was to play a retired cat burglar who, after a series of jewel robberies, is trying to clear his name. The character was suave, handsome, and crafty. A contemporary Raffles, he was elegantly dressed whether in a turtleneck sweater and gray flannel pants or in formal evening wear.

"Cary always looked smashing," says NANCY REAGAN. "Ronnie thought the mock-turtleneck sweaters Cary wore in *To Catch a Thief* were so good-looking. I mentioned this to Cary, and he sent Ronnie two of his sweaters."

During the filming Grant came to realize he was working

with a woman who was much more than a pretty face. Thereafter he admired Grace Kelly tremendously and was a devoted friend until her death in 1982, when he paid her a monumental tribute:

> CG: I think the most memorable and honest actress I've ever worked with was Grace Kelly. Don't misunderstand. I appreciated Ingrid Bergman, Audrey Hepburn, Deborah Kerr, Irene Dunne, Kate Hepburn, and all the women I worked with. . . .

Grant always disliked being asked, "Who was your favorite leading lady?" whether by the press or by his public. Tactfully he would reply, "They were all my favorites." In the company of his friends, Grant wondered what was behind that question. "What are they really asking? Did we have an affair? Which actress worked the hardest? Who was the easiest to work with?" In spite of his diplomacy, Grant allowed his special feeling for Grace Kelly to come out:

> CG: Grace had a kind of serenity, a calmness, that I hadn't arrived at at that point in my life—and perhaps never will, for all I know. She was so relaxed in front of the camera that she made it look simple. She made acting look as easy as Frank Sinatra made singing appear. Everyone thinks they can sing after an evening at the theater listening to Frank, but to create that sense of ease takes a tremendous amount of knowledge and experience and talent.
>
> Grace was astonishing. When you played a scene with her, she really listened. She was right there with you. She was Buddha-like in her concentration. She was like Garbo in that respect.

Grant was impressed too with Grace Kelly's other attributes as an actress, particularly her ability to ad-lib:

> CG: In the picnic scene—where we eat chicken in the car—we exhausted all the film in the camera but went on talking anyway. I asked her, "How is it that you're so experienced at dialogue?" She told me she had done dozens of soaps. Soaps were live in those days, and you

With Grace Kelly shooting To Catch a Thief, *1954.* CG: *"Her death [1982] hit me very hard because it was so horribly, horribly unexpected."*

sometimes had to ad-lib. I was awed by her. We all loved her very, very much.

Grant's deep affection was well known to his friends. "Every time he got a letter from Grace Kelly, he told me about it," says MICKY ZEILER. "She was the kind of woman he liked. Barbara Grant is like Grace Kelly—very elegant and ladylike." LESLIE CARON confirms Grant's taste: "Cary liked women who had a distinction and a certain education about them. That's what he liked about Grace Kelly."

One of Hitchcock's great strengths as a director was knowing how to work actors against type. He kept his audience in suspense about the true nature of his characters just as masterfully as he kept them on the edge of their seats with the intrigue of his plots. In *To Catch a Thief* Grace Kelly totters between hot and cold, while Grant balances perfectly between gravity and humor.

Hitchcock once explained this to PETER BOGDANOVICH: "Outwardly Grace was cold as ice, but, boy, underneath! That incongruity is epitomized by the scene in *To Catch a Thief*, where Grace Kelly and Cary kiss in the corridor. It's as though she'd unzipped Cary's fly." And JAMES STEWART observes how Hitchcock utilized Grant's sense of humor: "Cary had real, solid humor, something so important and so rare. He knew how to use it. For example in *To Catch a Thief*, he didn't let the humor overrun the dramatic part. He used it as a part of the performance he was giving. There are very, very few actors, when you get down to counting people, that have this ability."

During the filming of *To Catch a Thief*, Grant fell in love with the Riviera. He was to return many times, to Antibes, Cannes, Nice, St.-Jean-Cap-Ferrat, and Monte Carlo, where he was a frequent guest of Princess Grace and Prince Rainier. Grant's daughter, Jennifer, and Princess Stephanie were occasional playmates. "Grace loved and admired Cary and cherished working with him," says HSH PRINCE RAINIER III. "She was also proud and happy about the things Cary had said about her professionalism. But Cary was above all a friend. She valued his friendship and wanted me to share that with her. It was my great privilege to know Cary."

DAN MELNICK remembers one trip to the Riviera. "Cary and

I were at the Hôtel du Cap in Antibes, where Cary and Grace
Kelly filmed much of *To Catch a Thief*. Kirk Kerkorian insisted
we use his yacht, which was anchored off the hotel. One night
we took the boat and started out for St.-Tropez, but it got so
late we went to Cannes instead. On the way over, Cary realized
he hadn't arranged for a car. I told him there were always cabs.
Well, we got there very late, and there were no cabs. We hitch-
hiked from the outskirts of Cannes into the middle of town in
search of a restaurant whose specialty was bouillabaisse. It was
terribly funny. We stood on the side of the road, thumbs in the
air, with cars passing and then slowing down. You could just
imagine the conversation—women telling their husbands, 'My
God, that was Cary Grant.'"

By January 1955 Grant, Betsy Drake, and her poodle, April,
were spending most of their time in their Palm Springs home.
They owned a lovely old Mexican house, an authentic hacienda,
with thick adobe walls and a sloping tile roof set amid tall rose-
bushes and citrus, date, and olive trees. Drake played the guitar
and sang. She dedicated a great deal of her time to writing. Always the perfectionist, Grant improved his swimming and became increasingly more interested in horses.

The Grants would rise early in the morning and ride out
across the desert to see the sunrise. At night, after a long ride,
they would cook steaks under the desert moon.

In the spring of 1955 Grace Kelly introduced Grant to Judy
Quine. She and Grant remained friends for the next thirty years.
"I met Cary right after Grace Kelly won her Oscar for *The Country Girl*," says QUINE. "Grace had never been to Las Vegas. She
asked my then-husband Jay Kantor if we would take her if she
won the prize. Jay was her agent at the time. We agreed. Grace
then discussed the trip with Cary and Betsy, and we all went for
Easter weekend right after the award ceremony.

"Cary arranged for penthouse apartments with a private elevator at the Sahara. We darted back and forth to one another's
rooms in our bathrobes because we had the whole floor to ourselves. We were feeling very clubby, congenial, and *entre nous*.
Even when we went down into the public rooms, we went as a
group.

"Cary didn't gamble. He never went to a table. He said it
didn't interest him. But he had obviously been to Las Vegas a

great deal. Everybody was delighted to see him. He sat with a soft drink or coffee in the lounges. The pit bosses, hotel owners, entertainers, and just folks wandering around the casino would stop by to talk to him.

"While we were there, Cary secretly arranged a little Easter surprise. Not telling anybody, he ordered three enormous baskets from the hotel's gift shop, each one topped with a funny-looking stuffed Easter bunny. He enclosed cards saying, 'Love and kisses from the Easter Bunny away from home.' Early Sunday morning we each opened our doors to collect the newspapers and found the baskets. Cary was in the shower when Betsy opened their door. We decided to play a joke on Cary, to hide the baskets and not mention them.

"We ordered a huge breakfast in Cary and Betsy's living room. Cary waited for a reaction. None came. You could see the wheels turning, but he kept quiet. The food came; everybody laughed and chatted and carried on. It was beginning to get to him.

"Finally he opened the door to the living room. We heard him scuffling around in the hallway and tried not to laugh. He checked the service entrance. When he came back, we pretended not to notice. When he couldn't stand it any longer, he said, 'Didn't you see anything outside your doors this morning?'

"'Our newspapers,' we said.

"Then he mumbled about how people have no sense of responsibility. We finally asked him what he was muttering about, and he told us about the baskets. And we said, 'Oh, but how sweet of you. It was a lovely thought anyway.' The more we thanked him, the angrier he got. He walked around, listing from side to side, and said, 'I know what happened. Some people came up in the elevator, saw the baskets, and took them to get my card. They're taking home Cary Grant's autograph.'

"This was Betsy's opportunity. 'Well, how would they prove to anybody in Des Moines that the Easter Bunny away from home was really Cary Grant?' At that we all collapsed in laughter, got out the baskets, and hugged him and kissed him.

"What I love about the story is that one night when my husband Don and I had dinner with Cary and Barbara in the summer of 1986, I told the story to Barbara. Cary was still amazed at himself and laughed about how foolish he was to have presumed anybody wanted his autograph that badly. He said, 'That shows what your mind can do. When you get accustomed to people pursuing you, what silly stuff goes on in one's head.' His humility was wonderfully appealing."

"Meanwhile, a Los Angeles doctor who was after Grace found out we were going to Las Vegas. He wanted Grace to notice him and had failed in Los Angeles, so he flew to Las Vegas. He had just published a major medical paper and was in the news everywhere. He saw himself as a great celebrity and, of course, the savior of the world, which he might have been. He also thought he was God's gift to women. He expected Grace Kelly to fall all over him. She didn't, but that didn't deter him.

"He lurked behind a pillar in the lounge ready to pounce on Grace when she sat down at a blackjack table. He was the last person any of us wanted to see. We dodged him all over town, but he was like a piece of flypaper. Everywhere we went, he emerged. He skulked in the doorways and watched as we took off in cabs and then followed us.

"Cary came up with wonderful ploys to get rid of him. He staged melodramatic car chases and had us skip out the side door so this guy wouldn't see us leave. We got a lead on him before we moved to the next casino. But he'd show up again, and Cary would say, 'Ah, that didn't work.' And he'd think of another scheme."

BETSY DRAKE remembers an occasion when an old friend of Grant's was equally unsuccessful: "When Grace tried to avoid Howard Hughes, she didn't use any makeup and wore glasses. He came to the house specifically to go on the make for Grace, *but he didn't recognize her*. Howard was on the make for every woman. He would make it a project. He went to such pains to get his various women, but he never got Grace."

Grant had a percentage deal on *To Catch a Thief*. So, in July 1955 he was asked to promote the picture by appearing at previews in various cities, to answer questions from the audience. Paramount asked former Cleveland television host JOHNNY ANDREWS to prepare Grant to go onstage. He remembers: "Paramount said they had a problem with Cary Grant. He wanted to promote the film but was scared to death. He was amenable to some coaching, but the studio insisted nobody could know.

"In July they scheduled a preview in Cleveland. I built it up on the air but said only that a major star from the picture would appear onstage. They warned me that Grant might back out at the last minute.

"Cary came to Cleveland the Tuesday before the Monday preview. He met me at the door of his suite at the Statler. He was wearing the bottoms to his blue pajamas and had a mouthful of toothpaste.

"When we got down to business, he told me he hadn't slept all night. He said, 'I cannot get out in front of an audience. I've never done it. Look at my knees. They're shaking.' He was so simple and honest about it. He was thinking about it as a chore. I told him that for twenty-five years people had been giving him love but that he had never heard it or felt it. He *owed* the people the chance to meet him, and he owed himself the opportunity to get that feeling from them.

"I talked to him and worked with him on relaxation exercises until Monday. We developed a format. I was to talk to the audience, introduce him, he would come onstage, and I would go into the audience with a hand mike to get questions. When he wanted to call a halt to it, he would take his thumb and first finger and rub his left lapel. By Sunday he was raring to go.

"When we got to the theater, there were sawhorses in the street and people lined up for blocks. In the wings he looked through the curtain and said, 'My God, Johnny, I've never seen so many people in one place in my life. I can't do it.' He was shaking and started to walk away. I grabbed him by the lapels and told him he had worked too hard and if he didn't do it now, he'd never come back. He finally agreed but said he would do only five minutes. He wanted to be sure I'd stay onstage after introducing him.

"People knew it was going to be either Grace Kelly or Cary Grant. They loved the picture. When I announced his name, there was thunderous applause. When the spotlight hit the wings and he walked out, the second wave of love hit him. He was stunned. He stood there for a moment, his eyes twinkled, and he smiled. Then he dipped his shoulders and confidently strode across the stage. He loved it. It was more than an hour later when he gave me the lapel signal."

Grant didn't mind the burden of publicity and even liked

being photographed if it was done in a professional manner. When writer EVERETT MATTLIN interviewed Grant in his desert wardrobe at his Palm Beach home for *Gentlemen's Quarterly* in 1964, he observed as much: "During the morning shoot he was endlessly and contagiously enthusiastic and cheerful. He laughed often, joshing with us, and was totally cooperative. Most celebrities we photographed for the magazine despised the whole business and wanted it over with as quickly as possible."

PETER BOGDANOVICH remembers Grant's advice on being photographed: "One time I was going to sit on a dais and Cary said, 'Never eat on a dais.' I said why. 'Because they'll be taking pictures and they'll catch one of you eating—and *that's* the one they'll use—with your mouth wide open.'"

On April 19, 1956, Grace Kelly married Prince Rainier of Monaco. The preparations had dominated all the headlines. The American public was dazzled by the real-life fairy tale of the Philadelphia-born actress and her European prince.

Grant and Betsy Drake shipped their wedding present, a lovely antique desk. Grant was due in Spain on April 1. JUDITH CRIST, who was working for the New York *Herald Tribune* when Grant stopped in New York on his way to Europe, recollects: "He was staying at the Astor Hotel, four short blocks from the *Tribune* building, before leaving for Spain to make *The Pride and the Passion*. My editor had given me five different stories to cover by phone, and Grant was one of them. He was flirtatiously charming when I telephoned and said, 'Why don't you come over?' I looked at the piles of stuff on my desk and said, 'It's snowing.'

"It was any female's dream invitation, and the pure idiocy of my reaction has stuck with me forever. It apparently stunned him, too. So he went on to invite me to come to Spain with him, where sunny weather was guaranteed. Ha! I was a married lady and—ever the idiot—came up with babblings about a vacation schedule. But I established my niche in the history of fools as the gal who turned down Cary Grant."

Grant's schedule for *The Pride and the Passion* prevented him from attending the royal wedding, but some weeks later, when the newlyweds honeymooned in Spain, Betsy Drake enjoyed filming the princely couple herself.

The Pride and the Passion, like *The Howards of Virginia*, was a historical drama. Based on a novel by C. S. Forester, the epic romance took place in Spain during the Napoleonic Wars. STANLEY KRAMER was chosen to direct. He recalls: "I was a new director, having only directed *Not as a Stranger*. I thought *The Pride and the Passion* was an opportunity for Cary to break a certain chain of acting, and he agreed. Cary's performance was singular and very, very interesting. He was playing strict drama in heroic proportions, a real departure for him."

Kramer's casting of the other principals was equally daring. Frank Sinatra played the rebel leader of Spanish guerrilla forces, and a young Italian actress, virtually unknown to American audiences, was chosen to play Juana. "When Stanley Kramer cast me in *The Pride and the Passion*, I was only twenty years old," says SOPHIA LOREN. "Neither United Artists nor Cary Grant (who had contractual cast approval) wanted to use an unknown Italian girl who was still wet behind the ears! But Kramer fought for me and they finally gave in.

"Stanley Kramer gave an elaborate cocktail party to commemorate the start of the film. I had never been to an American-style cocktail party. I felt so unprepared. I knew everyone would be speaking English, and I was still far from fluent.

"But it was the thought of facing the judgment of Cary Grant that was really paralyzing. I have never been as nervous as I was that night. Getting ready, I must have changed my dress a half dozen times.

"When Stanley Kramer introduced us, Cary teased me about my name. 'How do you do, Miss Lolloloren, or is it Lorenigida? Ah, you Italian actresses, I can never get your names straight.' He was debonair and charming, even more handsome than he appeared on the screen. I immediately felt at ease with him, and I could tell from the look in his eyes that he approved of me."

STANLEY KRAMER thinks all would have gone well with the film if Frank Sinatra had not walked off the picture. He remembers: "We only had five weeks to go when he left. Cary's stature as a human being came to the fore. He came to me and said, 'Look, life is filled with pitfalls and disappointments. You can let this ruin the entire situation, or you can rally above it and be a mensch. That's what I'm counting on you to be.' It touched me very much. He said, 'Whatever it takes, no extra charge to you, I will fill in.'

"That meant doing close-ups with coat hangers as the foreground because Frank Sinatra wasn't there. Sophia Loren cooperated, too. But it couldn't salvage the film because Sinatra was a key part of it. I finally settled with his agent for one week in Los Angeles. We used palm trees on a stage instead of finishing in Spain. Cary was extremely cooperative and did not play the big star at all. He was very human and very thoughtful. I am eternally grateful to him."

As he often did, Grant involved himself in aspects of production and even exploitation. STANLEY KRAMER remembers Grant's concern about Loren's publicity: "Cary had a thing about Sophia's presentation to a worldwide audience and to the American audience particularly because it was her first film in English. He didn't want her to have the image of an Italian sex symbol. He didn't want her to fall into that pit. He thought she was beyond that.

"It was her first English-speaking film, and Cary was thoughtful and very helpful to her. He never hesitated to say, 'Why don't we do another take? I don't think her line was clear there.' Or, 'I think she can do a little bit better, don't you think so, Sophia?' He encouraged and bolstered her. As he did everybody."

Grant was particularly disturbed about the décolletage of the dress worn by Loren in an Al Hirschfeld drawing that had been commissioned for the film's promotion. Grant personally requested that Hirschfeld reduce Loren's cleavage and make it more modest. He also questioned the little "nubbin" the artist had rendered on the six-thousand-pound cannon, which he found phallic and in bad taste.

During the weeks in Spain the personality conflicts and the difficulties presented by a foreign location put a strain on the entire cast and crew. Grant's initial reaction to Sophia Loren as a pretty Italian actress quickly changed. He responded to her vulnerability and natural talent. She was captivated by his confidence and his wisdom. Before they realized it, they were in love.

SOPHIA LOREN remembers, "We were shooting on location in a remote part of Spain. For six months Cary and I were together constantly.

"At first Cary was reserved with me. If our conversation became serious or introspective, he would try to make a joke out of it. When he got too close to his center, his true feelings, he would hide behind a mask of humor. But more and more he confided in me and trusted me. It disturbed him that although he had been married three times, he had never really sustained a relationship with a woman. He talked about his life in London and his early struggles. He disclosed his deepest self-doubts. He wanted to be open and honest and direct, yet he could not make himself vulnerable. He was afraid to be touched. And of course, one cannot have it both ways.

"Slowly our relationship grew, and his trust in me grew. He realized that trust and vulnerability went hand in hand. When his trust was strong enough, he no longer bothered with his mask. I was just as open and trusting with him.

"Evening after evening we dined on the craggy hilltops to the accompaniment of flamenco guitars. We drank the good Spanish wine and laughed and confided in each other . . . and fell in love. I was fascinated with him, with his warmth, affection, intelligence, and his wonderfully dry, mischievous sense of humor.

It was no passing fancy, according to IRENE MAYER SELZNICK: "He was desperately in love with Sophia Loren." And GEORGE BARRIE admits, "Cary never talked much about romances with famous women, but he did tell me he loved Sophia Loren."

"Cary showered her with flowers during the filming," says STANLEY KRAMER. "I was aware of the romance, but I didn't want to get involved in it. It was just an added complication for me."

It also complicated the lives of Betsy Drake and of Carlo Ponti, Loren's married lover. Betsy Drake visited the Spanish location, as did Judy Quine and her husband. QUINE remembers: "After the wedding [in Monaco], Jay and I went to Rome and Paris. We ended up in Madrid at the end of April and spent a few days with Betsy and Cary in their hotel suite.

"I had known Carlo Ponti since I was sixteen, when he was married to his first wife. I knew about his relationship with Sophia, but I did not have a clue about Cary and Sophia. Betsy said not one word. In fact, Cary and Betsy always seemed as though they were having a very good time. We all had dinner, Cary, Betsy, Sophia, Carlo, my husband, and I."

SOPHIA LOREN reveals, "I was also in love with Carlo Ponti, who was still a married man and not yet prepared to leave his family. Now, here was Cary Grant, who was ready to renounce everything. He wanted me with no strings attached. I was very confused and needed to be away from the magic of those Spanish nights to make my decision."

In July Betsy Drake decided to go back to the United States. Judy Quine and her husband had returned to her parents' house in Westchester, on Long Island Sound, and had booked a room for Drake at the St. Regis in New York City. QUINE says: "Betsy had boarded the *Andrea Doria*. My husband, Jay, and John Foreman, an agent with Jay at MCA, planned to meet Betsy's boat when it docked.

"It was July 26, 1956. I was still asleep when Jay called from the office with the news that the *Andrea Doria* had been hit by another boat off the coast of Nantucket the night before and was sinking in the Atlantic.

"For several hours we didn't know whether Betsy was alive or dead. Finally there was a report that a boat had come to the accident scene and had picked up several survivors and would arrive in New York in midafternoon. I drove in from the country with some things of mine because if Betsy was there, in all likelihood, she was going to be without luggage. I bought lingerie at Bergdorf's, made a quick trip to a drugstore for basic things, and headed for the St. Regis, where I got a message. Betsy was okay.

"Sure enough, a little while later, John and Jay drove up in a limousine with Betsy, whose hair was very neatly combed. Since she never wore much makeup, she didn't look much different from when she wore the minimum amount. She was wearing a charming little Ben Zuckerman silk suit with a little pin on the lapel. It was all adorable except that on her feet were huge, bulky white sweat socks loaned to her by a sailor. Betsy had lost her shoes. But thank God, she was all right."

Drake was among the 1,134 persons rescued. Among her lost belongings were a manuscript she had been working on in Spain and the footage she had taken of Princess Grace and Prince Rainier on their honeymoon.

QUINE continues: "Upstairs Betsy immediately called Cary. I don't think he had heard about it because they had been out on location. That's my recollection. He had just come back in when she reached him by phone and was simultaneously hearing the news and hearing from her. We all decided I should stay with her. It was very frightening."

Settled again in the house in Palm Springs, Grant and Betsy Drake redecorated their house with the furniture they purchased in Spain. His retirement had ended, and he began making films again at a slow but steady pace.

In February 1957 Grant started filming *An Affair to Remember*. Leo McCarey, who had cowritten and directed *Love Affair* (RKO, 1939), was remaking his own film. The original had blended humor, romance, and melodrama. The witty repartee between Dunne and Boyer had beautifully balanced the tear-jerking elements in the simple black-and-white love story. In *An Affair to Remember*, the story was to be blown up with color and CinemaScope into a four-hankie tragedy.

When Grant was making *An Affair to Remember*, a young actor at the studio, ROBERT WAGNER, took every opportunity to watch him work. He recalls: "One day I walked on the set, and Cary was very excited. I had watched him for days and hadn't seen this kind of exhilaration. 'R.J.,' he said, 'I've just learned the most wonderful thing. I've finally solved a problem I've been having for years. Today, for the first time, I learned how to breathe during a scene. It's going to make all the difference in the world.' It's true. You say a line and wait for somebody to answer so you get enough air in there to fill up the diaphragm. Cary was something else. It was his sixty-second picture, and he was still honing his craft."

As part of the promotion for *An Affair to Remember*, Grant did something he had always shunned: He endorsed a product, possibly because it was a tie-in with a picture. He was photographed standing with a TWA pilot at the nose of a TWA Jetstream. The ad copy mentions the film, and Grant claims, "I always fly TWA. I've been a TWA customer for years. And I'm delighted to say the new Jetstream makes the habit even more pleasant. It is noticeably quieter and the seats offer more legroom. I have never traveled on a more comfortable airplane." The sentiment was sincere. He did travel TWA whenever possible.

On May 2, 1957, Grant began work on *Kiss Them for Me*, a film directed by Stanley Donen. It was the first of three movies that Grant made with the young director. Two personalities new to motion pictures were cast in prominent roles, the model Suzy

Time Warner chairman and CEO STEVEN J. ROSS: "An Affair to Remember *has one of the great closing lines in cinema history. Cary says to Deborah Kerr, 'If I can paint, you can walk.' It is my favorite film. It always makes me cry. Cary knew that and told me it also made him cry.*"

Parker and the comedian RAY WALSTON, who says, "I consider myself lucky to have been involved with Cary. He was such a brilliant technician. And he was always prepared, so I was surprised one day when during the rehearsal, he didn't know the lines. Then, just before the camera rolled, he picked up a piece of paper and went over it. They started shooting, and he did some business like brushing off the top of the couch, but he was actually looking at his lines on the floor. He'd gaze down, get the line, look up, and say it perfectly."

STANLEY DONEN reveals Grant's shrewdness in filming a scene with Suzy Parker: "This story about Cary may sound vain, but in fact, it isn't. We were doing a scene in which Cary and Suzy kissed. She was lying back on the bed, and he was supposed to lean over and kiss her. Cary said, 'We're not going to do it like that.' He lay on the bed and asked me to stand over him. I immediately understood his point. When I leaned down, gravity made my face fall. I never would have noticed it if I hadn't been in the actual position myself. I could feel it on my own skin. Suzy was only twenty or so. Her face wouldn't fall. Cary knew a lot, and I was happy to learn some of it."

RAY WALSTON remembers, "In one scene he is in bed with malaria having chills. The covers are over him. Jayne Mansfield pats him on the stomach, and says, 'Now, now, darling, you're going to be all right.' She patted him right below the navel. On one take, just to be extremely mischievous, he scooted up in the bed so she patted him on his genitals."

Grant's joke on Jayne Mansfield was typical of the bawdier side of his sense of humor.

"When we went to the commissary," RAY WALSTON recollects, "people at other tables would get annoyed with our raucous laughter at Cary's stories."

According to GEORGE BARRIE, "Cary told the funniest stories, with southern accents, ethnic accents—any kind of accent. Dirty ones, too. You'd never think those things would come out of him." And GREGORY PECK says, "He was a great one for jokes, and they were sort of risqué. It was a curious side of his personality. I think it was English music hall humor—those funny, bawdy postcards that they sell at Blackpool and Brighton. English humor often has to do with bare bottoms and somebody's knickers coming off. Both he and Barbara had that streak of British humor. They enjoyed slightly off-color jokes."

BEA SHAW confesses that "Cary and Prince Rainier would call one another and tell dirty jokes. Some of Cary's jokes were really raunchy." David Mahoney and Grant traded dirty stories. MAHONEY adds: "He could tell my jokes to mixed audiences, and I couldn't. He told them, and they all laughed. I told them and got into trouble."

And once Merv Griffin put one of Grant's favorite poems to music:

> They bought me a box of tin soldiers
> I threw all the generals away
> I smashed up the sergeants and majors
> Now I play with my privates all day.

CHAPTER TEN

AN ACTOR'S LIFE FOR ME

CG: How the devil do I know what I would have become if I hadn't become an actor? I did what I did without paying much attention to the consequences . . . and there were a lot of consequences I could have done without, believe me.

A nationwide poll in *Popularity* asserted that the all-American favorite actors of 1957 were Rock Hudson, William Holden, Cary Grant, Frank Sinatra, Gary Cooper, Marlon Brando, James Stewart, Burt Lancaster, Glenn Ford, Yul Brynner, Clark Gable, and John Wayne.

Audiences and motion-picture exhibitors had welcomed Cary Grant back from retirement. He was exactly the shot in the arm that a sagging box office needed. The high-water mark for ticket sales had been 1946, and the postwar years looked increasingly bleak for the future of movies as a national pastime.

During the late 1940s and 1950s the impact of television and the rapidly changing structure of American life were a double threat. Families preferred to stay at home and watch "Uncle Miltie" than go out to a movie.

The industry fought back by relaxing its censorship code and making more adult films like *A Streetcar Named Desire*. Wide-screen formats like CinemaScope and VistaVision combined with more location shooting—*Three Coins in a Fountain* in Rome, *Love Is a Many-Splendored Thing* in Hong Kong—offered the public scope and sweep the square boxes in their living rooms couldn't provide.

The studios went so far as to forbid their contract stars to appear on television, and legend has it that Jack Warner would not allow writers to include scenes with television sets in them. Screenwriters found opportunities to poke fun at the limitations of the medium. In *Angels in the Outfield,* when a TV set is given to an orphanage of little girls, all they can tune in is a wrestling match.

In this atmosphere it was not surprising Grant refused to work in television. To him, television was a "diminished" medium. Compared with the grandeur and potential elegance of motion pictures, early television was a crude, limited, and virtually experimental medium. This is not to say everyone in motion pictures held this attitude. On the contrary, Dick Powell's *Four Star Playhouse* enlisted the talents of Powell, Charles Boyer, Ida Lupino, and David Niven.

Television was also exclusively *live*. The pressures of shooting live drama, comedy, or talk shows are entirely different from the slow, careful process of making a movie. Especially during the 1930s, 1940s, and 1950s, when Grant was working regularly, filmmakers had the time, money, and resources to work in a leisurely fashion. Early television was manic by comparison, attracting a whole new breed of young directors and actors who throve on the pace.

Additionally, and maybe most important as far as Grant was concerned, live television eliminates editing, and the actor has no opportunity for retakes. For a perfectionist like Grant, this would have been an unbearable aspect of the medium even if he had been interested in it. By the time editable film and tape became the norm in television production, Grant had already taken a stand on the issue.

"It was obvious why he didn't want to be seen on television," PETER BOGDANOVICH says. "He was larger than life. And TV tends to make everything smaller than life." Every time MERV GRIFFIN tried to get Grant to appear on his show the answer was cheerful but firm: "Cary would say, 'No, no, no. I can't stand talking about myself.'" And when JACK HALEY, JR., suggested Grant do a television special about his career, "Cary said, 'No. Well, if they paid me a million dollars, I might consider it.' Six weeks later I called him back and said, 'CBS will go for the million.' And he said, 'Oh, Jack, you didn't!' and backed out right away."

Grant's dislike of television ran so deep that even later in life when it came to appearances designed to please his daughter, Jennifer, or charitable causes he strongly supported, he could not make an exception. STEVE ROSS remembers, "When Jennifer was about four or five years old, Cary said he was interested in doing a television project which had a message for young people—something educational in an entertaining form. He wanted to dedicate it to Jennifer, but we were never able to come up with a show."

Over the years television aired an increasing number of awards shows, and friends such as PEGGY LEE expected Cary Grant to receive his due. She says, "I never understood why Cary didn't get any awards. Why did it take the academy all those years to give him an Oscar?"

It wasn't that organizations didn't *try* to give Grant awards; it was that he continually refused. He was forced to decline awards that meant live acceptance speeches in front of millions of viewers. GEORGE STEVENS, JR., explains, "In 1970 and 1971, the early days of the American Film Institute, when it was struggling, the head of the National Endowment for the Arts said to me, 'We'll give you a five-hundred-thousand-dollar matching grant to help solve AFI's immediate problems.' And I thought—matching grant, matching grant, Cary Grant! That's how the idea for the Life Achievement Award was born. Cary sparked my thinking about retrospectives of filmmakers' lives. So I proposed to Cary an evening showing his work at the Kennedy Center." He declined when he learned it was to be televised.

"A couple of years later," STEVENS continues, "I devised the AFI Life Achievement Award and defined it as recognizing those people who throughout their careers had made a contribution to the art of film and whose work had stood the test of time. Again I talked to Cary. This time he said, 'I can't stand up there and make a speech. I get absolutely terrified.'"

As ROBERT WISE recalls, there was at least one other reason: "When I was on the board, I called him on behalf of AFI. He said, 'Oh, no, Bob. I just can't bear to face the public and make a speech. Even *worse*, I can't stand to be there when people get up and say all those things about me. It's too difficult to take.'"

"In March of 1973," STEVENS remembers, "John Ford was chosen as AFI's first recipient. Nixon, his Cabinet, and Kissinger attended. It was the first time in the history of Hollywood when the President of the United States came to an event. The [Washington] Hilton was packed to the rafters. There was terrific excitement. The Marine Band was playing when Cary came through the door, and he said, 'Oh, George, this is just wonderful.' I looked at him and said, 'Cary, this should have been your night.' He smiled with a tear in his eye, just as you would expect Cary to do."

MONTY HALL recalls, "When Variety Clubs [a show business charity] did its salutes every year, Cary sat in the audience. We toasted Reagan, Burt Reynolds, and John Wayne. . . . He always delivered a line or two. He would turn to the camera from where he was sitting and read his lines. He didn't mind saluting others, but he wouldn't let us honor him."

RICH LITTLE even suggested a scripted acceptance to entice Grant into the AFI award: "I said to Cary, 'At the very end of the evening you'll get up, and they'll applaud. You'll go up to the podium, and I'll go with you. The two of us will walk up there, the applause will die down, and then you will lean over and whisper in my ear. Then I'll go to the mike and say, [Little imitating CG] "Thank you very much." And then we'll sit down.' Well, he screamed at that."

Grant's aversion to accepting awards included untelevised ceremonies. It may have been his incredible modesty that made him decline, but whether the event is televised or not, being an honoree means giving a speech, and for Cary Grant giving a speech that wasn't broadcast was just as intimidating as giving one that was.

> CG: I've always been apprehensive about serving as a master of ceremonies since introducing my colleague Walter Pidgeon one night and hearing myself say, "Mr. Privilege, this is indeed a pigeon."

When the Film Society of Lincoln Center originally offered Grant a tribute, he declined. Some years later, William Lockwood (executive director of Lincoln Center's Great Performers Series) tried again personally. Lockwood, who is also a Princeton graduate and director of special programs for Princeton's McCarter Theater, where Grant staged one of his *Conversations* on April 17, 1985, was scheduled to spend two days hosting Grant. Confident he could talk Grant into accepting the award, he told Grant he would arrange the acceptance so he wouldn't have to say anything. A grateful but unbending Cary Grant reminded him that since all the previous honorees had given a speech, it had become an expected part of the program, and he didn't want to be treated differently.

Grant did, in fact, make an occasional exception. He spoke when saluted by the New York Friars Club in 1982 at the Waldorf-Astoria Hotel. It wasn't televised. And he sometimes appeared on the Academy Awards show to present an award to a colleague. In 1970, when the academy awarded him a special Oscar, he was stuck. He had to make a speech.

In December 1981 the fourth annual Kennedy Center Honors feted Grant, Jerome Robbins, Rudolf Serkin, Helen Hayes, and Count Basie for their lifetime contributions to the performing arts in America and to the nation's culture. GEORGE STEVENS, JR., explains, "I think he was so pleased and willing to accept the Kennedy Center honor because even though it was televised, he didn't have to make a speech.

"In the years following Cary's acceptance of the award, he did read the citations to the other recipients at the dinner preceding the show. At the last awards program Cary attended, Budd Schulberg was supposed to toast Elia Kazan from his table. Instead, he went to the podium with a sheath of papers, read his comments, and sat down. When Cary walked to the podium to read, his cue cards were gone. Apparently Schulberg had clutched them to his papers. Fortunately my wife, Liz, had a second set of cards. What would have been a sixty-second glitch for anyone else was a panic for Cary, and he said he'd never do it again. All that ease and grace was part of his craft and part of his work. He didn't want to stumble. He needed to be goddamn good. Well . . . he needed to be 'Cary Grant.'"

In a profitable irony, and to the delight of his fans, Cary Grant's movies frequently appear on television. But he only once appeared in a role written for television, and it gave him an opportunity to use his expert skills as a pantomimist.

In 1950 he was an unbilled guest for Cliff Arquette and David Willock, radio actors who wrote and produced a Los Angeles television show called *Dave and Charley*. Grant liked the show so much he agreed to appear in a sketch. He plays a hobo with just two lines of dialogue.

Grant also made an unscheduled appearance on *The Jack Paar Show*. MERV GRIFFIN remembers that Grant never said a word: "It was the funniest thing. He was seeing a beautiful girl who was a guest on the show, and he sat in the audience. He refused to be on camera, so Jack Paar interviewed the man in front of him. The camera pulled back, and there was Cary sitting in back of the man. Jack never referred to Cary at all. He just interviewed this anonymous man right in front of him. Of course, the audience at home is saying, 'Isn't that Cary Grant sitting behind him? Why is he interviewing. . . .'"

In July 1957 Grant and Betsy Drake went to England, and he made his first trip in five years to Bristol. She stayed in London to make a film. By August 5 Grant was back in Hollywood to film *Houseboat* with Sophia Loren.

Loren had arrived in Hollywood that spring, when United Artists released *The Pride and the Passion*. She and Grant saw each other in the months before they began shooting *Houseboat*. RAY WALSTON says, "On *Kiss Them for Me*, in May and June of 1957, we would break at about six-thirty each night to go to the rushes. All of a sudden Sophia Loren started showing up. She wouldn't come every night, but she was there often. You could tell she and Cary were very fond of one another."

Sophia Loren and Grant had talked about marrying while they were still in Spain, but eventually she married Carlo Ponti. LOREN says, "Cary and I were filming *Houseboat* when Carlo and I were married by proxy in Mexico. Just a few days later playacting and real life mingled when Cary and I filmed our make-believe wedding. I was a radiant bride dressed in a long white gown of antique lace and carrying a bouquet of white roses. It was a vision that returned me to the darkest days of my girlhood in Pozzuoli, where I had cut bride pictures out of old magazines and pasted them in my scrapbook. Now I was living that fantasy wedding with Cary. Mendelssohn's wedding music was playing and Cary was waiting at the altar with a white carnation in his buttonhole.

"I was aware of how painful it was for him to play this scene with me, to have the minister pronounce us man and wife, to take me in his arms and kiss me. It was painful for me, too, his make-believe bride. I could not help thinking of all those lovely times in Spain."

FREDERIQUE JOURDAN says, "He wanted to marry Sophia and would have if she had been available."

On the Houseboat *location, 1957.* IRENE MAYER SELZNICK: *"He was desperately in love with Sophia Loren."*

In 1957 Grant's next project was with his friend Stanley Donen. Their first experience working together was so congenial he agreed to make *Indiscreet* without seeing a script. To produce the film, Grant, Stanley Fox, and Donen decided to form Grandon Productions, Ltd. Donen and Grant, as business partners, quickly became sparring partners.

CG: Stanley and I disagree about many points of picture making, but no disagreement disturbs our mutual regard. Someone once said that if two partners in business are in constant agreement, one of them is unnecessary!

According to DONEN, "Sometimes our lawyers would be locked in battle over the share of the spoils on a movie, and my lawyer would say to me, 'We're never going to get this contract finished. It's impossible.' I would go to Cary and say, 'Cary, for God's sake, won't you just give this up and settle this? In the end you're not even going to know how much money you have. It's just a number on a page. It doesn't mean anything to you. It's just going to be another digit on your numbers.' He didn't see it that way. And eventually I didn't care. The picture got made because of Cary. We got the backing and other actors because he was in it. Cary was lavish in his giving to me. He gave me lots of gifts, always thoughtful ones. Something was always arriving. But in making a deal, it was a struggle."

And DONEN made trenchant observations on the subject of actor-director conflict: "When the director insists or cajoles or implies something about an actor's performance, especially the wonderful ones, he is going right to the core of the most important thing in the actor's life. If you don't get the actor to understand it and agree with you, then there's conflict. Sure, Cary and I had conflicts. If it didn't matter, I gave it up. If it did matter, I tried my best to arrange it."

Donen thought Grant and Ingrid Bergman had been "magical" together in *Notorious* and proposed that they could recapture the chemistry in *Indiscreet*. "When I flew to Rome to see Ingrid," says DONEN, I had an idea of how to make the play *Kind Sir* into a movie. That much was on paper. We hadn't met before. She picked me up at the airport and drove me back to her apartment and explained, 'Before I take you to the hotel, you obviously want to talk to me about the movie. Let's do that first, and then you can go rest.' She took me into a room and closed the door. And said, 'Cary likes you. I've asked about you. Cary wants to do the picture. I'm going to do the picture. Just tell me what it is.'"

Bergman's screen image of the wholesome, virtuous woman had been shattered in 1949, when she left her husband, Dr. Peter Lindstrom, and daughter, Pia, for the Italian director Roberto

Rossellini. To add to the shame of deserting her husband, she was pregnant with Rossellini's child. She was attacked by religious groups and by U.S. senators and was blacklisted by American studios. Bergman and Rossellini married in 1950. Together they had a son and twin girls.

Throughout the widespread industry denunciation, Grant took her side as a friend:

> CG: Ingrid Bergman is a fascinating, full-blooded, yet temperate woman who has the courage to live in accord with her needs and strength enough to accept and benefit from the consequences of her beliefs in an inhibited, critical, and frightened society. Ingrid needs no uninvited busybody to proclaim her debts. She knows and pays them herself.

In March 1950 Bergman wrote to him from Rome, "I shall never forget that you were the first one to give me a kind word of encouragement." They corresponded and talked to each other frequently. On July 28, 1952, she thanked him for his good wishes upon the birth of her "double daughters."

Ingrid Bergman was nominated in 1957 for an Oscar for her performance in *Anastasia*. She was in London playing in *Tea and Sympathy* and asked Grant to accept the award for her if she won. When the academy gave her the Oscar that night, it was Hollywood's vote of confidence in her both as an actress and as a woman. She was forgiven. His acceptance speech was heartfelt:

> CG: It's a privilege to have been asked to be here in case Ingrid won this award and to accept it and try to thank all of you on her behalf. But I have no way of knowing or properly conveying to you the degree and depth of her emotion when she learns the news. I only wish she could be here to have felt the warmth of your enthusiasm when her name was announced as the winner. So, dear Ingrid, if you can hear me now or will see this televised film later, I want you to know that each of the other nominees and all the people with whom you worked on *Anastasia*, and Hitch, and Leo McCarey, and indeed *everyone* here tonight, send you congratulations and love and admiration and every affectionate thought.

CG in one of his favorite scenes, Indiscreet, *1958*.

On March 29, 1957, she wrote Grant to tell him just how she received the award:

> I got the news about the Award in the morning at six o'clock. I said on the phone, "I got it?" The answer was "yes," and I fell asleep again. This seems a very indifferent way of accepting an Oscar. . . . [S]everal hours later [when she was taking a bath, her seven-year-old son rushed into the bathroom with the radio in his hands and] I heard your voice. . . . "if you can hear me now," and I said, "I am here, Cary, in the bathroom!" . . .
>
> That was the moment I really received the Oscar and I felt tears coming to my eyes, having known about it all day but still not getting IT. I got IT in the bathroom. What a place to get an Oscar.

In an interview in May 1957 Grant was asked by a reporter to name his ideal female companions for a hypothetical dinner. His favorite dozen included Ingrid Bergman. He rounded out the list with his first, second, and current wives because "they are all fascinating women, or I wouldn't have married them." Others were Grace Kelly, Deborah Kerr, Suzy Parker, Irene Selznick, Bea Lillie, Janet Gaynor, Mrs. William Paley, and Fleur Cowles Meyer. He said, "The reason I like them is that all can be candid without being tactless about it. In this age of hypocrisy, these women can mentally afford to tell the truth. . . . Some are especially beautiful but, more important, all of them are interesting or amusing . . . very easy and delightful conversationalists."

After Grant made *Indiscreet*, he wanted to give Ingrid Bergman a memento of the picture. BEA SHAW recalls: "He remembered one day on the set she had shown him her children's baby teeth. She didn't know what to do with them, but she couldn't bear to throw them away. Cary said, 'I took the baby teeth to a jeweler and had them set in a gold bracelet for her. She loved it.'"

> CG: *Indiscreet* was one of my favorites, and one of the most economical to make because there was a small cast. We did very well with it. It successfully contrasted with a new wave of violence in films.

To promote *Indiscreet*, Grant again went on the road speaking in theaters. In Great Britain alone, Grant traveled to nine cities—Kingston, Hammersmith, Glasgow, Edinburgh, Dublin, Birmingham, Liverpool, Leeds, and Belfast. He stepped onstage in each city and answered questions for up to forty-five minutes following the film. People asked questions ranging from "Are you in love with Ingrid Bergman?" to "Why are credit titles so lengthy?" Warner Bros. officials were impressed with Grant's energy and enthusiasm and called the promotion a success.

RODERICK MANN first realized how shy Grant was in Dublin when he was promoting *Indiscreet*. He recalls: "He was a nervous wreck. Later, on other occasions, I noticed he would look around and not want to be recognized. He dreaded having eye contact with people when they came up to see him."

MONTY HALL says, "Cary fluctuated between 'Leave me alone' and 'What do you want me to do?' We were in Seattle for a convention in the late 1970s, and I was going into a meeting of forty or so presidents of Variety Clubs when I saw Cary walking down the hall. He had just finished breakfast. I said, 'Do you want to do something good? Just pop in and make an appearance.' And he said, 'Okay.' Now that's not Cary. Cary didn't say okay to those things. He shied away from them. So I went inside and told the meeting I had found someone strolling the halls, would they make him feel comfortable? They looked at me as though I were crazy. Cary walked in. They just fell apart. They couldn't believe the waif I was bringing in was Cary—bigger than life—Grant. I never saw anything like it. He kibitzed with them in that other Cary Grant attitude, the one that's giggling and smiling. There was the one who shied away from people and then there was the one who could just walk in a room with that seventy-million-dollar smile and that shy, captivating giggle.

"I don't think it was a question of his having a good day or a bad day. It was different facets of his personality. You had to catch him in the right mood. He fluctuated in his confidence in himself, which amazed me. He was one of the three greatest actors of our generation. When he walked on the set and the cameras were on him, he could do no wrong. He knew he had command. Being out of that milieu made him uncomfortable."

According to GEORGE BARRIE, "He didn't know how to express himself away from the film industry until he got involved with Fabergé. He was brilliant when he could ad-lib. He got to the point where he could get up and volunteer to speak."

Grant and James Stewart appeared on the Academy Awards show together in 1984. They both experienced stage fright, and Grant later speculated that it "had to do with being with our peers." JAMES STEWART explains the depths of his own stage fright: "Oh [gesturing with his hands to indicate nervousness], I'm al—I'm—I'm worse than that. I've had stage fright ever since the first time I went on the stage in New York. I was in a stock company in Falmouth, Massachusetts, which I figured was a way to spend a summer vacation. But when I got interested in acting and learned the demands that were going to be made of me, I developed stage fright. I still have it. Even if I'm only cutting a ribbon. I'm going to Washington with [wife] Gloria [Stewart], and while I'm there, I'm lunching with a few senators to try to get colorization killed. And I'm frightened. I have stage fright about it. Then there's a tribute to Bette Davis in New York. I'm going to introduce Bette. I've started the fright now, and it's two weeks away.

"But it's an amazing thing. The minute you get started, you're all right. Kim Novak and I gave the awards for sound at the Academy Awards this year, and I was like this [again gesturing with his hands to indicate nervousness]. It went fine, but I was glad when it was over.

"I always resented Henry Fonda. He would eat an enormous steak dinner right before an appearance, then go on, give a great performance, go someplace afterward, and have another steak. I would want to shoot him."

Grant insisted it was impossible to be good, no matter what one's profession was, unless you were nervous. STEWART continues, "Well, I've heard that, too. But the minute you get into something and start doing it, the fright leaves.

"I did several productions of the play *Harvey*. The last time was in London, and my hearing was going bad. I couldn't hear my cues, although I was standing backstage right by the door. So I bought flashlights for the stage manager, who was stage left. When I was center stage, he'd station stagehands with flashlights, and they'd just flash the lights for me to come in. Once I got onstage, I could hear and everything was just fine. But standing there was awful.

"I don't know where it comes from. I've talked to athletes that have it. I don't know whether it's a disease or whether it's just something you're lacking in your mind. I haven't had anybody explain to me what it is. I've heard it said that if you are completely satisfied with what you are doing, then you don't have stage fright. But if I have the least question about what I'm doing, I have it."

> CG: I studied the problem, and it finally came to me that the audience wasn't making me nervous. I was making myself nervous. Nobody ever buys a ticket hoping to see a lousy show. Or to hear a terrible speech. Or to see any performers fail. They want every actor to be Olivier. They want every ballplayer to hit home runs and make impossible catches. That way they can tell their friends they were in the theater or the ball park when it happened. . . . Most audiences are pussycats. Give them half a chance and they'll love you.

JOHN FORSYTHE and Grant discussed the problem of nerves: "Cary asked me one day, 'How are you when you start a movie?' I said, 'Nervous. Why do you ask?' He said, 'Nervous? You should see me. I was so bad that when I started to own part of the movies I was in, we generally scrapped the first and second day of work.' You really have to have a lot of muscle to do that on a picture because it costs a lot of money to scrap two days. Obviously Cary did."

Grant told BEA SHAW, "The only time you give a bad performance is when you're self-conscious. Inside, everyone is beautiful. You just have to let the child come through."

CHAPTER ELEVEN

"MADAME, WE'RE MAKING A MOVIE"

CG: All my films were favorites in many ways. In one I loved the director but not the leading lady. In another it was the script but not the cast. Still another would be a box-office hit. An awful lot of stuff goes into the making of a film. If it all jells, then you've got a pretty good one.

So said Grant in public. Privately Grant admitted he especially liked *The Awful Truth, His Girl Friday, Bringing Up Baby, Gunga Din, The Philadelphia Story, None but the Lonely Heart, Notorious, To Catch a Thief, Indiscreet, Charade, Father Goose,* and *North by Northwest.*

North by Northwest was to be his last film with the enigmatic but brilliant director Alfred Hitchcock. It was a record-breaking smash hit. It was Grant's twenty-third picture to play Radio City Music Hall, a record unmatched at the time. He had seventy-five weeks to his credit. Fred Astaire, with forty-eight weeks, was his closest competitor. Grant's single-longest run was eight weeks in *Notorious*.

When *North by Northwest* was released, Grant was thrilled to have been part of it, but during the production he had reservations that terrified the film's screenwriter, ERNEST LEHMAN, who says, "Cary was charming, thoughtful, and at times surprisingly worrisome.

"We were in the last weeks before shooting began. Jimmy Stewart had badly wanted the leading role, but Mr. Hitchcock and I wanted Cary. The ink on the deal had dried, and suddenly all Cary could think about and talk about was how desperately he wanted out of the movie.

"The role was all wrong for him. The picture would be a disaster, et cetera, et cetera. Apparently Hitch was accustomed to this sort of thing from Cary, so he just shrugged his shoulders and held fast. MGM held on, too. But I was unnerved by all his doubts. Did he know something we didn't know? I wondered.

"Now Hitch was shooting the Plaza Hotel sequences in New York. The scenes were supposed to be amusing, but Cary frowned darkly as he muttered an aside to me: 'The trouble with Hitch is he doesn't know how to do comedy.'

"Then we were out in Bakersfield, California, doing the crop duster sequence. It was a hundred and ten degrees in the shade, and between takes Cary requested my presence in the backseat of his air-conditioned limousine—to hear his complaints about my screenplay: Why did his character have to carry all the exposition? 'And what about this dialogue? You think you've written a Cary Grant picture? This is a David Niven picture.'

"It came time for the first sneak preview up in Santa Barbara. Everyone connected with the picture was there—except me. I was taking no chances. I had heard enough from Cary to know it was going to be a disaster. Let the others be trapped in it but not me!

"The next day, all the next day, I paced the carpet of my office. Finally it was late afternoon, and not a soul had called me. Obviously Santa Barbara had been a catastrophe. I couldn't stand it any longer. I had to get out of the office, get in the car, drive somewhere—anywhere—just get away from the awful truth. . . .

"Then, the phone rang. It was my secretary. 'It's Cary Grant,' she said.

"'Cary Grant!' I said. 'Tell him I've left for the day!'

"'But I already told him you were in. . . .'

"I braced myself. 'Ernie! Wasn't it marvelous?'

"'Wasn't *what* marvelous?'

"'Santa Barbara. Last night. Weren't you there?' he asked.

"'No.'

"Ernie, you missed the most fantastic preview I've ever been to. You never *heard* such audience reaction. They laughed; they gasped; they cheered. And the response cards! You should

On the set of North by Northwest *with Alfred Hitchcock, 1958. It was CG's last film with the director, who said, "Cary's the only actor I ever loved in my whole life."*

see those cards. I can't begin to describe what an exciting night it was. I'm calling just to tell you how thrilled I am for you. For all of us!'"

"Just as I said. Charming, thoughtful, but at times . . ."

Grant modestly acknowledged during his career that his box-office successes were directly linked to the quality of directors he had chosen since becoming a free-lance actor:

CG: I gravitated to men such as Hitchcock, George Stevens, George Cukor, Howard Hawks, Stanley Donen, and Leo McCarey. They understood me. They permitted me the release of improvisation during the rehearsing of each scene. They let me discover how far out I could go with confidence. I got accustomed to being with certain people, and I am deeply indebted to each of them.

Hitch and I had a rapport and understanding deeper than words. He was a very agreeable human being, and we were very compatible. I always went to work whistling when I worked with him because everything on the set was just as you envisioned it would be. Nothing ever went wrong. He was so incredibly well prepared. I never knew anyone as capable. He was a tasteful, intelligent, decent, and patient man who knew the actor's business as well as he knew his own. He could be very calm in the most difficult of situations. A fire broke out once on the set, and he just looked around and asked someone to take care of it so we could finish the shoot.

Hitch also had a wonderful sense of humor. On the set he would make up names for the crew members. We called it the Hitchcock Comedy Crew. This will give you an idea of what we thought was funny:

Cameraman: Otto Focus
Cutter: Eddy Tor
Hairdresser: Herr Dresser
Script girl: Mime O'Graph
Publicist: Bill Board
Director: Fay Doubt or Manny Takes

Villain: Mike Shadow
Gag man: Joe King
Production manager: Bud Get

Grant's files contain a listing of more "crew members":

Assistant cameraman: Phil Mer
Ingenue: Dolly Shot
Electrician: Alec Trician or Xavier Arcs
Body make-up woman: Mae Kupp
Stand-in: Stan Din
Ballet dancer: Pan Ova
Camera crew: Matt Box or Otto Frame
Lens cleaner: Anna Morphic
Drapery department: Cy Clorama
Writer: Ty Pwrighter
Wrangler: E. Z. Trot

Grant loved this kind of wordplay and told RICK INGERSOLL about the games he and Stanley Donen played between scenes: "One was called Mixed Emotions—dry wit, shredded ego, warm handshakes, and so forth. Another was Unlikely Couples— Tennessee and Esther Williams. As a joke, he threw in Gene and Betsy Kelly, because they were married but an unlikely couple.

"I told Cary the name game would make a wonderful feature for publication. He said, 'I was thinking that. Let me get my friend Bennett Cerf on the phone.' From his dressing room he called Cerf, who was writing a Sunday supplement called 'This Week.' Cerf loved the idea. In effect, Cary had devised it. We made up all these unlikely couples, and they ran it as an important feature."

> CG: I've always liked playing with names. Shirley Synagogue instead of Shirley Temple. Gregory Bushel. Kirk Boeing. What about Bob Despair? Red Zippers. Ben Purple. Ed Wynn—Place or Show. Stan Eucalyptus and Oliver Softy. What about Sid Caligula and Imogene Ovaltine? Elaine September and Mike Quarters.
>
> I also liked to make up fractured French. *Coup de grâce:* a lawn mower. *Vin ordinaire:* a Volkswagen bus.

Tête-à-tête: tight brassiere. *Café au lait:* whorehouse.
Mal-de-mer: Mummy's sick. *Chateaubriand:* my hat's on
fire. *Pas de deux:* father of twins.

JILL ST. JOHN remembers "playing a word game with Lance
and Cary and Betsy Drake related to food. Instead of ground
meat, it was ground floor; fresh bluepoints/fresh viewpoints;
sweet peas/sweet talk; buttered carrots/buttered up."

QUINCY JONES's daughter and grandson loved spending
Sundays at Grant's house playing word games, especially "My
Aunt Loves Coffee, but She Hates Tea." He recalls: "Sometimes
I would get into a lot of mixed metaphors. The way I expressed
things cracked Cary up because it was so un-British. For instance,
I would say, 'I'm getting to the age where I've got to start making
some more horizontal money.' He asked me what that meant. I
explained, 'Well, when I'm up in the studio conducting, that's
vertical money. But when you're at home watching TV and *An
Affair to Remember* comes on, that's horizontal money.' Cary
talked about that for years. He told all his friends."

While Grant was filming *North by Northwest,* he enjoyed
Hitchcock's lighter side:

> CG: Hitch's humor was droll and quick. A newspaper-
> man once upbraided him, asking, "Why do you always
> make these terrible murder things?" Hitch quipped
> back, "Why do you always put them on the front page?"

"Cary and Hitchcock had a mutual respect for one another,"
says RICK INGERSOLL. "Hitchcock liked people he felt comfortable
with—people he didn't *have* to direct. He loved working with
James Stewart for the same reason."

Grant prized his relationship with the director and proudly
introduced him to George Barrie. Shortly before Hitchcock died,
he told BARRIE, "Knowing Cary is the greatest association I've had
with any film actor. Cary's the only actor I ever loved in my
whole life."

Grant invested in *North by Northwest* and negotiated an unusual contract that gave him approval of nearly every aspect of
the film. "I was told to read Cary's contract thoroughly because
it spelled out exactly what he expected," remembers RICK INGER-
SOLL. "Cary was wonderful as long as you obeyed the letter of his

contract. He would do whatever you asked. If there was a violation and he didn't feel like doing it, he wouldn't do it. He told me his contract had been developed over the years. He said that each time something happened on a film that he didn't like, he would remember to cover that in the next contract.

"In *North by Northwest,* for example, his name, Cary Grant, is nine letters. Eva Marie Saint is thirteen. You put them side by side, and Eva Marie Saint dominates. You put them one on top of each other, and Eva Marie Saint dominates simply because her name has more letters. So Cary not only got top billing, but his name covered the same amount of space as his costar's. In this case, 'Cary Grant' is stretched out to fill in the same space as 'Eva Marie Saint.' When they were pictured in advertising, his photo always appeared on the left, not on the right.

"All these conditions were there for a reason. They were not capricious or temperamental. His contract also provided a limousine solely for his use. Nobody else could use it. He said, 'Too often I've been on location, ready to go the forty miles back to the studio when they say, "You'll have to wait for so-and-so." Then I wait forty minutes for the leading lady to get ready. Then we have to wait for her makeup man to come along, and suddenly I'm not only waiting a full hour, but I'm scrooched in between a dozen people. It's terribly uncomfortable for everybody. So I have an agreement that only I can invite someone to come with me.' Now, he was always inviting someone to ride with him. He never kept it selfishly for himself. But why should he wait forty minutes for somebody rude enough to keep him waiting?"

Grant's personal involvement extended to other members of the cast, crew, and staff. RICK INGERSOLL recalls, "Cary included us in everything. In Chicago he insisted Eva Marie and I have lunch in the Ambassador Hotel in the Pump Room. At that time it was the room of rooms in the hotel of hotels. And of course, we got a wonderful table. I ordered a bacon, lettuce, and tomato sandwich on white bread. When it came, it was a four-by-four-inch-square double slice of bread with the crusts cut off. Cary said, 'Wait a minute, Rick. What is that?' I told him, and then Cary asked the waiter what it was. When the waiter told him, Cary said, 'This looks like a bacon, lettuce, and tomato canapé. Mr. Ingersoll ordered a bacon, lettuce, and tomato sandwich. You've cut it practically to the bone. There's nothing left, and look at what you're charging for this. (The charge was probably four dollars and fifty cents, which in those days was a huge amount of money for a sandwich.) I insist you take this back to the kitchen and bring Mr. Ingersoll a proper bacon, lettuce, and tomato sandwich!' The waiter hustled off saying, 'Oh, yes, Mr. Grant. Yes, Mr. Grant.' Eva Marie and I sat there dying. I would have eaten it meekly, not said a word, and paid the bill. I told Cary he had more guts than I had, and he said, 'You owe it not only to yourself but to future customers.'"

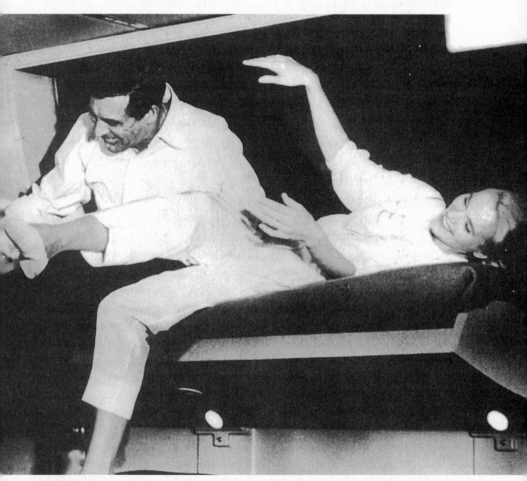

Off camera with Eva Marie Saint in North by Northwest, *1959, CG's twenty-third picture to play Radio City Music Hall, a record unmatched at the time.*

221

Throughout his life Grant never hesitated to demand what he thought was right, especially when it came to food. His displeasure with the English muffin service at the Plaza Hotel is now legendary. Instead of two halves of an English muffin, he was served one. Outraged, Grant spent a fortune on international telephone calls to track down his friend Conrad Hilton, then owner of the Plaza, to ask him if this was the way he ran a first-class hotel. Such stories led to the gossip that Grant could squeeze a dollar until Washington cried.

Understandably Grant did not like to feel taken advantage of. MICKY ZEILER points out: "He wanted one hundred cents on the dollar. I admired him for that. It wasn't that he was tightfisted because he was a very generous man. Every time I went to Bergdorf's to buy Jennifer's baby clothes, Cary would look at the bill and say, 'These things are not too expensive, are they?' He didn't mind the cost, but he wanted to be sure he wasn't paying too much."

During the filming of *North by Northwest* Grant and Betsy Drake decided to make their estrangement public. A news release went out on October 17, 1958:

> After careful consideration and long discussion, we have decided to live apart. We have had, and shall always have, a deep love and respect for each other but, alas, our marriage has not brought us the happiness we fully expected and mutually desired. So, since we have no children needful of our affection, it is consequently best that we separate for a while. We have purposefully issued this public statement to the newspaper writers who have been so kind to us in the past, in order to forestall the usual misinformed gossip and conjecture. There are no plans for divorce, and we ask only that the press respect our statement as being complete, and our friends to be patient with, and understanding of, our decision.

Grant handled the highly emotional situation with professional ease. RICK INGERSOLL describes his methodical approach: "He brought out four different photographs of him and Betsy Drake. He said, 'This picture is for Louella Parsons, this one is for Hedda Hopper, this one is for the Associated Press, and this is for the United Press. Be sure and give this story to Louella immediately so she can get it in the bulldog edition. Then, at five-twenty, give the story to Hedda Hopper. Now, she will have it at the same time Louella has it, but she will not be able to beat Louella's break on the news. Then you give it to the Associated Press at seven o'clock and the United Press. . . .' He had the whole thing mapped out—the deadlines of the columnists. He knew exactly what to do. I was overwhelmed. I was amazed. Cary had the most knowledge of public relations and publicity of anybody I've ever known. He knew exactly what made news and what didn't make news."

But his adroit handling of public relations was designed in the main to minimize press interference in his personal life. LESLIE CARON explains, "He thought too much publicity wasn't necessarily good for a star, that revealing your private life made you into someone average. He thought mystery was essential. When we were shooting *Father Goose*, the press was hounding me because I was getting a divorce. Cary advised me not to do interviews—and he was right."

Grant gave PETER BOGDANOVICH similar advice in the mid-1970s, when Bogdanovich was in the midst of a very public love affair: "[Bogdanovich imitating CG] People *do not like* beautiful people, Peter, remember that. And they do not like *happy* people either. Don't ever tell anyone you're *happy* because most people aren't at *all* happy. And certainly do not *ever* tell people you're in love."

Generally Grant cooperated with the press and the public when he thought he could, but there was one issue on which he took a *very* firm stance: autographs.

RICK INGERSOLL explains: "Cary was always pleasant to people. He was only very strict in terms of autographs. During the filming of *North by Northwest* at Mount Rushmore he came out of the men's room, furious. He said, 'You ask why I don't like to give autographs? I'll tell you why. I'm standing there at the urinal, and there's a man standing next to me at a urinal. His right hand is occupied holding himself while he urinates. He looks over, sees me, and says, 'My God, it's Cary Grant!' He switches his penis to his left hand and takes his right hand and slaps it into my hand. Now that's the last place in the world I want to be interrupted.'

"Because we were a captive audience at Mount Rushmore (and I understand he had done this before), he would charge tourists a quarter for his autograph. He got Eva Marie to agree to the same thing. Then they took the money and donated it to the Motion Picture Relief Fund."

CG: Autographs are ridiculous. When I sign one, it starts a chain reaction. I'm not able to do anything else for the rest of the day.

CLEVELAND AMORY recounts his experience at Dodger Stadium: "It was really incredible. People would come up, and he would use these wonderful lines to turn them off in such a way that was both funny and nice. But we literally didn't get to watch any of the practice and everything baseball fans like to watch because he had to talk to this steady stream of people who were coming up to him."

CG: This kind of thing goes on from the time you leave your hotel until you go to bed at night. One time I was walking through an airport loaded down with luggage. I had a bag in each hand and one under my arm, and a guy running after me asking for an autograph. I turned and asked him, "Now, how do you expect me to do that? With my foot?"

"Cary got his way without offending anyone," ABIGAIL VAN BUREN says. "Maybe they didn't go away with an autograph, but they certainly got a lot of cute patter."

STANLEY DONEN believes most people were reasonably gentle when they asked Grant for his autograph. But, he adds, "Adults are embarrassed and feel odd about it. We were having dinner one night, and a man walked over to Cary with a piece of paper and a pen. And he shoved them under Cary's nose. And said, 'Sign this.' Just like that. And Cary looked up at him and said, 'No.' And the man said, 'What do you mean, "No"?' And Cary said, 'No.' And the man said, 'Who do you think you are?' And Cary said, 'You know perfectly well who I am, but I don't know who you are. So go away.' He normally would have signed it, but the man had no grace, no polite quality."

At one of Grant's *Conversations* a man explained to Grant that an autograph was an opportunity to meet him. Grant smiled and told him, "Well, you can do that by coming up here to shake my hand." So, while the man was making his way to the stage to shake his hand, Grant said to the audience: "I've heard every excuse to get an autograph: 'I've always wanted to meet you' or 'Oh, they'll never believe I met you!' And I'll ask, 'Your relatives won't believe you?' If they say, 'My wife will kill me if I don't get your autograph!' Then I say, 'You have that kind of relationship with your wife?' Or they say, 'I hate to do this, but . . .' And I say, 'Wait a minute, never do anything you hate to do.'"

On February 15, 1984, when Grant was doing an evening's *Conversation* at Johns Hopkins University in Baltimore, Maryland, a woman in the audience begged to shake his hand. He agreed to have her join him. When she got to the stage, she leaned forward and kissed him right on the lips. In his inimitable style Grant looked around her and said to the audience, "Just a minute. We'll be right back."

When Grant spoke at the La Mirada (California) Civic Theater on January 31, 1986, an elderly woman also prevailed.

CG: She was very old . . . probably in her nineties, but she had a lot of spunk. She was very insistent and also quite amusing. She wanted to have her picture taken with me. Of course, I had to tell her that it would start a chain reaction. But she kept on and said, "But my friends won't believe me." So I asked her what kind of friends she had. And she said, "They won't believe that you were actually here and that I got to meet and talk to you." I finally invited her to come to the stage. She made her way in her walker, with her nurse giving her assistance. It took a long time for her to get to me, but she was determined.

The only time RICK INGERSOLL saw Grant become impatient was when he was shooting a scene for *North by Northwest* in front of the United Nations: "Hitchcock was hidden with the camera across the street. Cary was to drive up in a taxi, jump out, and run into the United Nations Building. As Cary pulled up and jumped out of the cab, a woman recognized him and said, 'Cary Grant!' She ran over to get his autograph. He said, 'Madame, *we are making a movie.*' It was so funny because she couldn't see a camera."

It wasn't always funny. "Cary told me how frightening it could be to be mobbed by crowds," BEA SHAW remembers. "He said, 'I've learned to relax. You can get hurt if you tense up and you're being pushed this way and that.'"

"Sometimes Cary needed police protection," ABIGAIL VAN BUREN says. "People mobbed him. They wouldn't let him alone. They were in such awe of him. They told him he was the one person they wanted to meet. We often escaped through a side door."

And CLEVELAND AMORY recalls how impossible it was for Grant just to take a walk down Fifth Avenue: "It started slowly, with people gathering and then walking fast to keep up. It was really like the beginning of a parade. As we marched down the sidewalk, it got really hopeless. We were totally blocked. I ran for a cab. In all my dealings with celebrities, I have never seen such a draw.

"Once Cary was staying at the Sherry-Netherland in New York, and he ordered up tea. When the waiter brought it, Cary went to the door, and the waiter went right by him and put the tea down. Then he looked around and for the first time saw him. 'Jesus Christ!' he said. And Cary just grinned that grin of his and said, 'No, Cary Grant.'"

CHAPTER TWELVE

COMING FULL CIRCLE

CG: I get stared at all the time. It's annoying. And I certainly do get tired of it. I don't like to be ungracious, but I scowl at times. It goes on all day long. As soon as I get into an elevator, a silence falls, and I know everyone is looking at me. Then why do I get up here on this podium? I don't actually know why. Maybe, after all these years, I'm used to it and no longer want to avoid it. Maybe I even like it.

Everywhere Cary Grant went in 1958, he was mobbed. At fifty-four he evoked the kind of response usually reserved for teen idols like Elvis Presley.

After filming *Indiscreet* in London, Grant took a pleasure trip to Moscow and Leningrad. Film producer Sam Spiegel had invited Grant and Howard Hawks's former wife Slim (then Mrs. Leland) Hayward, who was accompanied by her close friend, author Truman Capote. The Russians had invited Spiegel to show three of his films, *The Bridge on the River Kwai*, *On the Waterfront*, and *The African Queen*. In return, Spiegel and his guests would see some Soviet films. Grant was able to relax completely and enjoy himself because he was in a world cut off from American movies.

CG: Nobody knew who I was. It was the first time in twenty-five years I could walk down the street without people pointing at me.

Perhaps the man in the street didn't recognize him, but the *Moscow News* didn't miss the opportunity. Interview, March 5, 1958:

> CG: . . . I have always regretted the tensions and relations between our countries. I came here from London just out of curiosity. . . . Moscow gave me the opportunity of a real rest in the most friendly conditions. And without the annoying and really stupid autograph collectors.
>
> I have noticed here a mutual attraction of the Russians and Americans in the field of art. In particular, I value very highly the work of the late [Sergei] Eisenstein, the Soviet film director, who is quite famous in America, and here I saw the antiwar picture *The Cranes Fly Over [The Cranes Are Flying]*, which is a marvelous creation reminiscent of Eisenstein productions. I am not a politician. I am an artist. And I hope the recently concluded U.S.-Soviet cultural agreement holds in store for me an opportunity of coming here again as an actor.

When Grant returned to the United States, he said he admired the people in Russia. They were obliging and had no animosity toward Americans. When asked about Russian women, he said, "It was really quite difficult to see them because they bundle themselves up from eyebrows to anklebone and wear heavy scarves over their heads." He was amused that he had created a stir by walking around hatless. "All the men wear black fur hats. They stared at me as though I were crazy."

Grant went to England for Christmas in 1958 and spent the holiday in Bristol with his mother.

Desite his popularity, Grant now limited himself to making one picture a year. He was one of the best-paid actors in Hollywood, in the company of Frank Sinatra, Marlon Brando, and William Holden. He worked on a percentage basis, averaging five hundred thousand dollars per picture against 10 percent of the gross and could easily make seven figures if the film did well at the box office.

By 1959 he was paying 91.3 percent of his income in taxes. Yet tax havens never attracted him.

CG: I could have been [one of] the first to use the Swiss escape route from taxes, back in 1939. Forget the tax. You can't run away from it. Go to Switzerland and what happens? You're trapped. Hemmed in. You sacrifice your freedom. And you'd be surprised at how many stars get homesick. They have to make quick nocturnal forays into the outside world. Money isn't worth it.

On January 24, 1959, he started *Operation Petticoat*. Blake Edwards directed the Stanley Shapiro and Maurice Richlin screenplay from an unpublished story by Paul King and Joseph Stone. MAURICE RICHLIN explained, "The first choice of romantic comedy writers was Cary Grant. *Operation Petticoat* was supposed to be a studio picture costing about a million dollars and shot in black and white. But Robert Arthur, the producer, had a friend who slipped Cary the script. When Cary said yes, the budget jumped to more than three million (a lot in those days) and went into color. If the film had been black and white, the now famous pink submarine would have been white. It was the pink submarine that led me to *The Pink Panther*, which I did a couple of years later. Pink strikes comedy writers as a funny color."

The pink submarine became the most memorable character in the film. Unable to procure gray paint, the supply officer (played by Tony Curtis) mixes the paints he gets, which turn out to be red and white.

CG: It actually happened to a submarine during the Second World War. It's taken right from the submariner's log.

It was Grant's idea to cast DINA MERRILL in the film. She recalls: "Cary asked me to be in *Operation Petticoat* and wanted me to play the part of his girl friend, which called for a woman with an enormous chest, which I, unfortunately, didn't have. I was devastated. I said, 'What about padding?' He said, 'No, no, no. That would never do.'" In the end she was cast as Curtis's girl friend.

MERRILL also remembers Grant's generosity toward a much younger member of the cast: "There was a darling little five-year-old Cuban girl who played one of the native children being herded on board the submarine when they heard the Japanese were going to bomb the island where they lived. This little girl was absolutely thrilled that she was going to be an extra. She thought she was going to get dressed up in a pretty dress. She was in tears when she found out she had to wear just a little cotton shift with tatters because she was playing a native islander. She cried and cried, which worked fine for the scene, but the poor child was really upset.

"So Cary, seeing all of this, sent his assistant down to the store and bought her the most beautiful little pink party dress with tulle. And at the end of the day, when she was finished with her work, he presented it to her. You've never seen such an expression on a child's face in your life. It was so thoughtful and kind and loving of him to do that."

Grant and Tony Curtis became close friends on the picture. PETER STONE remembers, "One day Tony said to Cary, 'You live in Palm Springs. I'd like to get a house there. Do you know of any good houses?' And Cary said, 'I'll sell you my house. I'll give it to you for a hundred thousand dollars.' Tony said, 'What do you mean? That's nothing.' Cary said, 'I know.' Tony wanted to know the catch. Cary said, 'You will it to me.' Tony was outraged by the notion—that Cary felt he was going to outlive him and get the house back. Cary thought he was going to outlive everybody."

"Cary had been a star years before most of us had even thought of going to Hollywood," MAURICE RICHLIN said. "Everyone on the picture was in awe of him. Tony Curtis thought that being in a film with Cary Grant was the greatest moment in his life. But he was also worried. He had just played the lady-killer in *Some Like It Hot,* in which he used an impersonation of Cary Grant's voice for a characterization."

When Grant was asked who did the best Cary Grant impersonation, he said, "I do, although Tony Curtis does a pretty good job."

CG: When Tony was living aboard ship in the Navy during World War II, the crew would go out for long periods of time. They only had a limited number of films on board. One of them was *Gunga Din*. They got so tired of listening to it over and over that they turned the sound off and acted out the different roles. Tony played me.

There have been many impersonations of Grant, of course. In addition to Curtis, his friends Peter Bogdanovich, George Stevens, Jr., and Steve Lawrence all do excellent imitations. Steve Allen once sent Grant a tape of Peter Sellers and Allen addressing the other in the guise of Cary Grant. His most successful mimic, RICH LITTLE, who also became his friend, remembers: "Cary would see me coming at a party. He'd light up and say: [Little imitating CG] 'Oh, my God, here I come.' Then he'd turn to Barbara and say, 'I'm looking younger every day, aren't I? Look at me.'

"His voice changed as he matured. When he was younger, the voice was up here like this in *Gunga Din*. It was more cockney and much higher. 'Now listen, Sergeant Ballantine, I'm telling you—' At the end of his life everything was down here like this. His voice was very husky. . . . The later Cary Grant is the most interesting one for me and the easiest.

"Cary knew I imitated him at different ages. At parties he'd say, 'Do Cary Grant,' as though I was just doing some other actor. So I'd do a little joke or something, and he'd get a big thrill out of it. Then he'd say, 'What age were you doing? I'd say that's about thirty-five, right?' And I said, 'No, thirty-two.' 'Oh, thirty-two. Yes, of course.'

"Some stars are a little self-conscious about being imitated. They don't really want to hear it. Maybe I exaggerate them too much or pick up on a mannerism they don't want to be reminded of. Some don't want you to show that little idiosyncrasy around others. But Cary was never self-conscious. He loved it. . . .

"He had such a great sense of humor. One time we were in Denver for Marvin Davis's Carousel Ball, which benefited diabetes, and Cary was trying to explain something to a reporter. He turned to me and said, 'Rich, you do me better than I do. Tell him what I'm thinking.'

"I did a children's album with 'Peter and the Wolf' on one side and 'Babar the Elephant' on the other. I narrated the whole thing as Cary. I sent the album to him, and he said, 'It's too bad you weren't around when I was dubbing movies. We could have saved a lot of time.'"

Operation Petticoat was a huge hit, even with the military. Representatives of the Army, Navy, and the Office of the Assistant Secretary of Defense praised the film. A letter in Grant's files addressed to Robert Arthur, the film's producer, from the Office of the Assistant Secretary of Defense shows appreciation that "the story shows the wonderful ingenuity and spirit of a crew to keep the ship afloat and in the battle." They were so enthusiastic they even offered to help develop another picture.

Grant liked the relaxed atmosphere and sense of camaraderie on the lot at Universal. He decorated his office, which he shared with Stanley Fox, with a blend of burgundy-colored leather couches and Spanish, Portuguese, and Brazilian furniture and mementos from his trip to Spain.

PETER STONE describes the bungalows at the studio: "There were about twenty-five charming little duplexes. They were surrounded by lawns, with rabbits running around. Each bungalow had two offices and two different entrances, with little kitchens, and secretaries' and writers' rooms. Stars, producers, directors, and writers had their own bungalows. Hitchcock had more than a bungalow; he had a building—a whole production unit. Jack Benny, Rock Hudson, Marlon Brando, Cary, Tony Curtis, Jimmy Stewart, Doris Day, Audrey Hepburn, Shirley MacLaine, and Elizabeth Taylor were all on the lot. We all used to sit on the front porch of our bungalows in the afternoon and chat with everybody." Maurice Richlin and Stan Shapiro and Robert Arthur worked in the bungalow that adjoined Grant's. RICHLIN recollects: "There was a doorway between the two, and he would saunter in, lie down on the couch, and talk. He was always telling us to see our mothers whenever we got the chance."

NICKY BLAIR remembers that Stanley Shapiro never washed his car and adds, "None of us could stand it anymore, so one day on the lot we all washed his Rolls-Royce—including Cary."

These pleasant days at Universal came to an end when MCA took over. A black high rise replaced the bungalows, and a new commissary, without any windows, was built.

The bungalows gave Grant an opportunity to mingle with writers. According to MAURICE RICHLIN, "A writer in Hollywood, even when he's doing well, is looked down upon by everyone else. In radio, television, and motion pictures, all writers were called the boys. 'Call the boys in,' they'd say. Cary called us authors. You can't realize what a compliment that was."

JERRY D. LEWIS says, "At every studio there used to be a writers' table in the commissary. Nobody could sit there unless they were a writer. One time at Paramount Adolphe Menjou sat at the writers' table, and all the writers got up and left. But they invited Cary to join them."

SIDNEY SHELDON believes that comedies were often written with Grant in mind, adding: "If he turned the project down, we would have to drop about ten levels for the next actor. It was never 'Cary or—' He was absolutely in a class by himself."

PETER STONE explains Grant's prejudice when it came to stories set in foreign countries: "You couldn't do a foreign script with him where the people spoke English instead of the other language. *The Pride and the Passion* cured him of that. He said, 'It's ridiculous. You're supposed to be speaking French and so you speak English with a French accent?'"

MAURICE RICHLIN discovered Grant's prejudice when he and Stanley Shapiro wrote a script for him: "Stan and I were told by Universal that they wanted to pair Gina Lollobrigida and Cary Grant in a picture set in Italy. So we wrote *Come September*. In it there were a lot of young people from various countries in the film, and Cary wanted them each to speak their own language. We told him that was difficult, that we'd have to use captions. I said, 'What about Romeo and Juliet? They spoke English.' And he replied, 'That's Shakespeare.' For which there is no reply. He wouldn't do it, so we ended up with Rock Hudson and Lollobrigida."

Some of Hollywood's best screenwriters and journalists became Grant's friends. "I spent a lot of time with him," BILLY WILDER says. "In the early years I would see him in Palm Springs, and then we became friends when we became members of the board of directors of the Norton Simon Museum in Pasadena. We would meet there and at friends' houses—mostly the [Gregory] Pecks. We always had a good time together. We talked about life, food, paintings, collecting, about music—a wide range of things. We exchanged addresses of good restaurants. This was the type of relationship we had. He would come to the house, and we would talk about art. Or I would play a new CD for him. There was one he liked especially by a German composer. And he was very much interested in where I got my loudspeakers. He was a man full of curiosity. He was always drinking everything in."

HENRY GRIS first met Grant when he was working at Universal. He recalls: "Cary kept notes on everything, including interesting words. Elegant words that meant something different. Words with meaning and sophistication. He wrote them down in a very fine, calligraphic longhand, in alphabetical order."

Grant listed the words at the back of one of his notebooks, along with their definitions: "avuncular," "attrition," "exacerbation," "hypertrophies," etc., continuing right through the alphabet. GRIS had never seen anyone do such a thing and he remembers "asking Cary why he did it, and he told me it was because he was in love with the English language."

Grant kept several large binders full of notes. Two contained his collection of jokes. Two others kept information about anything from shoe repair to reminding himself to "Vote for Proposition 65." He kept track of the latest medical advances, of travel destinations (including the possibilities of a trip on a 1928 Dutch sailing barge), of a man who raised white sturgeons in a holding tank at the University of California at Davis, and of classes in public speaking. He made notes to remember a yacht for a "possible Jennifer wedding." He wanted to know about everything. One note to himself says: "Like everyone else, I shall die before accomplishing even an infinitesimal fraction of what my imagination will—a will of its peculiar own—suggests to me."

When he traveled, he carried a large black notebook, on the front of which he wrote: "THIS IMPORTANT BOOK BELONGS TO MR. CARY GRANT. HE WOULD BE GRATEFUL IF IT IS RETURNED TO . . ." and he listed Beverly Hills and Fabergé addresses, Monte Carlo, Warwick Hotel (New York), and Athenaeum (London) telephone numbers.

Betsy Drake was now living at 1717 Westridge Road, off Mandeville Canyon, in Los Angeles, in a house Grant bought for her when they separated. She decorated it with great style and taste and invited friends for dinner. Judy Quine and John Foreman and his wife were frequent guests, and occasionally, so was Cary Grant.

In 1959 Drake sought treatment with a Dr. Mortimer A. Hartman, a radiologist and internist, who was practicing in Los Angeles and experimenting in the field of psychotherapy. Although DR. HARTMAN was not a psychiatrist, he had undergone five years of classical Freudian analysis in New York. He says,

"When I moved to Los Angeles, a friend and professor at Southern California University told me about LSD, which was created by a Swiss chemist, Albert Hoffman, in 1938. My friend said LSD was different from other drugs because people who took it could remember what they experienced. Both my wife and I took LSD over a long period of time. Our judgment would be off for about twenty-four hours, but we were always clear about what happened."

His first session sold Grant on the powerful possibilities of the drug. DR. HARTMAN remembers, "Betsy Drake came first, but I don't remember who referred her. And then Cary came. I was not part of the Hollywood scene, and yet many Hollywood people came to me. I chose my patients on the basis of their creativity. One recommended another."

Drake was particularly interested in psychodrama, a technique in which she could combine her theatrical training and the insights she had gained through years of personal psychoanalysis. During the 1960s she studied with Dr. Alfred Cannon at UCLA's Neuro-Psychiatric Institute. She began doing volunteer work at the institute and eventually directed the psychodrama program.

Dr. Hartman found that Grant had gained intellectual insight from reading Freud but looked for emotional insight when he started taking LSD. "He was searching for answers," DR. HARTMAN recalls, "but the deterministic approach doesn't work. Things just happen. He was a highly introspective man and an excellent patient." As RICHARD BROOKS puts it, "He wanted to 'feel' life, no matter where it led him."

JUDY QUINE, who found Grant's openness very appealing, says, "Cary had a constant curiosity about everything. Life was a process and an adventure. There was always more to learn, which was certainly a lot different from the sort of current, popular, jaded boredom that one finds in a great many people who have had it all. It made him seem young to me."

> CG: There is a great misconception about LSD and a great deal to explain. . . . I used it about one hundred times before it became illegal. Each session lasted about six hours.

"He came over a period of three years, from 1960 to 1963," DR. HARTMAN continues. "During the periods when he wasn't working, he came once a week. He arrived at nine and left around three. His driver picked him up, and his maid kept an eye on him for the next twenty-four hours. He never called me to say he was having any difficulty."

Although Grant never called Hartman about serious physical difficulties after a treatment, his experiences had long-lasting emotional ramifications:

> CG: I ran the gamut of emotions, from deep pain with tears to light-headed laughter. For me, it was an experiment, and it was always monitored under Dr. Hartman's care. . . . I had become dissatisfied with me. I took LSD with the hope it would make me feel better about myself. I wanted to rid myself of all my hypocrisies. I wanted to work through the events of my childhood, my relationship with my parents and my former wives. I did not want to spend years in analysis. I found it extremely valuable. It did me a great deal of good. It brought up all those guilts, all the nightmares I'd been holding down.
>
> When you take it once a week, the way I did, it knocks you flat.

DR. HARTMAN concludes, "LSD was not recreational for Cary. It was a very serious experiment."

> CG: LSD permits you to fly apart. I got clearer and clearer. Your subconscious takes over when you take it, and you become free of the usual discipline you impose upon yourself. I forced myself through the realization that I loved my parents and forgave them for what they didn't know. I became happier for it, and the insights I gained dispelled many of the fears I had prior to that time.
>
> I began to realize that I was my own worst enemy. You can't blame anyone else for what you've done in your life. You must keep in mind that you are always part of the action. Once you realize that, you're home a little freer.

LSD was a government-licensed experiment. JUDY QUINE talked with both of the Grants about their experiences: "Sometimes I picked one or the other up from a session (because you couldn't drive afterwards), and the nature of the communication was so different from classic analysis it convinced me that it was something I wanted to do. What I had with Cary and Betsy was a kind of soul-baringness that the culture didn't start to deal with until years later. We continued to have that even when our lives went off in different directions."

DR. HARTMAN never discussed his patients with anyone, not even his wife. He says, "And while I have no personal opinions about patients, I can tell you I liked Cary. And he liked me. Cary called me Mahatma, the wise one. He liked my sense of humor and my street talk. He liked my intellect. We exchanged a lot of jokes, and he told me I should dress better."

Indeed, Grant left money to Hartman in his will.

JUDY QUINE believes that the greatest change in Grant was a sense of peace. "I think," she says, "he realized he was coming closer and closer to becoming the person he always wanted to be and thought he was. My sense was that the fundamental simplicity of committing oneself to the life process happened for Cary somewhere in those years. Cary said, 'I invented the person I wanted to be, and I had to find that person.' I think he had done that long ago on the screen, long before he was able to do that in a more spiritual sense inside of himself."

RICHARD BROOKS says, "I didn't recognize that the changes in him were from taking LSD, but under LSD he was too placid. He was not his questioning self."

STANLEY DONEN believes that Grant was always looking for something and thought he'd discovered what no one else knew, that "LSD gave him the belief he had found the real answer to the miracle of how to live. Did I notice any real changes? Not really. He was still exactly Cary Grant after LSD. He had the same attitudes, except he felt more secure perhaps."

Grant introduced Peter Stone to Dr. Hartman in London. "Everything was uncritical after LSD," Stone reports. "It wasn't real. It was beatific. You'd say, 'Cary, stop it. You're making me crazy.' He'd say, 'I'm not making you crazy. *You're* making you crazy.'

"I never saw him raise his voice. I never saw him yell at anybody. I never saw him have a tantrum. It gave him equanimity. It was cosmic in its scope. Up was down. Black was white.

In was out. Everything was a cycle. What's the difference? He could literally stop any discussion by one of these tautologies.

"But some of it was proper. I'd smoke, and he'd say, 'Why do you want to kill yourself?' I'd say, 'I don't want to kill myself.' He'd say, 'Then why are you doing that if you don't want to kill yourself?' Every defense was useless. Finally you stopped smoking because he was at you all the time."

By the mid-1960s the dangers and side effects of the drug had become more apparent. Active research projects on LSD dropped almost overnight from seventy-two to a dozen. The surgeon general of the United States and the commissioner of the Food and Drug Administration condemned the drug. Federal laws against manufacture and sale of such dangerous drugs already existed, and some states, including California, enacted their own bans on possession and use of LSD. Grant said he discontinued use when the drug became illegal, and so did Dr. Hartman.

> CG: It isn't my responsibility to decide whether someone should go to jail, but taking LSD is, after all, illegal. I don't advocate it for anyone else. If a man takes LSD, he must realize the consequences.

Grant began *The Grass Is Greener* on April 2, 1960. It was his third film with Stanley Donen. Grandon Productions, Ltd., produced the picture. Grant headed a stellar cast with Deborah Kerr, Robert Mitchum, and Jean Simmons. Grant's old friend Noel Coward wrote the music and lyrics.

DEBORAH KERR, like others, believes that working with Grant was without doubt a high point in her career and says: "His elegance, his wit, his true professionalism were outstanding, and I learned so much from just watching him work. The ability to ad-lib, the timing of a double take . . . in fact, all his timing—so essential for true comedy.

"As a person, apart from his talent, he was warm and affectionate and a joy to have as a *friend*. He lived simply and was not tremendously social—a very private person. He was also a keen and shrewd businessman; in fact, there was no end to his talents. I treasure my memories of him. . . ."

By January 15, 1961, Grant was in a new picture, *That Touch of Mink*. This time his costars were Doris Day, Gig Young, and

AUDREY MEADOWS, who recalls: "One day, while I visited Jerry Lewis in his dressing room at Paramount, there was a knock on the door, and there stood the most gorgeous man I had ever laid eyes on. The excitement on Cary's face when he saw me had me absolutely dumbstruck because I didn't know he was a fan of *The Honeymooners*. He said, 'I'd love to walk through the door and be in that set with all of you.' Now, can you imagine him in that broken-down terrible set, the way he dressed and the way he looked?

"A couple of years later my agent read the script for *That Touch of Mink*, which had a part for 'an Audrey Meadows type.' We had gone off the air, but Cary didn't realize I was available. My agent let him know I was. When Cary said something about getting together on the deal, I told him the part was so good and the movie so funny I would consider paying him.

"Pat Scofield, my English housekeeper, desperately wanted to meet Cary Grant. The first couple of days she sat very quietly in my dressing room. I told her that when Cary came to the set, I would see what I could do. She had very short, hennaed red hair and huge blue eyes with very thick lenses that made them even larger. She asked to borrow my makeup man and hairdresser to get fixed up for him. When I told Cary about her, he said, 'Where is she?' And he came to my dressing room. He was so dear to her. She wasn't tongue-tied and was in full control of her personality. As soon as he left, I thought she was going to collapse.

"Every day after that when he came on the set, he made small talk with her. He was overseeing everything on the picture, plus being in it, and yet he was aware of what it meant to Pat: It was her whole life. She never got over it. Every elevator man and doorman in New York heard about her meeting Cary Grant. She sent postcards to everybody she knew. For years after that on her birthday, I sent her flowers and signed the card 'With much love from Cary Grant.' She showed the card to all the elevator men, who believed the flowers were coming from Cary."

In 1961 Cary Grant, like most Americans, watched television regularly. Always interested in young talent, he was particularly attentive to newcomers who had a chance to break in on network programming. On Wednesday nights at seven-thirty most of America was watching *Wagon Train*. It was one of the top three

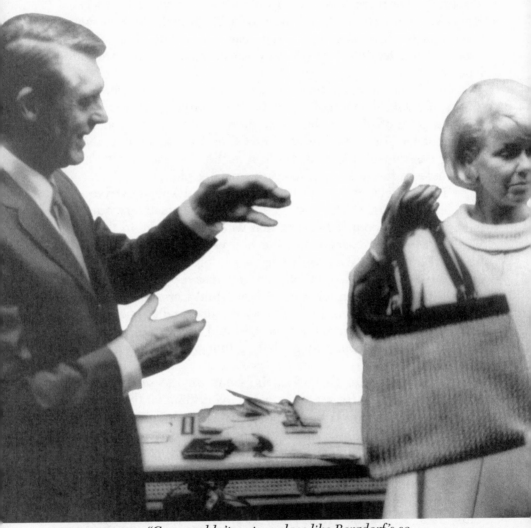

AMY GREENE: *"Cary couldn't go to a place like Bergdorf's so [photographer] Milton [Greene] took him to Richard Bienen's New York showroom to shop for Doris Day for* That Touch of Mink *[1961]."*

shows. Not very many people saw its competition, *Malibu Run,* a one-hour show about two skin divers who ran a shop selling diving equipment. The producer of the show, PERRY LAFFERTY, knows Cary Grant did: "I had seen a young actress in a soap opera who absolutely enchanted me, but I didn't know who she was. When we needed to cast a kind of a Judy Holliday part, like in *Born Yesterday,* I tried to get Elizabeth Montgomery but couldn't find her because she was driving across the country with her then fiancé, Gig Young. So the casting director located the girl in the soap opera. It was Dyan Cannon. I read her for the part, hired her, and directed that particular episode. The day after it aired she told me Cary Grant had called her and wanted to interview her. I presumed it was for a film he was making."

CHAPTER THIRTEEN

"DYE MY HAIR?"

CG: I'm getting too old for certain types of comedy. If you watch my recent films, you'll accept my none-too-soon evolution into older roles.

Once Cary Grant saw Dyan Cannon on *Malibu Run*, he was determined to meet her. As JACK HALEY, JR., remembers, his motive was decidedly personal: "Cary desperately wanted to meet her. I dated a girl Dyan was living with, and the number of calls Cary made to her was embarrassing."

Grant persisted but did not actually meet Cannon until the summer of 1962. That was the July that he and Betsy Drake finally made their long separation legal. She divorced him on the basis of mental cruelty, the charge used by his two previous wives. Their incompatibilities had outweighed the strength of their feeling for each other. Later she said, "I still love him very much." At the time Grant said: "I've known that Betsy has been contemplating a divorce for some time. We have discussed it together, and the step is a sad one for both of us; but it's useless for me to dwell upon what might have been, and I can only hope that Betsy will find the happiness she deserves."

On July 19, 1962, he wrote to his mother in an attempt to explain Drake's actions.

MY LOVE,

The last few weeks have been difficult ones for me, and I've been unable to write or telephone you as happily as I would have wished. But everything's all right now and I plan to come back to Bristol and you for a while, as soon as my business, which I've recently neglected, is in order again.

I hope the news of Betsy's divorce from me has not disturbed you. It was inevitable and probably the best for both of us. At least I shall try to think so. We have remained friends and we both love you. So please be patient with us; we seemed unable to resolve matters in any other way, and I know that if Betsy were here as I write this she would add her loving thoughts to mine.

Stay well, dear Mother. I look forward to seeing you, darling, and will telephone you very soon.

Always, ARCHIE

Certainly his spirits lifted when Dyan Cannon finally responded to his attentions. Grant was fifty-eight, and the striking, vivacious actress was twenty-three.

She was born Samille Diane Friesen on January 4, 1939, in Tacoma, Washington. The daughter of Ben Friesen, a Baptist insurance broker and his Jewish wife, Clara, Cannon sang at a Seattle Reform temple. After two years at the University of Washington she moved to Los Angeles, where she worked as a showroom model. In the early 1960s she played minor roles in films and appeared in a number of television programs and a few unsuccessful Broadway shows. Her Broadway debut was *The Fun Couple* in 1962.

While Cannon was in New York in the play, she stayed with Grant at the Plaza Hotel. There he met with Peter Stone, the author of his next project. Stone and Marc Behm had tailored an original screenplay called *The Unsuspecting Wife* for Grant and Audrey Hepburn. Unable to sell it, Stone had turned it into a novel and renamed it *Charade*. After it appeared in *Redbook* magazine, Stanley Donen bought it, and STONE had a chance to realize his original conception: "Cary said he would make the film if I would meet with him to go over certain objections."

CG: Stanley Donen promised me that Peter Stone would rewrite the central characters to bridge the wide age difference between Audrey and me.

243

It was PETER STONE's first picture. He recalls: "I was scared to death. I flew from my home in Switzerland and knocked on Cary's door at the Plaza. He'd just stepped out of the shower and opened the door wearing a towel.

"We talked and joked for three days and got to know each other. We argued endlessly about the shower scene. It was one of those really dumb, funny, charming scenes only Cary can pull off. In it Audrey gets him into her room and insists he take a shower and change for dinner. He takes the shower but fully dressed in a drip-dry suit. Everything he is wearing is water-resistant, including his watch.

"Cary didn't want to do the scene. He thought it was foolish. At that point I realized something about Cary. There were certain things he was interested in doing, but he didn't want to take the blame if they failed. He begged us not to do the scene, but we *made* him. He had set it up so that if it didn't work or was foolish, he was in the clear."

Audrey Hepburn and Grant had never met, and STANLEY DONEN looked forward to introducing these two magical personalities. He remembers: "I arranged a dinner at a wonderful Italian restaurant in Paris. Audrey and I arrived first. Cary came in, and Audrey stood up and said, 'I'm so nervous.' He said, 'Why?' And she said, 'Meeting you, working with you—I'm so nervous.' And he said, 'Don't be nervous, for goodness' sake. I'm thrilled to know you. Here, sit down at the table. Put your hands on the table, palms up, put your head down and take a few deep breaths.'

"We all sat down, and Audrey put her hands on the table. I had ordered a bottle of red wine. When she put her head down, she hit the bottle, and the wine went all over Cary's cream-colored suit. Audrey was humiliated. People at other tables were looking, and everybody was buzzing. It was an horrendous moment. Cary was a half hour from his hotel, so he took off his coat and comfortably sat through the whole meal like that."

HEPBURN agrees: "He took it so well, rather like he did in *Charade* when I dropped the ice cream on his suit. That scene came out of the experience in the restaurant. Can you imagine how I felt? I wanted to crawl into a hole. I felt terrible and kept apologizing, but Cary was so dear about it. The next day he sent me a box of caviar with a little note telling me not to feel bad."

Filming started on October 18, 1962. GEORGE KENNEDY discusses one of the unexpected advantages of working in France: "Walter Matthau, Jimmy Coburn, Ned Glass, and I had the marvelous advantage of commanding Cary's and Audrey's attention because we were the only people who spoke English. Cary talked about himself in the third person, which I thought was remarkable. He would say, 'A Cary Grant can't be in a picture like that.' Or 'A Cary Grant can only be in a picture like that.'

"He followed it up with a haymaker that has meant so much to me. He said, 'You must always remember that you—George Kennedy—are a property, and you must treat that property with respect.' I have found it to be immensely true and helpful. You must sell yourself like somebody would sell real estate or automobiles or anything else. If you treat the property with respect, everybody else falls in line. It is the single best piece of advice I've ever had in our business."

Grant celebrated his fifty-ninth birthday in France, and STANLEY DONEN realized Grant was beginning to feel his age. He recollects: "There was a scene in which he had to run. When I asked him to do it again, he said 'I'll do it just once more.' I asked him why, and he said, 'I'm nearly sixty, and I don't like having to run that fast.'"

While he wasn't self-conscious about his age in "real life," Grant was increasingly aware of his age on-screen. He dated and married much younger women, but he didn't want to appear "lecherous" as a romantic lead. Howard Hawks told PETER BOGDANOVICH, "'That's one of the reasons he didn't do *Man's Favorite Sport*, which cast Paula Prentiss as the female lead. Hawks had tailored the film for Cary, but it was eventually made with Rock Hudson."

PETER STONE believes Grant had decided he was too old to get the girl. He says: "He thought he'd be called a dirty old man. He made me change the dynamic of the characters and make Audrey the aggressor. She chased him, and he tried to dissuade her. She pursued him and sat in his lap. She found him irresistible, and ultimately he was worn down by her.

"I gave him lines like 'I'm too old for you, get away from me, little girl.' And 'I'm old enough to be your father.' And in the elevator: 'I could be in trouble transporting you beyond the first floor. A minor!'

"This way he couldn't get in any trouble. What could he do? She was chasing him. He wasn't coming on. There's even a line where she kisses him—on the *bateau mouche*—and he says, 'When you come on, you come on.' And she says, 'Well, come on.'"

Grant continued to work closely with Stone, taking every precaution to assure that what went on-screen was precisely the way he wanted it. STONE says: "Cary had never made a mystery like *Charade*. He was chased in *North by Northwest*, he was the suspect in *To Catch a Thief*, and a menace in *Notorious*, but he had never solved a crime or murder in a picture.

"About two thirds through the movie there's an obligatory scene for a mystery. It's a reviewing the bidding scene, where you go over what's happened so the audience can keep up. Cary didn't want to do that scene. When we insisted, he said, 'No, that's all exposition. Stars don't do exposition. Other people do exposition.'

"We agreed, but told him that in this case he was playing both the victim *and* the detective. There was no one else who could do the scene. 'Well,' he said, 'I'm sorry, but I didn't learn the lines.' So I told him I would write it on the blackboard, and he agreed to read from a three-foot-by-two-foot slate.

"When he finished the scene, we told him it was just great. He said, 'Yes, that was good, wasn't it? Do you want me to do it again?' We were amused that he was so proud of himself.

"The next day at the dailies Cary saw his scene. It was in close-up, and he did do it well. Immediately after his take we cut to an enraged-looking actor saying, 'You're reading off a blackboard!' Cary jumped a mile. 'What is that?' Everybody fell down laughing."

STANLEY DONEN describes the day they shot one of *Charade*'s funniest scenes: "It's the sequence where Cary tries to take an orange from beneath a stout matronly woman's neck using only his head and neck—no hands. The orange rolls down her body, and Cary and the matron find themselves in some awkward and embarrassing positions while Cary tries to maintain his savoir faire. It required instant improvisation since we couldn't predict where the orange might rest and where Cary's head might be required. He found himself against her ample bosom, or belly, and so on. It was a sequence invented just for him."

CG: It was one of my favorite scenes. I did it with such concentration that it looked like my life depended on it.

STANLEY DONEN continues, "But that was the day President Kennedy blockaded the Russian warships from bringing missiles to Cuba. [The situation] held the possibility of the beginning of the end of the world, but Cary gave a concentrated and amazingly inventive performance. Think of that the next time you watch the picture."

AUDREY HEPBURN found Grant an extremely sensitive person, with "lots of antennas. He was very gentle and very dear with me. Working with him was a joy. There was something special, which is quite undefinable, about Cary. He was expressive and yet reserved. He was a quiet man basically, for somebody who dealt in comedy, and yet very much to the point. He led a very quiet life. I do, too. I think a lot of it has to do with shyness and wanting to be with people you're comfortable with instead of having to always break new ground.

"I think because he was a vulnerable man, he recognized my vulnerability. We had that in common. He had more wisdom than I to help me with it. There was something mystic about Cary, which I've never been able to put my finger on, but I think he had a deep perception of life. He said one thing very important to me one day when I was probably twitching and being nervous. We were sitting next to each other waiting for the next shot. And he laid his hand on my two hands and said, 'You've got to learn to like yourself a little more.' I've often thought about that."

Dyan Cannon visited Grant for the Christmas holidays and joined him for New Year's Eve at what was supposed to be a splendid party. PETER STONE, who was among the guests, recalls: "Audrey had a marvelous château outside Paris and an Italian staff that served with white gloves. It was very formal, very fancy living. For New Year's Eve there were eight of us, Audrey, her husband, Mel Ferrer, Cary and Dyan Cannon, Stanley Donen and his then wife Adele, a great beauty who had been married to Lord Beatty, and my wife, Mary, and me. Audrey served enormous Idaho-type baked potatoes, and everybody spooned sour cream and Russian caviar from Cary's five-pound tin into the baked potatoes.

"It was as glamorous an evening as one can imagine, but it

CG, fifty-eight, with Audrey Hepburn off camera while making
Charade, 1962. HEPBURN: "He knew what I was feeling before I did, or
anybody else for that matter."

was truly boring. It wasn't anybody's fault. Nobody there was boring. Far from it. But it was just one of those terrible evenings where nobody got any conversation going. Nobody was in great humor. Cary and Dyan were arguing a bit, Mel and Audrey were arguing a bit, and Stanley and Adele were arguing a bit. The only ones still happily married to each other are Mary and me."

In spite of Grant's age, the magnetism was unmistakable and unique. He carried off the romantic lead in *Charade* with the same aplomb he'd had twenty years earlier. PETER STONE says, "He wore gabardine Botany suits in *Charade* that were eighty-five bucks off a rack. He loved them. They looked like they were made by a Savile Row tailor."

According to RICK INGERSOLL, "Everybody used him as an example of the well-dressed man, and he put that down by saying he didn't focus on being well dressed; he merely dressed moderately. I once told him, 'If what you wear isn't in style, it becomes the style because you're wearing it!'" JOHN FORSYTHE, who always found Grant meticulous about his appearance, says: "Once he advised me against wearing a particular suit. He said, 'It's too extreme. Wear classic clothes. I've got suits that are twenty-five and thirty years old. They look brand-new.' He was impeccable in every aspect."

CG: When I was a young man, if I was hanging out with the crowd and was inclined toward a loud suit or a loud pair of socks, my father would say, "Hold on a moment. Remember, that's you walking down the street, not the socks." My father always said, "Buy the best of something. Inferior brands wear out."

While it was true Grant occasionally bought ready-made clothes and liked to tell people he did, almost all his suits and sports coats were tailor-made. Most of his shirts and shoes were made for him in London and Hong Kong, and many of his friends have stories to share about Grant's wardrobe.

"Cary had suits from all over the world," RICHARD BIENEN says. "He bought from Schiffanelli in Rome, and he had them made in Hong Kong. One time in New York he took me to Dunhill's, introduced me to the men who run it, and then watched while they measured me for a cut, make, and trim suit. It's up to you whether it's three-button or two-button, slash pockets, high double-vent, single-vent. It wasn't a custom suit; but you got it the next day, and it was Cary's little secret. It was the best suit for the least amount of money I ever owned."

GEORGE BARRIE says, "Cary used to get his clothes in England from Sir Charles Abrahams, who owned Aquascutum. One time when we were there, their tailor measured him for a couple of suits, and then a photographer took pictures of him getting fitted. I said, 'Are you crazy?' He said, 'Why? I get all my clothes here free.'"

JUDY QUINE remembers, "The first time he had clothes copied in Hong Kong, he took a shirt he loved from London, gave it to this great copyist, and ordered a dozen *exactly like it*. When Cary went back to pick them up, he saw the man had copied the shirt, identically. Now he had twelve new shirts with this little fray in the identical place on the collar!"

Not only could Grant successfully wear a suit off the rack, but he could have his hair cut by any barber and walk out of the shop looking like a million dollars. PETER STONE remembers one surprising trip to the barbershop with Grant during the making of *Charade:* "We were walking in the village. He suddenly said, 'I need a haircut.' I didn't think it was a good idea. He said, 'No, no, I'll just get one here.' We walked into this back street barbershop. I reminded him that he still had a scene to shoot, and his cut wasn't going to match. He said, 'Oh, nonsense, nonsense.' I thought he had lost his senses and considered calling the production office. But the haircut he got was perfect. He knew a barber couldn't hurt his hair. It cut itself. You could have cut it with pinking shears."

At home, in Beverly Hills, Grant, Burt Reynolds, John Forsythe, Jule Styne, and Mervyn Le Roy all went to ROBERT COX, who says, "I cut his hair for almost twenty years. The layered cut I gave him reminded him of the club cut he got in England. It's tailored, and it grows out evenly. The only thing we discussed about his hair was the length in front. He liked it to be very short. I was hesitant but always gave in."

In September Grant matched the thousand-dollar donations by Attorney General Robert Kennedy and President John Kennedy for the Stay in School Fund campaign. The fund sponsored the world premiere of *Charade* in Washington, D.C., on September 24. While he was there, Grant visited local schools with

Robert Kennedy to help raise funds to get school dropouts back into classrooms. Dorothy McCardle covered Grant's visit for *The Washington Post*. He told her: "As a youngster in England, I didn't get all the schooling I would have liked. In my day, the best school was the school of experience in the theater and that's the school I graduated from. But that's not true today. Any child who wants to make a decent living in this world has got to stay in school until he has prepared himself to make it."

Less than two months later President Kennedy was assassinated. After hearing the news, PETER STONE went to bed in California and awoke in the middle of the night in a cold sweat, remembering that: "There were two lines in *Charade* that referred to assassination. Standing in front of Notre Dame, Audrey said, 'Do you realize any minute we could be assassinated?' Then she asked Cary, 'Could you do that?' And he says, 'What, assassinate somebody?' And she says, 'No. Swing down out of there like Quasimodo to save the woman you love?'

"It's hard to imagine how sensitive the word 'assassinate' was at that particular moment. But I felt it had to be changed. Stanley was in Europe, and *Charade* was opening as Radio City Music Hall's Christmas show at the end of November.

"I called Cary, and he said, 'We can dub it immediately.' We substituted the word 'eliminate,' which had the same number of syllables and read the same."

In the spring of 1964 Elsie Leach went to live at the Chesterfield Nursing Home in Bristol. She was now eighty-seven. Grant's handwritten notes remind him to turn off her television and questions whether he should turn off the gas at her home. DR. FRANCIS PAGE first met Grant at the Royal Hotel in Bristol. He recalls: "We met to discuss Mrs. Leach. Her behavior had become unpredictable, and I finally convinced her to move into the Chesterfield, a private acute-care home, where I visited her for social rather than medical reasons. She was very fit and tough physically and would forcibly prevent any attempt on my part to carry out a medical examination.

"I never did know the official psychiatric diagnosis used years earlier to keep Mrs. Leach in the mental institution. It was always presumed she was a chronic paranoid schizophrenic. She could be very suspicious and convinced that others were trying to impose upon her or do her down.

With Robert Kennedy in Washington, D.C., 1963, at the Shaw School, in support of the Stay in School Fund.

"Her recollection for details of events going back to her youth was minuscule. It wasn't possible to discuss coherently the significance of her circumstances or surroundings at the time.

"I took her for rides in my car. On these outings she would sometimes recognize parts of Bristol as it used to be and tell me a snippet of some event but never enough to form a distinct picture. Yet some of her observations on humanity were remarkably shrewd.

"If she decided to buy anything, which would be unusual, it was clear that her concept of the value of money had not changed since she was a girl. She was totally uninterested in material things. She hardly ever accepted the results of Cary's position or wealth and would order the nurses to remove any flowers or presents he sent her.

"She would sometimes describe how 'Archie' wanted to take her back to America to live with him, but she didn't want to go. At other times she believed he was going to live in England or Ireland to be with her.

"Mrs. Leach could behave in quite an impossible manner toward Cary and was highly critical of him, but he showed astonishing patience. She had a hold on him and treated him as though he were a naughty boy. As a result, he behaved like a little boy in her presence because her demands were impossible. She chided him the whole time he visited her in the nursing home. When it came time for him to leave, she wouldn't let him go. The staff had to take strong measures to get him out. She was a very strange woman—more than eccentric. She had a mind of her own, and no one in the nursing home could tell her what to do. She was sometimes hopeless to deal with, yet when she died, everyone missed her terribly."

CLARICE EARL remembers, "Mrs. Leach persisted in wearing blouses or jumpers [sweaters] with a skirt, but when she knew Cary was coming, she dressed up. She would sit by my office and look along the corridor toward the front door. When she saw him, she'd give a little skip and throw up her arms to greet him.

"In stature, she was fairly short, very thin and wiry, and light on her feet. She always held herself absolutely straight whether sitting or standing.

"Cary, to his mother, was always the character he portrayed. 'He's a much better doctor than any of the doctors here,' she'd say. Or 'He's a very good ship's captain.' When she saw him in the shower scene in *Charade,* she said, 'Look at him, getting soaked through. He's spoiling that nice new suit he's wearing!' And when she saw his beard in *Father Goose,* she roundly told him off for being slovenly.

"Sometimes Mrs. Leach's TV wouldn't work, usually because she pressed the wrong buttons. A senior consultant orthopedic surgeon had his consulting rooms near her room, and she would order him to come and put it right, which he did with amused good humor. On one occasion I suggested she shouldn't bother him because he was a doctor, a specialist, to which she replied, 'Rubbish! He's my television man!'

"She would occasionally show me a picture of her husband, an extraordinarily handsome man, with striking and compelling eyes.

"Everyone had a deep affection for her, although she was totally exasperating. She will always be remembered by those who knew her."

BETSY DRAKE says that when she first met Grant, he told her a great deal about his boyhood, adding, "I was touched. Years later he showed me his school, and we visited his cousins Eric and Maggie Leach many times. When Cary would go see his mother, I would wait for him in a hotel. Finally he took me to meet her. I put my arms around her, which completely disarmed her. His mother was a strange little woman. She was always criticizing and attacking him. One time she greeted him with 'Archie, I've never seen so many wrinkles in all my life.'"

> CG: Once when I was home in Bristol, I took my mother for a ride in the car. I sat in the front. She was in the back. She was in her eighties. I was in my sixties, and my hair was turning gray. She said, "Archie, you should dye your hair." And I asked her, "Why on earth would I dye my hair?" And she said, "Because it makes me look so old."

GEORGE BARRIE also went with Grant to visit and recalls: "It was about four years before Mrs. Leach died. She had him under her thumb in a way. He was somewhat afraid of her."

To BEA SHAW Grant admitted "he loved his mother but said she was not a terribly warm or demonstrative person. He talked about how beautiful she was—dark with dark eyes." FREDERIQUE JOURDAN remembers that "he talked about his mother taking the bus in Bristol and riding for two hours, from the start of the line to the end and coming back. He said she did it every day. It was sweet how it amused him."

On April 9, 1964, Grant started working on *Father Goose*. The screenplay was written by Frank Tarloff and then rewritten by Peter Stone. The two writers never worked together in person and did not meet until the 1965 Academy Awards, when they won for best screenplay. Grant was thrilled with the role. He said he was most like himself.

> CG: I was a bum. I was all broken down, in jeans and a beard. It was me. After dressing so carefully for my films for so many years, I wanted to do the opposite. It wasn't the most successful film by any means, but it was a very happy occasion for me.

LESLIE CARON agrees: "He was comfortable and relaxed in old clothes and a beard. For once he was not so spick-and-span." According to PETER STONE, "Cary had wanted to be the old poker player in *The Cincinnati Kid*, which was ultimately played by Eddie [Edward G.] Robinson. We prepared a lot of it, but he lost interest. Then Cary got hold of Frank Tarloff's script, a war adventure story about an alcoholic, unshaven bum in dirty clothes. I told him that if he committed to the character—a drunk, disgusting, irascible, misanthropic curmudgeon—I'd do the picture."

LESLIE CARON had received an Academy Award nomination for *The L-Shaped Room*, but she was surprised when Cary Grant asked her to be in *Father Goose*. She says, "It wasn't the same style of film. We met at Universal, and I thought that maybe he would see me differently—that he was mistaken."

When they met, she adds, "He was impeccably dressed, and yet he gave out a feeling of animal strength—almost like a jaguar ready to pounce. He was very compelling and had enormous energy about him. I've always been shy, so I was apprehensive about meeting him. But he was just as he was in his films, only more so. His presence was very commanding, and his eyes were burning and alert. He was watching everything . . . watching me . . . thinking very fast. He was extremely alive."

Playwright/screenwriter PETER STONE: *"Father Goose is a war-adventure story about an alcoholic, unshaven bum in dirty clothes. I told him that if he committed to the character—a drunk, disgusting, irascible, misanthropic curmudgeon—I'd do the picture."*

Grant wanted Cy Coleman to score the picture and invited the young New York composer of such songs as "Witchcraft" and "The Best Is Yet to Come" to lunch. "It was a big moment in my life," COLEMAN remembers. "We met at his bungalow at Universal. He was exceedingly warm. He told me he knew every song I had written and then *sang them to me*. I was dumbfounded. I left there about five feet off of the ground. I thought, *If he never calls, what's the difference? I've had lunch with Cary Grant. How many people can say that? And he sang my songs to me!*

"Eight months later Universal called, and our next lunch was with Robert Arthur, the producer. Cary put his arm around me and said, 'Now, when I was in the English music hall, I used to sing these kinds of songs. And he sang something like 'I've got a loverly bunch of coconuts. . . .' All the songs he sang had the same tempo.

"I got increasingly nervous with Cary singing at me and the entire commissary looking at me. Bob Arthur's stern visage didn't help. I was eating scrambled eggs, the easiest thing to digest, but I couldn't get the fork up to my mouth. I would get frozen halfway between the plate and my mouth, and then my hand started to shake. So I decided not to eat. At the end of the lunch Cary said, 'You haven't finished your eggs.' And he finished them.

"Robert Arthur, who was a nice guy but a staunch company man, resented that my agent had negotiated fifty percent of the publishing [music publishing income] for me. In the movies they generally don't give you any of the publishing. He told me I should stick to composing and keep out of business. Cary got really angry. 'I don't want you telling creative people they don't have any business heads. If I'd listened to that kind of thinking, I'd have been finished. Look at me, I own the picture, I hire you, and I hire Cy. That's what creative people can do!'

"As we left the commissary, somebody stopped me and Cary walked ahead. As I tried to catch up with him, I became fascinated with his walk. He walked in the same jaunty tempo of those English music hall tunes he sang to me at lunch. 'I've got a loverly bunch of coconuts. . . .' I studied his walk, and from that came the theme for *Father Goose*—'Pass Me By.'"

The starting date of the film was delayed, and LESLIE CARON was told by her agent that Grant was making changes in the script. "Finally we got to the first day of shooting," she remembers, "and Cary was annoyed at all the postponement costs. He was responsible for the postponements; but he was the producer, and it cost him money. Throughout the film it became a leitmotif: 'I'm getting ruined with this. I'm getting ruined with this.'"

CARON also comments on acting with Grant: "I had a tough time keeping a straight face during my drunken scene because he was trying to break me up. Finally he turned around, and I played the scene to his back.

"During a scene he would say a punch line and tell me not to move. He wanted me to be stunned by it. That was his technique: Say the punch line and freeze. It wasn't realistic, but it certainly worked. It's what he had learned on the stage, and I use the trick whenever I play a comedy. It was certainly very useful when I played Feydeau.

"Cary could be in the best of moods—full of joy and light-hearted—and then change like a storm on the Mediterranean Sea. For instance, he was basically left-handed, but he had trained himself to be ambidextrous. One time the propman set a bottle he was to use in the scene by his right hand, and Cary flashed very angrily. 'How do you expect me to pour the bottle with this hand?' It was a sudden storm. The funny thing is that just half an hour before, he had told me I should raise my children to be ambidextrous. I don't think he saw the humor of that, but I did.

"Cary kept you on your toes. He electrified the set. You felt inspired. It was essential to have a quality far superior to the average. You had to be as bright and brilliant as possible. He was one of those people who *generated* that demand. Vincente Minnelli was another. You were at your best with them."

As usual Grant was involved in details. This time he also had advice for CY COLEMAN: "Cary knew every facet of making a movie—a real moviemaker. He said to me with supreme confidence, 'I'll tell you where you'll get a laugh.' Now I was skeptical. Musical jokes are hard to get. They don't sit well—like a bad pun.

"He asked me how I planned to score the scene in which he is in a little, dumpy, run-down boat and Trevor Howard is following him in a big boat. I told him I wanted to do something offbeat. I was looking for a distinctive sound and planned to use the ocarina. His character was so offbeat that the out-of-tune, airy, hollow sound of a toy ocarina was perfect.

"Cary said, 'That's very good. When you see me on-screen, use the ocarina and use a small orchestration. The minute the bigger boat comes into view, let all hell break loose. Take the same theme and go big, very, very big. Use the full orchestra.' I said, 'That'll give me a laugh?' Cary said, 'Guaranteed.'

"I ran it for the first preview, and it was a roar."

PEGGY LEE helped make a hit of the *Father Goose* theme song. She also gave a party: "I was living in the penthouse of a Tower Grove apartment in Los Angeles, where I was actually trying to break my lease. I had a big sound system blasting with 'Pass Me By' [sings]: 'Ten, five toes to wiggle in the sand. . . .' Cary organized and led about thirty-five marching people down the hall to two elevators, and everybody got in. We were on the thirteenth floor, and the sound was coming out of the sides of the building. We marched around the lobby and got back in the elevators. They didn't break the lease. They loved it!"

In 1967 Cy Coleman and Peggy Lee, who had tried before, finally got Grant to record two songs, with a full orchestra behind him, in Columbia Records' New York studio. LEE wrote the lyrics: "One was a Christmas lullaby for little Jennifer, with music by Cy Coleman. The other was a New Year's Eve song, called 'Here's to You.' The music was by Richard Hazard."

Columbia had agreed to use the lullaby on its all-star Goodyear Christmas album and issued Cary Grant as a single, using 'Here's to You' as the flip side.

When Peter Stone and Frank Tarloff won their Oscar for *Father Goose*, STONE said, "I want to thank Cary Grant, who keeps winning these things for other people." When Grant received his Oscar in 1970, he returned the favor and thanked Stone and other writers, crediting his directors and writers for making his career possible.

In spite of the excellent reviews Grant received for *Father Goose*, the public didn't accept him in the role. BURT REYNOLDS observes, "*Father Goose* wasn't a terribly successful film because it wasn't the Cary Grant everybody was used to and wanted to see, but for me, it was some of his best work." Grant explained to John Forsythe that the transition didn't work in his case. FORSYTHE comments: "It's very hard for somebody that looked the way he did to get involved with character parts. His acute perception of what he wanted himself to look like and be was part of that decision to stop acting when he did. His image of himself was that of a leading man in a Hitchcock picture, commanding everything." LESLIE CARON believes that "people wanted him to be fantastically sophisticated, so the film wasn't a big success. I think he was hoping to start on a new career, more like Spencer Tracy or Humphrey Bogart. I think he had some ambitions to play dramatic parts."

But FRANK TARLOFF says the film finally found its audience: "Writers are paid a rerun payment when a film goes to television. I have had easily over a hundred residual payments for *Father Goose*. It's a nice family picture which does better on television than it did in the theaters."

Grant was now sixty years old. He felt uncomfortable playing romantic leads. He had "failed" in a character part. What had worked for Tracy and Bogart had not worked for Cary Grant. Retirement beckoned again.

CHAPTER FOURTEEN

"HELLO, THIS IS CARY GRANT"

CG: The only really good thing about acting in movies is that there's no heavy lifting.

As the years went by, it became more and more difficult to get an interview with Cary Grant. He thought the press often misinterpreted his remarks, although he said his statements were sometimes "improved by misquotation." Yet he had developed a trusting camaraderie with a few journalists and writers, among whom were Jerry D. Lewis, Roderick Mann, and Henry Gris.

He was closest to Roderick Mann. Their association had begun in the late 1950s. Not only were they friends, but Grant also admired Mann as a writer. In 1968 he helped Mann promote his novel *The Headliner*, saying, "His writing is always worth reading and recommending. It was difficult to put down. It was also difficult to hang on to. I never realized I had so many friends."

RODERICK MANN thought of Grant as an older brother. He says: "Most actors are empty. He was a very sage person—almost like a prophet. A thinking man. What I liked most about Cary was that I could talk to him seriously—about anything. You could tell your troubles to Cary.

"Before I married, I sometimes took my romantic woes to him. We would sit on the steps going down to his garden, and Cary would tell me where I was going wrong. Then I'd say, 'You're a fine one to give advice!'

"It was flattering to find he was as interested in you as you were in him. Most actors couldn't give a gazumba about you. They want to know, 'What do you think of me?'

"He was a loving man, a kind man, probably because he'd been starved of love and affection in his early days. He handed it out in great dollops as he got older."

Grant liked Henry Gris's honesty. GRIS observes: "Cary viewed me as the man from the outside looking in. Hollywood was merely a human laboratory where human destinies are accelerated through the magic, the joys, the disappointments of moviemaking. Human lives are concentrated into a couple of years—like mice in the lab, used because they live two years.

"As a human being and as an intellectual Cary rated very high with me. There was some depth to Cary, which I enjoyed."

It was difficult to get an interview out of Grant, but JERRY D. LEWIS, who knew Grant was a nut about baseball, says, "I got my first interview when I told him I had been a baseball writer."

Grant always kidded Henry Gris about a hidden tape recorder. "Of course, I never had one," GRIS says. "One time we were sitting in first class on Aer Lingus, and I tried to persuade him to let me turn on my tape recorder. I think the reason he said no is very simple. He felt he would not be in total control. He was afraid that a reporter, whatever his integrity, would get something out of him he would later regret."

You could get to Grant by staying off certain subjects, too. RODERICK MANN says, "I never talked to him about movies. That bored the bejesus out of him. Almost all the columns I wrote were about personal things, his private views."

In January 1965 Grant gave columnist Bob Thomas two items for his column. Thomas published the one in which Grant described the "films that appeal to *me*"—Grant's least favorite subject. He did not print the following, which reflected the thoughtful side of Grant, the side the journalists he gravitated toward instinctively brought out:

> CG: Doesn't it strike you as curious that society has so carefully collaborated to avoid discussing the actual acts of birth or death, the two most important experiences of each individual's life? Why is it we avoid reference to almost every natural biological function? Who is omnipotent or wise enough to decide each new standard of

good taste? Of sensitivity? It certainly isn't old Mother Nature herself. Because old Mother Nature goes on about the business of birth and death and peace and violence in the same old cyclic way, no matter how much today's society strives to close its eyes or acknowledge such behavior. Old Mother Nature eventually has her own way, so perhaps the best procedure is to accept what old Mother Nature or God, if you will, dictates. Accept it and you'll get along better.

Grant might not have been cooperative about most feature stories, but he could be *after* the fact. According to RODERICK MANN, "Cary called numerous people to tell them he liked what they wrote. Can you imagine? He called Sheila Benson, the *Los Angeles Times* film critic. She didn't believe it. He said, 'Hello, this is Cary Grant.' And she said, 'What?'"

Sheila Benson's response was characteristic of almost everyone. Although Grant lived by the telephone and used it constantly, calls in response to letters, to his bank, the florist, a department store, or a business executive were frustrating. No one believed him at first or, sometimes, at all.

Grant and Henry Gris had frequent phone conversations. GRIS recalls: "Calling him was a simple matter because he always answered his own telephone. But every so often he got the phone slammed in his ear. Cary would say, 'I *am* Cary Grant,' but the caller would refuse to believe it and demand the impostor get off the line."

NORMAN ZEILER received a call from Grant after he saw an advertisement for a raincoat manufactured by Zeiler's company. He remembers: "Cary called and told me he thought the coat was perfect for Doris Day in *That Touch of Mink*. I didn't believe it was Cary Grant, so I told him if he wanted to see our collection, he'd have to come up himself. And he did." A similar story comes from RICHARD BIENEN: "He told the receptionist who screened my calls, 'Hello, this is Cary Grant,' and she said, 'Well, hello! This is Elizabeth Taylor. What can I do for you?'"

Although Grant loved to use the telephone, he also enjoyed writing and editing. He always welcomed the opportunity to correct an article about himself before it went into print. Sometimes he insisted on it, according to JERRY D. LEWIS, who says,

"Whether I agreed with his changes or not, I always made them. One time he wanted me to put in a reference to Shakespeare. Here was the sentence as I wrote it: 'Born beside the river Avon, just as another British actor who became rather well known, Cary's birth certificate read Archibald Leach.' He asked me to put in 'Who became rather well known—one W. Shakespeare. . . .'"

Grant was a great letter writer. He painstakingly drafted many in longhand before giving them to a secretary to type. QUINCY JONES always recognized a letter from Grant: "Although his secretary typed it, Cary wrote in ink, 'Dear Quincy.' It was the first time I'd ever seen anyone do that."

The letters friends most treasure are those entirely written by hand. It was Grant's practice to send gracious and sometimes witty notes of thanks to friends, colleagues, merchants, restaurants following a great meal, airlines, the local fish market, the postman, his dentist, and the personnel at Disneyland. If he enjoyed something on Tuesday, Grant thanked you for it on Wednesday. Almost all his notes and letters to friends were signed "Happy Thoughts from me" or "Happy Thoughts," an expression he also ad-libbed in *An Affair to Remember* as he says good-bye to his Italian grandmother.

In his letters Grant demonstrated compassion, humor, and wisdom. He was able to communicate his feelings freely and eloquently, as in this note to a friend who was grieving after a loss:

DEAR ———

There is an unreality, an unacceptability, that protects the emotions of each of us when we lose someone to whom we've been close who shared our emotions and thoughts: none of us can know the degree of another's sadness, so I send this message as I would reach out a comforting hand to bring you sympathy and affection, dear friend.

He wrote compassionately to an acquaintance who was coping with a friend's terminal illness. He shared his insights with her, and this, perhaps, is what Grant himself would have wanted, were he the dying friend.

DEAR ———

. . . I am so sorry for you and those he loved. Go to him, never mind what others except the doctor think is proper for him. Go before he is snowed under with drugs. You'll give him courage.

The most difficult thing a man has to do is die. And no one should do it alone.

Sit with him. Comfort him; not with tiring small talk, but with your quiet presence when he opens his eyes and sees you sitting there between his periods of rest.

It is too late for vanity; he won't mind how he looks if you don't mind. Your very presence will help him face the unknown and assure him that he did not live unloved or without being understood; and, therefore, life was not without purpose. This is especially necessary for ———— who was childless. You'll be brave, dear. . . . Such sufferers frequently feel hot and burning. Gently apply cooling compresses to the back of his neck. It is soothing to be quietly nursed. His illness is not infectious.

When the ABC Vending Corporation wrote to its shareholders in November 1963 for suggestions about a new name, Grant happily and quickly wrote:

GENTLEMEN:

Please permit me, as an interested stockholder of many years, to suggest that in renaming your corporation you consider calling it

"ABC Dispensing"

It retains ABC and uses the "D" of dispensing in rhythm and self-explanatorily. Too, such a name requires less type-changing on all newspaper stock quotation pages, and keeps the same listed position for readers interested in the corporation's daily market activity.

With good wishes and continuing growth and success, no matter what name is eventually chosen.

Grant enjoyed gift giving. To his friends he sent sterling silver picture frames from Cartier, ice-cream makers, wheels of cheese, baked hams, cases of wine, and miniature paintings. According to RICHARD BROOKS, "He rarely exchanged gifts on Christmas or birthdays. If he was in Hong Kong, Rome, or Paris, he would send a gift because it was a nothing Tuesday. Once it was a Chinese silver pipe from Singapore. Another time it was a twenty-dollar gold coin, issued in 1900, he had had made up as a money clip."

His feeling for presents was precise and not all-embracing. "Cary objected to the commercializations of holidays," recalls RICK INGERSOLL. "He felt they were merely an excuse to force people to buy presents they didn't necessarily want to buy or give. He felt they made people feel guilty or obligated, and he did not like to give presents under those conditions. One time he said to me, 'That's a very good-looking suit you have on. I have the perfect tie for that.' I thought no more of it, and the next day he came in with a beautiful, very expensive tie, which I still have."

Grant and Dyan Cannon enjoyed spending time in "his favorite place on earth"—Palm Springs. They talked of marriage (and of children), but Grant was reluctant. He had "failed" three times before. HENRY GRIS remembers additional considerations: "Dyan told me that Cary took her to Bristol twice to get Cary's mother's approval of the marriage. Dyan said it was his condition. He wouldn't take the step without it. They went twice because the first time she didn't meet her. Cary was scared. She said Cary spent all his time with his mother in the nursing home while Dyan read books, walked through churches, and spent her days with Eric and Maggie Leach. Eventually she was presented to Mrs. Leach and was approved. Dyan said that thereafter they had good times, she and Mrs. Leach, eating fish and chips and drinking white wine. Mrs. Leach called her Betsy some of the time, but Dyan said she didn't mind."

DR. MORTIMER A. HARTMAN, who went to London with Grant on one of these trips, recollects: "One day he asked me to accompany Dyan to Bath and Bristol. I later pointed out to Cary that I thought Dyan looked like a younger Sophia Loren.

"My second trip to Bristol was with Cary, who wanted me to meet his mother, who appeared to be a very strong woman. He had great love and respect for her, and I got the sense she returned that affection. She admired him."

Reservations set aside, Grant and Dyan Cannon were married on July 22, 1965. Grant said he chose the Dunes Hotel in Las Vegas for their wedding at the "happy instigation of Charles Rich." Stanley Fox was the best man. SYLVIA FINE KAYE recalls,

Riding about the dunes in Palm Springs in 1964 with great panache and control. Actress VALERIE ALLEN: *"Cary was perfect on a horse. He rode as well as everything else he did."*

"He brought Dyan to the house a great deal so we could get to know her better. Cary asked Danny [Kaye] to put Dyan on his show, something Danny never did for anyone. But he did it for Cary."

On October 11, 1965, Grant went to work on *Walk, Don't Run*. It was an updated remake of *The More the Merrier*, a 1943 comedy that had been done with Jean Arthur, Joel McCrea, and Charles Coburn. The movie is set in Tokyo during the Olympics, with Samantha Eggar playing a British Embassy secretary and Jim Hutton an American Olympic athlete. Grant appears as a British industrialist. Charles Walters directed, and Sol C. Siegel produced.

Again Grant hired the composer, this time choosing Quincy Jones. They had first met in 1961. JONES recalls: "I was conducting for Peggy Lee, who introduced me to Grant at Basin Street East. I saw him one other time, at a great party at Peggy's. Tony Bennett sang, then Peggy sang, and then Judy Garland. There were musicians everywhere. It was the kind of house party jam session Peggy was known for.

"And then in 1965, Cary said, 'Mr. Jones, you probably don't remember that we met, but I'd like you to do my last film.' Everybody was retiring. Frank Sinatra, for whom I was also conducting, was in his second retirement. So I didn't believe him.

"Cary asked me to meet him at Columbia at two o'clock. It was the most important day of my life. My wife had the car but would return in time to drive me because I don't drive. At a quarter to two I knew she couldn't make it. I jumped in a laundry truck and asked the guy to let me out at the newsstand at the corner before Columbia. He insisted on taking me right there. I kept telling him to let me out. I wore my Italian suit and carried an attaché case. Since there was no place to sit down, I stood up. When the guy did a U-turn, he drew the attention of Cary and Sol Siegel, the film's producer. It was so embarrassing to have them see me get out of that truck.

"For me, *the* movie stars at that time were Marlon Brando, Cary Grant, Humphrey Bogart, Elizabeth Taylor, and Katharine Hepburn. I'd learned that behind the reputation is a human being. People have a frequency range of common interests and chemistry. They like each other, tolerate each other, or can't stand each other—*immediately*. The connection with Cary was instantaneous, starting with the laundry truck.

"At first Cy Coleman was going to do the score. I didn't have any name at all, so I was happy to get the job."

Grant told GEORGE BARRIE that after *Walk, Don't Run* was completed, he decided "That's it. I'm through." STANLEY DONEN, who remembers that Grant had been discussing retirement for a long time, says, "I never could understand why, but he was determined." IRVING LAZAR suggests that it wasn't vanity, that "he wasn't a vain man. I think he was a great professional who felt he had done as much as he could. There was no ambivalence. He knew he didn't want to act anymore. Perhaps it was for the same reason Garbo didn't want to. He wanted to be remembered as a leading man, the best of his kind, and didn't want to get into movies which he felt were inferior to the ones he had made."

The man closest to him, STANLEY E. FOX, believes that it was an issue of age, that "he really didn't want to play a romantic lover any longer. He said he didn't feel he was believable."

Many of Grant's friends disagreed. "Even in the last minutes of his life, he looked better than most forty-year-olds," says GEORGE KENNEDY. And BILLY WILDER protests, "At any age, Cary Grant would still be a heartbreaker. He would still be the most attractive man on the screen. He did not age one bit. His hair got gray. That's all."

"Cary knew when to stop," observes LORETTA YOUNG. "I think that was part of his genius." LOUIS JOURDAN agrees: "Moving a career into character parts or secondary parts is what an actor should do. But not Cary. You cannot possibly picture Cary Grant not being Cary Grant anymore."

BILLY WILDER expresses his disappointment at never making a film with Grant. He recalls: "When I directed *Sabrina*, we wanted Cary and Bill Holden. At the last minute he slipped through our fingers and Humphrey Bogart played the part. We also wanted him to play opposite Audrey Hepburn in *Love in the Afternoon*. But maybe three days before shooting there was no deal. So we went with Gary Cooper.

"When Cary retired, I started concocting stories for a man with gray hair in his early seventies, but he told me, 'No, I'm not going to do it anymore.' He guarded the last few years of his life brilliantly. But to the very end I can assure you there were several pictures for which the studios wanted Cary, but he was just not available."

He had his reasons, mundane and profound:

CG: I got tired of getting up a six o'clock and tripping over all those cables and drinking coffee out of styrofoam cups. It's not as glamorous as you might think.

You can never go back. It's not possible. I could make another film, but I'd be playing a different man. People are used to me as a certain kind of fellow, and I can't make that kind of film anymore. It would have been a great disappointment for an audience to see an aging actor that they knew when he was young. It reminds you of your own age. You'd think, "Oh, my God, do I look like that?"

LOUIS JOURDAN muses, "Can you imagine the wonderful parts he must have turned down in the last twenty years?"

It wasn't only the parts after retirement that he turned down. Like all actors, as noted, he had declined some great roles.

JOURDAN remembers one of them: "He was offered Rex Harrison's part in *My Fair Lady*. He refused. He told my wife, 'It's because I can't do better than Rex Harrison. That's not for me. I cannot play a dialectician—a perfect English professor. It wouldn't be believable.' His judgment was extremely intelligent and instinctive and overpowered the vanity of being offered that part." PETER STONE has a similar anecdote: "When Jack Warner asked Cary to do *My Fair Lady*, he said, 'You don't understand. My accent is cockney! I sound the way 'Liza does at the beginning of the film. How can I play Henry Higgins?' Cary said, 'Not only won't I play Professor Higgins, but if Rex doesn't, I won't even see it!'"

CG: Jack Warner also begged me to do *The Music Man*, but I declined because nobody could do that role as well as Bob Preston.

HENRY GRIS says, "Bob Taplinger [former chief of publicity at Warner Bros.] told me Grant was offered a million dollars to star in *Man of La Mancha*." According to PETER BOGDANOVICH, "He could have been paid three, four, five million a picture." IRVING LAZAR adds, "He didn't need the money, so he wasn't even tempted. I once offered him three million dollars to do a movie, which today would be twenty million, and he wouldn't do it. He said, 'It's not a question of money. I wouldn't do it for any amount.'"

In 1977 Warren Beatty was producing *Heaven Can Wait* and was considering Peter Bogdanovich as the director. BOGDANOVICH remembers: "Warren said that Cary was interested in doing the Mr. Jordan role. I very much liked the Elaine May script *and* Warren, but the main attraction was Cary Grant."

"One morning I called Cary to ask him about the picture. He was out. A couple of hours later Warren dropped by, and while we were making a sandwich, Cary phoned back. I hadn't yet told Warren about placing the call. I bit the bullet, pretended Warren wasn't there, and asked if Cary was in fact going to do the part. Cary said, 'I've told Warren I'm not going to do that picture. I wouldn't tell Warren, but it's not a good part. Long speeches. Stands around a lot. Everybody else gets the jokes. Claude Rains did it quite well in the first picture,' he said, referring to the original version of the story, *Here Comes Mr. Jordan* (1940), 'but I'm not going to do that.'

"I outlined some simple but drastic changes, but he stopped me, saying, 'No, if you rewrite the role for me and I don't play it, then you won't be able to find anyone else.'"

STANLEY E. FOX, who wanted him to go on, says, "There was one script, called something like *Counsel for the Defense*, which was set in a small town in England. Cary would have played the role of a barrister whose daughter was kidnapped. Cary said, 'I'm a new father, and a kidnapping could very easily happen to me. I don't see the humor in any of this.'" And PETER STONE says, "He said the only thing he would do was a part with no lines in a wheelchair. He didn't want to move, and he didn't want to talk. It was his joke."

There was at least one more major missed opportunity:

CG: I had to back out of *The Bridge on the River Kwai* because of another commitment. I slimmed down a lot to do the part, but you know you can't do them all. I was sorry to have missed it . . . but Bill Holden was very happy. He got that one—and ten percent of the gross.

271

CG at sixty. Attorney-partner-friend STANLEY E. FOX: *"He really didn't want to play a romantic lover any longer. He said he didn't feel he was believable."*

As late as 1958 Grant still hoped to produce Jonathan Swift's eighteenth-century novel *Gulliver's Travels*. Touring the provinces as a boy had appealed to Grant and may explain his attraction to the *Travels*. In 1949 Grant had telephoned Thornton Wilder at the Hotel Jerome in Aspen, Colorado. He and Howard Hawks were contemplating an adaptation and wanted Wilder to write the screenplay.

On August 23, 1949, Wilder responded by hand, in pencil, on three-ring binder-type lined paper. He had pages of suggestions but wrote, "If I ever work on a movie again, it will be an 'original.'" However, STANLEY DONEN says, "Cary never mentioned *Gulliver's Travels* to me. I'm glad he didn't do it because there are just too many around—cartoons and live actions. It would not have been a good idea." Eight years before his retirement Grant had said, "Don't laugh. I'd give a tasteful performance as Gulliver."

"The worthiest of men retire from the world" is a quotation scribbled in one of Grant's ever-present notebooks. He wondered who wrote it. He never found out, but he lived it. Grant's unannounced retirement remained unannounced. He never made a formal statement. Nevertheless, it was, to him, official. At the age of sixty-two his life was about to take on new meaning. Just as he returned from Tokyo and making *Walk, Don't Run*, his life permanently changed. The most important person, then and for the rest of his days, came into his life. Her name was Jennifer.

CHAPTER FIFTEEN

IT'S A GIRL!

CG: I could have gone on acting and playing a grand-father or a bum, but I discovered more important things in life. I retired when I became a father because I didn't want to miss any part of my daughter's growing up. Jennifer is the best production I ever made.

Grant was filled with wonder about the birth process. On February 25, 1966, the day before his daughter's birth, he wrote his mother:

> Watching, and being with, my wife as she bears her pregnancy and goes toward the miraculous experience of giving birth to our first child, I'm moved to tell you how much I appreciate, and now better understand, all you must have endured to have me. All the fears you probably knew and the joy and, although I didn't ask you to go through all that, I'm so pleased you did; because in so doing, you gave me my life.
>
> Thank you, dear mother, I may have written similar words before but, recently, because of Dyan, the thoughts became more poignant and clear. I send you love and gratitude.

The next day, February 26, 1966, Dyan Cannon gave birth to their only child at St. John's Hospital in Los Angeles. They called her Jennifer and left her second name open so she could make her own choice later in life. Grant said Jennifer's "little turned-up nose looked quite Irish, the result perhaps of our honeymoon trip through Ireland last summer." And he proudly told friends he was "sixty-two years, one month, and nine days old" when Jennifer was born. Grant gave his wife a beautiful diamond and sapphire bracelet as a keepsake.

They received congratulatory letters from people all over the world and conscientiously answered each one. One reply reads:

> Thank you for such happy words about the delightful new addition to our family. I have just dictated the word delightful. It's such an inadequate word; Jennifer is not only delightful but attractive, quite beautiful, sweet-smelling, unblemished and incredible. In every way the unusually wonderful baby of all proud parents, a joy.
>
> We'll be taking Jennifer to England during the summer to visit my mother, who is 89 years old and naturally eager to see her first grandchild.

They formed a book of congratulatory notes for Jennifer to see as soon as she could learn to read. (Her proud father thought: *It could easily be tomorrow*.) They unfailingly sent novel letters of thanks for gifts:

> Our little daughter Jennifer can see your pretty rattle and can hear your pretty rattle, but can't yet write to thank you for sending it to her, so we will. Especially because it's a very attractive rattle bearing a mellow dulcet, pleasing tone that, unlike other rattles, won't rattle her. Which, come to think of it, probably explains the expression's origin.

Walter O'Malley, then owner of the Los Angeles Dodgers, even offered to install diaper service at Dodger Stadium.

The happy parents were deluged with requests for interviews and photographs. They knew if they gave in to one source, they'd antagonize others. If they obliged everyone, it would result in an endless procedure and a lifetime of harassment to the child. They decided no interviews or photographs would be given until the event became less topical. They planned instead to release an official photograph at a later date.

Thelma Orloff and Dyan Cannon's friend Addie Gould gave a baby shower at the Bevery Hills Hotel for about thirty women. According to ORLOFF, "When Cary walked in, they all dropped dead. He sat right down and talked to everyone, and the women were absolutely beside themselves. He surprised Addie, me, and Dyan with a beautiful gold watch. I still have mine. Addie had a child about Jennifer's age. As they got older, Cary often took her along to romp with Jennifer."

BEA SHAW remembers a dinner at Danny Kaye's house one night when Kaye's daughter was a teenager: "Dena came in, threw her arms around Danny Kaye, and said, 'Hi, Daddy.' Cary turned to me and said, 'Just think . . . someday Jennifer will come in and throw her arms around me and say, 'Hi, Daddy.'"

RICHARD ANDERSON says, "Cary's telephone calls about Jennifer and what it was like to be a father sometimes lasted for more than an hour." SYLVIA WU recalls, "He always had a stack of pictures of Jennifer in his pocket. If I hadn't seen him in a while, he would pull out the pictures and say, 'This is why.'" And according to PEGGY LEE, "When he had Jennifer, that was the main event. The wonder of having a child never left him. I've seen fathers look at babies but never the way Cary looked at Jennifer."

BEA SHAW admired Grant as a father: "Cary was a real pro at everything. I watched him diaper her one day, but when he tried to put her frilly panties on over her diaper, she kept squirming away from him. He said, 'Come on, give me a hand.' And then, to Jennifer's great delight, he slipped the panties over her feet and held her upside down by the ankles while I pulled the panties up over the diaper." THELMA ORLOFF observes: "His whole life was Jennifer, starting with the day she was born. He put pictures of her completely around the top of his bedroom between the ceiling and the bookshelves."

On April 18 Grant wrote to his cousins Eric and Maggie and asked them to inquire about renting a secluded and fully staffed house for July, August, and September. The family planned to leave for England by boat on June 27, with a possibility of going to Paris during August. Dyan Cannon inquired about the availability in Bristol of certain baby foods, appliances, and diaper services. THELMA ORLOFF, who saw them off, reports: "They took with them the folding crib I bought for Jennifer. They were like two young kids on a honeymoon with a baby."

They sailed for Southampton aboard the SS *Oriana* and returned by way of the Orient, stopping in Hong Kong.

Mindful of tradition and eager to affirm his allegiance to his origins, Grant wished to have Jennifer baptized in the same parish church where he had been christened sixty-two years earlier. The baptismal form, however, required that he and Dyan Cannon agree to raise their child as an Episcopalian. Since the minister wouldn't waive the condition and they didn't wish to impose a religious point of view on their daughter, she wasn't baptized.

BEA SHAW recalls, "His mother had said, 'I don't want to see too much of this baby because I'll fall in love with her and then you'll take her away again.' Cary understood but felt sorry for her."

Elsie Leach was nearly ninety. DR. PAGE wrote: "I see no reason why she shouldn't live to be 100. . . . She is just as active in her body as ever she has been." When Grant was asked to describe his mother after a visit, he said, "She is active, wiry, and witty. She doesn't eat very much. And never did. It might be the secret to her longevity."

By the summer of 1967 Grant's fourth marriage was in trouble. Dyan Cannon had left him, rented a house—and taken Jennifer with her. Johnny Maschio and his wife, Constance Moore, tried to get the couple back together. MASCHIO says, "We got some champagne and caviar and invited Cary and Dyan for an overnight sail on our forty-eight-foot cruiser. We all got loaded and showed up barefooted for a late breakfast at the California Yacht Club, which sent us back for shoes.

"Cary said, 'I want to take Dyan and you and Connie to New York for a couple of weeks.' I couldn't go; but Connie did, and they stayed at the Sherry-Netherland. They were out every night at Twenty-one or El Morocco. They had a ball.

"But Dyan and Cary didn't stay together. He came to live with us in our three-bedroom, three-bathroom apartment at the Churchill on Wilshire Boulevard in Westwood because he was fixing up his house. He was with us for four months. Stanley Fox came every day. Connie picked up Jennifer and brought her to the apartment so he could play with her. He was so upset about that divorce. It really was heartbreaking."

With Jennifer at advertising executive Bea Shaw's house. SHAW: "Cary was a real pro at everything. I watched him diaper her one day, but when he tried to put her frilly panties on over her diaper, she kept squirming away from him. He said, 'Come on, give me a hand.' And then, to Jennifer's great delight, he slipped the panties over her feet and held her upside down by the ankles while I pulled the panties up over the diaper."

PETER BOGDANOVICH, who saw Grant and Cannon together on only two occasions, observes: "But I somehow felt Cary was more in love with her than she was with him. Certainly he doted on her and seemed to do whatever she asked, and she appeared to enjoy showing him off. 'Sing 'em that song, Archie!' she cried out on the way back from a ball game."

At the time of the separation Grant's first goal was to protect Jennifer from the press. He became even more protective when Cannon tried to serve him with a subpoena demanding he appear in court to decide the terms of Jennifer's custody. Distraught, Grant called BEA SHAW, who remembers: "Cary asked if anyone was staying in my guesthouse. I told him it was vacant and he was welcome to move in. He said, 'Dyan is trying to subpoena me to come to court, and I cannot put Jennifer through that. Barbara Hutton went through this, and it just ruined her. Even though Jennifer is a baby, she'll read about it when she's older, and people will tell her about it.'

"Aside from the members of my household, nobody ever knew he was there except Stanley Fox and the secretary who brought Cary his mail every day. He kept his Rolls-Royce parked in back. The car was tan with a black top. It looked like Cary. That particular visit he stayed a couple of months, maybe longer."

THELMA ORLOFF says, "The whole thing was difficult, but it's nice that Jennifer was brought up so beautifully by both her mother and her father. Whatever they did, they did right because she's a lovely girl."

Dyan Cannon took the baby to New York, where Cannon was appearing onstage. Grant followed them to be close to Jennifer.

The publicity surrounding the breakup of his marriage made it impossible for him to stay in his usual apartment at the Plaza Hotel. Reporters and photographers camped out day and night, hoping to catch him coming and going with Jennifer. Robert Taplinger saw what was going on and offered to put Grant up at his Forty-ninth Street town house. Grant was sequestered there for five months. On Sundays he used David Tebet's apartment on East Fifty-fifth Street. HENRY GRIS says, "Taplinger told me it was a terrible period for Cary. Dyan was being difficult about his seeing their child, and that gave him anguish. Taplinger said Cary waited in the house all day for word from the nurse as to when he could get to see his little girl for an hour or two. He'd just sit and hope the phone would ring. He wouldn't make plans with *anyone* if he thought there was a chance he could see his child."

Taplinger, who was now doing public relations work for George Barrie, the founder and president of Fabergé, suggested to Barrie that Grant join Fabergé's board. Not surprisingly Barrie jumped at the suggestion. So Taplinger arranged a dinner party to introduce the two men. Grant told GRIS that George Barrie became a frequent, almost nightly visitor and that "gradually they started talking shop. By the time Barrie made his offer, Cary was hoping he would ask."

BARRIE remembers, "Cary was nervous about what he would have to do for Fabergé. I told him that he'd just have to be associated with the company and we'd go around and meet people." But HENRY GRIS observes, "If Barrie had merely been another business tycoon, Cary wouldn't have . . . but George fascinated him."

CG: What a background. Son of a Brooklyn house painter. Started in life as a musician playing the saxophone. Came up from the very bottom. Put in years in show business. He spoke its jargon. I told myself: "I wouldn't be going anywhere if I joined him. I'd be coming home."

Grant and Barrie became inseparable. In March 1968 Cannon left New York and took Jennifer back to California. Grant wanted to follow immediately. To send him off, Taplinger arranged a dinner party, inviting George Barrie and his then wife, Gloria; Grant and his date, Gratia von Furstenberg; and Micky and Norman Zeiler. After dinner the Zeilers' chauffeur, Troy Lindahl, drove Grant and von Furstenberg to the airport. Grant would not let anyone accompany them. MICKY ZEILER says, "It was a terrible night. There was an awful rainstorm. We begged him not to go to the airport, but he wouldn't listen. The next day was his day to be with Jennifer, and he wouldn't give that up for anything." BARRIE says, "There was no doubt about his leaving. I wanted to see him off, but Cary insisted it wasn't necessary to accompany him on such a night."

ZEILER continues, "On the way to the airport a huge trailer van came from the other side of the highway. Its caboose got loose and smashed right into our car." HENRY GRIS says,

"Taplinger told me that Barrie was still at the house when the hospital called, and they rushed out to Queens, numb with fear and reproaching themselves for letting Cary go."

Grant and Von Furstenberg were taken to St. John's Hospital in Elmhurst, Queens. According to MICKEY ZEILER, "Gratia was badly hurt and had a brace from her foot to her waist. Cary's nose was smashed, and his ribs were broken." The next day the hospital was deluged with telephone calls, gifts, and bouquets. Peggy Lee sent Grant his favorite springtime flowers, yellow and white daisies. Sylvia Fine Kaye sent a blossoming dogwood tree. For seventeen days he was ably cared for by Sister Thomas Francis. All of Grant's friends rallied around him.

Later, when Grant read in a newspaper that St. John's Hospital needed money, he phoned and asked what he could do to help. Grateful for the care he had been given, he agreed to pose with 450 men and women for pictures at five dollars a shot. The place was bedlam.

While Grant was in the hospital, the divorce proceedings in Los Angeles went as scheduled for March 20. Dyan Cannon made her lamentations public. On March 21 all the newspapers reported what she had to say.

DAVID TEBET, who went to the hospital the very day Cannon's story hit the newspapers, recalls, "She beat up on him in the press. It made me angry. I said, 'Cary, what do you want to do? Aren't you going to answer any of this?' And he said, 'No. I'm not going to do anything. The poor dear doesn't know what she's doing.' His words stuck with me all these years. They could only come from a man like Cary."

GEORGE BARRIE explains, "He never wanted Jennifer to be exposed. She was his main concern." HENRY GRIS recounts: "Taplinger told me that all Cary ever said was 'After all—she's the mother of my child.'" Eventually Grant's trial lawyer released a statement: "If Miss Cannon feels a need to seek public sympathy and approbation through a press agent, that is up to her. As Mr. Grant's legal representative we have good reason for our decisions, and each action is carefully considered, and taken, in accordance only to what is best for his child's welfare."

When Grant left the hospital, George Barrie flew him to Los Angeles, where he returned to Bea Shaw's guesthouse to recuperate. All he wanted was to be as close as possible to Jennifer.

George Barrie was now a brother to him, and Grant never forgot it. BEA SHAW says, "For a while, if Cary stood up too quickly, he would feel dizzy and have to steady himself. Otherwise, he recovered quickly from the accident and rarely mentioned it."

Dyan Cannon gained custody of Jennifer in a Santa Monica court. She was awarded twenty-five hundred dollars per month in alimony and two thousand dollars per month, including the nurse's salary, in child support. Grant got visitation privileges. Cannon lived in the Malibu Colony. More than once when Grant came to pick up Jennifer, he couldn't get past the Colony's guard because there were no instructions to admit him. So he solved the problem and moved himself in behind the gates, renting a place two buildings away from their house.

PETER BOGDANOVICH, whose oldest daughter was just a year older than Jennifer, says, "One of the points of interest between us over the years was our daughters and our mutual divorces and how they affected the children. Cary said to me, 'The women always win in the end. You might as well just face it and give in, because they're going to win anyway.'"

Grant and Dyan Cannon agreed that to avoid spoiling Jennifer, the staggering deluge of dolls, books, toys, and boxes of still unknown contents received at Christmas would not be opened all at once but three or four days apart. HENRY GRIS explains, "Both Cary and Dyan kept a cupboard filled with packages. There were so many presents that they were never able to exhaust the supply from year to year. When Jennifer behaved particularly well or had done a kindness, Cary said he told her, 'When we give, we get,' and he would hand her a box out of the cupboard."

When he wasn't at the beach with Jennifer, Grant continued to stay in BEA SHAW's guesthouse. She recalls: "My kitchen pantry was always in disarray, and Cary was always straightening it. He'd go into this cockney accent, 'Oh, blimey, look at this cupboard. The mustard goes with the mustard, the ketchup with the ketchup, all the labels facing front.' I was on the telephone one day in my office, with a really important call, and Cary came in and said, 'Do you know you have seven jars of mustard all in different places?' That Christmas he gave me a beautiful pin—a little gold teddy bear with sapphire eyes and a ruby mouth. On the card he wrote, 'Here's a little fellow to keep you company until I can find something you really need. Like a pot of mustard . . .'

"He showed me the diaries he kept. He would pretend to read while I looked at them, but if I chuckled, he'd say, 'What? What are you reading?' I'd tell him, and sometimes he'd say, 'I don't feel that way anymore. I've outgrown that.'"

When Bobby Kennedy was shot in Los Angeles on June 5, 1968, Grant was deeply affected. BEA SHAW recalls, "We were having dinner when we heard the news. Cary shook his head and said, 'When you're too good, it makes the world angry and they try to kill you.' Then he told me the most touching story. He said, 'One night Bobby and Ethel and I left a dinner and dashed through a heavy rain to the car. Ethel was drenched, her makeup streaked, and her hair streaming into her face. Bobby looked over at her and said softly, 'You're so pretty.' And Ethel's face lit up like a schoolgirl's.'

"The next day, at Ethel's invitation, Cary flew to the funeral."

Following Kennedy's death, Grant taped a plea for gun control to be played on radio stations across the country. His sentiments were heartfelt.

> CG: The flags are still at half-mast for Robert Kennedy. Suddenly July Fourth—a jubilant day—becomes a day for reflection. Since 1900, seven hundred and fifty thousand Americans—three quarters of a million, have been killed by private guns in private hands. What about that? Today those hands may be the hands of murderers, psychopaths, delinquents, all with legal access to guns. The man who wants a gun badly will probably get one, whatever laws we pass. But in the name of sanity, why do we make it so easy for killers to kill? Responsible gun owners agree that two safeguards are needed. First, a ban on mail-order guns; second, licensing and registration. This is Cary Grant begging you to write or wire your senator or congressman, urging them to vote for sensible gun control.

In September 1968 Grant took another excursion into analysis. He attended at least one session directed by the American Behavioral Institute. In preparation for the seminar, he wrote a biographical summary. It beautifully encapsulates Cary Grant's state of mind in the fall of 1968 and the attitude he held for the future:

> I am a sixty-five-year-old professional man, recently divorced for the fourth time, and father of a two-and-a-half-year-old daughter. I am happier than I have ever been, yet not as happy as I intend to be.
>
> I am often pessimistic, yet mainly optimistic. I no longer resist, or inhibit, the penetration of knowledge which I trust will eventually result in wisdom!
>
> I enjoy the boundless feeling of love and intend to let it grow forever within me. I intend to try to set a good example to, and live with consideration of, others.
>
> Looking back upon my life, I occasionally wish I had known enough to choose a profession that could have been more directly beneficial to others. But, since I didn't, I must take that into consideration in all future endeavors.
>
> I have learned to accept with understanding the behavior of society, and each individual, even tho' sometimes I give vent to what I consider justified anger.
>
> I am enjoying the self-exposure and, therefore, hope others also will enjoy self-revelation.
>
> It's a good day and a good life!

CHAPTER SIXTEEN

THE INTERNATIONAL BUSINESSMAN

CG: If I had continued in motion pictures, I would have had to commit six months or a year in advance to be in a certain place at a certain time for a certain job. I wouldn't have been able to leave for ten weeks or more. I wanted to spend more time with my daughter. Her mother was off making movies, and I had to fly to different places to be with my child.

Commercial airlines were too public. Besides, by the time I got there, I never had any time alone with her. So I joined different companies, sat on various boards, and was provided with private jets. I had easy movement at a moment's notice with no questions asked. This way I visited my daughter and still had a job.

In May 1968 Fabergé announced that Cary Grant had been elected to the board of directors of Rayette Fabergé, Inc., the cosmetics and toiletries company. In commenting upon the announcement, George Barrie said Grant's "business acumen and creativity, his awareness of public taste, and identity with good grooming will prove invaluable to the company." Grant's first corporate affiliation outside the motion-picture industry took everyone by surprise.

Why had the leading actor of the day chosen to represent a fragrance company when he had turned down millions of dollars in offers for films, for commercials, and for writing his autobiography?

GEORGE BARRIE says, "Cary didn't want a salary. I insisted he have something, so I started him off at five thousand dollars a year. I don't think he ever made more than twenty-five thousand dollars a year with the company. He had about twenty thousand stock options when the stock was seven, eight, or nine dollars, but he let them lapse. He got new ones when the stock was about twenty and finally picked them up. When we sold the company, he got thirty-two or thirty-three dollars a share. It's a nice appreciation, but he would have had a lot more if he hadn't lapsed the previous options. He was interested in a private plane and expenses, not money."

To Barrie's surprise, Grant requested a small prop plane instead of a jet. BARRIE remembers: "He wanted to cross the country, caravan style, in an old DC-3, which flew at a hundred and twenty miles an hour. So I got it for him. It was hilarious. Soon he was flying coast to coast with his French girl friend, Clotilde [Barot] Feldman [the pretty young widow of agent-producer Charles Feldman; she lived in Los Angeles but kept an apartment in Paris]. They'd stop in St. Louis and other places and spend the night. The plane had to fly low because it wasn't pressurized. It took them *days*.

"I thought the DC-3 was ridiculous and convinced him he ought to have a Convair, which is pressurized and can fly over weather. We changed its configuration to seat seventeen, fixed it up with a piano, and had a crew of two hanging around, but he hardly used it. Finally we sold it, and Cary used one of the company jets."

RODERICK MANN points out, "There is something inherently glamorous about travel by private jet. I am reminded of the scene in *That Touch of Mink* where Cary sends Doris Day to Bermuda for the weekend in an empty Boeing 707. I asked Cary one time whether he had ever done that in real life. He said, 'Yes.' I asked him whether the girl was anyone I knew. 'No,' he said, 'it's somebody I know.'"

Grant's association with Fabergé began in 1968 and lasted for eighteen years. He had an office on the first floor of the old Vanderbilt townhouse at 5 West Fifty-fourth Street and stayed up the street at the Warwick, the hotel that William Randolph Hearst had built for Marion Davies and where Grant was pampered by the staff. Eventually Fabergé moved to the Burlington House, on the Avenue of the Americas between Fifty-fourth and Fifty-fifth streets. A company helicopter kept by the East River near the Queensboro Bridge was at his disposal. He used it for vacations at Barrie's house in Connecticut or to visit the Zeilers in Westhampton, on Long Island. Until Jennifer was five or six years old, Grant often visited MICKY ZEILER in Westhampton. She says, "He would bring Jennifer, a little friend of hers, and his housekeeper, Willie." Willie Lee Watson, a grandmother from Tulsa, Oklahoma, was one of Jennifer's first nurses. When she left Dyan Cannon's employ, Grant asked her to come work for him. Willie was always a comfort to Jennifer when she visited. She accompanied Grant whenever he traveled with Jennifer, including several trips to Bristol and vacations in Paris and Monte Carlo. She was Grant's all-around housekeeper.

They stayed at the Zeilers' for two or three weeks at a time. "Cary included Jennifer in everything," says MICKY ZEILER. "You never saw such devotion. She was the apple of his eye. He would patiently explain everything and read to her for hours and hours. He was the most charming houseguest. I can still see him in his watermelon-colored pajamas." NORMAN ZEILER adds, "Cary would get up in the morning, sing a few songs, jump in the pool, and spend the rest of the day with Jennifer on my boat." MICKY ZEILER continues, "I had been a swimming instructor, so I taught Jennifer how to swim. She took to it right away."

BOBBY ALTMAN, who lives just down the road from the Zeilers' in Westhampton, remembers: "Cary and I spent a lot of time together during these weekends. He never liked to wear shoes. He'd always show up barefoot for lunch or at night when we went to eat at Casa Basso."

STEVE ROSS, who met Grant many times at Norman Zeiler's house, says, "My heart would go out to him. Everyone sits back and thinks it's fantastic to be Cary Grant, which it was, of course, but a nanny had to take his daughter onto the beach. You could see how wistfully he would watch Jennifer go. He couldn't take two steps on a public beach without people asking for his autograph."

During these years when he came to New York, Grant called CHARLOTTE FORD, who remembers: "My daughter Elena and Jennifer were the same age, and I invited Jennifer for lunch. When Cary came to get Jennifer, I told him I thought it'd be fun to take

CG, Jennifer Grant, and Micky Zeiler at her Long Island home. ZEILER: *"He was the most charming houseguest. I can still see him in his watermelon-colored pajamas."*

the kids to the park. And he said, 'No, I can't do that.' . . . So I took the kids to the park without him."

His total lack of privacy in public places was the aspect of stardom Grant disliked.

In time he preferred to talk about almost anything other than his film career. The public wouldn't let him forget it, but he made it clear to his friends he didn't want to live in the past. DAN MELNICK says, "In his later years Cary would pretend (I say pretend because I don't believe it really was his attitude) that acting wasn't for grown-ups. He said he was more interested in business and politics and life. But when you got him talking about pictures, he had a good time. We were sitting around after dinner, and someone mentioned *Talk of the Town*. And he said, 'I played with Jean Arthur.' When I mentioned that he had played Leopold

From left, *housekeeper Willie Lee Watson; Gerald Ford; Jennifer Grant, ten; and CG, seventy-two, March 26, 1976.*

Dilg, he said, 'How did you ever remember that? If my life depended on it, I couldn't tell you the names of the characters.' He pretended not to be connected emotionally to all the films he made."

Grant once said to Gregory Peck, "Well, it's all a put-on, isn't it?" PECK, who agreed with Grant's philosophy, says, "I thought that was a wonderful way to express it because Cary had a little conspiracy going with the audience. They were just having fun."

RICH LITTLE, who was amused by Grant's ambivalent attitude, recalls: "We'd sit on planes, or we'd be at a party, and we'd start talking about his movies, and he'd say [Little imitating CG], 'Now, wait a minute. I don't want to talk about that.' 'Why?' I asked. He would say, 'I don't want to talk about my old movies. . . . My movies are a thing of the past. I'm only interested in real things.' But within ten minutes we'd be talking about his movies again."

George Barrie and CG on Fabergé business in Madrid, May 12, 1980. BARRIE: *"He would tell people not to use makeup—that makeup was a turnoff."*

Grant liked his new occupation. "Somehow Cary seemed to think the life of a businessman," MICKY ZEILER says, "was more respectable—or admirable—than acting. He enjoyed being on the board of various companies." KIRK KERKORIAN appointed Grant as a director for MGM and Western Airlines because he was a good businessman, because he was "well respected and serious about contributing. He had an excellent point of view. He rarely made comments at board meetings, but when he did, they were well thought out and succinct. He went straight to the issue." DAVID MAHONEY adds, "When I was chairman of Norton Simon, Cary came to my annual stockholders' meeting three or four years in a row. People thought I asked Cary to come to divert the audience, but it wasn't true. Cary was interested in how big business worked."

MARJORIE EVERETT and Grant met after she was made a director of Hollywood Park in 1971. She recalls: "Cary became an investor and went on the board on October 13, 1977. I relied a great deal on his judgment. He had great respect for women in the business world. For example, he respected Irene Selznick tremendously. A lot of men like women, but he was almost deferential. He was very, very supportive and helpful.

"We were going to have a proxy ballot, and a group who had very little stock wanted to take over Hollywood Park. Cary agreed to run on our slate, against the other group. And I thought, *Why would this famous and popular man want to get into a battle?* He phoned people and asked them to vote for our slate. We won. Cary showed a great deal of courage and guts."

Being a "businessman," however, had its drawbacks as far as Grant was concerned. Again he had to confront his fear of public speaking. GEORGE BARRIE recalls Grant's first Fabergé sales meeting: "We had a thousand people in the ballroom at the Americana Hotel in San Juan, Puerto Rico. Nobody knew he was there. All we wanted Cary to say was a few words. He agreed if I would walk out with him. I started the meeting, but Cary didn't arrive. Somebody else kept talking while I went to Cary's suite. He was scared stiff. I said, 'Cary, you've got to start this sooner or later. Just come down and say hello. That's all you have to do. You don't have to take questions, and you don't have to sign autographs.'

"I went back to the meeting, saw him coming, and introduced him as a new member of our company. The applause was incredible. He came up to the platform with me and spoke to the audience. It was fantastic. It was a great moment for him and for us.

"Little by little he started to loosen up. All the key people in the organization knew him, and they all got very friendly. He told jokes and stories and cursed like anybody. There were no formalities."

However, there were ironies. "Cary was anti-cosmetic," BARRIE continues. "He would tell people, 'Don't use makeup. Makeup is a turnoff.' I didn't really care because it made him more real, and we weren't heavily in cosmetics. Fabergé was primarily a fragrance business."

CG: I don't like an abundance of makeup or perfume. When a woman overdoes it, it becomes immediate evidence of her insecurity. I find a woman attractive for her lack of artifice. I like a woman to come on straight—for everything to be just what it is. It's nice, and you feel comfortable that way. It's awful to be doing an act all the time. Just be whatever you are. If you're accepted for that, so much the better.

Once I was established, I used to create a stir on the set by not using makeup. I'd let them put it on me, so that everyone was employed, and then I'd wipe it off. Later, I found if I kept a suntan, it wasn't necessary to wear makeup.

LESLIE CARON observes, "Cary was dark-skinned naturally and took the sun very well. But during *Father Goose* he learned why a suntan doesn't always work. We were shooting the scene where he shaves off his beard for our marriage. When the beard was shaved, it revealed his very white chin! He had no choice. This time he had to use makeup. He was furious. I said, 'Well, you see, Cary, this is exactly what happens to us girls. Not all of us can go in the sun, and we want to have the color even out. This is why we wear makeup. Without it we'd have splotches and a red nose!'"

Women were not his only targets.

CG: I just can't believe any newscaster who uses makeup. When I see an orange anchorman, I think, *How can I take this man seriously?*

Among Grant's personal papers there was a short poem that summarizes his attitude toward makeup:

SHADOW AND SUBSTANCE
Most women wear eye shadow
I don't know why they do
That bluish stuff must cost enough
Takes time applying, too.
A lot more fun I'd think it,
At least with most adults,
To stay up late and dissipate
And get the same results

[Author unknown]

Being a "businessman" also meant handling an expense account. Grant, whose reputation for prudent and conservative spending preceded him, spent Fabergé's money the same way he spent his own—watchfully. GEORGE BARRIE claims Grant never abused his expense account: "He was extremely cautious about money. I finally opened charge accounts for him in different restaurants because he'd look over a bill, read it, and add it over again. It was embarrassing. And it wasn't even his money!"

Long before he started spending Fabergé's money, Grant had a reputation as a tightwad. He told BEA SHAW, "People accuse me of reading the check in a restaurant before I pay it. Of course, I read it. It's a bill. Do you pay your bills without looking at them?"

JOHN FORSYTHE says, "Cary wasn't a wasteful man, but he wasn't cheap either." And HENRY GRIS offers his opinion on Grant's "stinginess": "One morning in Ireland I remember Cary wore a cardigan with holes in the elbows. He noticed my look and said, 'I'm having it mended. It's my favorite cardigan. I bought it here in Ireland, and I just love it. I don't care if it has holes.' People would make a point of how stingy he was. But I don't think that was stinginess. It was his love for the cardigan."

JUDY QUINE was charmed with what she saw as Grant's lack of snobbery: "He had made an enormous success and yet seemed never to forget that money was something very real. And that's all it was. Money. It wasn't image. It wasn't self-esteem. It was just dollars. It bought stuff. It bought freedom. It bought safety from certain things. It's comfort of a certain kind but not label stuff you have to splatter all over yourself to identify that you're a success in some way. And I always thought that was such a delicious, wonderful trait about him."

"When an actor is intelligent about his money, he becomes a tightwad," BURT REYNOLDS observes. "If he was in any other profession, a banker, a lawyer, or an architect, he would be smart about money. Cary was smart. There was nothing tight about him at all. He picked up checks and bought you dinner and did lots of things for people. He just didn't go crazy with his money, which everybody out here does. People who didn't know him at all love to say he bought people hot dogs. Well, I think that's terrific. I love hot dogs. And I would rather have a hot dog with Cary Grant than steak with about anybody I know."

BEA SHAW remembers, "In a restaurant when he saw young people whom he felt couldn't quite afford it, he paid their check on the way out. They found out after he left. If he heard on the news that a tragedy had taken place, he sent money but never with his name attached to it."

"You'll hear that he was tight with a buck," says MARVIN DAVIS. "Well, I used to have to fight him for the check!" SYLVIA WU found him a difficult man to repay: "Because I was his guest so often, I didn't want him to pay when he came to the restaurant. We had terrible arguments. He used to call and say, 'We won't come unless you give us the check.'"

STANLEY E. FOX, too, found Grant an extremely generous man: "He never allowed me, or people who joined us at the table, to pick up the check. I would get very angry with him and tell him he should let me pay once in a while, but he wouldn't hear of it. Sometimes he would give money to the captain before we'd sit down and tell him not to bring the bill to me. It went on all through the years. He never let me pay for anything."

IRVING LAZAR says, "Cary told me he was tight. I never saw any evidence of his being the penny pincher he said he was. Frankly he was extremely generous and thoughtful with me and Mary. He, more than anybody else, started the idea that he was tight." And DAN MELNICK, who had heard stories for years about Grant's pinching his pennies, says, "I certainly never saw it. Quite the contrary. Cary was prudent, and he enjoyed quality. He had made millions, but he wasn't affected by it. He still turned off the lights and put a nickel in the meter rather than pay two dollars every quarter of an hour at a garage and then wait forever to get the car back. But people confuse turning off the lights with greed and avarice. If the man was avaricious, he sure had the opportunity. He had a sense of values. And that's what I loved in the guy."

Yet, according to QUINCY JONES, "He threw dollars around like manhole covers. He would get mad at me when we were at the racetrack and I got crazy. One time I ran out of money and wanted to keep going. I asked Cary for a thousand dollars, and he said, 'I won't do it. I don't want you to lose your money.' He wouldn't give it to me. No way."

BEA SHAW believes that Grant's experience during World War I permanently affected him: "I think we forget what living through the war meant for the British. Cary was a young, impressionable boy then, and it probably taught him to be careful about how he spent his money, to squirrel it away and not be frivolous. Even in his later years he kept saying, 'I want to be careful for Jennifer and Barbara.'"

Over the years there was only one detail concerning Grant's "stinginess" he thought he had to correct. It was a story told by his former employee Dudley Walker:

> CG: When I was married to Barbara Hutton, my valet gave an interview saying that I was so cheap I would keep the buttons when I threw away my shirts. Well, I did do that, but it seemed like a sensible thing to do. After all, the buttons were special bone buttons made in England, they were still perfectly all right, and I would need them in case the buttons on my shirts were lost or mangled when they were laundered. Besides, my shirts were made of fine Egyptian cotton, and when they wore out, my housekeeper used them as dusters. She removed the buttons so they wouldn't scratch the surface of the furniture. We'd put the buttons away until we needed them.

Grant never failed to tell the button story during his *Conversations*. "He had a self-deprecating sense of humor," says STANLEY E. FOX, "and he knew the audience was dying to hear that stuff."

His friendship with George Barrie, which had already transcended their connection at Fabergé, included another aspect of mutual interest. Barrie, an accomplished musician, and Grant shared a love of jazz. According to BARRIE, "We had jam sessions and Cary played the piano, but he was shy about playing with other musicians around."

QUINCY JONES was surprised to learn that Grant loved jazz piano. "He loved Oscar Peterson, Bill Evans, and Count Basie. Only a few actors understand music the way Cary did. Tony Perkins is one. Warren Beatty is another. Cary and I went to the Comedy Store, the Crescendo, Shelly's Man Hole, Dante's, or Memory Lane—wherever the jazz people were playing. We would just sit there and enjoy it."

George Kennedy and Grant "whistled and hummed together passages out of Dave Brubeck's 'Take Five,' one of Brubeck's biggest hits," according to KENNEDY.

Grant picked up jazz expressions, says JONES. "He understood them. Absolutely. I used to kid him and call him Boogie. 'Boogie' has a lot of meanings—having a good time or making love. I'd say, 'How's your boogie going?' And he would answer, 'You'll have to ask Barbara.'"

STEVE LAWRENCE remembers, "Whenever we were at parties and gathered around a piano, everybody looked to Cary for the words because he knew the verse of every song that was ever written." IRVING LAZAR was impressed that Grant always knew the chorus *and* the verses: "Cary appreciated the gifts of Jerome Kern, Gershwin, Berlin, Cole Porter, and Johnny Mercer."

When Grant traveled for Fabergé, he continued to read assiduously. He still thoughtfully cut out stories and sent them to friends. They fondly referred to these mailings as Cary Grant's Clipping Service. VALERIE ALLEN remembers, "Cary found my name in the June 1981 'Screen Actors Newsletter,' listing hundreds and hundreds of actors and actresses for whom the SAG residual department in Hollywood was holding checks. He sent the whole newspaper to me aboard the TSS *Fairwinds*, docked in Fort Everglades, with a note saying, 'I'll split it with you!'"

Grant's work for Fabergé included attending benefits across the country. GEORGE BARRIE recalls: "Cary appeared at charity events and drew enormous crowds. When we were in Cincinnati, the mayor gave him a key to the city. Cary thanked him and said, 'This is the first time I've been given a key to anything. My wives always locked me out without a key!'"

Grant was no stranger to charity. He had learned its value as a Boy Scout, and he continued throughout his lifetime to give generously to hundreds and hundreds of philanthropic organizations, more often than not giving anonymously. During World War II Grant donated his salaries from two films to the British war effort.

In November 1942 Grant was thanked by the lord mayor of Bristol: "Our city is grateful to you for the generous help which you accorded her at the time of her affliction."

On April 18, 1947, His Majesty King George VI awarded Grant the King's Medal for Service in the Cause of Freedom, citing his "Outstanding service to the British War Relief Society."

"He gave before you had a chance to ask," recalls BINNIE BARNES. "He would call and ask if I needed money for Variety Clubs. He gave a lot of money to Variety—anonymously."

In Grant's early, lean days he had helped support his family. To provide security for his father, Grant made him beneficiary of a New York Life Insurance Company policy on January 8, 1927, just before Grant's twenty-third birthday. Later he helped his cousin Eric Leach. After his cousin's death Grant supported Maggie, his widow.

With fame and success had come a sense of noblesse oblige. He gave generously and in the style in which he lived his life—quietly and honorably. Other recipients of his largess were grateful. On one of the many occasions that Grant gave to the Joseph P. Kennedy, Jr., Foundation for the retarded, Ethel Kennedy wrote, in October 1972, referring to "Your extraordinary check . . . with all those miraculous zeros. . . ." Pepperdine University was enriched by Grant's interest in some Riverside property. His personal papers identify hundreds of organizations over the years.

BARBARA SINATRA recalls, "When we had art auctions to raise money to build the Barbara Sinatra Children's Center for Abused Children, Cary got right in the midst of the bidding and bought three or four paintings every time. I never did know what he did with all of them, but he really was very, very generous. After the center was built, he sent the children money on every holiday."

He sent large sums of money to Jewish charities. On October 20, 1953, Grant participated in "City of the Ages, the Great Historical Drama and Tribute to Three Thousand Years of Jerusalem," along with Edward G. Robinson, José Ferrer, Jan Peerce, and Gregor Piatigorsky. On November 28, 1953, he served as the narrator for the Israel Bond Event when Jerusalem had its 3000th Anniversary Festival in Chicago. President Harry S. Truman was the guest speaker, and Charlton Heston and Jeff Chandler also appeared. When he gave his entire salary for *Arsenic and Old Lace* to various charities, twenty-five thousand dollars went for milk for children in Palestine, an impressive sum of money in the early 1940s. As a result of these activities, some people assumed Grant was Jewish.

Once Walter Matthau tried to confirm the rumor by asking Grant if he was Jewish. Grant said he was not. "So," MATTHAU says, "I asked him why everyone thought he was. He said, 'Well, I did a Madison Square Garden event for the state of Israel and I wore a yarmulke.' He pronounced the *r* in 'yarmulke.' An Englishman wouldn't pronounce the *r*, so I still thought he might be Jewish. Besides, he was so intelligent. I'm extremely prejudiced. Intelligent people *must* be Jewish."

On April 14, 1983, Grant received a letter from a Debbie Rosen, of Pompano Beach, Florida. Ms. Rosen said she understood Grant's mother was Jewish. As was his custom, Grant indicated at the bottom of the letter that on May 6, 1983, he had telephoned Ms. Rosen and told her that his mother was not Jewish.

Grant was eager for Dyan Cannon to get a job in one location so he could spend longer periods with his daughter. Sammy Cahn remembers that when Cannon was on the road with *How to Succeed in Business Without Really Trying*, Grant traveled to every town. BINNIE BARNES relates Grant's coup when he called her husband, Mike Frankovich, and asked him to offer Cannon a part in *Bob and Carol and Ted and Alice*: "Mike tested her, and she was absolutely wonderful."

PETER BOGDANOVICH explains, "Cary was thrilled when Dyan's career bloomed. It meant she would be out of town and Jennifer could be with *him*."

Grant went to Palm Springs as often as he could with his daughter. When Jennifer was almost three and a half years old, he wrote this to her.

Today, Sunday, July 20, 1969, man landed on the moon. The lunar module . . . "Eagle" . . . touched down on the moon's surface at 4:17 PM Eastern Time here in Miami, where I am . . . and where I miss you . . . and at 1:17 PM in Beverly Hills, where you are. Some four hours later, Commodore Neil Armstrong took man's first step on to the moon's surface. . . . The attached brochure, brought from the Florida launching site of Apollo 11, the missile which blasted them out into space, explains how their historic mission was accomplished. By the time you are grown up, such space journeys may be commonplace and even the longer journey to Mars, which seems more able to support the continuance of life as we human beings know it, might be taking place. However, to date, it is Man's greatest achievement in space.

It is late Sunday night as I write so, unfortunately, your envelope cannot be stamped with the actual date of the landing on the moon; where both astronauts now rest inside the lunar module prior to an attempt to project their vehicle back into space and rejoin Astronaut Lieutenant-Colonel Michael Collins, who orbits in the mother space ship that hopefully will carry them back to earth.

Yesterday and today the people of our nation and throughout the entire world are united in prayer for safe being of these three brave Americans. You are always in my thoughts, Jennifer, and my dearest wish is to live long enough to read and study the enclosed brochures with you . . . perhaps on our way to Mars.

I love you.

Over the years he took many opportunities to express himself in writing to Jennifer. On her eleventh birthday, February 26, 1977:

You are eleven years old today and about to embark upon the second ten years of a wonderful life.

Ten years have passed since I first saw your dear face. Ten years. Ten years of loving you. Ten years of regarding you, of thinking of you, and of being with you at every opportunity possible to me. In those ten years you and I have

Restaurateur SYLVIA WU: *"He always had a stack of pictures of Jennifer in his pocket. If I hadn't seen him in a while, he would pull out the pictures and say, 'This is why.'"*

shared the kind of love and companionship I could not have shared with anyone else.

I am proud to know you. Proud to be seen with you. Proud and happy while watching you swim, ride, and play tennis; and in each of our activities together: The baseball games, the races, every day at Greenhorn Ranch, the Malls; Everything; Everywhere. I am admiring of, and deeply affected by, your manner, your kindness, and each new accomplishment. I respect your quiet loyalty to your friends and to each of your parents.

You may have noticed that most of the previous sentences begin "I." Yet they could not begin with "I" if it weren't for YOU. You are the dearest daughter a man could have. You have never caused me a moment's anguish or disappointment. Your qualities are of the best, and if you persist in those qualities throughout life, you will enjoy ever-growing happiness, and, by so doing, understand the happiness you bring to others who know you, especially to me.

Grant's penthouse apartment at the Warwick, in New York, Suite 2704, had earlier been occupied by Marion Davies. It had two large bedrooms on the twenty-seventh floor, with two entrances off the foyer, a spacious living room, a small kitchen, and a big terrace all around. GEORGE BARRIE says, "He wanted the terrace so he could take the sun. He tried sitting there only once. Everybody looked at him from the windows of surrounding office buildings."

BEA SHAW reaped the benefits of the Warwick apartment: "I would use it, and he would stay at my house because his was always under construction. He'd say, 'I have to get out of here. The workmen stand around and smile at me instead of working.'"

In the early 1970s Grant's hilltop house overlooking Benedict Canyon was undergoing its first face-lift in more than twenty-five years. Grant was remodeling the whole place; Jennifer could enjoy it as she got older. His daughter seemed to figure in his every plan for the future. According to HENRY GRIS, "Cary said he had owned it so long and had let so many people use it whenever he wasn't there during his marriages, it was about to fall down. He had to put it in shape or let it slide down the hill."

THELMA ORLOFF, who visited one day during construction, says, "Jennifer was running on the roof. I said, 'You know, Cary, she could fall off there and get killed.' And he said, 'Oh, no, she knows every nook and cranny.' So what do you say? Anything she did was fine with him."

On April 7, 1970, the Academy of Motion Picture Arts and Sciences gave Grant a special award for his achievements in film acting over the past four decades. Although he had been nominated twice, it was his first Oscar. The inscription reads:

TO CARY GRANT
FOR HIS UNIQUE MASTERY
OF THE ART OF SCREEN ACTING
WITH THE RESPECT AND AFFECTION
OF HIS COLLEAGUES

GREGORY PECK, who wrote the inscription, says, "I've never told that to anyone before because it would have seemed as though I was trying to grab some reflected credit or glory."

JACK HALEY, JR., who produced the awards show, remembers the hitch that developed: "A private plane was bringing Princess Grace to Hollywood so she could give Cary the award. All of a sudden Cary wouldn't let her do it. . . . Some dame was going to file paternity papers on him and as much as he wanted to accept the Oscar from Grace, he didn't want to embarrass her in any way."

One of Grant's notebooks contains a statement dealing with the threatened paternity suit, demonstrating the reason for his reluctance and his strength and, as always, his humor:

Well, at my age it may seem flattering to be labeled a swinger but surely not a careless swinger. However, I've never known a public person of so-called means who did not become a target for petty gossip, character assassination, envy and baseless law-suits. And it was almost inevitable I would someday be selected to join the long list of men who have endured similar allegations. (A list that includes Clark Gable, Charles Chaplin, Grover Cleveland, Lloyd George, and on and on.)

302

CG, sixty-six, in 1970: "Probably no greater honor can come to any man than the respect of his colleagues."

I'm told that Mrs. Bouron is in her mid-thirties, been married and divorced twice, and has grown children; so why the lady indulges in fantasy and persists in using my name as her newborn child's father is inexplicable and ridiculous. But it's a free country and anyone can say anything they like, I suppose. I'm extremely sorry for her innocent baby, but I have my own family to protect from such unnecessary actions or implied threat of scandal and, I am relieved to say, my lawyers are fully prepared and confident.

Subsequently it was proved that Grant was not the child's father.

JACK HALEY, JR., adds, "In the end, of course, Cary accepted the Oscar and made a stirring speech about collaboration, which he wrote himself." Grant's papers contain a draft of his acceptance speech:

I'm very grateful to the Academy's Board of Governors for this happy tribute . . . and to Frank [Sinatra] for coming here *especially* . . . to present it to me . . . and to all the people who must have spent so much time searching for, and assembling, those *wild* film clips!

I may never look at this [the Oscar] without remembering the quiet patience of the directors who were kind enough to put up with me more than once; some, even, three and four times. Extraordinary men. Howard Hawks, Hitchcock, the late Leo McCarey, George Cukor, George Stevens, and Stanley Donen . . . oh, and the writers, Philip Barry, Dore Schary, Bob Sherwood, Ben Hecht, Charlie Lederer, dear Clifford Odets, Sidney Sheldon, and more recently, Stanley Shapiro and Peter Stone. I trust they, and all the other directors, writers and producers have forgiven me for the things I didn't know.

I realize it's conventional to praise one's fellow-workers at these occasions, but why *not?* Ours is a collaborative medium. We all need each other. And what better opportunity to publicly express one's appreciation and affection for those who contribute so much to our welfare.

I've never been a joiner or member of any particular social set, but I've been privileged to be a part of Hollywood's most glorious era. Yet, thinking of all the empty screens waiting to be filled with marvelous new images, ideologies and points of view . . . and considering all the students who study film techniques at universities throughout the world . . . and the astonishing young talents coming up in the industry today . . . I think there's an even more glorious era just around the corner.

And now before I leave, I want to thank all of you very much for signifying your approval of this. I shall cherish it until I die . . . because . . . probably no greater honor can come to any man than the respect of his colleagues.

The next day Grant wrote and thanked Frank Sinatra for standing behind him during the "astonishing ovation." Without Sinatra's support, Grant admitted, "I might have burst into tears rather than laughter."

On September 2, 1970, Grant reinstated his membership in the academy, after receiving a gracious and appealing letter from Daniel Taradash, then the academy president. Grant offered the explanation for his resignation many years before: "At a time when because of what may have since become outmoded principles, I deplored commercializing a ceremony, which, in my estimation, should have remained unpublicized and privately shared among the artists and craftsmen of our industry. I'm not at all sure that my beliefs have changed; just the times. . . ."

On November 18, 1970, Grant attended a reception at Buckingham Palace and the Royal Gala Cabaret in aid of Prince Philip's wildlife charity. Fabergé sponsored a telecast of the evening for American television. Two years later Grant was organizing a March 1972 trip to Las Vegas with a member of the royal family. Lord Louis Mountbatten wrote that he was particularly keen on seeing Frank Sinatra again. He also said, "I am really looking forward to this long awaited weekend in Las Vegas with you and Mike [Frankovich], particularly if you are able to arrange for Jane Fonda to be there at the same time!"

BINNIE BARNES remembers, "We stayed at Caesars Palace and

CG, Lord Louis Mountbatten and producer Mike Frankovich with the cast after the show, Dunes Hotel & Casino, Las Vegas, **facing the camera,** *March 26, 1972.*

CG: "Lord Louis said, 'Smile, everyone!'"

took Mountbatten to all the shows—just Mike and I and Cary and Mountbatten's equerries. He couldn't get over the place. I remember we went to see Jack Benny's show. Because Mountbatten was on London time, he had a great habit of falling asleep, but he could still hear what was going on. He'd take cat-naps and somehow know when to wake up. He did this at every show. It was the most amazing thing. He was exhausted, but he didn't want to miss anything."

Several of the bare-bottomed chorus girls in the Dunes Hotel show were English. Grant and Lord Mountbatten went backstage to meet them, and they agreed to be photographed. BARNES continues, "The girls were trying to be discreet about their bare bottoms. They stood facing the camera. Then Mountbatten invited them to turn around. . . ."

> CG: Mountbatten asked the girls to stand in a line so that he and I could be photographed in the center. Naturally they had to cover their scanty costumes, and then Lord Mountbatten suggested we all turn around and have just our backs photographed. The result was that the cleavage at the base of their backs was quite . . . uh . . . interesting!

Grant wrote to Charles Rich on March 31, 1972, to thank him for the show and dinner at the Dunes. He also speculated about the photographs. "Neither of us can guess at what Queen Elizabeth's reaction will be to that backstage photograph with the showgirls, which amused Lord Louis so greatly, but it's almost certain that he will show it to her and, from all we gathered, his nephew Prince Philip and probably every one of his friends when he returns to England. . . ."

Grant confirmed it in his eulogy for Charles Rich on April 18, 1986, in Las Vegas: "Well, one of those photographs was taken to Malta, blown up large, and hung in a prominent place in a corridor of the queen's yacht by Lord Mountbatten, who sent a wonderfully amusing and appreciative note of thanks to Charlie."

By 1972 Grant was traveling to Europe five to ten times a year. According to HENRY GRIS, who saw him in London with George Barrie, "They were staying at the Inn on the Park. Cary preferred the sedate Connaught but switched because Barrie opted for the Inn. They had come over in the company jet, a four-million-dollar Grumman G-two luxury job which earlier in the year had won a gold medal for excellence in design. There was a sleeping couch aboard, but Cary had let a younger company executive have it, insisting he would be fine on the floor, where he said he slept for a couple of hours."

BARRIE recalls one trip to Czechoslovakia: "We were detained at a checkpoint to get some information, and someone brought us a big bottle of plum brandy. They call it slivovitz. We drank and talked . . . and finished the whole bottle. We were absolutely paralyzed. We had a hell of a time, but we finally got through. Cary had read up on the iron curtain countries. He had a memo from AT&T that said, 'Be careful of who you talk to, everything is bugged.' After we got into our suite, Cary, who's half shot, or maybe all shot, crawled for an hour under the beds, looking for bugs. He looked behind the pictures on the wall in the kitchen and the living room. I kept laughing and asking him what he was doing, and he'd say, 'Shhh. Shhh.' It was so funny.

"Another time we were in a European department store, and when it was announced that Cary Grant was there, *nothing* sold in the store. They just mobbed. It happened everywhere we went. We had a lot of bodyguards and people around so he could get through the crowds. He wouldn't go anywhere without me. I would hold on to his arm or pull him along."

RICHARD BIENEN tells of going "to Macy's to buy a watch he had seen advertised. Cary was like the Pied Piper. The main floor of Macy's was so packed with people trying to get near him, they didn't do any business. Strauss, who was running Macy's, sent Cary a letter saying, 'We're thrilled you want to shop here, but next time, let us bring whatever you'd like to your apartment.'"

Grant was approaching seventy. He enjoyed his Fabergé association and was delirious about his daughter. Fatherhood was everything he had hoped. Maybe more so. In spite of his age, he wanted to father more children. His reasons were not shallow sentiment. When HENRY GRIS asked Grant if he would ever remarry, he answered, "I may or may not. I intend to have more children, but I don't know whether I'll get married. Creating children is the only reason we are here. Furthermore, it's one's only ticket to eternity. I don't have any other."

Chapter Seventeen

"WOMEN . . . ONE OF MY FAVORITE CAUSES"

CG: My mother died peacefully one afternoon at the age of ninety-five, claiming to be ninety-three. She died in a perfect way. She was served a cup of tea, and when they came back to see her, that was it. I often wonder how I'm going to do it. Do you ever wonder whether you are going to embarrass someone or do it in your sleep?

Elsie Leach died on January 22, 1973, less than two weeks from her ninety-sixth birthday. Grant and his cousins gave Mrs. Leach a quiet funeral in Bristol.

In the early 1970s Grant became a partner in an elaborate holiday resort, called Shannonside, rising up on 555 acres, to attract American tourists to Ireland. It included a modern township a half hour's drive from Shannon Airport. Situated between the villages of Ballynacally and Kildysart, the project envisioned 1,850 houses, a hotel, and an eighteen-hole golf course.

HENRY GRIS, who visited the property with Grant, says the project first appealed to Grant when the architects showed him plans for their school of tomorrow because he "thought Jennifer needed a good, solid, permanent environment, and this was a promising place to bring up children—away from violence and pollution."

Grant planned to build a house on five acres overlooking the golf course and the Atlantic Ocean.

He made many trips to the Shannonside site and even lent his name to publicity for the project. However, by 1974, when an American investment company did not advance further funds, the venture collapsed.

During this period Grant talked to George Barrie about buying an apartment in London. Nothing came of it, but that idea, coupled with his plans in Ireland, indicate he was serious about spending more time near the place where he was born.

Grant's friends do not recall any serious or meaningful relationship during the early 1970s. Grant stated publicly many times that he would not remarry. According to GEORGE KENNEDY, "He had enormous affection, respect, and admiration for women, but I thought he was in awe of them . . . a little abashed around beautiful women. He had a little-boy quality, not feigned, not trying to gain position, and felt—shy is the word, I think."

Other Grant friends classify him as a gentlemanly ladies' man. HAL ROACH says, "I never knew any man that was in love with so many gals as Cary was." But, JOHNNY MASCHIO adds, "He wasn't a swinger. He was a one-gal-at-a-time guy."

BINNIE BARNES remembers, "Cary would come to the projection room at our house and see pictures all the time. He'd always bring a different girl. But the minute he married, I would lose him. Then when he wasn't married, he'd call again. It was the funniest thing in the world. He was like an errant husband." JEAN DALRYMPLE clarifies the point: "Cary wasn't a womanizer, but he loved women. He was always looking for one to make him happy. I don't know why his wives didn't in the beginning."

> CG: You marry them, and they've got you. You have a child with them, and then it's completely over.

Only too aware of California's joint property laws, Grant had no plans to share his estate. He resolved that Jennifer would get everything he had.

Grant's position with Fabergé, undefined, meant no title, no set hours, and no demands on his schedule. He gave his time only by mutual agreement. Grant told HENRY GRIS, "I do what I like and go where I like. I am never sent. I go because I think I should."

When Fabergé launched a new line, Grant got involved with testing buyer reaction. He met with potential buyers but did not do any of the actual selling. He told GRIS, "I open a door that might have been shut tight. I am the first in the door. They look at me. They know me. But then, why not? They've been brought up watching my pictures. An instant trust is established."

GEORGE BARRIE says, "If Cary heard about somebody not liking something, he volunteered to write a letter." He wrote once, "Your helpful comments and kind suggestions regarding the possible improvement of Fabergé lipsticks have been passed on to the proper department for study and consideration, which hopefully will result in your eventual satisfaction. . . ." A soothing letter from Cary Grant theoretically would alleviate any woman's discontent.

Grant spent hours with Barrie and his executives participating in "think sessions." Indeed, he thought about Fabergé continually. He sniffed, viewed, and appraised fragrances and followed the progression of marketing a product to the public.

His travel logs show that despite his frequent jaunts for Fabergé, Grant had time to visit the Hathaway Brown School in Shaker Heights, just outside Cleveland. LEIGHTON ROSENTHAL recalls that the children in his daughter Jane's class wanted Grant as their commencement speaker. "He was all set until a week before, when he said he couldn't stay for commencement but would meet informally with the class. When he got there, the kids were sitting in a circle, and he got right down on his haunches and said, 'I'm your new headmaster. What would you like to ask me?' He spent some time with them and went back to the airport."

He carried only an attaché case with papers from his office. He never took even a toothbrush. He had complete wardrobes on Fabergé's planes and kept evening clothes in London, Paris, New York, and Tokyo. He also kept a Rolls-Royce in London. HENRY GRIS remembers, "It carried license plate CG 1, which someone presented to him. He had to get rid of it after spending a fortune on paint jobs. Whenever the car was left unattended, someone would scratch across the hood in large letters, 'We Love You, Cary.' After that, he drove a Rover."

Meanwhile, Grant had obtained regular, court-approved fortnightly visitations with his daughter. Scheduled to meet Barrie in London to fly on to Tokyo to open Fabergé's new office, Grant instead stayed in Los Angeles to spend the weekend with Jennifer.

Barrie picked him up in Los Angeles, and they continued to Tokyo. Ten days later Grant left Barrie in Hong Kong, dashed back to spend the weekend with Jennifer in Palm Springs, and then rejoined Barrie in Hong Kong.

It's inconceivable that during this time Grant could have seriously considered writing an autobiography. He was far too busy to write a memoir. But following the publication of three autobiographical pieces he had written for the *Ladies' Home Journal* in 1963, he was deluged with lucrative offers from publishers to write a total account of his life.

CG: I'm too busy living my life to write about it.

It wasn't just a question of being busy. Grant's perfectionist nature would have turned writing into an obsession. His research notes and drafts of the articles he did write indicate he was satisfied with the pieces when they were published. However, when he reread the articles a few years later, he concluded the writing wasn't very good. Had Grant attempted a full-fledged autobiography, he would have been writing, rewriting, and correcting until the day he died.

CG: Besides, I don't think anybody else really gives a damn. Who tells the truth about themselves anyway? A memoir implies selectiveness, writing about just what you want to write about, and nothing else. To write an autobiography, you've got to expose other people. I hope to get out of this world as gracefully as possible without embarrassing anyone.

RICHARD SCHICKEL laments Grant's procrastination: "If only he had done it and left it behind him—written an autobiography for posthumous publication, say, twenty-five years after everyone's death." But Grant told HENRY GRIS, "Call it superstition if you will. I call it belief. I firmly believe that if and when I write about myself and carry the events up to the day of writing, I'll be close to my end. We are taught by religions that a man's life passes through his mind as he goes to meet his maker. The drowning man sees his life go by as he goes down, and so does the man who goes back over his memories to write about them."

If Grant never wrote a book about his life, inevitably others did. Grant chafed over books by people he didn't know but seldom publicly articulated his feelings about the sometimes gossipy and misinformed tales. Public fuming simply increased sales for the author. It was the one area of his carefully orchestrated public life Grant couldn't control. At one *Conversation* he said, "I don't care what they're saying. I've developed a skin like a rhino's." Still, his hostility toward unauthorized biographers occasionally rose to the surface.

CG: There's so much junk written. I never understand why people write these wicked and malicious things. They keep stacks of "information" on you—much of it misinformation—and then shove it into a book.

Hanging on a wall in Grant's office vault is a framed version, beautifully scripted, of parts of Iago's speech in *Othello*, sent to him by an admirer: "He who steals my purse, steals trash. But he that filches from me my good name, makes me poor indeed." Attached to one of his notebooks was a poem, "Word of Myth," by Marian Gleason:

You can't believe the things you see in print
You can't believe the facts or trust the telling
Through gossip, allegations, rumor, hint
And, nowadays, you can't believe the spelling.

The *Conversations* provided the perfect forum for his more positive criticism:

CG: A person like me is subject to certain indignities. I've had biographies written about me by people I've never met. One was a real hatchet job. I never read the one by Schickel, although I heard it was a quality job. It certainly had a good look to it.

LOUIS JOURDAN appreciated Richard Schickel's book: "I told Cary and Barbara it was irresistible. I told them to read it, and they did." Richard Schickel recalls that his conversations with Grant over the years were unfailingly pleasant. "He knew I was a sympathetic witness to his career and didn't view him as a subject for gossip," SCHICKEL says. "He expressed a benign, distant, skittish interest in my book [*Cary Grant: A Celebration*]. After my publisher sent him an early copy, he called and thanked me. He was very pleasant, and said, 'Of course, I haven't read it.'

"Later, when I was making a documentary in San Francisco, he telephoned and got me out of the cutting room. (This is how I know he read the book.) He had found two little errors or what he thought were errors. It was funny because they weren't gigantic. He took exception to a critical interpretation, which I disputed and explained that I felt the comment had to stand. The other was a hard fact, but something minor, such as a date. I called my publisher and asked that it be fixed."

Grant expressed his thoughts about the behavior of some people toward celebrities and his contempt for unauthorized biographers in a letter he wrote to Nancy Sinatra, for her book, *Frank Sinatra: My Father,* published in 1985.

> . . . Forty years ago, coming out of the old Astor Hotel on Broadway, I'd been buttonholed by a casual acquaintance who, while I was trying to recollect his name, suddenly went into a tirade about a young man who was blocking the sidewalk, impeding progress, showing off, stopping traffic. The inequity of my acquaintance's remarks . . . has persisted in me ever since. That young man, who eventually became your father, was merely trying to walk from his car to the Paramount's performer's entrance. He had not blocked the sidewalk . . . the crowd had. They were responsible for blocking the sidewalk in their efforts to touch him, photograph him, pull at him for autographs or other unfathomable reasons.
>
> . . . [W]hy should a publicized person cause special excitement? . . . Why is it not sufficient to see and enjoy the performance of a great entertainer or athlete and then leave him or her alone?
>
> Why invade privacy? . . . It's extraordinary how many uninvited people find it necessary to make personal remarks, occasionally uncivil, to a celebrity. What prompts them? Is it their need for attention? . . . This is the constant plight of your father. . . . I, at least, spent most of my working days in the comparative security of a studio, whereas your father works before huge live audiences throughout the world, surrounded by people of all kinds. . . .

It's a sad paradox that the people whose acquaintance one would most like to make are the people least likely to introduce themselves. Yet I've been approached by strangers, while sitting quietly reading, captive in a commercial airliner, and been forced to listen to incredible anecdotes about notables—exaggerated yarns gleaned from already exaggerated gossip columns—written by second-class writers who may never have met the persons about whom they write so knowingly. I've often read innuendos or implications about myself that were so blatantly wrong that I was staggered by the writer's imagination. . . .

In the *Conversations* Grant felt free to negate accusations:

CG: It is just ridiculous that Errol Flynn was a Nazi spy. And the book written about Hitchcock that paints a very black picture is absolute nonsense. I don't agree that there was anything indecent about him. Anyone who worked with him knows that. And they say that he was homosexual. It's just not true.

He elaborated this point in his letter to Nancy Sinatra: "The victimized dead cannot defend themselves. Though the fabrications are refuted by others close to them, the damage has been done. I've already conditioned my wife and daughter to expect the biographical worst. . . ."

Contradicting himself, Grant, preceding a *Conversation* in Dallas on March 23, 1986, told Phillip Wuntch, the film critic for the Dallas *Morning News* that he had read some of the publications about him: "And . . . Whew! They all repeat the rumors that I'm a tightwad and that I'm homosexual. Now I don't feel that either of those is an insult, but it's all nonsense."

KATHARINE HEPBURN says boldly, "Everyone is called a homosexual in Hollywood." Garson Kanin, who knows Hollywood as the home of gossip, says, "Facts don't interest people. Everyone likes to be in on the inside story. Whether it's true or not is a secondary consideration. If it's spicy, then it's interesting."

BINNIE BARNES offers an insight: "Some people want you to think they knew Cary, so they make up things. They think it's the truth. They will exaggerate to tell you they knew him—when they probably only said hello to him from across the room."

DAVID TEBET agrees that Grant attracted all kinds of flagrant gossip: "I was *amazed* at what I heard. They never could have known him. I'm probably one of the most cynical people out here. I don't pay attention to any of the gossip."

CG: Those kinds of people actually hope you'll sue them. They know that if you do, you'll help bring attention to the book.

While he was alive, Grant did use the courts to protect himself from what he saw as slander and libel. On Tom Snyder's November 1980 NBC show *Tomorrow*, Snyder was interviewing Chevy Chase. When Grant's name came up, Chase said, "He really was a great physical comic, and I understand he was a homo. . . . What a gal!" Grant filed a ten-million-dollar lawsuit against Chase.

He was furious and told PETER BOGDANOVICH, "[Bogdanovich imitating CG] He can't go around like that, saying whatever comes to his head. And I'm not going to let him get away with it."

The suit was eventually settled out of court, and Grant told Bogdanovich he felt Chase was sorry and had learned his lesson. BEA SHAW remembers, "When Cary bumped into Chevy Chase at the Los Angeles Olympics in 1984, he walked right up to him, said hello, and shook hands as though nothing had happened. Only Cary would do something like that. He was a very gentle man, and he never bore a grudge. Cary felt that a vicious person would ultimately hang himself."

After death, however, the libel laws in the United States do not protect an individual from attack (although, as DOUGLAS FAIRBANKS, JR., points out, "They don't even protect you when you're alive if you're a public person").

Grant prepared his wife and daughter to expect an onslaught upon his death. Still, the feeling of helplessness against this kind of victimization is staggering. BURT REYNOLDS believes that "these books—each one worse than the last and having the most bizarre things to say—can do nothing to take the shine off Cary Grant's star."

Grant never gossiped about other people:

CG: Some people think that if they say something bad about someone, it makes them feel more important. In

316

fact, it doesn't. It makes them more insignificant. People should say something good about others or keep it to themselves.

This is substantiated by ABIGAIL VAN BUREN: "He never said anything malicious, and he never gossiped. You would never hear him say, 'Don't tell anyone, but . . .'" RICK INGERSOLL says, "He seemed a little put out when people asked him even seemingly innocent questions that sounded as though they could be gossipy."

This doesn't mean Grant hesitated to say what he felt. MARJORIE EVERETT explains: "Cary wouldn't knock people openly, but he'd be very candid if you asked him specifically. He was smart, very level-headed, and perceptive." IRVING LAZAR says, "Cary was a singularly straitlaced and extremely correct fellow. He had a sense of kindness. If he didn't like somebody, he'd say so and then avoid them, but he didn't make a big deal of it."

Periodically Grant was approached to do commercials. People proposed he promote everything from his own line of clothing to airlines to diamonds. No matter how lucrative the offer, he never succumbed to what would have amounted to millions of dollars in royalties.

RICHARD BIENEN remembers one offer Grant almost took: "It was for a staggering amount of money, and Cary said, 'Well, it would be some more for Barbara and Jennifer. . . .'" Still, BEA SHAW recalls, "He turned down millions and millions of dollars when he refused to have a line of men's clothes. He said he didn't want to be the one who told people to wear something one year and throw everything out and start over the next."

But Grant's savvy promotional skills were put to use in 1973, when George Barrie's Brut Productions launched its first feature film, *A Touch of Class*. The title had been inspired by Grant himself. BARRIE says, "Cary loved the film and talked to film editors and writers all over the country. We did the country by sections, giving them a number to call at a certain time, just the way Cary promoted his own films. He told them, 'If I was younger, there's no way George Segal would have done that film without my playing the lead. It's my type of film, but I'm too old for this stuff now.' Imagine the publicity we got—and on a film he *wasn't in!*"

The film earned five 1973 Academy nominations. Glenda Jackson won as best actress, and Barrie received his second nomination for an original score.

On January 18, 1974, Grant turned seventy. He told Army Archerd of *Daily Variety:* "I'm not even certain that it is my 70th birthday because the records of my birth were destroyed in a Bristol fire during the First World War and, only by gathering information among various members of my family, who affirmed that I'd been born pretty early in the century, was I eventually able to obtain an acceptable birth certificate and passport."

Grant joined the board of Metro-Goldwyn-Mayer in 1975. In 1980, when MGM split into two companies, MGM Grand Hotels and Metro-Goldwyn-Mayer Films, Grant sat on both boards. In 1981 MGM acquired United Artists, becoming MGM/UA Entertainment Company, and Grant remained a director until his death in 1986.

WALTER SHARP said, "Cary's background in entertainment was invaluable to us. He knew what worked and what didn't. His contribution was tremendous."

DAN MELNICK grew up believing there were just two movie stars—Fred Astaire and Cary Grant. Much to his delight, he got to know both of them. He recalls: "I came from New York to become head of MGM, and Cary called me the day after my first meeting with the board. . . . He made me feel so good. We were together initially at business functions, and then we became friends. I was very much aware of the difference in our ages, although he was much less so. Part of his graciousness was his ability to treat me as a peer. His enthusiasm was extraordinary."

The year before Grant joined MGM, Kirk Kerkorian and Jim Aubrey convinced him to take a look at Jack Haley, Jr.'s compilation documentary *That's Entertainment!* HALEY, who wanted Grant to narrate a section in the film, remembers: "Cary, little Jennifer, and her nurse sat in MGM's big theater, and I ran the film. Cary started to cry when he saw Jean Harlow and was trying to hide it from Jennifer.

"It was late afternoon when we finished, and Cary said, 'Let's you and I walk.' The nurse took Jennifer to the car, and we walked down the deserted studio street.

"'I can't, Jack,' he said. 'I just can't. I can't go in front of that camera.' When he overheard Gene Kelly recording a voice-over, he thought he'd found a loophole. 'Well . . . I'll do it, but not on camera.'

"I said, 'I can't have ten people on camera and one voice-over. The audience would wonder what happened to Cary Grant? Did his nose fall off?'

"He said, 'I suppose you're right. . . . And I'd really love to do this, especially for MGM . . . but I just can't. But I do have one question. You know that beginning number with Fred Astaire and Eleanor Powell? Who do you suppose was Fred's tailor?' Here it was 1974, and he was asking about a costume from *Broadway Melody of 1940!*"

During these years Fabergé sponsored annual Straw Hat Award events in New York, honoring young show business talent. Jean Dalrymple & Associates handled the publicity. She had given Grant his first speaking role in the 1920s. Now he and DAL-RYMPLE were to work together again. She says, "I had quite a lot to do with George Barrie and Fabergé. We got a lot of publicity out of those big parties. Archie did the presentations and handed out the trophies."

CG: Before introducing you to our next recipient, I'd like to tell you a story. My young daughter goes to a nursery school with the children of other theatrical people. Recently she came home, very excited and said, "Daddy, I know the story of Adam and Eve."

I was a little worried about the version she had heard, but still, I asked her to tell it to me. She did, and I got a version that could only have been concocted by show people.

My daughter told me, "Adam and Eve were the first man and woman acting team, the original Paul Newman and Joanne Woodward. They performed in an outdoor playhouse called the Garden of Eden, which was run by a manager named God.

"They were doing fine until backstage one day came an agent called Snake. He saw Eve and said, 'Psst . . . pssst . . . hey, lady, you're pretty good, but you're stuck here. There are other places I can get for you. Trouble is—you need a new vehicle. That Adam's rib number has had it.'

319

"Eve asked Snake what he could suggest, and Snake said, 'Hey, how about doing the apple bit?' Eve got real excited, told Adam, bugged him until he agreed.

"So they broke in the apple bit. Well, God caught the first matinee and canceled them. He said, 'You play my house, you do the show I bought.' He threw them out.

"Well, after that they tried other things, like Cain and Abel . . . no laughs. And when last heard of, they were in a lost road company of *West Side Story.*"

Grant was always in demand to say a few words at a dinner or introduce a dignitary, but in the 1970s he appeared to speak more frequently. On October 26, 1977, Grant prepared and delivered a speech at the Variety Club dinner honoring Prince Charles at the Beverly Hilton Hotel in Los Angeles. He talked about the prince's great interest in the theater and the world of entertainment and the fact that Prince Charles had written many of the sketches for a revue in which he had appeared at Trinity College, Cambridge.

CG: I also learned that [he] played the trumpet and Macbeth. . . . I wish I'd seen that. I've never heard Macbeth played on a trumpet.

I learned, too, that Prince Charles plays the cello, played rugby, broke his nose, is an excellent fisherman, excels in seamanship. . . . He's done almost everything and even flies a helicopter . . . and perhaps on some occasions might have been tempted to fly the coop. But I read something recently that *particularly* appealed to me. An interviewer asked Prince Charles why both he and his father walked with their hands behind their backs . . . like so. "Because," the prince answered, "we have the same tailor who sews the arms in funny."

Departing from his earlier refusals to get involved in politics, he gave a speech at the Republican National Convention on August 19, 1976, in Kansas City, introducing Mrs. Gerald Ford:

CG: Oh, I know you have *many* remarkable women in your party—after all, what's *any* party without remarkable women?—and in this party, of course, I think of *dear* Nancy Reagan, Happy Rockefeller, Elizabeth Dole, and many others. . . . But I'm here to talk about only *one*, my own personal nominee. . . . I can assure you of her sincere love for all people and her hope to further the cause of women's rights (women have always been one of *my* favorite causes, too).

His speech was one of the longest he ever gave. During Ford's reelection campaign Grant escorted the First Lady to a fund raiser in Beverly Hills.

LORETTA YOUNG remembers that night: "We were all gathered downstairs in the lobby, and Cary brought her down the main stairway. He came down first, and he left her two or three steps behind. She looked particularly lovely, and Cary kind of walked down backwards and off to the side as though he were presenting her. He wouldn't stand in her spotlight, but he wouldn't get out of his own either. He knew exactly how to handle himself at all times. It was so pretty. He looked just like a dancer. He was so graceful. That's the last time I saw him make a public appearance. It was such a gentlemanly, attractive, animal movement. And I thought, *'That's where you belong, Cary. Don't do anything unless it's with the top.'* And he didn't."

BETTY FORD didn't take her evening with Grant lightly. She reports: "Karl Schumaker, the photographer who traveled with me, took a color picture of Cary Grant and me dancing, and when we got home, he blew up the picture and hung it on a wall right smack as you walked into the East Wing, which housed the offices of my staff. I took one look at that handsome, handsome man, and me in his arms, positively pink with pleasure, and I wrote on the picture, right across my dress, 'Eat your hearts out, girls.'"

Chapter Eighteen

"MY BEST PIECE OF MAGIC ..."

CG: Most women are instinctively wiser and emotionally more mature than men. They know our insecurities. A man rushes about trying to prove himself. It takes him much longer to feel comfortable about getting married.

Cary Grant and Roderick Mann arrived in London at the Lancaster Hotel for the May 1976 annual Fabergé trade show and were immediately attracted to the Lancaster's young, beautiful public relations officer. MANN remembers, "Barbara Harris graciously welcomed us to the hotel, but she was distracted and paid us very little notice. Cary was really taken with her. But she rushed past us and dashed down some stairs to the press conference she had organized for Margaux Hemingway, whose plane was late.

"Sometime later, when Cary and I were sitting in the lobby-bar area, she walked by. I asked her whether she was going to take us to lunch. She knew we were coming on to her. Her back rose, and she said, 'No, I won't be taking you to lunch, but I would be happy to make you a reservation.' She thought we were being fresh. However, Cary talked her into it, and she did eventually have lunch with us. Then he invited her to Fabergé's cocktail party that evening.

"I dressed early and went down to the lobby-bar to wait for Cary, and Barbara came along. Cary and I got our signals crossed, and he was waiting for me someplace else. He finally strolled into the bar and saw me talking to Barbara. My God, he was furious! He didn't talk to me again for two or three days. He thought I was stealing her away. I finally went out and bought him a gold pen as a peace offering. It touched me greatly that Cary asked Barbara to give the pen to me after his death."

Born in Dar es Salaam, Tanganyika, on September 30, 1950, Barbara Harris is one of three daughters of Lesley and James Harris, the youngest major in the Royal Army during World War II. Her father served in many locations and received the military cross for bravery in Italy and the Order of the British Empire for serving with the Australian Army in New Guinea. Harris and his wife lived for eighteen years in East Africa, where Harris was a provincial commissioner, and where Barbara Harris first went to boarding school. In 1960 she went to boarding school in England. Her father died in March 1979. Today her mother lives in Devon, England.

Grant was beguiled by the hazel-eyed, open-faced, simply dressed woman with brown hair—and no makeup. She impressed Grant with her honesty and with her wisdom for one so young. She embodied all the qualities he admired in women.

It was serendipitous that Grant's Fabergé association and Barbara Harris's Lancaster job were responsible for their meeting. She drove him around London in her Mini Minor, a car so small Grant's knees came up to his chin when he sat down. They ate and drank in pubs. Soon, however, Fabergé and the Lancaster played no role at all. Grant's visits to London became more frequent, Harris introduced him to her friends, and they often traveled in her car to the southwestern part of England.

For two years Grant's relationship with Harris was one of ardent friendship. He habitually telephoned from his home, gave her a beautiful gold watch on one of his trips to London, and invited her several times to visit him in California. In January 1978 she watched him plant a tree at Lord Mountbatten's historic home, Broadlands. Soon Grant was visiting her parents in Devon. LESLEY HARRIS says, "I had never seen Barbara so happy. He was so easy and friendly. The two of them would laugh the whole time they were here. It was an extraordinary thing. One wondered to begin with, my goodness, there was quite a difference in age, but it worked perfectly."

The man who said he would probably never remarry was

smitten. Harris, too, had fallen in love but wanted to be sure of the intensity of her feelings. Grant was, after all, forty-six years her senior. She would have to make a serious commitment. Although he seemed ageless, full of energy and curiosity, a flirtation was unfair and, she felt, would be ultimately devastating to a man his age. In 1978 Grant was seventy-four. Barbara Harris was twenty-eight. She was troubled about the disparity; she had never dated a man more than ten years older.

In July 1978 Grant and the Sinatras were guests of Gregory and Veronique Peck in the Pecks' villa at St.-Jean-Cap-Ferrat in the south of France. They all had been invited to attend Princess Caroline's wedding in Monaco.

At dinner one night at the restaurant Chaumière, Grant expressed his loneliness. They were in France. Romance was in the air. Everyone except him had somebody. BARBARA SINATRA recalls the evening: "Frank and Greg asked if there wasn't someone special in his life. And he said, 'Well, there is a wonderful girl I've known for quite some time in London.'"

They implored Grant to fly her down. According to GREGORY PECK, "Cary said, 'No, no. I don't think she'd come.' He was shy about asking her. I said, 'Well, you're Cary Grant. You don't have to be alone. You can have any woman you want. Call her up!'"

And he did. When Harris agreed, she knew the direction of their relationship had changed. Grant met her at the airport in Nice and drove back to the Pecks' villa, where they spent the next two days before moving into the Hôtel de Paris in Monte Carlo.

BARBARA SINATRA liked her at once: "I fell in love with Barbara. She was very special and captured everybody's heart. You could really see the great love she had for Cary."

The following day Grant, the Sinatras, and the Pecks attended Princess Caroline's wedding. Grant was so eager to get back to Harris that he started and finished eating the wedding luncheon before any of the other guests, excused himself, and dashed back to her. GREGORY PECK reminisces: "Yes, that was a happy weekend. It seemed to me from that time on Cary spent the happiest years of his life. We were acquaintances in the 1940s, 1950s, and 1960s. We became close friends after he met Barbara. It was a wonderful last chapter in his life. Getting to know Cary better was for us a new chapter. I suppose we drew

Barbara Sinatra photographed Gregory Peck, CG, seventy-four, and husband Frank Sinatra returning from Princess Caroline's wedding, 1978, aboard Fabergé's G2 plane. PECK: *"That was a happy weekend. It seemed to me, from that time on, Cary spent the happiest years of his life."*

closer together because we had such fun in the south of France and because, in a way, we had stage-managed his romance. The fact that Barbara and Veronique struck it off so well and liked one another so much also pulled us together. From that time on until he died, we saw them frequently—here, up at their house, and in Palm Springs, at the Sinatras'. We even took a trip to Hong Kong and Macao together."

Grant and Barbara Harris flew to London. This time when he asked her to come to California, she said she would. Grant

At the International Velvet *premiere in London, July 20, 1978. Left, producer Brian Forbes. Businessman Kirk Kerkorian is standing next to Queen Elizabeth.*

flew back to Los Angeles while she prepared for her three-week visit. He returned immediately to London and met up with Kirk Kerkorian for the premiere of *International Velvet,* after which they flew back to Los Angeles in Kerkorian's plane.

Grant took Harris to Las Vegas and Palm Springs and introduced her to twelve-year-old Jennifer. Meeting Jennifer was one of Harris's chief concerns. Nervous, she knew how much Jennifer meant to Grant. She wanted Jennifer to like her as much as she hoped she would like Jennifer. They took to each other right away. Friends even remarked about how much alike they looked. Grant couldn't have smiled more. Harris flew back to London, sold her apartment, and gave notice to the Lancaster.

THELMA ORLOFF believes that "he was the luckiest guy in the world. She always looked divine, and he adored her. He was so affectionate and loving toward her. And she got along beautifully with Jennifer." ABIGAIL VAN BUREN says, "Barbara is a consummate lady. It was a match made in heaven."

AUDREY HEPBURN thinks the relationship was exactly what Grant had longed for: "It really was marvelous that he met Barbara, who is darling and so lovely. She made him happy the last years of his life. Cary was searching for serenity, and I think he found it. That was what he was trying to impart to me, and to others—the search for a calm, an inner serenity. How he went about it I don't know, but I think that's what he was searching for always."

According to HSH PRINCE RAINIER III, "Cary had not been a happy man. . . . It was only when he met Barbara that he found what he had been searching for: the everyday happiness that lasted all day, all night, day after day, month after month, year after year."

BEA SHAW observes, "When I went to the house, he'd say, 'Let me go get my old lady.' He touched her all the time. You know, when a man is really in love, how he wants to touch the woman? He touched her hand; he put his arm around her; he stroked her. And that said more to me than anything he could say about her. And she was that way with him." According to DAVID TEBET, "They were a real team. You didn't think about one without the other."

BEA SHAW continues, "Barbara has a disarming sense of humor. Once at Hollywood Park Cary said, 'I'm going to go home and share a wonderful bottle of wine and some lovely smoked salmon with the most beautiful woman in the world.' Barbara said, 'I didn't know we were having company.'"

After living with Grant for six months, Barbara Harris went to work for a short time in the newly opened Los Angeles office of a British public relations firm. She arranged a flexible schedule so she could accompany Grant on holidays and business trips. After they married, however, Grant persuaded her to stop working. She occasionally drove him to appointments in the white

Cadillac that had replaced his Rolls-Royce. ABIGAIL VAN BUREN remembers, "Cary didn't like riding in limousines unless he really had to. Barbara pulled up to the front of a hotel or public place and gave the car with the keys to the doorman, who left the car right where she parked it. They'd leave a few minutes early, before the crush, and hop into the car. She whisked them away without drawing any attention."

Grant was dazzled by her competence and sense of organization. DAVID MAHONEY says, "Barbara is one of the smartest women I know. She is a computer bank of information. Cary knew her strengths and absolutely idolized her." BURT REYNOLDS thinks the marriage was unique: "I saw a lot of those kinds of relationships—younger women taking care of the older man—and there would be real affection and devotion, but I never saw that kind of loving sexuality and fun. . . . They were like two thirty-year-old kids."

Barbara Harris was fascinated with Grant's agile mind and affected by his understanding and kindness. She found his stories hilarious and laughed uproariously when he mugged, donning a top hat in his pajamas and walked like a camel. It was a relationship of few arguments. The age difference, which had concerned them both in the beginning, served only to remind them of how precious their time together was. Neither wanted to waste a minute of it.

BEA SHAW believes, "If anything, the difference in their ages was a plus. Barbara's youthful energy was helpful to Cary and fun for Jennifer. And Cary's counsel was important to Barbara."

When Harris came to live with him in 1978, Grant had been remodeling his Beverly Hills home for more than five years. Bags of cement, lumber, sawhorses, and workmen were everywhere. The never-ending upheaval and difficulties surpassed even the mishaps in *Mr. Blandings Builds His Dream House*.

Soon she was in charge of coordinating the work. "That was a terrible house until Barbara took it in hand," says BEA SHAW. "Barbara did all the decorating. But every time I said that, she would say, 'No, we did it together.'"

For the first year and a half they practically lived in the master bedroom and Grant's library-office. There was no dining room, and they couldn't use the living room because everything was packed in crates. Besides, almost everything was open to the

Photographer BERNARD FALLON: "Cary, Barbara, and Jennifer were always joking about strangers standing at their security gate, so one day I suggested they imitate them."

elements. The windows hadn't yet been installed. The kitchen was pulled apart, and the housekeeper slept with a refrigerator in her room. Jennifer and Barbara shared a bathroom. The workmen started every day at seven, and the constant banging ended at four.

> CG: The head carpenter came to me one morning and said he'd like to have a word. I thought he wanted to discuss my career when he said, "I really admire you, Mr. Grant." Instead, he said, "Imagine a man your age going through all this."

When the house was finished, DAN MELNICK was invited to the first dinner party. He recalls: "There were six of us. Cary was so proud of what Barbara had done and kept saying, 'Barbara did this, and Barbara did that.' Barbara cooked the meal. They entertained so graciously, starting the meal with caviar." IRVING LAZAR remembers, "All their dinners were gay, pleasant, and unique. They always served caviar."

It seems Grant was a caviar gourmand. His notebooks show he studied the ways of the sturgeon and the history of caviar. He ate mountains of it . . . his and other people's. ANGIE DICKINSON, who was often seated next to Grant at dinner parties, recollects: "I would get an elbow in my ribs when I passed up the caviar. I don't like caviar. So I would say, 'No, thank you,' and he would jab me, and I would say, 'Oh, just—yes, thank you very much.' I was always slipping him my caviar. It was enchanting because he was just so real. He didn't have to pretend that he also wanted my share."

Grant's Moorish-style house sits atop a hill off Benedict Canyon, high above Beverly Hills. Totally white, inside and out, the monochromatic scheme reflects the simplicity of the design. The quarters for the household staff were placed opposite Jennifer's wing, a large apartment with sliding glass doors opening out into a garden.

The floors are wide, oak-planked, and perfectly smooth, reminiscent of old French barns. Grant loved his house and wanted to enjoy it for a long time. He expected to live to be a hundred. He told BEA SHAW, "I'm going to put a ramp in my house. Who knows? I may need it. I may be in a wheelchair someday."

The corridors in Grant's house are open and wide. A ramp

leads from the kitchen out to a garden. Most of the house faces glorious gardens and a swimming pool, overlooking the Wilshire corridor all the way out to Santa Monica and the ocean. One can see the Harold Lloyd mansion, the Beverly Hills Hotel, Century City, and indeed, the city of Los Angeles as far as the airport. Off one long corridor near the living room there is a room-size vault containing Grant's papers, scripts, and memorabilia. There are fireplaces in the living room and dining area. The guest bedroom, called the English Room, contains the secretary William Randolph Hearst gave Grant in the 1930s.

Grant's library-office off the living room and master bedroom contains several prized objects: his Oscar; a large gold lion made by Cartier and inscribed "1984, The MGM-UA Entertainment Company;" and a gold clock inscribed "For 16 Years of Devoted Service to Fabergé." There is also a magnificent sculpture of Grant's head by Wei Li ("Willy") Wang of Houston, Texas, a gift to Grant from the artist. A painting by Ben Herring and W. C. Dodd, "Welsh Mountain Ponies" (1856), hangs over his desk.

His eclectic collection of sheet music dates back to the 1920s and includes everything from English sacred music to songs made popular by Judy Garland. Countless songbooks, from which he played selections on his ebony grand piano, include Tchaikovsky, Johann Sebastian Bach, and Mendelssohn as well as Noel Coward, Gilbert and Sullivan, and Comden and Green. At Christmas Grant played carols for his guests.

The enormous beamed living room is delightful for entertaining. Grant's extensive art book collection occupies four enormous shelves that wrap around two walls. Other shelves are variety itself—from Thomas Mann to O. Henry. Books range in taste from the nine volumes of *The History of India* to *Literary England, London Perceived, Sophie's Choice, Don Quixote,* and *Noble House.* Modern couches and ottomans in white fabric complement antiques, mostly French.

Considering the demands of Grant's public life, his home was understandably his sanctuary. Barbara Harris liked to stay at home as much as he did. It was another important aspect of their compatibility. She cooked on weekends and prepared exceptional meals for Grant's birthday and special occasions. She enjoyed having him watch her work in her garden and challenged him in card games. They were tutored in French, read voraciously, listened to music while they took lovely quiet swims in their pool, and, in the early evening, drank a glass of wine on their patio and observed the setting sun. With Jennifer, they played backgammon, word games, and Trivial Pursuit.

Harris made clothes for Jennifer, knitted sweaters for Grant, and sewed him brightly colored cotton shirts, patterned after those she had seen in North Africa and in the south of Spain. He wore these over white pants with black velvet slippers. GREGORY PECK recalls, "He used to stroll in here during the summer months in those ankle-length caftans Barbara made for him. He felt very much at ease and comfortable at our house, and we always felt very easy when we went up there. He dropped his defenses with us, and I don't think he did that with everybody. We felt lucky. . . ."

Grant took caftans when he visited MERV GRIFFIN in Carmel, California, who remembers, "Barbara, Cary, and Jennifer spent a weekend with me and Eva Gabor, along with Lucille Ball and Gary Morton, and the Armand Hammers. Both Cary and Barbara wore caftans that weekend, and Lucy kept saying, 'Here comes the high lama.'

"Kathryn and Arthur Murray and Clint Eastwood and Sondra Locke came for dinner. Clint was flying in from his ski place in Sun Valley. He's probably my oldest friend. He kept calling and saying that it was another one of my practical jokes. Why would Cary Grant come to Carmel Valley to my ranch? 'If this is one of your jokes, I'll kill you. What'll I say to him?' And I said, 'Well, try a hello.'"

GARY MORTON played golf with Eastwood and reports: "He said, 'Oh, my God, I'm going to finally meet Cary Grant. What should I wear?' And I said, 'It's very informal, Clint—just a sports jacket and an open shirt.'"

Grant surprised Morton by saying, "I'm going to meet Clint Eastwood. God, I really enjoy his work." Then Grant expressed concern about what to wear, wondering if his caftan was appropriate. Morton suggested a sport shirt with a pair of slacks.

"We changed," says Morton, "and met back in the living room for cocktails. Cary walked over to me and said, 'Is this all right?' And I said, 'Cary, it's perfect.' He had on a beautiful pair of slacks and a sport shirt."

Merv Griffin met Eastwood at the gate and brought him in.

According to GRIFFIN, "Before Clint could get out 'Hello,' Cary said, 'Well, I just think you're the best director-actor. You really are an amazing talent.' And Clint turned to the whole room and said, 'Oh, my God. He talks just like he does in the movies.'"

"Clint was so excited about meeting Cary Grant," says GARY MORTON, "that suddenly he sounded like Jimmy Stewart."

"Cary and Barbara held hands and walked the grounds all weekend," remembers GRIFFIN. "It was almost a meditative experience for them." Their gardener, ADOLPHO NAVARRO, recalls that Grant walked in their gardens every day when he was home: "He loved plants and flowers, especially *Tecomaria* (Cape honeysuckle), high bushes with orange flowers that surround the front of the property. Orange was his favorite color."

Large ficus and eucalyptus trees and beautiful, mature bushes of bougainvillaea and gardenias greet the visitor at the tranquil entrance to the Grants' house. Inside the iron gate, daisies, impatiens, and roses in massive, sweeping beds line the driveway. Barbara Grant commissioned a salmon-colored rose for Grant for Valentine's Day 1986. An unusually beautiful species and color, corresponding closely to Grant's favorite shade of orange, the flower is named the Cary Grant Rose. Hundreds of these line the Grants' driveway. More have been planted in Monaco in the extensive rose garden built by Prince Rainier in memory of Princess Grace.

Cary Grant and Barbara Harris were married quietly before a judge at home on April 11, 1981. The attendants were Jennifer Grant and Stanley and Jewel Fox.

> CG: When I first told Jennifer that I was going to marry Barbara, her eyes filled with tears. For a moment I thought she was upset. She was just the opposite. She was thrilled for me.

The bride made the wedding lunch, which included avocado soup. She wore a white suit and a coffee-colored silk blouse; the, groom a gray suit and gray tie. That night, they were at Dodger Stadium for a baseball game.

They wanted a serene wedding without reporters present. Barbara Grant telephoned her mother immediately, but the news didn't break until eight days later. First, the Grants wanted to tell their friends Prince Rainier, Princess Grace, and their children; the Pecks; the Sinatras; and the Roger Moores when they

Jennifer Grant with Barbara Grant and CG on their wedding day, April 11, 1981, on the steps leading down to the garden. Opposite, the more formal picture they gave to friends.

met over Easter weekend at the Sinatras' Palm Springs home. Veronique and Gregory Peck had been expecting a wedding, but when the announcement finally came, it was a surprise. "The fact that they waited for that moment to tell their close friends was very nice," says PECK. "Everyone was happy. It was a celebration."

BARBARA SINATRA, who found it very touching and very romantic, says, "And it was the same weekend Prince Rainier and Grace celebrated their twenty-fifth anniversary. Prince Albert, Cary, Frank, and others made toasts. Then Rainier stood up. He was at my table, and Grace was at my husband's table with Cary. I must say, Grace had a very special relationship with Cary. And with Frank. They were very, very close. Rainier seems a staid, stern sort of fellow, and it isn't easy for him to say what he really feels in his heart, but he toasted Grace and told her what she had meant to him and to the three children. It was a very special moment—one I certainly shall never forget. There wasn't a dry eye in the whole room. Grace was crying. I looked at Cary, and the tears were running off his chin.

"Cary was a very sensitive man. We called him Leaky Eyes because every time he attended one of my husband's benefits, the tears rolled down his cheeks. I don't know whether it was the way my husband sang, or whether he identified with the lyrics, or whether he thought of my husband living some of the songs, but he got very emotional."

NANCY REAGAN also recalls Grant's vulnerability: "We were at a dinner, seated at a podium, Cary started to talk about his daughter, and I started to talk about mine, and then Cary teared up and I teared up. And finally I said, 'Cary, they're going to wonder what's wrong with us. We're sitting in front of thousands of people, and we're both crying.'"

At home in Beverly Hills the Grants settled into the marriage that Grant had hoped for all his life.

CG: My best piece of magic was marrying my wife Barbara.

On July 1, 1986, their marriage was blessed in a church wedding. In fact, "Cary said he wanted to remarry Barbara every five years," recalls ABIGAIL VAN BUREN. "Barbara always wanted a church wedding. A few months before he died, their vows were blessed in the small village church where her father is buried and near her mother's home in Devon."

The Grants' housekeeper, Gemma Camins, an amusing woman from the Philippines who was remembered by Grant in his will, recalled that although Barbara Grant was a cat lover, Grant was not—until Sausage came into their lives. CAMINS recalls: "A stray cat appeared at the door, and Mr. Grant called to Mrs. Grant and said, 'Come, darling, look what we have here!' He picked up the cat, stroked it, and asked the houseman how he thought the cat got there. The houseman said, 'Oh, he must have used the Map of the Stars.' Mr. Grant doubled over with laughter."

BEA SHAW tells about a second feline member of the Grant household: "EQ was a white cat with one blue eye and one yellow eye. Someone had given the cat to Barbara and Cary. Cary said, 'We don't know what EQ stands for.' I told them that when you're recording music, 'EQ' means 'equalization.' A few days later Quincy Jones stopped by the house. Barbara said he cracked up when he heard the name and said, 'EQ! Man, that cat hasn't even got two eyes the same color!'"

Neither of the Grants cared about late nights on the town, but he had certain obligations to the Hollywood community. Many charities continued to invite him to attend dinners, and Grant often obliged because his attendance helped them fill their tables. Barbara Grant limited these black-tie parties to no more than two evenings in succession.

JACK HALEY, JR., discounts the idea that Grant was reclusive: "It's not true at all. He went to benefits, but he wouldn't perform. But when he showed up, the photographers went crazy." ROBERT WAGNER says, "He had a lot of exposure, but when he wanted privacy, he worked it out."

The Grants went to the Magic Castle and to the Variety Club in downtown Los Angeles. Grant enjoyed the old music hall ambience. They rarely went to movies because as always, everyone looked at him instead of the film. They drove to Palm Springs and stayed with Charles Rich. Later, they started spending weekends, which Grant called love-ins, at the Sinatras. Sometimes Jennifer went with them. They traveled to Las Vegas on business for MGM and to Hawaii and Spain for Fabergé. They went to Alaska and to Calgary for the Stampede. They traveled often to London and were at Wimbledon in 1985, when Boris Becker won his first singles championship. They visited Barbara Grant's mother, Grant's cousin Maggie, and the pubs and lovely old hotels throughout southern and southwestern England.

After Thanksgiving every year they went to Paris and to Monaco, where Grant was a judge at Prince Rainier's world-famous circus, the Monte Carlo International Circus Festival. HSH PRINCE RAINIER III, who shared Grant's love of the circus, recollects: "We had a fascination with the artists, their work, and their devotion to their profession. Cary especially enjoyed watching morning rehearsals. When the artists noticed him in the tent,

CG, David Niven, and Princess Grace at the Monte Carlo International Circus Festival, watching a trapeze act, 1978.

they would go right over to him and talk. When we met for lunch, Cary would be full of stories and told us what to expect."

In May 1981 Grant took his new wife to her first of many White House dinners. The evening was in the Reagans' private upstairs quarters in honor of Prince Charles, who was returning from Australia, just before his marriage to Princess Diana.

JAMIE NIVEN recalls that his father, David Niven, had been invited but "elected not to go because he had been diagnosed earlier in the year with a terminal illness. He was uncomfortable about going out in a situation like that. For reasons that still defy my imagination, my wife and I were invited to join this august group of thirty-two people. I told my father that I was very nervous about going to the White House, and he said, 'Don't worry about a thing. Seek out Cary Grant and tell him you're nervous and ask him what to do.' I did exactly that. Without batting an eye, Cary turned to a waiter and said, 'We'll have two large vodka martinis.' And we hammered them down."

SAMMY CAHN remembers, "The Reagans had exactly four tables of eight in the Yellow Room. At the end of the evening I did some special lyrics: "I'd say tonight is the loveliest night of the year / Because the loveliest people we know have all gathered here / Can I ignore him? / No, I can't / How do you ignore Cary Grant?' . . . Everyone's name was in the lyrics."

While not affiliated with any religious denomination, Grant occasionally attended church services. On one occasion he was happy to join his friends to raise money for a new Catholic church in the Southern California desert. GREGORY PECK recalls, "The church at La Quinta was designed by Franco Zeffirelli. It's a smaller version of the famous chapel—with the Giotto murals—at Assisi." BARBARA SINATRA says, "Everybody decided to help our friend Father Bluett, who had raised the money for the church single-handedly. My husband, Frank, Greg Peck, and Roger Moore agreed to read. Cary decided to take up the collection.

"He started from the back on the side. People were facing straight ahead. You could see they didn't want to stare. They'd glance to the side and whisper, 'Is that. . . ? Oh, no. Oh, yes. Oh, no. It couldn't be!'"

From January through April 1983 the Grants started on a trip to sail around the world, leaving Los Angeles during an atrocious storm. The *Royal Viking* rolled for five days, but the turbulence didn't disturb Grant. He loved the nostalgia and "calm" of being on the water. However, until she got her sea legs in Hong Kong, his wife begged to get off. They stopped in Singapore, Sri Lanka, South Africa, and South America. They especially loved the Seychelles Islands. They read books on the balcony outside their stateroom. Grant read the prayer he used in his *Conversations* at the *Viking*'s services on Sundays and informally answered questions about his career for the crew in the ship's pub.

Virtually all the jewelry Grant gave his new wife was designed by him. Nonetheless, he found an exquisite sapphire and diamond bracelet in Thailand absolutely irresistible. BOBBY ALTMAN explains: "Cary studied gems, and his taste was irreproachable. None of his selections were impulsive. He knew exactly what he wanted. He designed a brilliant sapphire and diamond ring for Barbara's birthday shortly after she came to live with him. I remember a diamond necklace with about forty diamonds and a bracelet to match. And lots of pearls with diamonds. Barbara loves pearls. He designed another diamond necklace with graduated stones starting with one three carats in size, together with diamond earrings shaped like flower petals. The pear-shaped diamond in the ring he gave her when they married is one of the most brilliant and exquisite I've ever seen."

ABIGAIL VAN BUREN told "Barbara one night that I couldn't take my eyes off the pin she was wearing. Cary said, 'That was one of the first gifts I gave to Barbara.' And then he turned to her and said, 'Why don't we let her copy it?' Barbara gave it to me in the Verdura box it came in, and Harry Winston in New York copied it. It was such a generous thing to do."

Chasen's and Madame Wu's were the Grants' favorite Los Angeles restaurants, but they preferred dinner at home with friends, with good conversation, and limited to eight or twelve people.

While the contrast in their ages was invisible to them, Grant made a list of what he called May-December marriages:

Hayley Mills, when she was twenty-two, to Ray Boulting, fifty-five. (Age difference, thirty-three years.) Kathy Crosby, when she was twenty-three, to Bing Crosby, fifty-three. (Thirty years.) Jacqueline Picasso, forty-three, was wed to Pablo Picasso, eighty-seven. (Forty-

Barbara Grant finally got her sea legs in Hong Kong, 1983.

four years.) Bogart, forty-five, and Bacall, twenty. (Twenty-five years.) Oona O'Neill, at eighteen, married Chaplin, when he was fifty-four. (Thirty-six years.) Marta Casals, forty, to Pablo Casals, ninety-two. (Fifty-two years.) T. S. Eliot was married to a woman thirty-nine years younger. . . .

Grant was convinced he would be blessed with a very long life, and when Henry Gris wrote *May You Live to Be 200!* with coauthor Milton Martin, Grant was eager to try the Russian secret for longevity Gris had "discovered." Gris had spent six weeks with the famous centenarians in the Caucasus Mountains. "The subject of our banter over the telephone for a long time," says GRIS, "was the Caucasian centenarian aphrodisiac, honey and crushed, tree-fresh walnuts, a mixture the Caucasians ate every morning before breakfast."

They spoke often about producing and selling this simple formula through supermarkets. GRIS remembers, "I always reminded Cary that he was probably the best subject for old age because his mother lived to be ninety-five and was active right up until she died. Cary was fascinated that the centenarians of the Caucasus live to be a hundred and thirty, a hundred and forty, and didn't finish their lives in wheelchairs. They are physically and mentally active, totally and completely, and Cary wanted very much to meet them, to go with me to Russia. We always talked about the day we'd have the time to do it together. Cary was anxious to live a long time, and I felt he deserved it. If I had gotten him with the centenarians, probably I would have succeeded. You become rejuvenated after meeting them."

Grant kept to a regular schedule, attending board meetings for Fabergé, MGM/UA, Hollywood Park, and the Norton Simon Museum. In 1980 he was appointed by President Reagan as a trustee for the John F. Kennedy Center for the Performing Arts. He rose each morning before six to follow the New York stock market. He constantly reviewed his portfolio of mostly blue-chip stocks to safeguard the future of his wife and daughter. His only flyer was the Harris Corporation stock he bought because of his wife's maiden name. Even it did well. He and Stanley Fox talked business weekly. FOX says: "I loved to play golf, but Tuesday was ladies' day. Often I would go to Cary's because there was always a houseman or a maid who could bring us coffee and lunch. Cary would occasionally come here because he liked the cookies. He had an unbelievable sweet tooth. Tuesday was our day."

Jennifer went to high school at the Santa Catalina School for Girls in Monterey, California. Her graduation in 1983 was filmed by cinematographer Cary Grant. RICHARD HENNING recalls: "The nuns and counselors thought the world of Jennifer at Santa Catalina. At a father-daughter weekend one year many of the students and their fathers joined Cary and Jennifer for a trail ride and picnic. They also played backgammon and volleyball.

"On Saturday night they presented the musical *Hello, Dolly!*, and Jennifer played Dolly. She sang; she danced. She was incredibly talented. She seemed quite pleased to be praised so highly, but she was very modest."

ANGIE DICKINSON saw Grant soon after: "He was exuberant. 'Oh, she was glorious,' he said. 'She was wonderful!' He was so happy with her coming into adulthood."

Grant confided to GREGORY PECK, "'I just want to see Jennifer have a child. I want to see my grandchild. Then I'll be ready to shuffle off.' I think that nicely expresses his state of mind at the end. He had no fear. I hope he had a feeling that he had accomplished a lot with his talent, determination, and hard work. I hope he had an inner feeling of having done a good job and having made something of himself. I think he did."

BEA SHAW recalls, "Jennifer said that until the Kennedy Center awards in December 1981 she never really thought of her father as being Cary Grant the superstar. At home he was just Daddy." According to MARJORIE EVERETT, "Cary worshiped Jennifer, of course, but he also wanted to make sure that she was a fine girl. He didn't spoil her, but that doesn't mean he would deprive her of anything. Jennifer's now a strong-minded, bright, warm, compassionate, gracious young woman, with lovely manners. I've never seen her do anything in excess. She helped us prepare the Breeder's Cup in 1987. She was very organized, very capable. She's going to be successful."

BEA SHAW admired the father-daughter relationship: "She liked the same kinds of jokes, and she wasn't afraid of him or awed by him, as some girls are by their fathers."

Angie Dickinson saw CG soon after Jennifer Grant played the lead in Hello, Dolly. DICKINSON: "He was exuberant. 'Oh, she was glorious,' he said. 'She was wonderful!' "

Dyan Cannon and CG, almost fifteen years following their divorce, proudly smiling and talking about their talented daughter, Jennifer (between them), after her performance as Dolly in a school play.

Jewel and Stanley Fox, Barbara Grant and CG, 1986. FOX: *"I took care of everything for him because his mind was completely taken up with his profession. But he could have done everything for himself. He was the most capable man. . . ."*

One day David Tebet told Grant that Jennifer made Brooke Shields look like a boy. "Cary loved it," TEBET comments. "He told the whole town."

> CG: Whatever she does is all right with me so long as she's happy. From the time she was born, she's been the joy of my life. We have an honest relationship. I don't think she's always looking at me and thinking, How can I get a BMW out of this old codger?

Jennifer's excellent grades at Santa Catalina earned her admittance to Stanford University. BEA SHAW recognized how difficult it was for Grant to leave his daughter off at college: "Cary said it was very emotional for him. The campus was huge, and he thought it must be frightening for her to be left there, with about twelve thousand other students, to fend for herself. I laughed, because Cary was more worried about it than Jennifer."

After graduating with honors from Stanford in 1987, Jennifer worked on projects for the homeless with a public-interest law firm in San Francisco. Today she is studying to become an actress and sees Barbara Grant frequently. "Their relationship certainly disproves the wicked stepmother theory," JUDY QUINE says. "It's special, and it has survived Cary's death. Jennifer has a best friend and second mother, and Barbara has a friend and the daughter she never had."

Under "LOVE IS" in his yellow notebook binder, Grant kept the following undated letter to his daughter.

> I want to thank you for being my daughter and for many loving memories I have of that. How proud I am to have you as a daughter and as my friend. I may not have been right all the time, or pleased you all the time, but I did and said everything with the utmost of good intentions. Dear Jennifer, resolve to enjoy life to the fullest, but unselfishly. In fact, *only* unselfishly can you enjoy life to the fullest. Be considerate, respect endeavor, strive for excellence and good taste, be pure in mind and, therefore, in turn, behavior. You may judge yourself to have good and bad points. Strengthen the good and forget the bad.
>
> One short sleep past and I shall awaken eternally is a paraphrase of English poet, John Donne. And even if I do

not awaken, as we know awake, I shall live within you, dearest daughter. Or if I do awaken, my first concern, and thought, will be of you. Take care, good care, of your dear sweet self. Be kind and risk loving and no harm can ever come to you.

Be thankful for ears that can listen to Beethoven and a bird singing on a telegraph wire. For being able to see the face of good people and the sweetness that lies behind their eyes. For the young friends and the children whose voices make the sweetest music in the world. By those books that light up the mind. For simple songs to sing. For the sun by day and the moon by night. For the flowers that dance in the wind and for the grain that lifts its head above ground and gives us our daily bread.

I'd like my child to know that whatever she does we'll always be with her. No father or no mother can be with her for all the time. She has to live for herself and if she wastes or abuses her life, she is the one who must live with the consequences.

Parents must accept the child they get, but *you* are just what I, and your mother, would have ordered. Jennifer, you've brought great joy to my life.

CG: Jennifer is one of the two most exciting things that ever happened to me. The other is my wife Barbara. And now Barbara and I are working on other children.

Barbara Grant told friends that she hoped to have a son, that she wanted a part of him throughout her life.

Retirement and a more settled life gave Grant the perfect opportunity to pursue his sporting passions. One was for horse racing. QUINCY JONES says, "Going to Hollywood Park was a ritual. He'd have a different group every time. And he had all the English guys out there—Roger Moore, Michael Caine, Dudley Moore, Michael York . . . and me. He was such an amiable host. I come from the South Side of Chicago—the heart of the ghetto—and that approach to graciousness was something I hadn't come across."

"We were always looking for a cheap tip, somebody who knew more about horses than we did," RICHARD BROOKS remembers. "I never saw him place a bet larger than two dollars." JOHN FORSYTHE teased him about the bets he made at the window: "He thought for hours about how he was going to make a two-dollar bet. It was like another man going up there and betting five thousand dollars." When RICHARD HENNING asked him why he bet only two dollars, he replied, "Because they won't let me bet a dollar fifty."

Hollywood Park, left to right, *Loni Anderson and Burt Reynolds, Carol and Dom DeLuise, Barbara Grant and CG.* REYNOLDS: *"When a reporter asked me if I wanted to be the next Cary Grant, I said there would never, ever be another Cary Grant. Then I was shocked to get a complimentary note from Cary saying he had read the piece. Soon we had little notes going back and forth."*

JOHN FORSYTHE recalls Grant's popularity at the track: "In the big races celebrities—from Elizabeth Taylor to Omar Bradley—are often asked to present the cup to the owner in the winner's circle. The only time people flocked to the winner's circle was when Cary made the presentation, proof of the incredible hold he had on people. At the racetrack people work on their racing forms and care only about the next race, not who's making a presentation."

One of Grant's other great pleasures was baseball. "He and Barbara were always at Dodger Stadium opening day and at the play-offs and the World Series," says PETER O'MALLEY. "From April until October each year, they averaged fifteen of the eighty home games.

"Cary walked in like everyone else. He went down to the club level, past third base, and into the first door on the left to my box, which sat a maximum of sixteen people. We'd have lunch or dinner, watch the game, have a glass of wine, and sometimes, for dessert, Barbara's homemade ice cream.

"Danny Kaye brought fresh lime juice, and we supplied the tequila and Cointreau for the margaritas he stirred in a pitcher. Cary gave his season box on the club level to friends when the Grants were out of town or with us.

"Once in a while he'd go downstairs before the game and wish someone well. For example, he closely followed the career of Fernando Valenzuela, who was one of his favorites. Cary was always warmly greeted by the players, the media, the manager, the coaches, the ushers, and the parking lot attendants. He was truly loved here.

"For several years Cary and Gregory Peck participated in an annual pregame ceremony honoring heroic policemen and widows of policemen slain in the line of duty. The chief of police presented each with a citation medal. Cary [reluctant public speaker] would be on the field at home plate before fifty-five thousand people talking about what these men had done. . . .

"The fans would recognize him, wave, and he'd wave back. Soon thousands of people would be waving to him. And he enjoyed that. If it was a big crowd, or if it was a game that had ended suddenly and most of the people were still here, I'd offer to have somebody walk them out to the car. Nine times out of ten Cary would say, 'No, no, don't be silly. We're not in any hurry.' They walked through the crowd like you or I. He felt totally secure here."

Grant frequently gave baseball tickets to his housekeeper, GEMMA CAMINS, another Dodger fan, who recalls: "One time a voice called out, 'Gemma, are you enjoying yourself?' and I turned and there he was. Suddenly all these heads turned, looked at me, and then back at Mr. Grant and then back to me again. They must have been wondering, 'Who's *that*?'"

CHAPTER NINETEEN

HOW OLD CARY GRANT?

CG: I would have thought that medical science would have had the problem of death all sorted out. I was sure that by the time I reached the age I am now, they would have found a cure for it, that they would be able to transplant everything and we'd all just keep right on going forever.

David Tebet and George Barrie conspired to get Grant's consent to a New York Friars Club Man of the Year dinner at New York's Waldorf-Astoria Hotel on May 16, 1984. It was the first one ever held in Grant's honor and the largest dinner in the history of the club. Always before, he had declined. When David Tebet told him all he had to say was "Thank you," he accepted.

PEGGY LEE, who sang "Mr. Wonderful" to him from the balcony, recalls: "He looked up at me—and I could see that he was moved."

Peter Duchin's Orchestra played as Joe Williams sang "The Star-Spangled Banner." Tony Bennett, Sammy Cahn, and Cy Coleman offered musical tributes. Frank Sinatra was the toastmaster. He sang Sammy Cahn's special lyrics to the melody of "The Most Beautiful Girl in the World," changing "girl" to "man." There were more than sixty people on the dais.*

---

*They included Muhammad Ali, Richard Anderson, George Barrie, former New York Mayor Abraham D. Beame, Richard Bienen, Jacqueline Bisset, Tom Brokaw, George Burns, Red Buttons, Charlie Callas, Governor and Mrs. Hugh L. Carey, Howard Cosell,

Grant had prepared three typewritten pages of notes. He joked, told stories, and reminisced about his friends. DAVID TEBET said, "He gave a long speech and became so overwhelmed by the moment that he cried."

CG: I find myself tearful with happiness quite often these days. I cry at great talent. I'm deeply affected by the works of certain painters, by the words of certain writers, by certain singers, phrases of music, the perfection of Fred Astaire, the national anthem at the baseball game. Such things can trigger off a complexity of emotions, but you see, to indulge in one's emotions, publicly and unashamedly, is a privilege permitted the elderly.

TEBET continues, "Fifteen hundred people went absolutely berserk. I can only compare it with Tallulah Bankhead playing *Rain*. The audience stood on their seats and wouldn't let her off the stage, and that's what happened to Cary." RICH LITTLE remembers, "It was heartwarming. The love was incredible—not a dry eye in the house. I turned to my wife when he finished and said, 'And he says he can't talk.' He consented to the dinner because it wasn't televised and because he adored the people who were there." The evening ended with a private party hosted by Frank Sinatra.

Bobby Altman and Kirk Kerkorian were invited, but at the last moment Kerkorian had to fly to Europe. ALTMAN recalls: "He insisted on flying Cary's friends to New York and chartered another plane for himself. Once Kirk gives his word, that's it. The day after the dinner we were sitting in the bar of the Hôtel de Paris in Monte Carlo when Cary called and said, 'You guys really went out of your way to avoid the party.'"

A few days later Myrna Loy wrote to Grant: ". . . I didn't blame you for weeping a bit. It would not have been you if you hadn't. It was so sweet. I was trying to get word to you down the

Tony Curtis, Marvin Davis, Marjorie L. Everett, Farrah Fawcett, Stanley Fox, Mike Frankovich, Alexander Godunov, Benny Goodman, Jack L. Green, William Randolph Hearst, Jr., Jack H. Klein, John W. Kluge, Ralph Lauren, Myrna Loy, Dina Merrill, Joe Namath, Louis Nizer, Ryan O'Neal, Mr. and Mrs. Gregory Peck, Clifford Perlman, Charles J. Rich, Jilly Rizzo, Harry Reasoner, Cliff Robertson, Frank Rosenfelt, Daniel Schwartz, Irene Mayer Selznick, Walter M. Sharp, Sidney Sheldon, Mr. and Mrs. Norton Simon, Mrs. Frank Sinatra, George Steinbrenner, George T. Stevens, Jr., Jule Styne, David W. Tebet, Jack Valenti, Joe Williams, William B. Williams, Sylvia Wu, and Norman Zeiler.

line to say 'blow your nose and clear your voice.' . . . I wish your mother could have been there. . . ."

There were other honors equally as touching. On October 3, 1984, MGM celebrated its diamond jubilee and named its theater on the MGM lot the Cary Grant Theater. Grant said, "I've never had anything named after me." He thought for a moment. "Oh, my mother once named her dog Archie." And on May 2, 1987, the year after he died, Hollywood Park honored him with the Cary Grant Pavilion.

On January 18, 1984, Cary Grant was eighty years old. He grew a beard for the occasion, an idea he got after seeing Prince Rainier with one. When his friends objected, Grant shaved it off. ADOLPHO NAVARRO wished him a happy birthday, Grant thanked him, "and then went into the house and came out with presents for *me* to bring home to my family."

MARJORIE EVERETT remembers, "Barbara had a little surprise party and invited Charlie Rich, Jennifer, the Sinatras, and me. Barbara called earlier in the day and was beside herself. All the power was out, and she couldn't cook the dinner. She wanted us to slip into the house without being seen by Cary. Somehow we all came in through the back of the house, hid in Jennifer's bedroom, and came out at the appropriate time. We ate by candlelight, and suddenly, at eleven-thirty, the lights came on. We had the best time."

According to BEA SHAW, "Barbara prepared for Cary's birthday a year in advance. Everywhere they went, she slipped a blank audiotape to Cary's friends and ask them to record a birthday message.* One night Cary played the tape for Charlie Rich, the Gregory Pecks, Kirk [Kerkorian], and me.

"We all recognized the first voice, which was our President saying, 'Cary, Nancy and I want to wish you . . .' and then the First Lady's voice came in and said, 'Don't say Nancy, he'll know who you are,' and then the President said, 'Oh, is this supposed to be a surprise?' 'Well, I don't know if it's a surprise,' she said, 'but he's supposed to guess from our voices who we are.' It was the perfect introduction to the rest of the tape. Ingrid Bergman said, 'When we made *Indiscreet*, I told

*Barbara Grant gathered recorded birthday greetings from George Burns, Bobby Altman, George Steinbrenner, Cy Coleman, Walter Cronkite, Irene Selznick, Cubby and Dana

you our combined ages were eighty-one. You didn't think that was funny, so I don't think I will tell you what our combined ages would be now.'"

"There was a serenity about him at eighty," PETER BOGDAN-OVICH observes. "He never became an old man. He could be scrappier than ever, and was surprisingly open and candid over the phone—pungent, acerbic, very honest." BEA SHAW thinks "his curiosity kept him young. When you concentrate on your age, you lose your agility. Cary had such a fertile, inquisitive mind. And he never lost his almost militarylike walk. He walked with authority right to the end."

> CG: There's no point in being unhappy about growing older. Just think of the millions who have been denied the privilege.

As the years went by, Grant was steadily saddened by the deaths of close friends. Howard Hughes and Rosalind Russell died in 1976; Howard Hawks in 1977; Lord Mountbatten in 1979; Alfred Hitchcock in 1980; Princess Grace, Ingrid Bergman, and his cousin Eric Leach in 1982; David Niven in 1983; and Charles Rich, who was six months younger than Grant, in 1986. "When your mates start dropping off, it puts little dents in your longevity," said RODERICK MANN.

In late 1982 Grant embarked on yet another "new" career. To the astonishment of his friends, over the next four years, Grant made thirty-six public appearances in his one-man show, *A Conversation with Cary Grant*.

Before each engagement, Grant gave two telephone interviews to local press. He rarely did in-person press interviews for these appearances but made an exception for Carrie Dolan, of *The Wall Street Journal*, who spoke to him in San Francisco in June 1984. She said, "I tried to appear professional. I thought I might fall down." Her article began:

Broccoli, Jimmy Stewart, Danny Kaye, Peter O'Malley, Dan Melnick, Stanley Donen, Peter Bogdanovich (who also did messages in Hawks's and Hitchcock's voices), Sammy Cahn, Katharine Hepburn, Tom Lasorda, President and Mrs. Gerald Ford, Ingrid Bergman, former President and Mrs. Ronald Reagan, Jennifer Grant, Charles Rich, Fred De Cordova, Johnny Carson, Glenn and Cynthia Ford, Roderick Mann, Frank and Barbara Sinatra, Norton and Jennifer Simon, Gregory and Veronique Peck, Princess Grace, Irving Lazar, Stanley Fox and his family, and Maggie Leach.

Recently, I was alone in an elegant hotel suite with Cary Grant. My life has not been wasted.

Sure, it was a Sunday morning, and we only had coffee. And actually, we were alone for only a few minutes while his wife went downstairs to mail a letter. It doesn't matter. There are only two good reasons to become a reporter: to help change the world or to meet Cary Grant.

At the dedication of the Cary Grant Theater, on the MGM lot, October 3, 1984, CG, Barbara, and Jennifer Grant. Businessman MARVIN DAVIS: "He was a very modest man. He wasn't looking for honors, but you could tell how proud he was."

Mr. Grant is perhaps the only living man who can inspire lust in any red-blooded American girl—and her mother and her grandmother. He has been doing this for quite a while. He was the one Mae West invited to come up and see her sometime. Mr. Grant is 80 years old. I am 24. It doesn't matter.

His popularity was enormous. When appearances at the La Mirada (California) Civic Theater were announced, two within one year, all 1,264 seats sold within twenty-four hours. A woman shopping across the street at a supermarket left her groceries at

LOUIS JOURDAN: "It fits him . . . because it's delightfully absurd. It's his joke, his game. He said, 'You just put a spoon on your nose and try to keep it there.' Cary was the master of the absurd." October 1986 at the Pecks' house, one month before CG died. Frederique Jourdan is on CG's left, Veronique Peck behind him, Jeanne Weymers, Barbara Grant, Gregory Peck, and Tina Sinatra.

CG with beard inspired by Prince Rainier. PETER BOGDANOVICH:
*"Although there was a serenity about him at eighty, he never became an
old man. Often he could be scrappier than ever. And he could be
surprisingly open and candid over the phone—pungent, acerbic, very
honest."*

the check-out counter and ran to the ticket office as his name went up on their marquee. A woman from Washington, D.C., flew across country just to see him. Tom Mitze, the managing director of the theater, received telephone calls from Wyoming, northern California, and London for reservations. Desperate fans mailed blank checks with their ticket requests only to have them returned—without tickets.

It was at the second of these La Mirada appearances, in March 1985, that Grant conceded that age was catching up with him. In October 1984, after days of refusing to go to a hospital, Grant had been admitted to Cedars-Sinai, in Los Angeles. He had suffered a mild stroke. A *Conversation* in San Francisco was canceled and rescheduled for January 29, 1985, with the explanation that Grant was suffering from postflu syndrome. At the time he lamented that he had never canceled an event. Several other *Conversations* had to be postponed.

JUDY QUINE says, "Some of us knew he had had a stroke, but he said he didn't want anyone to make a fuss over him. It was kept very quiet. I was stunned when he stood on that stage at La Mirada and told the whole audience about it."

Grant didn't slow down much and was amazed to receive invitations from all over the United States, Canada, Great Britain, and Australia. He actually believed he had been forgotten. Once when RICH LITTLE was performing in Las Vegas, he introduced Grant to the audience. He recalls: "He happily stood up and took a bow. Later he asked [Little imitating CG], 'You're not really doing me in your show?' I told him that I was. 'You're kidding. You're just doing it because I'm here.' I told him I did it every night. 'Do they remember me?' I said, 'Of course, they do.' 'They do? And it gets a good reaction?' Cary believed because he wasn't making films, people had forgotten him."

To prepare for a *Conversation,* Grant spent an hour on the day of the event working with the stage crew and specially selected microphone attendants, all of whom he treated as colleagues. They posed together for photographs, joked, and shared his ever-present pot of black coffee. Any feelings of intimidation were put to rest.

JUDITH CRIST says, "When the Ulster Performing Arts Center in Kingston, New York, near our Woodstock home, asked me whether I could do them a big favor and come there midweek to

Christmas morning, 1984, in top hat . . . and pajamas! JAMES STEWART: *"Behind all that polished ability was his extra-special quality of completely open, wonderful humor . . . not only in acting but also in the way he looked at things. That's what set him apart."*

introduce a program they were presenting, I glanced at my calendar and thought about the excuse I could use to decline. Almost incidentally I asked, 'What's the program?' And they said, 'Cary Grant.'"

In her introduction on April 18, 1985, CRIST said she became tongue-tied at the thought of introducing Grant. She didn't know where to begin. "I went to a friend, a top movie person, and said, 'What on earth would you say if you were about to introduce Cary Grant?' My friend's advice was 'You gush.'

"Meeting him at UPAC was the ultimate thrill. After his engagement I got a call saying 'Hello, this is Cary Grant.' And—wouldn't you know it?—I said, 'You're joking!' He wasn't, and our last encounter—on the phone—was as charming as the first, in 1956."

An eight-minute film clip opened the evening. The montage was the one put together by Jack Haley, Jr., and Mike Frankovich when the Academy of Motion Picture Arts and Sciences gave Grant his special Oscar in 1970.

The film illustrated Grant's versatility. He dances, does somersaults, falls on his face, gets water dumped on his head, is slapped by a half-dozen leading ladies, is run down by an airplane, and, in that famous moment from *The Philadelphia Story*, pushes Katharine Hepburn back through a doorway. Lifted out of a half dozen love scenes, he kisses Eva Marie Saint, Grace Kelly, Ingrid Bergman, Katharine Hepburn, Irene Dunne, and Rosalind Russell.

In the film Grant moves toward Frank Sinatra, who is about to present his Oscar. Then the real Cary Grant, a beat behind his shadow on film, steps to center stage. His timing was perfect.

Grant took his place on a simple wooden stool. Jittery backstage, he told the stagehands, "You can't be good unless you're nervous." Grant reminded himself that many great performers got the jitters. In his notebook he wrote, "Vladimir Horowitz, in his early days, was stricken with panic and horror akin to nausea at the thought of facing a huge audience."

Yet once Grant was seated on his stool, he looked as though he were lounging in his own living room preparing for a chat with old friends.

DICK HENNING believes, "He had a need to show Jennifer and Barbara that he still had vitality and star attraction. He enjoyed interacting with people. He was truly interested in them. But if he hadn't had these two wonderful women in his life, I don't think he would have ventured out on that stage."

"When he retired, he stepped away from all the adoration," says BEA SHAW. "And I think it was important for him to know people still loved him and wanted to see him and hear him speak. It was invigorating."

Grant got prolonged standing ovations from capacity crowds before he even uttered his first word. He invited ABIGAIL VAN BUREN and her husband to see him in La Mirada. "He's the only person I know," she says, "who can get a standing ovation for just walking out onstage."

"If you won't sit, I'll sit," he'd say to quiet the audience. The hoarseness and thickness in his voice were momentary, but he let the audience know he was shaking inside. Still, he looked very comfortable and happy, displaying the mannerisms and gestures everyone knew so well.

He'd grin. "I never quite know how to begin these things." He'd mention something that had just happened. "I have to apologize for what I'm wearing on my feet. Somehow I managed to leave my dancing shoes back at the hotel." Or "You won't believe it, but just a moment ago, I busted a button off my coat. Anyone got a needle and cotton?"

CG: I don't have the vaguest idea of what to do up here. I've done a few of these, but I still don't know how to get it going. I can't make a speech. I'm a rotten speech-maker. Making speeches has never been my forte . . . not even my fifty or sixty or seventy. No one wants to listen to what I have to say anyway. I read a book once about giving speeches, and I learned that you're supposed to say something amusing to get the audience warmed up.

This is about a woman who has a parrot that can only say, "Who is it?" One day the woman goes shopping with her neighbor, and while she's away, the plumber arrives. He knocks on the door, and the parrot says, "Who is it?" "It's the plumber," the plumber says. Nothing happens. The plumber knocks again. The parrot says, "Who is it?" *"It's the plumber!"* the plumber shouts. Nothing happens. He pounds on the door. The parrot says, "Who is it?" The plumber screams, "*It's . . . the . . . plumber!!!*" And becomes so angry he drops dead. At this point the woman and her neighbor return from shopping and find a dead body on the doorstep. The neighbor gasps, "Who is it?" And the parrot says, "*It's the plumber!*"

The evening had begun. "Are there any general questions," he asked. And to the side: "Ah, General Questions, I knew him well."

His audiences ranged from movie fans who remembered Grant when he was a young man to college students who watched his films on late-night television. They wanted to know his thoughts on acting, his leading ladies, the LSD experiments, and his views of life, youth, and women. They became noticeably still whenever he talked. Some women practically swooned and visibly trembled when they asked a question. On one occasion, a woman stood and sang "You Made Me Love You." On another, a woman asked him to father a child.

In this unstructured, unpredictable format, he demonstrated his ability to absorb quickly and respond to lines with the same sort of wit and sophistication and style he showed in his screen personality. He was sharp, fast, and perceptive. He was a master at repartee.

Often there were people who had crossed paths with him on a cruise ship, an airplane, a film location, a hotel, or having breakfast with his daughter at Rumpelmayer's, in New York City. The evening was lighthearted and convivial, a rare opportunity for intimacy between a celebrated man and his admirers. It was human and warm. And it was always filled with laughter.

Grant had learned in earlier times how to evade or parry searching questions politely.

CG: The audience knows when I'm ducking a question. They know because I tell them that's what I'm doing. At my age you might as well be honest. Honesty is not only the best policy; it's rare enough to make you pleasantly conspicuous these days.

Many of his replies were short and diverted attention away

from himself. A number of the questions were predictable. His answers were not.

"Why are you here?" was often the first question. People were curious. Advertising and publicity included "in person" to avoid telephone blitzes from admirers wondering whether or not it was Grant on film. For some it was inconceivable that he would come to their small town. Early on he told audiences, "I'm here to regain my self-confidence. Somehow this helps me." Sometimes he called it "ego fodder." And toward the end: "I'm here because it's fun. I like hearing your opinions and thinking about the questions you ask. And besides, it gets me around. I'm enjoying this. I hope you are, too."

Grant and his wife were often transported in private jets. When he flew commercially, he usually disembarked at planeside. Grant rarely walked through a terminal. Even at New York's busy John F. Kennedy Airport, Grant was given red-carpet treatment. A private jet owned by the Champion Corporation met the Grants' flight from Los Angeles on TWA's runway, collected their baggage, and lifted off, all in a period of less than ten minutes, for Schenectady, New York. He went where he wanted to go on short notice and eagerly showed his wife new places as well as those he had visited or played in vaudeville.

His fee was based on the capacity of each theater, its budget, and the ticket price. If it exceeded twenty-five dollars, he wouldn't go.

Playing on his age, Grant often referred to himself as an old geezer. He grinned, said, "Put the wrong set of teeth in tonight," flipped his fingers under his top teeth, turned to someone in front, and asked, "I didn't get anything on you, did I?" One time Grant said something similar to a French journalist. She took him literally and wrote that "Cary Grant has false teeth."

The pace of an evening was a rapid series of questions and answers.

WHAT DID YOU THINK OF YOURSELF ON FILM?

CG: I could have done it better if I'd known what I know now. It's such a shock to see your face standing eighty feet high on the screen. The bags under my eyes were bigger than you are.

CG: *"Who wants to listen to an old geezer like me?"*

DOES YOUR DAUGHTER WATCH YOUR MOVIES?

CG: If she does, she's staying up too late. I took her to a screening of *Bringing Up Baby* when she was about twelve or thirteen. She didn't seem to like it at all. But we're still friends.

DO YOU WATCH YOUR OLD FILMS?

CG: I might watch something occasionally, to oblige my wife. If the phone rings and it's six o'clock in the evening New York time (just when I'm having a drink), and friends say, "I bet you can't guess what we're doing," I know exactly what they're doing. They're watching one of my old movies. And then it gets to be nine o'clock in the evening in California, and friends call and say, "I bet you can't guess what we're doing?" And I say, "I hope you're in bed making love."

DID YOU CREATE THAT SUAVE, SOPHISTICATED IMAGE, OR IS IT REALLY YOU?

CG: Of course, it's me!

LEGEND HAS IT THAT SOMEONE CABLED, "HOW OLD CARY GRANT" TO WHICH YOU REPLIED, "OLD CARY GRANT FINE HOW YOU?"

CG: It never happened, but it's one of the things I wish I had said.

COULD YOU PLEASE TAKE OFF YOUR GLASSES?

He reached up to his face with both hands, removed his black-framed glasses, and after the slightest, perfectly timed pause, he looked back at the woman and said, "Is there anything else you'd like me to take off?"

HOW DO YOU FEEL ABOUT THE FILMS OF TODAY?

CG: They lack a certain kind of ease and graciousness about life. I deplore the language used in today's films. When I was making pictures, we couldn't even say "damn." We were not permitted to make sexually explicit films, and I don't know if I would have if I could have. The whole business today is blood and heavy breathing.

WHAT GIFT WOULD YOU LEAVE TO THE CHILDREN OF THE WORLD?

CG: Love. The children in turn would give love at home and to their friends. Love would spread, and we would have world peace.

WOULD YOU PLEASE SAY "JUDY, JUDY, JUDY"?

CG: Why, is your name "Judy"?
—No, but I'll change it if you want me to.

CG: What is your name?
—Dina.

CG: Well, I won't say "Judy," but I'll say "Dina, Dina, Dina."

WERE YOU EVER HURT WHILE MAKING A FILM?

CG: I've been injured many times doing my own stunts, had ribs and knuckles broken. You nearly always get hurt in a fight scene.

HOW DO YOU FEEL ABOUT YOUR AGE?

CG: I feel about my age much as I did when I first went to New York and watched a street parade of veterans from the American Civil War. Each year I noticed how those guys kept getting fewer and fewer. So now I feel like one of those guys in the Civil War parade.

WHAT ACTORS DO YOU ADMIRE?

CG: I had special admiration for Spencer Tracy and Humphrey Bogart. Among the living, I've most enjoyed Mickey Rooney, who doesn't hesitate to expose his own feelings and failings, whether in drama or in comedy. And Larry Olivier, who arranges to submerge his own warm and distinguished personality behind fascinatingly true and incredibly effective character studies. Al Pacino, Jack Nicholson, and Dustin Hoffman all perform without inhibition. They have the ability to expose their inner selves to the utmost.

THE DICTIONARY WILL SOMEDAY REDEFINE THE WORD "CHARISMA" WITH THE WORDS "CARY GRANT."

CG: I'm glad they're waiting.

HAVE YOU ALWAYS BEEN THIS RELAXED?

CG: No. I haven't always been this way. I really didn't take time to smell the flowers. Oh, I smelled them, but I didn't appreciate them.

WHICH ACTRESS WAS THE BEST KISSER?

CG: The one whose nose didn't get in the way. You really don't get the essence of a kiss in a film. You're working, and you don't get the time to enjoy it.

HOW DID YOU MANAGE TO LOOK SO GOOD IN *North by Northwest* AFTER BEING CHASED THROUGH OPEN FIELDS BY A CROP DUSTER?

CG: Six suits and dozens of ties.

DID YOU HAVE ROMANTIC RELATIONSHIPS WITH YOUR FEMALE COSTARS?

CG: What do you expect me to say? My wife is in the audience.

WHO WAS YOUR TRUE LOVE?

CG: My wife Barbara. Until late in life I really didn't understand love. I wanted to be, you know, macho. And, of course, my daughter, Jennifer.

WHAT'S GOOD ABOUT BEING EIGHTY?

CG: The fact that one is living, I suppose.

WHY DON'T YOU RUN FOR PRESIDENT?

CG: I've been married quite a few times. The voters won't accept that.

HOW TALL ARE YOU?

CG: I was six feet one and a half inches, but I'm shrinking.

WHAT WAS THE BEST MOMENT IN YOUR LIFE?

CG: The day I was born.

DID YOU LEARN TO JUGGLE IN VAUDEVILLE?

CG: Only a few morals.

THIS IS A DREAM COME TRUE.

CG: Do you want to pinch me?

WHAT WOULD YOU LIKE FOR DINNER IF WE WERE MARRIED?

CG: The way you say that, I'd probably skip dinner.

WHAT ARE SOME OF YOUR PET PEEVES?

CG: People who call me "Car," denoting familiarity. Phrases like "She's a living doll," "Have a good day," "Enjoy," or mispronounced words like "otamobile" for "automobile," "tweny" for "twenty," "vichysoi" for "vichyssoise," or misused words like "anxious" for "eager," "infer" for "imply," or people who say to me, "You know, you know, you know," when I don't know!

WOULD YOU DO A PRATFALL?

CG: It's all I can do to walk.

YOU'VE [nervously] ALWAYS BEEN A FAN OF MINE.

CG: That's true. I have.

HOW DOES ONE ACHIEVE SUCCESS?

CG: Diligence, perseverance, and enjoying what you do.

DO YOU HAVE ANY REGRETS?

CG: I would have liked to have had more children. I was too self-centered when I was younger. I regret that I'm not better educated and the times when I was impatient with autograph hounds and pushy fans. I should have been more gracious.

He had a variety of answers at his fingertips for the inevitable questions about how he kept so fit. "I just breathe in and out." Or "Not a damn thing!" Or "I just have good genes." Or "How do you know I'm in such excellent shape? You can only see the outside!" Or "I keep smiling. It makes everyone wonder what I've been doing." He was candid about his habits. "I eat whatever is put in front of me. I don't exercise. I don't have any hobbies. I don't smoke. I drink red wine. And sometimes I have one too many." When pressed for advice, he'd say, "Don't drink to excess, try to relax. Enjoy yourself and like who you are. If you do things in moderation, you're fine . . . except, of course, when making love."

In answer to questions about his acting style, Grant worked up a short demonstration, a monologue designed to show audiences how he went about acting.

CG: I'm alone in front of the camera. There is no one else in the shot. Now let's suppose I'm doing the simplest thing—speaking a line to someone off camera. Perhaps I'm supposed to be speaking to Grace Kelly. But Grace is actually upstairs trying on a gown. I'm playing the scene only for the director, let's say it's Hitchcock, who is watching me carefully and for the sound man, who is listening just as carefully.

I have one line to do. I say to her, "What time can I see you tomorrow?" Hitchcock wants me to take a drink when I say the line. So I raise my glass of iced tea at the same time, which presents several problems. If I bring the glass up too soon, I sound like a man hollering into a barrel. If I put it in front of my mouth, I spoil my expression. If I put it down hard, I kill a word on the sound track. If I don't, it seems unreal. I have to hold the glass at a slight angle to keep reflections out of the lens. Then I must hold it a certain way so that the ice in the glass does not interfere with the sound. It has to be absolutely still to keep the ice from tinkling, since cellophane substitutes are not used in a close-up. And finally, I have to remember to keep my head up because I have a double chin. Now we've got the whole thing worked out. But no, there's one more problem. My elbow has to be bent and turned toward my body so as not to obstruct the view of the camera.

As he was finished, he exhibited his ability as a pantomimist and quickly ran through his technique: He picked up the glass, tilted it, bent his elbow toward his body, raised his head, drank the water, said, "What time can I see you tomorrow?" and gently placed the glass on the table beside him. Applause.

Grant was unwaveringly gracious about his former wives. He said, "They all decided to leave me." Someone once told him she thought Barbara Hutton seemed like a cold individual.

CG: She wasn't cold to me. She was a lovely woman who suffered unjustly at the hands of the press. It was not her fault that she was born rich.

Curious about Barbara Grant, people craned their necks to look at her as he talked to her from the stage. "My greatest love." He smiled. "Barbara's the woman who has made me the happiest." When she joined her husband onstage near the end of his show, he said, "Pretty good for an old geezer like me, isn't she?"

Instinctively Grant knew when to bring each evening to an end. He glanced at his watch, "Don't any of you want to go home?" He had answered questions, told anecdotes, joked, sang songs, and reminisced. When the timing was right, he read from an author unknown:

Now, Lord, you've known me a long time. You know me better than I know myself. You know that each day I am growing older and someday may even be very old. So, meanwhile, please keep me from the habit of thinking I must say something on every subject and on every occasion. Release me from trying to straighten out everyone's affairs. Make me thoughtful but not moody, helpful but not overbearing. I've a certain amount of knowledge to share; still, it would be very nice to have a few friends who, at the end, recognized and forgave the knowledge I lacked. Keep my tongue free from the recital of endless details. Seal my lips on my aches and pains; they increase daily, and the need to speak of them becomes almost a compulsion. I ask for grace enough to listen to the retelling of others' afflictions and to be helped to endure them with patience. I would like to have improved memory, but I'll settle for growing humility and an ability to capitulate when my memory clashes with the memory of others. Teach me the glorious lesson that on some occasions I may be mistaken. Keep me reasonably kind; I've never aspired to be a saint—saints must be rather difficult to live with—yet on the other hand, an embittered old person is a constant burden. Please give me the ability to see good in unlikely places and talents in unexpected people. And give me the grace to tell them so, dear Lord.

Grant had no exact recall of when the prayer had come to his attention. He discovered it among some old papers left over from his filmmaking days. During the reading his wife joined him onstage. Then the two walked off hand in hand to clamorous applause.

Beginning in the mid-1980s, for a period of a year and a half, Lois Jecklin tried to get Grant to visit Davenport, Iowa. She was then president of the Visiting Artists Series and in late November 1986, finally had a date that fitted into Grant's schedule. On his way to his annual visit to Monaco to act as a circus judge for Prince Rainier, he could stop over in Davenport.

He jumped at the opportunity. It was a part of America Barbara Grant hadn't seen. The date was set—Saturday, November 29, 1986. Grant's visit was to be a significant part of Davenport's first Festival of Trees celebration.

But on November 7, 1986, Prince Rainier canceled the circus. Strong winds on November 2 had torn his new circus tent to bits. Prince Rainier set January 29 as the new date. Grant never once mentioned canceling Davenport. He was prepared to keep his commitment and was willing to add a second engagement somewhere within a comfortable flying distance of Davenport.

Walter Gunn, executive director of the Sheldon Concert Hall in St. Louis, leaped at the chance to fill Monday, December 1st. Sheldon was built in 1910 as a chamber music hall, and its intimacy was perfect for a *Conversation*. Grant's suite at the Chase Park Plaza Hotel overlooked the Muny Theater, in which he had appeared in 1931. He was looking forward to showing his wife the town.

On November 28, 1986, the Grants flew to Chicago, where Doug Miller and his then wife, Vicky Palmer, met them for a flight in an eight-passenger King Air twin-engine Beechcraft. MILLER recalls: "Four plaincothesmen and two uniformed police officers, along with a beautiful, well-endowed American Airlines representative named Gwanda, made up our group. The policemen created a wedge so we could get through the terminal at O'Hare and get to where we had the plane waiting. People were making a terrible commotion. Two workmen looked up, and when Cary caught them looking at him, he winked. Everyone laughed.

"Cary hadn't missed the physical attributes of Gwanda. While we were waiting for the luggage, he recited an old music hall limerick about Wanda with the big boobs. He was so funny. It was a happy beginning. Meanwhile, Barbara was running around making sure everyone got tipped.

"It was a beautiful night. The sky was a cobalt blue, and the sun was setting on the horizon. We opened a bottle of California Chardonnay and talked about Thanksgiving, their cat EQ, Harry Blackstone (whom Cary knew from the Magic Castle), Bix Beiderbecke (who was from Davenport), the Festival of Trees, and the fact that Ronald Reagan's first job was at Station WOC in Davenport.

"We landed in Moline at five-thirty P.M. I saw right away that Cary didn't like people to make a fuss over him. He wanted to be treated like anyone else.

"The next day we met Cary and Barbara at two o'clock for a tour of the city. They enthusiastically told us about the twenty-minute stroll they had earlier taken along the Mississippi River. They came upon an eatery serving hot dogs and hamburgers. Cary thought it was a great discovery and had lunch there. The place was called Archie's.

"Cary asked about ticket sales. He said he was willing to make an adjustment in his fee if we were not coming out all right. In the twenty years I've been around show business, I'd never heard anything like that. I thanked him and assured him we were doing just fine. He was in great spirits, laughing and telling jokes.

"We visited the twenty-room Victorian house of Vicky's grandfather, Dr. B. J. Palmer, where over one of the fireplaces, written in a British Isles dialect, maybe Gaelic or Welsh, is a saying which Cary read and understood perfectly. He told us it meant, in essence, 'Come sit by the fire and warm yourself.'

"We drove through the little town of Le Claire, the birthplace of Buffalo Bill. Cary seemed to be fascinated with the history of our area.

"At about three-thirty Cary said he didn't want to be late for his four o'clock technical rehearsal, so we hurried back to the [Adler] theater, where the ushers and crew, about twenty people,

*Barbara Grant and CG, eighty-two, in Davenport, Iowa, during
rehearsal for an evening's* Conversation, *November 29, 1986.
Photographer* BASIL WILLIAMSON: *"I waited forty-five minutes for him to
give me a signal. I could see that something wasn't going right for him.
Just ten minutes before he left the stage, he said, 'Well, I guess you
better start shooting.'"* It was the last time CG was photographed.

were waiting. When he walked in, they all applauded. Cary said, 'I hope I deserve that.'

"The microphones and the stage were set. Cary described how the film would precede his coming out onstage. He instructed the light man to bring the houselights up full so he would be able to see the faces of each person in the audience. He watched patiently as the projectionist leveled and focused his film clips, and he quipped with the stagehands. Barbara sat down front in one of the orchestra seats. I remember telling him we hoped everything was just the way he wanted it, and he replied, 'Whatever happens happens.'

"Barbara joined Cary onstage toward the end of the rehearsal. At about five o'clock they left, and went to the dressing room. I thought they were taking a break and we would run through it again. After an hour or so Barbara came out and said they wanted to go to the hotel and asked me to get a doctor. Cary said he was sorry, but he didn't feel well. He complained of a headache and nausea and said if he rested at the hotel, he would be able to do the show. Both he and Barbara kept saying they were very sorry, that they didn't want to spoil the evening. We suggested he go to the hospital, but Cary was adamantly against it. He said that whenever he went to a hospital, there was always a big to-do about everything. All he needed was some rest."

"We stayed in the suite with him and Barbara, who called Dr. Gary Sugarman, Cary's doctor in Los Angeles. Cary kept saying he just wanted to go home and see his own doctor. He was determined not to go to the hospital. At that point I started to make inquiries about an ambulance plane.

"When Dr. Duane Manlove arrived, he looked at Cary, took his blood pressure, and told him he was very sick. He called in Jim Gilson, probably the best cardiologist in our region. Barbara again called Dr. Sugarman in Los Angeles so Gilson could get Cary's case history.

"Gilson and Manlove requested an ambulance, and Cary reluctantly agreed to go to the hospital. He wasn't happy about it.

"The police officers, Dave Holden and John Howard, were wonderful. We didn't want a gaggle of reporters and photographers. Barbara protected him and talked to him constantly in reassuring ways. She whispered in his ear, and he whispered back.

"When we got to St. Luke's, Cary was taken to cardiac intensive care. Barbara was upset that they wouldn't let her stay with him. It was the first time she cried. She really came apart after having been so strong in Cary's presence.

"I continued the search for a plane. In the meantime, the Gregory Pecks, who were in touch with Stanley Fox, called and spoke to Barbara. Kirk Kerkorian told Fox that his plane was ready to take off from Los Angeles, but Barbara felt it would take too long. Vicky and I finally found and rented a Learjet air ambulance from Bloomington, Illinois."

At 11:22 P.M., on Saturday, November 29, 1986, Cary Grant died. He had had a massive and fatal stroke.

DOUG MILLER says, "Barbara called her mother and Stanley Fox. She desperately tried to reach Jennifer, who was out for dinner. We didn't announce Cary's death right away because Barbara couldn't find Jennifer.

"The public affairs director of St. Luke's was out of town. Bill Bodnar, his counterpart from Mercy Hospital, just walked in and volunteered to help. Calls were coming from all over the country."

VICKY PALMER recalls, "Barbara was so sad, but she showed great courage, graciousness, and composure. The fifteen-minute drive from the hotel to the airport took an eternity. We didn't talk very much. We were all in a state of shock." DOUG MILLER adds, "Barbara wouldn't leave until Jennifer was found. We just sat in the darkness and waited."

Barbara Grant's sad and lonely three-and-a-half-hour journey got under way at 2:30 A.M.

The next day the roses intended for each woman in attendance at the scheduled show at the Sheldon in St. Louis and all the food for a reception beforehand were taken to local hospitals and nursing homes. Some of Grant's admirers kept a silent vigil at the door of the theater.

DOUG MILLER recalls, "Most of the people who bought tickets for Cary's show kept them. With that money we started the Cary Grant Residency, to support programs by major performing arts figures. Barbara Grant gave us money, and others gave us contributions."

Sunday at dawn, Stanley Fox was waiting for Barbara Grant in a remote location at the Los Angeles Airport. JUDY QUINE says, "It was a painful experience for Barbara—all alone in that tiny ambulance plane, with Cary's body right next to her."

Quine was at Grant's house before Barbara Grant returned. Over the next several days Quine answered telephones and assisted Barbara and Jennifer Grant, as did Bea Shaw, Marjorie Everett, Veronique Peck, and several other close friends. Barbara Grant's sisters, Catherine and Elizabeth, and her friend Dawn Jones came from London. Friends arrived.

QUINCY JONES remembers, "I held Barbara and Jennifer for a long time. There was nothing to talk about, so I just held them. Greg and Veronique Peck and Barbara Sinatra were there. And then Dyan [Cannon] came by. She was real gracious. She said to Barbara, 'You were the only woman he truly loved.' It was so giving and consoling. I'll never forget it."

According to JUDY QUINE, "Cary's will stated that he did not want a service and that he wanted to be cremated." RODERICK MANN says that when somebody asked Barbara Grant to put a flower on his grave, "Barbara didn't have the heart to tell whoever it was that there wasn't a grave. That was very much in keeping with Cary, the private man who didn't want the nonsense of a funeral." Grant told BEA SHAW many times, "'I hope I don't embarrass anybody.' And he didn't. He died just the way he lived. With dignity."

GREGORY PECK thinks, "It was in keeping with Cary that he went quietly and quickly, without any prolonged period of illness. Nobody saw any pain or suffering or unpleasantness. He certainly wouldn't have liked that—to have people know that he was ill or incapacitated."

RICH LITTLE says, "Cary radiated warmth and youthfulness. When he died, it shocked us so much. Some people get old and frail and slow down. With Cary, it was as though a young person had died." JILL ST. JOHN believes, "Cary died a very happy man. Everything was working a hundred percent. His relationship with his daughter, his marriage to Barbara, his health, and his lifestyle were what people dream about. He was at peace with himself. There was no room for negativity in his life. He'd gotten to the point where he could exclude it."

According to JUDY QUINE, "Hundreds and hundreds of telephone calls and letters poured in, and Barbara answered all of them. People she knew received notes completely written by hand, an impossible task, but she did it. For people they didn't know, each letter was typed, and then Barbara filled in the person's name and signed it." It read like this:

> Thank you for your card, and the kind words it contained. My beloved husband, Cary Grant, was the most unique of men—in every way. The happiness he brought to those of us privileged to know him personally, and to the millions who knew him through his films, is immeasurable. He so enriched all our lives and has left us the legacy of his laughter, grace, and elegance.
>
> I am touched by your thoughtfulness, and thank you for trying to ease this profoundly sad time.

ABIGAIL VAN BUREN says of the eulogy she wrote to her friend: "It was a whole column. It was a lovely, warm piece which expressed my personal feelings about him as a man. My readers didn't really know him, of course. They just knew the Cary Grant image. They had loved him for years and years. They didn't need me to bring Cary Grant to them. But they wrote so appreciatively and said they didn't know he was so real. That was the best thing about him. He was real."

On October 19, 1988, in the presence of HSH Prince Rainier of Monaco, the Princess Grace Foundation paid tribute to Cary Grant, who had been a foundation trustee. The thousand-dollar-a-plate black-tie dinner at the Beverly Hilton Hotel, in Beverly Hills, California, attracted 940 of his most ardent admirers and friends. Nearly a million dollars was raised to assist young talent in theater, dance, and film through scholarships. JACK HALEY, JR., comments, "I directed one Oscar show, and produced three, with less big names than the Cary Grant tribute. I was astonished at the numbers of people who wanted to say good-bye to him. Nobody wanted to be left out."*

"His friends told personal, happy anecdotes," Haley says. "People who couldn't be there did film clips. For example, at the

---

*The tribute's entertainment was by Shirley Temple Black, Michael Caine, Sammy Davis, Jr., John Forsythe, Merv Griffin, Quincy Jones, Henry Mancini, Walter Matthau, Dina Merrill, Liza Minnelli, Robert Mitchum, Roger Moore, Gregory Peck, Eva Marie Saint, Frank Sinatra, James Stewart, and Robert Wagner. Honorary chairmen were Nancy Reagan and Barbara Grant. Chairwoman Dina Merrill was assisted by co-chairs Merv Griffin, Veronique and Gregory Peck, Barbara and Frank Sinatra, Kirk Kerkorian, Judy and Donald Quine, and Edie and Lew Wasserman.

last minute Sophia Loren had to fly to Rome, so she paid for the cameramen to come into her home to record her message."

"It was the only ceremony in memory of Cary that Barbara and Jennifer Grant sanctioned," JUDY QUINE says.

DEBORAH KERR composed a poem as a tribute to her friend:

> For Cary—A few words in rhyme
> To celebrate this special time—
> To remember what a joy it was
> To work with him, and what a loss
> His absence is for those of us
> Who had the luck to know him
> And to watch him work—
> The looks, the grace, the "double-take"
> That no-one else could ever make.
> The fun, the laughs that made each day
> Something to look forward to, and hear him say
> "Good morning, darling—how are yew?!"
> Perfectionist he always was
> And how many "tricks" I learned!
> For these and many other things
> I thank, thank you.

Chapter Twenty

"HAPPY THOUGHTS"

CG: Most important to me is love and admiration of my family. I love to see it in their eyes and feel it in their hugs. If I'm to be remembered by my family and friends, then let it be as someone who didn't rock the boat, who did moderately well at his craft, and was polite to his fellow man.

BURT REYNOLDS: "Cary was magical. He was touched by the gods in the sense that he was different from everyone else. When he walked into a room, you *had* to look at him. Men liked him as well as women, and that is incredibly rare. Men found him nonthreatening. If a woman said, 'I'm in love with Cary Grant,' most men couldn't blame her."

PETER STONE: "Men don't find many men appealing, but Cary was attractive to everybody. Men wanted to look, dress, and be like him, but they couldn't."

ABIGAIL VAN BUREN: "Most celebrities are concerned with how they look and how people react to them. Cary reacted to other people. His success never went to his head. There are people who walk into a room and say, 'Here I am.' Cary walked in and said, 'There you are.'"

STEVE LAWRENCE: "When Cary walked into a room, not only did the women primp, the men straightened their ties."

MONTY HALL: "At a Variety Club convention in Monte Carlo in the mid-1970s we were surrounded by royalty. Prince Philip and Prince Charles were there. Prince Rainier and Grace Kelly were our hosts. To the crowd of a thousand delegates Cary was as much royalty as any of the others. No matter where he appeared, it was awe-inspiring."

HENRY GRIS: "One time I asked him what he thought when he looked in the mirror and saw that handsome face of his. He said, 'Come off it, will you? I say to myself, "You look more and more like your father." And since I liked my father very much, I don't mind it.'"

STANLEY DONEN: "I miss him. He used to write me jokes in a letter. The whole letter would be a joke. One said, 'Lady Hawthorne said to her butler, "Johnson, come into my bedroom." He said, "Yes, madam." And she said, "Now Johnson, take off my dress.' He said, "Yes, madam." She said, "Now take off my shoes." "Yes, madam." "Now take off my slip." "Yes, madam." "Now take off my stockings." "Yes, madam." "Now take off my panties." "Yes, madam." "Now take off my brassiere." "Yes, madam." "And if I ever catch you wearing them again, Johnson, you're fired."'"

GREGORY PECK: "He was comfortable in all aspects of show business: acrobatics, singing, music, comedy, drama, the circus. Underneath that suave manner and sophisticated style, he was dyed-in-the-wool, grass-roots, down-to-earth show business. A performer. He might have been a vaudevillian, or he might have been a band singer. In one way or another he was going to entertain people. But he finally weaved his way through and found he could be Cary Grant, the film star. He discovered that for himself."

BINNIE BARNES: "Whenever we went to London with Cary, we stayed at the Athenaeum. . . . [We'd] walk to his favorite pub on Haymarket, and get a couple of shandies (ginger beer and ale). Occasionally he'd ask for black velvet, which is champagne and stout. You put a hot poker in it and warm it up. There was a dart board there, and they served shepherd's pie—real old English food. This was Cary's favorite way of eating—the old pub."

ELIZABETH TAYLOR: "I remember his laughter. We always laughed a lot when we were together. . . . He was like a great fireplace. He warmed you and made you feel super. He was what one would hope a movie star would be like."

SYLVIA WU: "Cary was my only American friend. My whole

family respected him. When I wanted to sell the restaurant, he said, 'What will you do?' Cary talked me out of it."

FAY WRAY: "I have an enduring feeling for him that goes back to the joy of *Nikki*. I was loyal to that memory, and I felt he was, too. The last time I saw Cary was at Hollywood Park. When he died, not only was Cary gone, but an era had disappeared."

GEMMA CAMINS: "He always sang around the house. There was one song he'd sing over and over [sings]: 'There's a girl who's crazy over me, and I'm crazy over her. Ting-a-ling-a-ling, I'm waiting for the phone to ring. . . .'"

GEORGE STEVENS, JR.: "I think people like Cary who create work that lives have a kind of continuing presence."

RODERICK MANN: "It's nice to know he was on the planet with me. Rat, leaving me like that."

RICHARD BROOKS: "The thing that made Cary special, outside of his talent and his professionalism, is that he cared. He cared about people. In learning about him, I learned about me. His death affected me deeply. I loved him."

BEA SHAW: "Most of the time when I remember something Cary said or did, I find myself smiling."

CG: Happy thoughts!

THE OTHER VOICES

HSH PRINCE ALBERT OF MONACO met CG in the 1960s.

VALERIE ALLEN, writer-former actress, met CG in 1957.

BOBBY ALTMAN, owner of M. B. Altman Sons, New York jewelers, was introduced to CG by Los Angeles attorney Greg Bautzer in 1967.

CLEVELAND AMORY, author-social satirist-animal activist, met CG in the early 1950s.

RICHARD ANDERSON, actor, was "discovered" by CG in 1949.

JOHNNY ANDREWS, former NBC television personality, met CG in 1955.

BINNIE BARNES, actress wife of producer Mike Frankovich (who was active with CG in variety clubs), met CG in the early 1930s.

GEORGE BARRIE, businessman (founder of Fabergé)-musician-filmmaker, met CG in 1968.

RALPH BELLAMY, actor, costarred with CG in *The Awful Truth* (1937) and *His Girl Friday* (1940).

MILTON BERLE, comedian, met CG in 1925.

RICHARD BIENEN, Richard Bienen Handbags, New York, manufactured bags used in *That Touch of Mink* (1962).

NICKY BLAIR, owner of Los Angeles restaurant bearing his name, actor, worked with CG in *Operation Petticoat* (1959).

PETER BOGDANOVICH, director-producer-screenwriter-author-film commentator, was introduced to CG by Clifford Odets in 1960.

MARY BRIAN, actress-painter, dated CG in 1935 and 1936 and costarred with him in *Romance and Riches* (1937).

PHYLLIS BROOKS, actress, was engaged to marry CG in late 1930s.

RICHARD BROOKS, director-producer-screenwriter-author, directed CG in *Crisis* (1950).

GEORGE BURNS, comedian, met CG in the 1920s.

SAMMY CAHN, lyricist, cowrote theme song for *Indiscreet* (1958).

GEMMA CAMINS, the Grants' housekeeper (1985 to present).

LESLIE CARON, actress, costarred with CG in *Father Goose* (1964).

VIRGINIA CHERRILL, actress, was CG's first wife (1934–1936).

CY COLEMAN, composer-concert pianist-jazz musician, wrote theme song for *Father Goose* (1964).

ROBERT COX, barber, was introduced to CG in 1970 by director-producer Mervyn LeRoy.

JUDITH CRIST, film critic, met CG in 1985.

JEAN DALRYMPLE, vaudeville actress-writer-director-artists' representative-theatrical producer, met CG in 1926.

MARY LAWRENCE DAVES, wife of director-screenwriter-producer, Delmer Daves, who cowrote and directed CG in *Destination Tokyo* (1944).

MARVIN DAVIS, businessman-former owner 20th Century Fox, met CG in the late 1970s.

ANGIE DICKINSON, actress, was introduced to CG by Richard Brooks in the late 1950s.

STANLEY DONEN, director, directed CG in *Kiss Them for Me*

(1957) and directed and coproduced with CG *Indiscreet* (1958), *The Grass Is Greener* (1961), and *Charade* (1963).

BETSY DRAKE, actress, costarred with CG in *Every Girl Should Be Married* (1948) and *Room for One More* (1951), and was CG's third wife (1949–62).

IRENE DUNNE, actress, costarred with CG in *The Awful Truth* (1937), *My Favorite Wife* (1940), and *Penny Serenade* (1941).

CLARICE EARL, matron, Chesterfield Nursing Home, Bristol, England, where CG's mother lived (1964–73).

MARJORIE L. EVERETT, former chairman of the board and CEO of Hollywood Park, met CG in 1970.

DOUGLAS FAIRBANKS, JR., actor, costarred with CG in *Gunga Din* (1939).

BETTY FORD, wife of Gerald Ford, met CG in 1976.

CHARLOTTE FORD, author-former dress designer, met CG in the early 1970s.

JOHN FORSYTHE, actor, worked with CG in *Destination Tokyo* (1944).

STANLEY E. FOX, lawyer, CG's business partner, and closest friend, met CG in the early 1940s. At CG's urging, Fox gave up his law practice to get involved with films and became president of the companies formed to produce and own CG's films.

BETTY FURNESS, actress-presidential consumer affairs aide-NBC's consumer news reporter, dated CG in 1935.

DR. SEYMOUR J. GRAY, physician, met CG in 1949.

MERV GRIFFIN, TV personality-businessman, met CG in 1977.

HENRY GRIS, Latvian-born journalist-author-war correspondent, met CG in the 1960s.

FLORENCE HALEY, wife of actor Jack Haley, met CG in 1928.

JACK HALEY, JR., writer-producer-director, was introduced to CG by Richard Brooks in 1957.

MONTY HALL, former host *Let's Make a Deal*/Life-Time international chairman, Variety Clubs International, a beneficiary in CG's will, met CG in 1969.

LESLEY HARRIS, mother of CG's fifth wife, Barbara Harris Grant, met CG in 1977.

DR. MORTIMER A. HARTMAN, physician, was introduced to CG by Betsy Drake in 1960.

WILLIAM RANDOLPH HEARST, JR., publisher, met CG in the 1930s.

DR. RICHARD HENNING, Dean of Community Services, Foothill College, Cupertino, California, presented CG's first *Conversation* (1982).

AUDREY HEPBURN, actress, costarred with CG in *Charade* (1963).

KATHARINE HEPBURN, actress, costarred with CG in *Sylvia Scarlett* (1936), *Bringing Up Baby* (1938), *Holiday* (1938), and *The Philadelphia Story* (1941).

ROBERT HUTTON, actor whose maternal grandmother was related to the father of Barbara Hutton, CG's second wife, worked with CG in *Destination Tokyo* (1944).

RICK INGERSOLL, public relations executive, publicized *North by Northwest* (1959).

QUINCY JONES, composer-producer, scored *Walk, Don't Run* (1966), was introduced to CG by Peggy Lee in the early 1960s.

LOUIS JOURDAN, actor, and FREDERIQUE "QUIQUE" JOURDAN, his wife, met CG in 1946.

GARSON KANIN, director-writer, directed CG in *My Favorite Wife* (1940).

SYLVIA FINE KAYE, song and comedy writer of late husband Danny Kaye's material, met CG in the 1940s. Danny Kaye, Constance Moore, and CG celebrated the same birthday, January 18.

GEORGE KENNEDY, actor, worked with CG in *Charade* (1963).

KIRK KERKORIAN, businessman-former owner of MGM, met CG in Las Vegas and was reintroduced at New York's P. J. Clark's by Aristotle Onassis in the early 1960s.

DEBORAH KERR, actress, costarred in *Dream Wife* (1953), *An Affair to Remember* (1957) and *The Grass Is Greener* (1961).

STANLEY KRAMER, director-producer, directed CG in *The Pride and the Passion* (1957).

PERRY LAFFERTY, former CBS vice-president of programs, was introduced to CG by Danny Kaye in the late 1960s.

DOROTHY LAMOUR, actress, met CG in the late 1930s.

RALPH LAUREN, fashion designer, met CG in the late 1970s, when CG went to his New York office to thank him for some ties.

STEVE LAWRENCE, singer, was introduced to CG by his wife, singer Eydie Gormé, who met CG in Las Vegas in 1959 when CG sat ringside at her show three nights in one week.

IRVING LAZAR, literary and film agent-legendary Hollywood deal maker-party giver, met CG in 1950.

PEGGY LEE, singer-songwriter-actress, met CG in the 1950s, when CG first went to see her perform.

ERNEST LEHMAN, screenwriter-producer-director, wrote *North by Northwest* (1959).

JERRY D. LEWIS, television writer-producer, who began his career as a New York sportswriter in the 1930s, met CG in 1958.

RICH LITTLE, comedian-impersonator, got the idea for CG impersonations while watching CG accept Ingrid Bergman's Oscar in 1957 and met CG in the early 1970s.

SOPHIA LOREN, actress, costarred with CG in *The Pride and the Passion* (1957) and *Houseboat* (1958).

DAVID MAHONEY, former CEO of Norton Simon, Inc., met CG in the early 1970s.

RODERICK MANN, journalist-author, first interviewed CG in London in 1958.

JOHNNY MASCHIO, Beverly Hills real estate executive-former talent agent, met CG in the 1930s.

WALTER MATTHAU, actor, worked with CG in *Charade* (1963).

EVERETT MATTLIN, writer, interviewed CG in Palm Springs for *Gentlemen's Quarterly* in 1964.

AUDREY MEADOWS, actress, worked with CG in *That Touch of Mink* (1962).

DANIEL MELNICK, producer-former CEO of MGM, met CG in 1972.

DINA MERRILL, actress, met CG in 1942 and worked with him in *Operation Petticoat* (1959).

DOUGLAS MILLER, president of Two Rivers Consulting, Davenport, Iowa, and former wife Vicky Palmer brought CG to Davenport, Iowa, for a *Conversation* in 1986.

GARY MORTON, former nightclub comedian-husband of Lucille Ball, met CG in the 1960s.

ADOLPHO NAVARRO, the Grants' gardener (1981 to present).

JAMES G. NIVEN, businessman, son of David Niven, met CG in the 1950s.

PETER O'MALLEY, owner, Los Angeles Dodgers, met CG in 1962.

THELMA ORLOFF, actress-Beverly Hills real estate executive, met CG in 1939 and appeared in CG's MGM movies.

DR. FRANCIS PAGE, Bristol physician, met CG in 1964.

VICKY PALMER and Douglas Miller brought CG to Davenport, Iowa, for a *Conversation* in 1986.

GREGORY PECK, actor, met CG in the 1940s.

JUDITH QUINE, writer, daughter of Barney Balaban, former Paramount Pictures President, met CG in 1956.

HSH PRINCE RAINIER III OF MONACO met CG in 1955.

NANCY REAGAN, actress wife of Ronald Reagan, met CG in 1950.

BURT REYNOLDS, actor-director, met CG in 1970.

MAURICE RICHLIN, screenwriter, cowrote *Operation Petticoat* (1959).

HAL ROACH, producer-director-screenwriter-former stuntman and actor, produced *Topper* (1937).

LEIGHTON ROSENTHAL, Cleveland businessman, was introduced to CG by Mervyn LeRoy in 1969.

STEVEN J. ROSS, chairman and CEO, Time Warner Inc., met CG in the 1960s.

ROY, of Siegfried and Roy, illusionists, met CG in 1968.

JILL ST. JOHN, actress, met CG in 1958 when her future husband, Lance Reventlow (CG's stepson), brought her to meet his "father."

RICHARD SCHICKEL, film critic/author/writer-producer-director of TV specials, wrote, on the occasion of CG's eightieth birthday (1984), *Cary Grant: A Celebration*.

MARTHA SCOTT, actress, costarred with CG in *The Howards of Virginia* (1940).

IRENE MAYER SELZNICK, Broadway producer (daughter of Louis B. Mayer, founder of MGM) and one of CG's closest, most trusted friends, met CG in 1931.

WALTER SHARP, banker, fellow MGM board member, met CG in 1972.

BEA SHAW, broadcast advertising writer-producer-actress and former ABC-TV news reporter, met CG at a party in 1962.

SIDNEY SHELDON, screenwriter-author-director, wrote *The Bachelor and the Bobby-Soxer* (1947) and directed CG in *Dream Wife* (1953).

SIEGFRIED, of Siegfried and Roy, illusionists, met CG in 1968.

BARBARA SINATRA, wife of Frank Sinatra, met CG in 1972.

ALEXIS SMITH, actress, costarred with CG in *Night and Day* (1946).

RAY STARK, producer, met CG in the 1940s.

GEORGE STEVENS, JR., producer-founder of American Film Institute, met CG at age eight on the set of *Penny Serenade* in 1940.

JAMES STEWART, actor, met CG in 1936 and costarred with CG in *The Philadelphia Story* (1940).

PETER STONE, playwright-screenwriter, wrote *Charade* (1963) and cowrote *Father Goose* (1964).

FRANK TARLOFF, screenwriter, cowrote *Father Goose* (1964).

ELIZABETH TAYLOR, actress, met CG in 1947.

DAVID W. TEBET, longtime NBC production executive, was introduced to CG by Sammy Cahn in 1959.

ABIGAIL VAN BUREN, syndicated columnist ("Dear Abby"), was introduced to CG by industrialist Armand Hammer in the late 1970s.

ROBERT WAGNER, actor, met CG in 1957.

RAY WALSTON, actor, performed in *Kiss Them for Me* (1957).

BILLY WILDER, director-screenwriter-producer met CG in the 1940s.

ROBERT WISE, director-producer, edited *My Favorite Wife* (1939).

FAY WRAY, actress, costarred with CG in *Nikki* (1931).

SYLVIA WU, owner Madame Wu's Restaurant, Los Angeles, met CG in the 1960s.

JANE WYATT, actress, costarred with CG in *None but the Lonely Heart* (1944).

LORETTA YOUNG, actress, costarred with CG in *The Bishop's Wife* (1947).

MICKY AND NORMAN ZEILER, former owners Main Street Fashions, met CG when he took Doris Day shopping for *That Touch of Mink* (1961).

PHOTOGRAPH CREDITS

Cover. Courtesy of The Kobal Collection.

Page 2. "Destination Tokyo" © 1943 Turner Entertainment Co., an AOL Time Warner Company. All rights reserved. Courtesy of Turner Entertainment Co. Cary Grant Collection, courtesy of the Academy of Motion Picture Arts and Sciences.

Page 6. Courtesy of Barbara and Jennifer Grant.

Pages 25, 30, 32. Wilbert. Cary Grant Collection, courtesy of the Academy of Motion Picture Arts and Sciences.

Pages 34, 43, 63, 86, 87, 90, 252, 363. Cary Grant Collection, courtesy of the Academy of Motion Picture Arts and Sciences.

Page 60. Strauss. Cary Grant Collection, courtesy of the Academy of Motion Picture Arts and Sciences.

Pages 67, 70. Paramount Pictures. Courtesy of Paramount Pictures. Cary Grant Collection, courtesy of the Academy of Motion Picture Arts and Sciences.

PHOTOGRAPH CREDITS

Page 73. Cary Grant. Cary Grant Collection, courtesy of the Academy of Motion Picture Arts and Sciences.

Page 76. Courtesy of Betty Furness.

Page 80. Courtesy of Mary Brian.

Page 83. © 1936 RKO Pictures, Inc. All rights reserved. Courtesy of Turner Entertainment Co. Cary Grant Collection, courtesy of the Academy of Motion Picture Arts and Sciences.

Page 99. © 1937, renewed 1965 Columbia Pictures Industries, Inc. All rights reserved.Courtesy of Columbia Pictures. Cary Grant Collection, courtesy of the Academy of Motion Picture Arts and Sciences.

Page 114. © 1939, renewed 1965 Columbia Pictures Industries, Inc. "His Girl Friday" based on the play "The Front Page" (c) 1928, renewed 1955 Hecht & MacArthur. All rights reserved. Courtesy of Columbia Pictures. Cary Grant Collection, courtesy of the Academy of Motion Picture Arts and Sciences.

Page 117. © 1940, renewed 1960 Columbia Pictures Industries, Inc. All rights reserved. Courtesy of Columbia Pictures. Cary Grant Collection, courtesy of the Academy of Motion Picture Arts and Sciences.

Page 119. © 1940 Turner Entertainment Co., an AOL Time Warner company. All rights reserved. Courtesy of Turner Entertainment Co. Cary Grant Collection, courtesy of the Academy of Motion Picture Arts and Sciences.

Page 122. Paramount Pictures. All rights reserved. Courtesy of Paramount Pictures. George Stevens Collection, courtesy of the Academy of Motion Picture Arts and Sciences.

Page 131. U. S. Army Signal Corps. Cary Grant Collection, courtesy of the Academy of Motion Picture Arts and Sciences.

Page 136. © Sanford H. Roth. Courtesy of the Roth Estate. Cary Grant Collection, courtesy of the Academy of Motion Picture Arts and Sciences.

Page 142. Courtesy of Natalie Thompson Robinson.

PHOTOGRAPH CREDITS

Page 150. © ABC, Inc. All rights reserved. Cary Grant Collection, courtesy of the Academy of Motion Picture Arts and Sciences.

Page 155. © 1947 RKO Pictures, Inc. All rights reserved. Courtesy of Turner Entertainment Co. Cary Grant Collection, courtesy of the Academy of Motion Picture Arts and Sciences.

Page 165. Courtesy of Mrs. Ken (Bette Lou) Murray.

Page 171. © 1950 Turner Entertainment Co. An AOL Time Warner Company. All rights reserved. Courtesy of Turner Entertainment Co. Richard Brooks Collection, courtesy of Richard Brooks.

Page 173. Auguste. Cary Grant Collection, courtesy of the Academy of Motion Picture Arts and Sciences.

Page 185. © 1955, 1991 by Paramount Pictures. All rights reserved. Courtesy of Paramount Pictures. Cary Grant Collection, courtesy of the Academy of Motion Picture Arts and Sciences.

Page 197. © 1957 Twentieth Century Fox Film Corporation. All rights reserved. Courtesy of Twentieth Century Fox Film Corporation. Cary Grant Collection, courtesy of the Academy of Motion Picture Arts and Sciences.

Page 206. © 1957, 1991 by Paramount Pictures. All rights reserved. Courtesy of Paramount Pictures. Cary Grant Collection, courtesy of the Academy of Motion Picture Arts and Sciences.

Page 209. Paramount Pictures. All rights reserved. Courtesy of Paramount Pictures.

Page 216. © 1959 Turner Entertainment Co. An AOL Time Warner Company. All rights reserved. Courtesy of Turner Entertainment Co. Cary Grant Collection, courtesy of the Academy of Motion Picture Arts and Sciences.

Page 221. © 1959 Turner Entertainment Co., an AOL Time Warner company. All rights reserved. Courtesy of Turner Entertainment Co. Cary Grant Collection, courtesy of the Academy of Motion Picture Arts and Sciences.

PHOTOGRAPH CREDITS

Page 240. © 2002 From the Private Collection of Amy Greene, Courtesy of Amy Greene.

Pages 248, 256, 272. © Universal Pictures, a Division of Universal City Studios, Inc. Courtesy of MCA Publishing Rights, a division of MCA, Inc. Cary Grant Collection, courtesy of the Academy of Motion Picture Arts and Sciences.

Page 267. Hal Adams. © 1964 The Conde Nast Publications Inc. Courtesy of GQ. Cary Grant Collection, courtesy of the Academy of Motion Picture Arts and Sciences.

Page 278. Bea Shaw. Courtesy of Bea Shaw.

Page 288. Norman Zeiler. Courtesy of Micky Zeiler.

Page 289. Courtesy of the Gerald R. Ford Library. Cary Grant Collection, courtesy of the Academy of Motion Picture Arts and Sciences.

Page 290. © Antonio Tiedra. Courtesy of Antonio Tiedra. Cary Grant Collection, courtesy of the Academy of Motion Picture Arts and Sciences.

Page 300. Rich Martin. Cary Grant Collection, courtesy of the Academy of Motion Picture Arts and Sciences.

Page 303. © Academy of Motion Picture Arts and Sciences. All rights reserved. Courtesy of the Academy of Motion Picture Arts and Sciences.

Page 306. Dunes Hotel & Casino. Courtesy of Dunes Hotel & Casino. Cary Grant Collection, courtesy of the Academy of Motion Picture Arts and Sciences.

Page 325. Barbara Sinatra. Courtesy of Barbara Sinatra. Cary Grant Collection, courtesy of the Academy of Motion Picture Arts and Sciences.

Page 326. Harry Myers/REX USA. Courtesy of Harry Myers. Cary Grant Collection, courtesy of the Academy of Motion Picture Arts and Sciences.

PHOTOGRAPH CREDITS

Pages 329, 335, 356. © Bernard Fallon. Cary Grant Collection, courtesy of the Academy of Motion Picture Arts and Sciences.

Page 334. Stanley E. Fox. Courtesy of Stanley E. Fox. Cary Grant Collection, courtesy of the Academy of Motion Picture Arts and Sciences.

Page 338. The Monte-Carlo International Circus Festival. Courtesy of HSH Prince Rainier III of Monaco. Cary Grant Collection, courtesy of the Academy of Motion Picture Arts and Sciences.

Page 341. Courtesy of Barbara Grant.

Page 344. Dr. Richard L. Henning. Courtesy of Dr. Richard L. Henning.

Page 345. Jim Fox. Courtesy of Jim Fox and Barbara Grant.

Page 348. © Stidham & Associates. Courtesy of Stidham & Associates and Barbara Grant.

Page 354. © Peter C. Borsari. Courtesy of Peter C. Borsari. Cary Grant Collection, courtesy of the Academy of Motion Picture Arts and Sciences.

Page 355. Louis Jourdan. Courtesy of Louis Jourdan and Barbara Grant.

Page 358. Barbara Grant. Cary Grant Collection, courtesy of the Academy of Motion Picture Arts and Sciences.

Page 373. © Basil Williamson. All rights reserved. Courtesy of Basil Williamson.

INDEX

Page numbers in *italics* refer to photographs.